"Paul Copan and William Lane Craig are Christian scholars of the highest caliber and work at the top level of academic discourse. However, in this wonderful new collection of essays they have edited, they have given us all a real gift—a set of clear and powerful chapters filled with vital information lay people in the church need to know in order to be effective in their witness for Christ. This is must reading if you want to be up to speed for all the 'water cooler' conversations at work. The topics they have chosen are cutting-edge, the writers are stimulating, and, perhaps most importantly, all the chapters are very accessible for the average Christian reader."

Craig J. Hazen, Ph.D.
Christian Apologetics Program
Biola University
Author of the novel, *Five Sacred Crossings*

"Here are fresh answers to current challenges to Christianity, written with scholarly precision and yet in easy-to-understand language. It's a great resource for bolstering your faith while equipping you to defend it to others."

Lee Strobel
General editor, *The Case for Christ Study Bible*

COME LET US
Reason

New Essays in Christian Apologetics

Mary Jo Sharp
2 Cor 10:5

Paul Copan & William Lane Craig, *editors*

Foreword by Rick Warren

ACADEMIC
NASHVILLE, TENNESSEE

CONTENTS

Part 4
Ancient Israel and Other Religions

Part 5
Christian Uniqueness and Other Religions

FOREWORD

Rick Warren

As a pastor for over 30 years, I've noticed that the questions people ask me usually fall into two general categories. About half of the questions I'm asked could be categorized as "What does God want me to *do?*" questions. These deal with life, work, relationships, problems, and other personal needs. The other half I categorize as "What's the truth?" questions. How do I know what to believe and trust?

People want, and need, to know the answers to both types of questions. We need to know how to *behave*, and we need to know what to *believe*. Unfortunately, there are far more helpful resources for growing fruit in our lives (category #1) than developing the root of our lives (category #2). Beliefs determine behavior. That's why I am so excited, even overjoyed, that two of my friends, Paul Copan and Bill Craig, have created this new apologetic resource. It fills a deep hole in contemporary disciple making.

Both of these authors are intellectually brilliant (just read their other books!), but more than that, they know how to communicate profound truths in simple ways, as Jesus did. Einstein famously noted that you can be brilliant, but if you can't explain it in a simple way, your brilliance isn't worth much, and you don't *really* understand a subject until you can explain it in a simple way. Simple doesn't mean shallow or superficial. Simple means clear. That's the genius of this important book.

Bill and Paul have edited a powerful tool that addresses 16 contemporary challenges to the Christian faith in a way that presents the arguments in accessible, crystal-clear language. They present timeless truth in timely ways.

When Jesus stood before Pilate in judgment, Pilate asked Him *the* fundamental question of life: What is truth? Two thousand years later, we still ask that question, and with postmodernism infecting schools, many even ask, "Does such a thing as truth exist?" That's why this book is desperately needed.

In many ways, our culture parallels the days of Isaiah when he confessed, ". . . truth has stumbled in the streets, honesty cannot enter, and truth is nowhere to be found" (Isa 59:14–15 NIV). What makes this problem worse today is that the Internet allows the spread of erroneous ideas, foolish arguments, illogical conclusions, and false doctrine to be global, searchable, and permanent. People today are bombarded by nonsense. Bill Craig's essay on the world's 10 worst objections about God deftly deals with this reality.

God has called us to take His message of truth to the world. But we will hesitate to do this if we lack confidence in the reliability of the message, or feel unprepared to "give an answer to everyone who asks you to give the reason for the hope that you have" (1 Pet 3:15 NIV). This book answers both of these concerns. It shows that truth is knowable. You can test it; you can experiment with it; you can prove it.

At Saddleback Church, we've always emphasized the importance of knowing not just *what* you believe but *why* you believe it. We train our members to be experts in apologetics and Bible doctrine. Without a doubt, *Come Let Us Reason* will become a key part of our training program. My prayer is that you will not just read this book, but that you will pass it on, and even teach it to others, so the world may know that Jesus is *the* Way, *the* Truth, and *the* Life!

Dr. Rick Warren
www.saddleback.com
www.pastors.com

PREFACE

A s with the first and second apologetics books we have assembled with B&H (*Passionate Conviction* and *Contending with Christianity's Critics*), this third book we are coediting does several things. First, it raises classical questions in the philosophy of religion and apologetics, but it does so in a fresh way that interacts with cutting-edge scholarship and current discussion. For example, this book contains a fresh articulation of the argument against naturalism, and it responds to flawed reasoning used against the cosmological argument.

Second, the book addresses contemporary challenges for the church as well as current topics not typically covered in standard apologetics or philosophy of religion texts. The book has chapters on the much-discussed *Zeitgeist* film, on comparisons of Jesus' birth and resurrection to alleged dying and rising god myths in Mediterranean pagan religions, on the Qur'an as special revelation, on "slavery" and "genocide" in the Old Testament, and on Bart Ehrman's criticisms of the resurrection and of the New Testament's reliability. Third, the book undertakes the task of apologetics with pastoral concern undergirding it. It offers essays on when God gives humans the "silent treatment" and on navigating the question of God's hiddenness.

This book—as with the previous two books—makes cutting-edge resources available to the broader Christian community. Indeed, Evangelical Philosophical Society scholars and their evangelical comrades-in-arms in theology, biblical studies, archaeology, and history can help broaden and deepen the thinking of the next generation of apologists who would benefit from exposure to this wide range of topics.

Paul Copan and William Lane Craig
May 2011

Part 1

APOLOGETICS, CULTURE, AND THE KINGDOM OF GOD

Chapter 1

MAKING THE GOSPEL CONNECTION
An Essay Concerning Applied Apologetics

Gregory E. Ganssle

T he task of bearing witness to Christ is one to which anyone captured by the gospel is called.[1] The claim that we each have a role
as a witness will not strike believers as odd. It is simply part of what it
means to be a faithful follower of Jesus. The claim that each believer is
called to be an apologist—one who defends Christian belief and practice—might sound strange, however. Surely, the calling to be an apologist is a particular calling, such as the calling to be a pastor, an engineer,
or a father. It is not surprising that we often think of being an apologist
as a particular calling, given the way most of us think about the nature
of apologetics.

My aim in this essay is twofold. First, I wish to broaden our understanding of the nature and scope of apologetics in order see it more
firmly embedded in the calling of every believer. Second, I wish to
explain some conceptual tools that will help us in this high calling.

There are, I propose, three basic angles from which we can look at
the nature of apologetics. I like to think of them as the corners of a
triangle:

---

[1] The concepts in this essay were developed throughout the course of many seminars and
discussion groups I led at the Rivendell Institute. Portions of this essay were presented at the
national conference of the Evangelical Philosophical Society in November 2005 and the Jared
T. Burkholder Conference on Global Engagement at Grace University in Omaha, February
1–4, 2010. I am grateful to the many participants at these events. Thanks are due also to Paul
Copan. Mostly, I am indebted to my colleagues at the Rivendell Institute.

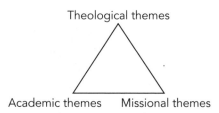

Theological themes

Academic themes   Missional themes

The first angle concerns the *theological themes* raised by the apologetic enterprise. This angle includes a variety of topics, such as the scope of common grace, the nature of general revelation, and the effects of our sinful condition on our reasoning. Exploring these topics theologically helps us develop a realistic understanding of what we ought to expect in our encounters with those who are not yet believers. Theological themes, then, are relevant to our thinking well about apologetics.

The *academic themes* include most of what people have in mind when they think about apologetics. This area includes the details of particular arguments for the existence of God or for other essential Christian claims such as the resurrection of Jesus. It also includes the investigation of challenges to Christianity, such as the problem of evil, or the notion that there is no objective truth. The academic themes include the *content* of apologetics, whether we are thinking about the content of a 30-second answer to a question or about the broad outlines of an academic treatise. As we know from experience, a 30-second answer quickly generates more questions that, in turn, lead us into deeper and more complicated answers. Somewhere along the way, what begins as apologetics becomes philosophy of religion, historical criticism, biochemistry, or physics.

The *missional themes* include what I am calling in this essay *applied apologetics*. These themes involve the dynamics of communicating to a particular audience, whether it is an audience of one or two or a larger group. We aim to communicate in such a way that the gospel is recognized as connecting with the deep needs at the core of every human being. I like to locate applied apologetics under a broader category: *Making the Gospel Connection.* This category covers many facets of our lives and ministries. Our own spiritual growth is largely about making the gospel connection to our own core values, identities, characters, and habits. Spiritual formation and discipleship are about helping other believers make the gospel connection to themselves. Evangelism and the missional themes in apologetics are about making the gospel connection to those not yet followers of Jesus. Our hope is to bring facets of the richness of the gospel to bear on the lives, beliefs, values, and identities of lost human beings. Thinking about apologetics under the category of *Making the Gospel Connection* makes it clear that applied apologetics is evangelism and evangelism is applied apologetics.

Each one of the three angles or themes concerning apologetics is legitimate and fruitful. Each is worthy of careful study. Despite this fact, there are two trends I wish to point out. First, most of the thinking about apologetics has been on the academic themes. While this weight of attention is not in itself a bad thing, it may allow us to forget the other angles of apologetics. Second, most of the criticisms of the usefulness of apologetics find their root in confusing the academic angle of apologetics with the entirety of the apologetic enterprise. Those of us who work in the academic angle bear much of the blame for this confusion. Sometimes we are overzealous about the strength of our arguments or how interesting they ought to be to nonbelievers. Sometimes we neglect the large distinction between arguments that are technically strong and those that might be persuasive to a given person. Sometimes we neglect the missional themes in the apologetic task and thereby reinforce the notion that coming to believe that Christianity is factually true is the main task in our witness. By articulating the importance of the missional angle, as well as of the theological angle, we can defuse many criticisms of apologetics.

Rather than entering the missional angle with a view to defending the apologetic enterprise, however, I shall enter it with a view to helping us be more effective and more faithful in our bearing witness to Christ. So, I will not be concerned with defending apologetics. I will aim to help you think better about how to make the gospel connection with those who are not yet believers. But I must begin by introducing one of my favorite writers.

Apologists as Diagnosticians

Walker Percy (1916–90) was trained as a medical doctor at Columbia University just after World War II. He specialized in pathology. While doing his residency, he caught TB from a cadaver. As part of his treatment, he spent a couple of years in various sanitariums in upstate New York. There was little for him to do except read. He pored over texts from Dostoevsky and Kierkegaard to Sartre and Susanne Langer. As a result, he made two life-changing decisions. First, he was converted to Christ. Second, he dropped medicine to become a writer.

Percy often reflected on the deep connections between his life as a pathologist and his life as a novelist:

> My point is that the stance of the physician is appropriate here. For his stance is that of the diagnostician. A diagnostician is a person who stands towards another person in the relation of one who knows that something has gone wrong with the other. He, the physician-novelist, has a nose for pathology.[2]

He observed that both the novelist and the pathologist begin with a hunch that there is something wrong, and each seeks to find and to name the malady. The pathologist pokes around (with a fairly sophisticated set of tools) until he can identify and name what caused the patient to get sick or die. The novelist has essentially the same calling. He pokes around in the remains of human behavior and culture to discern where they are diseased. They begin with a hunch, and they poke around until they identify and name what is wrong.

The notion that there is a calling to be a diagnostician of the human condition is one that ought to strike gospel-oriented people as right on target. It is fruitful to think about our mission as apologists and evangelists as involving a calling to be a diagnostician. We are the diagnosticians of our age, of the institutions of the world, of the global condition, and of the individual souls touched by all of these contours of the contemporary landscape. It is our calling to poke around and identify what it is that is wrong. It is up to us to find and name the maladies that are rampant throughout culture. How are these cultures, institutions, and

---

[2] Walker Percy, "Physician as Novelist," in *Signposts in a Strange Land*, ed. Patrick Samway (New York: Farrar, Straus Giroux, 1991), 193–94.

individuals resistant to thick gospel reality? When we set about diagnosing the ideas of the age or the currents of thought in an academic field or culture-shaping institution, we are involved in the academic angle of apologetics. Notice, however, that we also have the task of diagnosing the contours of an individual's beliefs and values. It is here that we inhabit the missional angle of apologetics. Rather than thinking about arguments that are generally strong or objections that might be raised, we are thinking about objections that are actually at work in a particular person's soul and reasons that might persuade him to turn to Christ.

Analyzing Soil Samples

Careful diagnosis is essential to our work as gospel-minded people, just as it is to the work of a pathologist or a novelist. Shallow diagnosis results in a fruitless prescription or a bad novel. Shallow diagnosis by missional apologists results in shallow and shortsighted recommendations and anemic articulations of gospel solutions. As people who aim to be faithful followers of Jesus, we need to cultivate our diagnostic skills so we can identify and articulate exactly how the remedy Jesus brings will meet the crucial need. Jesus told a story that illustrates our calling as diagnosticians:

> And he was teaching them many things in parables, and in his teaching he said to them: "Listen! A sower went out to sow. And as he sowed, some seed fell along the path, and the birds came and devoured it. Other seed fell on rocky ground, where it did not have much soil, and immediately it sprang up, since it had no depth of soil. And when the sun rose, it was scorched, and since it had no root, it withered away. Other seed fell among thorns, and the thorns grew up and choked it, and it yielded no grain. And other seeds fell into good soil and produced grain, growing up and increasing and yielding thirtyfold and sixtyfold and a hundredfold." (Mark 4:2–8 ESV)

When thinking about this story, it is important to recall that there is no growth or life unless the seed takes root. As we learn from 1 Cor 3:6, there are those who plant and those who water, but only God causes growth. The question this parable raises for humans, however, is not about what only God can do. It is not about what causes growth. It is about conditions that are necessary for growth to occur. Even when the seed falls on good soil, it is God who causes the growth. The question here is not about God's role. It is about our role. We are the ones who sow and who encounter various types of soil.

We have the sower, and we have four different kinds of soils. Only one of them is in the kind of condition that makes growth possible. The other three are in various conditions, each of which makes it impossible for the seed to sprout and grow well. There are different reasons that each of these soils is inhospitable to the seed. The effect of the soil on the ability of the seed to sprout varies with the condition of the soil.

Up to this point, I have summarized a pretty common understanding of this passage. There is, however, a question that Jesus did not ask but that everyone listening understood. The question is, "What next?" Thinking about the way we have farmed during the past few centuries, the question is: "What does the farmer do next year?" This year he sows and encounters various kinds of bad soil. What does he do next year? Sometimes we think about evangelism and apologetics as if the answer is: "The farmer throws the seed at the ground harder so that maybe more of it will stick." The answer to this question that I have heard most often is: "The farmer throws the seed only on the good soil." This cannot be the right answer. No farmer can afford to sow only on the shrinking patch of good soil. What does the farmer do? He goes out *before* he sows his seed, and he chops and plows the hard ground, pulls out the thorns, and pulls out the rocks. Those listening to Jesus would not have thought about what the farmer would do next year. They would have asked the question, "What does the farmer do next?" In Palestine, the farmer sowed the seed first and then plowed over the seed, to work it into the ground.[3]

I live in Connecticut. All over New England, there are beautiful rock walls. They stretch for miles by the roads. Where did they come from? Did the Pilgrims land and think to themselves: *The first thing we need to*

---

[3] For a discussion of this fact about sowing and plowing in Palestine, see Robert H. Stein, "Criteria for the Gospels' Authenticity," in *Contending with Christianity's Critics: Answering New Atheists and Other Objectors*, ed. Paul Copan and William Lane Craig (Nashville: B&H, 2009), 96; and Joachim Jeremias, *The Parables of Jesus*, rev. ed. (New York: Charles Scribner's Sons, 1963), 11–12. I want to thank Mark W. Linder for pointing me to this reference.

do is build miles and miles of beautiful rock walls? The walls are the results of generations of farmers prying the rocks out of the soil and lugging them to the edge of the field. They undertook this back-breaking task so they could plow effectively and sow the seed in better soil. The soil must be cultivated.

When we think about sowing the seed (doing evangelism), we must think about the preparation of the soil. Just as the task of the farmer is not only to sow, the task of the Christian is not only to present the gospel message. We need also to diagnose the condition of the soil and to discern the best way to prepare it so that the seed can take root.

Engaging the Individual

Although our diagnostic insight must be applied on a number of levels, I wish to focus on the level of the individual person we may engage in a conversation. Let's ask some questions. When encountering a person who is not yet a believer, what is it that shapes the ability of the seed to take root? What makes the soil hard? thorny? rocky? What is blocking the person's access to Jesus? What features in his loves, his thoughts, his habits push the gospel to the periphery of his consciousness? Of course, as gospel witnesses, we strive not only to name what is wrong; we also strive to recognize and to name what is right about individuals, the academy, and our fields. We want to find those points that resonate with the gospel and have potential to open up receptivity to its life-giving message. Not every trend is in the wrong direction. Some are movements in the right direction.

I recommend three tools that can help us become better diagnosticians of individual persons, of our work context, and of our communities. These tools are conceptual. They help us do one thing: They help us ask the right sorts of questions to aid us in our task to identify and name the maladies we face.

Upstream/Downstream

The first tool is a mental picture. Any culture is like a river. Whatever happens upstream has a great effect on what happens downstream. Downstream, we find the individual person and his relation to the gospel. Upstream, we find all of the culture-shaping institutions such as media, government, business, and the university. These institutions shape dramatically the loves and the beliefs of those downstream. They serve to make some notions appear plausible and worthy of consideration and other notions to appear ludicrous.

Of course this picture is an overgeneralization. The culture-shaping institutions are inhabited by people who are downstream as well as upstream. In other words, the people who shape culture are themselves just as subject to the effects of culture as anyone else. The ideas and values that come out of the university, for example, do not come into being out of nothing. They are developed, argued, and articulated by people who are shaped by culture.

In our calling as gospel apologists, we need to operate both far upstream and far downstream. We need to have believers who are engaging in research and teaching in the university, as well as in poetry and fiction in literature, and in film, government, and business. We need to be about shaping how these institutions affect men and women as far as their abilities to recognize the gospel is concerned.

We also need to operate downstream. We need to observe carefully what it is that actually forms resistance to the gospel in the lives of those people we would call ordinary people. What do they think or feel about the gospel? What do they think or feel about their own hopes and aspirations?

Thinking about upstream and downstream helps us think also about systemic and institutional influence. What shapes the human institutions such that they harm or help people? How does a corporation get to the point where it is exploitive of everyone except its shareholders and board? How can a corporation shape the people it touches and bring a touch of life and liberation rather than exploitation?

Incoming/Outgoing Questions

The second tool is to think in terms of incoming and outgoing questions. Ask yourself questions about the people you encounter in the course of your week. What shapes their assumptions? Why is Christianity not even an option for most of them? What are the options they might consider and why? How do they think of themselves and their lives? What do they deeply hold to make up the good life? What do they consider worth pursuing? What are they like as they walk into your office or greet you in front of your house?

These questions are the incoming questions. We ask them about people as they come into conversation with us. As you think hard about questions like these, figure out which answers have a connection to things you might naturally discuss. This thinking is not easy, but doing so might open up a conversation on a deeper level.

Then ask yourself: What do you want your coworkers to be like when they leave? That is, after the conversation or the week or the year or their time working closely with you is over, what do you want them to be like? These questions are the outgoing questions. What ideas can you counter in one conversation or in a few conversations? What vision can you open up a bit—like opening the window a crack on the first warm day in spring—to let some air into their lives? In what ways do you want to reshape their thinking a bit?

I am not talking primarily about conversions. But what new ways of thinking do you want them to begin to embody? What attitudes or assumptions do they come in with that hinder their giving the gospel a hearing and that need to be undermined? For example, many people in the United States embody values best articulated by Friedrich Nietzsche. This is not to say that they know their views are from Nietzsche. Rather, they think about their lives primarily in aesthetic categories. Moral reality, to the extent that they give it a thought, appears to be an alien intrusion that hinders their pursuit of the best life. One of my goals as a teacher is to get my students to think about their lives in terms of virtue rather than pleasure. I teach with this goal in mind. If a student walks out thinking about her life in terms of virtue, she is much closer to the gospel and she is closer to truth and she is closer to a better, richer life.

As another example, a lot of people embrace a false dichotomy about knowledge. Either we have 100 percent certainty, they think, or we have no knowledge at all. In order to know something, many think, we must have certainty. This notion is the wrong turn that René Descartes took. It led to all kinds of problems throughout the history of philosophy. We can help people see that they can and do know things even if they do not know the answer to every question.

Become a Spiritual Mapquest

The third item to cultivate is your skill as a spiritual mapquest. Mapquest, as you know, is the website where you can give any location where you are and any location where you want to go and directions will pop up. It disproves every instance of the quip, "You can't get there from here."

There are at least two sides to becoming a spiritual mapquest. First, we need to have a good grasp on just how far most of our students and colleagues are from the gospel.

In the early seventies, James Engel developed a scale to show that evangelism is a process and not simply an event. He marked the process as stages through which a person travels in order to grasp and apply the message of salvation. It has come to be called the "Engel Scale."[4]

The Engel Scale

-8	Awareness of Supreme Being but no Effective Knowledge of the Gospel
-7	Initial Awareness of the Gospel
-6	Awareness of the Fundamentals of the Gospel
-5	Grasp of the Implications of the Gospel
-4	Positive Attitude Toward the Gospel
-3	Personal Problem Recognition
-2	Decision to Act
-1	Repentance and Faith in Christ
**	NEW CREATURE
1	Post Decision Evaluation
2	Incorporation into Body

[4] Adapted from James F. Engel and Wilbert Norton, *What's Gone Wrong with the Harvest?* (Grand Rapids: Zondervan, 1975), 45. The following text is given (in a footnote) to explain the history of the chart:

This model as presented here has undergone an interesting history. In rudimentary forms, it was first suggested by Viggo Sogaard while he was a student in the Wheaton Graduate School. It was later revised by James F. Engel and published in such sources as *Church Growth Bulletin* and elsewhere during 1973. Since that time, modifications have been introduced as others have made suggestions. Particularly helpful comments have been advanced by Richard Senzig of the communications faculty at the Wheaton Graduate School and Professors C. Peter Wagner and Charles Kraft of the Fuller School of World Missions.

3	Conceptual and Behavioral Growth
4	Communion with God
5	Stewardship
*	Reproduction

       *   Internally (gifts, etc.)

       *   Externally (witness, social action, etc.)

Engel's scale brought significant insight and helped a generation of Christians realize that evangelism is a process. He wrote:

> Most people in most situations are at the very early stages of the decision process and cannot be reached with traditional evangelistic strategies presenting a truncated plan of salvation and calling for decision. How can people understand Jesus and accept him when they possess only a fragmentary knowledge at best of basic gospel truths?[5]

The process, however, was characterized largely as if it was about coming to understand the content of the gospel message. Today the process is quite different. Resistance to the gospel is rarely a matter of failure to grasp its content or implications.

I have put together a revised Engel scale, called *The Diagnostic Scale*, to show the progression as far as influences and ideas that a student or faculty member must go through before he can see his need for Christ. The purpose of this scale is to help us think very carefully about our diagnosis. To what degree do colleagues or fellow students consider God irrelevant to everything they hope for or value?

The Diagnostic Scale (Inspired by the Engel Scale)

-9   Suspicious of any truth claim—thoroughly secular, whether postmodern or otherwise.

-8   "God is completely irrelevant to everything I value or to which I aspire."

-7   Suspicion of theism and Christianity in particular.

-6   Engages with believers: "Even if there is truth, it is not found in God."

-5   Believers begin to shake up smug secularism.

---

[5] J. F. Engel, "The Road to Conversion," *Evangelical Missions Quarterly* (April 1990): 189.

-4   "Christianity is plausible. I still do not believe it."

-3   "I can begin to see myself as a Christian."

-2   "I want to be like you."

-1   "I see my need for Christon."

**   REPENTANCE AND FAITH IN CHRIST

1   Still largely secular and postmodern but committed to growing as a Christian.

2   Further involvement in the community of believers.

3   Sees how the life of Christ is lived out.

4   Begins to think biblically about relationships and issues of integrity.

5   Growing reliance on the Word and the Spirit of God in daily life.

6   Begins to think biblically about life and career.

7   Develops spiritual gifts, mentors others, engages the contemporary mind one person at a time.

I do not mean to claim that my points on this scale are exactly right.[6] I do want to emphasize that the steps have more to do with what a person *sees as valuable* than what he *understands*.

---

[6] See Don Everts and Doug Schaupp, *I Once Was Lost: What Postmodern Skeptics Taught Us About Their Path to Jesus* (Downers Grove, IL: InterVarsity Press, 2008). Everts and Schaupp summarize five major thresholds postmoderns typically cross on their pilgrimage to Christ:

Threshold #1: The move from distrust to trust: Many people can't get past the barrier of distrust of Christians. This requires faithfulness in relationships with relativists/postmoderns. Christians need to be a *safe place.*

Threshold #2: The move from complacency to curiosity: Through conversations/social time, people may come to show hints of curiosity. Rather than overwhelming them, we can present small-scale opportunities to think through the implications of the Christian faith.

Threshold #3: The move from resistance to openness to change in their lives: This takes patience on the part of the Christian; sometimes we can probe and ask: "You've said you're open-minded. Have you ever thought about looking at life from another perspective?"

Threshold #4: The move from meandering to seeking: The "come and see" invitations in John 1 suggest the opportunity to become more deliberate in one's spiritual quest, encouraging people to ask life-change questions.

Threshold #5: The move into the kingdom of God itself: This is where people turn from their old ways of operating to trusting in and following Christ, which leads to growing in faith and obedience.

The diagnostic scale can help us work on both the upstream/downstream issues and the incoming/outgoing questions. As far as up- and downstream is concerned, we can get a better grasp on what the obstacles to the gospel are and what shapes a student's resistance. If we take these observations and move upstream, we may be able to identify research projects that can contribute to undoing the effects of those ideas.

For example, in many cases, a person needs to see that Jesus connects to his deepest aspirations. In order for him to see this fact, he may have to have his aspirations reshaped. He needs to see that the best life is not comprised of the pursuit of pleasure. It involves virtue and deep relationships. The deeper his sense of what it is to flourish as a person, the better able he is to see that the gospel does take up his deepest concerns. In this way, rehabilitating a robust view of human flourishing is a downstream task. Most of the people we hope to reach live in an environment that does not help them to think of human flourishing in this way.

Rehabilitating a robust view of human flourishing is also an upstream task. It consists in many smaller pieces such as undermining reductionistic views of the human person. Those who work in philosophy of mind, metaphysics, sociology, or psychology can contribute to this task. By laying a metaphysical foundation for a human nature that is real and given to us rather than constructed, you can contribute to a theoretical framework that will have gospel implications.

The second part to becoming a spiritual mapquest has to do with the part of the website where you type where you are and where you want to go and then directions pop up. We need to be able to analyze where someone is on important issues and know what the next step for that person is to bring him closer to the gospel from that point. We need to be able to make steps toward the gospel from any and every point on the map. This is where we need to think theologically about everything. We need to think out the implications of all of our doctrines for each area of life and of our studies. It is fruitful to think about what it takes to draw a dotted line between our work and hobbies on the one hand, to some obstacle to the gospel that shapes the people we know, or to some opportunity to build receptivity to the gospel. In all we do, we want always to be aware of the connections to gospel issues.

To think about applied apologetics, then, is to think about how to connect the general features of the broad and cumulative case for Christianity to the particular needs and challenges of the individual person in front of you. No amount of knowledge of the technicalities of the academic issues will help us if we cannot show how these issues touch the very things he cares about most. The conceptual tools can help us by training us to ask the kinds of questions that might reveal fruitful paths to pursue.

Becoming a good diagnostician is part of the task of becoming a faithful follower of Christ. It is an element that requires careful and persistent thought and prayer. Our aim is to be faithful to articulate the riches of the thick gospel and to show its intrinsic relevance to the deepest hopes and dreams of those God brings into our lives.

Chapter 2

FOUR DEGREES
OF POSTMODERNISM

J. P. Moreland

T hese are tolerant, pluralistic times, or so we are often told. They are
also postmodern times, or so we are just as often told. Is there a
conceptual relationship between pluralism and postmodernism? I think
that one's answer to this question will depend on what one means by
the two terms in question. Clearly, one can be a pluralist and not a postmodernist, but given a fairly widely accepted understanding of postmodernism, it is far from clear that the converse is true. And even if
a specific form of postmodernism does not entail a relevant version of
pluralism, it still may be the case that the former provides a plausibility structure for making the latter go down more easily. It would seem
fruitful, then, to explore the relationship between different versions of
postmodernism and pluralism to see what can be learned. This is what I
propose to do in this essay. From time to time, I shall also offer a critique
of the version of postmodernism in focus.

In what follows, I shall distinguish four grades of postmodern
involvement from most to least extreme. In order, those grades are *ontic*,
alethic, *epistemic*, and *axiological/religious* (a.k.a. *nonempirical*) *postmodernism*. In speaking of "grades of postmodern involvement" I am referring to what we might call "degrees of ingression." What I have in mind
is this. The more deeply ingressed or strongly graded one's postmodernism is, the more pervasive is the impact of postmodern ideas throughout one's worldview. More specifically, with rare exceptions, ontic

17

postmodernism entails the other three (if one is an ontic postmodernist, then if one is consistent, one will also be a postmodernist of the other sorts); alethic postmodernism entails epistemic and axiological/religious postmodernism; and epistemic postmodernism entails axiological/religious postmodernism.[1]

Ontic Postmodernism

Ontic postmodernism denies the existence of a mind/theory/language independent world. For the ontic postmodernist, there is no such thing as an objective reality. On the face of it, this claim is pretty hard to take seriously. So before we tease out the implications of ontic postmodernism, we had better try to understand how someone could believe, or at least claim to believe, that there is no such thing as objective reality.

A fairly standard line of argument for this claim goes as follows: First, one refuses to talk about reality itself and, instead, talks about reality assertions, i.e., existence claims, reality-talk.

Second, one observes that existence claims are made relative to a background theory or linguistic community. "There are electrons" is made in the context of a broader theory of atoms, protons, and so forth, such that the assertion itself is given meaning by the role it plays in atomic theory. For example, an electron is something with negative charge, which attracts protons, circles the nucleus, and so forth. "Jesus is the Son of God" is similarly an assertion made relative to the Christian story.

Third, rival theories, different narratives, alternative communities have incommensurable stories—accounts that have no common ground that is theory-independent and on the basis of which those rivals could, in principle, be compared. Theories/narratives and their kin are imperialistic; they leave no prisoners. Nothing whatsoever is theory-independent. It follows that existence claims are simply assertions that play

---

[1] It is possible to deny the existence or relevance of truth and still affirm the objectivity of rationality if that objectivity is cashed out in an antirealist way. So, for example, one could hold that, for some person S, belief P is more rational to hold than belief Q just in case holding P solves more intellectual problems than holding Q, where a solved problem is not taken as an indication of truth and where it is taken to be an objective fact of the matter as to whether P solves more problems than Q. It would take us too far afield to examine these matters further and, in any case, a realist view of rationality is more relevant to the dialectic in focus.

certain roles relative to different narratives. There are no metanarratives, stories that exhibit an objective reality that is just there, existing for everyone. Advocates of different conceptual schemes live in different worlds because there is no such thing as reality itself.

If one asks whether there is something that is *really* real outside a community's narrative, then the ontic postmodernist will respond by saying that the questioner is using "*really*" in an abandoned modernist way, and the question should be disallowed as inappropriate given the postmodern viewpoint. If one does not believe in a narrative-independent reality, then the notions of objective truth, objective rationality (understood in a realist way, as we note below), and objective axiology will, like "Western Civ," have to go. There is a plurality of worlds, truths, rationalities, and values, each constituted by and relative to a different community and its narrative. It should be clear that this form of post-modernism entails a radical version of religious pluralism. Whether God exists and what God is like are literally reduced to linguistic practices relative to different communities. God exists relative to the Christian community because that community uses existence-language to talk about God. God does not exist in the atheist community because that community uses existential denial-talk as a form of life.

My main purpose is to clarify and not critique ontic postmodern-ism, but before we turn to the next grade of postmodern involvement, I should at least sketch out a line of response. First, it is self-evident that a language-independent reality exists. We are in direct contact with it all the time, bump up against it when our beliefs are false, and regularly experience acts of comparing our words, concepts, theories with the real world and adjust the former thereby. Indeed, we have more justification for believing in reality than we do for accepting any of the arguments for ontic postmodernism. This justification places a severe burden of proof on ontic postmodernists that they systematically fail to meet. Second, any attempted support for ontic postmodernism will be either self-refuting or something that should be ignored. If the attempted support (e.g., "linguistic studies demonstrate that various communities carve up 'reality' differently and, thus, there is no such thing as objective reality") is taken to be grounded in reality, then it is self-refuting (the studies must be of real communities and their actual linguistic practices if they provide a "demonstration"). If the alleged support is not even claimed to be rooted in reality, then why should anyone listen to it? It should be dismissed as neurotic ranting. If the postmodernist responds that my dismissal presupposes an outmoded modernist notion of reality, then I will just repeat the dilemma for this claim (either it is about reality and is self-refuting or else it is neurotic ranting).

Alethic Postmodernism

The second, weaker grade of postmodern involvement is *alethic postmodernism*, which denies the concept of truth—especially the correspondence theory of truth—but accepts the existence of a theory-independent world "out there." Accordingly, our descriptions of that world are neither true nor approximately true. Moreover, we are trapped behind our language (theories, conceptual schemes, narratives) and cannot get to the thing-in-itself; so for all purposes, questions about the existence and nature of the "real world" are moot.

The Correspondence Theory of Truth

A bit more needs to be said about the correspondence theory of truth. In its simplest form, the correspondence theory says that a proposition is true just in case it corresponds to reality, when what it asserts to be the case is the case. More generally, truth obtains when a truth-bearer stands in an appropriate correspondence relation to a truth-maker:

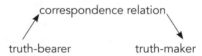

First, what is the truth-bearer? The thing that is either true or false is not a sentence but a proposition. A proposition is the content of a sentence. For example, *It is raining* and *Es regnet* are two different sentences that express the same proposition. A sentence is a linguistic object consisting in a sense-perceptible string of markings formed according to a culturally arbitrary set of syntactical rules, a grammatically well-formed string of spoken or written scratchings/sounds. Sentences are true just in case they express a true proposition or content.

What about truth-makers? What is it that makes a proposition true? The best answer is facts. A fact is some real state of affairs in the world—for example, grass's being green, an electron's having negative charge, God's being all-loving. Consider the proposition that *grass is green*. This proposition is true just in case a specific fact (viz., grass's being green) actually obtains in the real world. If Sally has the thought that *grass is green*, the specific state of affairs (grass actually being green) "makes" the propositional content of her thought true just in case the state of affairs actually is the way the proposition represents it to be. Grass's being green makes Sally's thought true even if Sally is blind and cannot tell whether or not it is true, and even if Sally does not believe the thought. Reality makes thoughts true or false. A thought is not made true by someone believing it or by someone being able to determine whether or not it is true. Put differently, evidence allows one to tell whether or not a thought is true, but the relevant fact is what makes it true.

Our study of truth-bearers has already taken us into the topic of the correspondence relation. Correspondence is a two-placed relation between a proposition and a relevant fact. A two-placed relation, such as "larger than," is one that requires two things (say, a desk and a book) before it holds. Similarly, the truth relation of correspondence holds between two things—a relevant fact and a proposition—just in case the fact matches, conforms to, corresponds with the proposition.

Two Arguments for the Correspondence View

What reasons can be given for accepting the correspondence theory of truth? Two main arguments have been advanced for the correspondence theory, one descriptive and one dialectical. The descriptive argument focuses on a careful description and presentation of specific cases to see what can be learned from them about truth. As an example, consider the case of Joe and Frank. While in his office, Joe receives a call from the university bookstore that a specific book he had ordered—Richard Swinburne's *The Evolution of the Soul*—has arrived and is waiting for him. At this point, a new mental state occurs in Joe's mind—the thought that Swinburne's *The Evolution of the Soul* is in the bookstore.

Now Joe, being aware of the content of the thought, becomes aware of two things closely related to it: the nature of the thought's intentional object (Swinburne's book being in the bookstore) and certain verification steps that would help him to determine the truth of the thought. For example, he knows that it would be irrelevant for verifying the thought to go swimming in the Pacific Ocean. Rather, he knows that he must take a series of steps that will bring him to a specific building and look in certain places for Swinburne's book in the university bookstore.

So Joe starts out for the bookstore, all the while being guided by the proposition that Swinburne's *The Evolution of the Soul* is in the bookstore. Along the way, his friend Frank joins him, though Joe does not tell Frank where he is going or why. They arrive at the store, and both see Swinburne's book there. At that moment, Joe and Frank simultaneously have a certain sensory experience of seeing Swinburne's book *The Evolution of the Soul*. But Joe has a second experience not possessed by Frank. Joe experiences that his thought matches, corresponds with an actual state of affairs. He is able to compare his thought with its intentional object and "see," be directly aware, that the thought is true. In this case, Joe actually experiences the correspondence relation itself, and truth itself becomes an object of his awareness.

The dialectical argument asserts that those who advance alternative theories of truth or who simply reject the correspondence theory actually presuppose it in their own assertions, especially when they present arguments for their views or defend them against defeaters. Sometimes this argument is stated in the form of a dilemma: Those who reject the correspondence theory either take their own utterances to be true in the correspondence sense or they do not. If the former, then those utterances are self-defeating. If the latter, there is no reason to accept them because they cannot take their utterances to be true.

Alethic Postmodernism and Truth-Denial

Alethic postmodernists deny the existence of objective truth, construed along the lines of the correspondence theory, which they often equate with absolute truth. According to Brian McLaren, making absolute truth claims becomes problematic in the postmodern context. Says McLaren, "I think that most Christians grossly misunderstand the philosophical baggage associated with terms like *absolute* or *objective* (linked to foundationalism and the myth of neutrality). . . . Similarly, arguments that pit absolutism versus relativism, and objectivism versus subjectivism, prove meaningless or absurd to postmodern people."[2]

Unfortunately, this postmodernist rejection of objective or absolute truth rests on at least two confusions. The first postmodern confusion involves metaphysical vs. epistemic notions of absolute truth. In the metaphysical and correct sense, absolute truth is the same thing as objective truth. On this view, people discover truth, they do not create it, and a claim is made true or false in some way or another by reality itself, totally independently of whether the claim is accepted by anyone. Moreover, an absolute truth conforms to the three fundamental laws of logic, which are themselves absolute truths. According to objectivism, a commitment to the absolute truth of some proposition P entails no thesis about a knowing subject's epistemic situation regarding P.

Objective Truth and Cartesian Anxiety

By contrast with the metaphysical notion, postmodernists claim that a commitment to absolute truth is rooted in Cartesian anxiety and its need for absolute certainty. Accordingly, they claim that acceptance of the absolute truth of P entails acceptance of the conjunction of P's truth in the objective sense *and* the possibility of a (finite) knowing subject having Cartesian certainty with respect to P. Thus, one postmodernist recently opined that commitment to objective truth and the correspondence theory is merely "an epistemic project [that] is funded by 'Cartesian anxiety,' a product of methodological doubt."[3]

As I have already pointed out, this claim is entirely false philosophically. Advocates of a correspondence theory of objective truth take the view to be a realist metaphysical thesis, and they steadfastly reject all attempts to epistemologize the view. Moreover, historically, it is incredible to assert that the great Western thinkers from Aristotle up to Descartes—correspondence advocates all—had any concern whatever about truth and Cartesian anxiety. The great correspondence advocate Aristotle was hardly in a Cartesian quandary when he wisely pointed

---

[2] Brian McLaren, "Emergent Evangelism," *Christianity Today*, November 2004, 42–43.
[3] Philip Kennison, "There's No Such Thing As Objective Truth, and It's a Good Thing, Too," in *Christian Apologetics in the Postmodern World*, ed. Timothy Philips and Dennis Okholm (Downers Grove, IL: InterVarsity Press, 1995), 157.

out that in the search for truth, one ought not to expect a greater degree of epistemic strength than is appropriate to the subject matter, a degree of strength that varies from topic to topic. The correspondence theory was not born when Descartes came out of his stove, and postmodernists lose credibility when they pretend otherwise. The claim that some proposition P is an objective or absolute truth is simply the claim that P corresponds to reality. Such a claim says absolutely nothing about the speaker's degree of certainty with respect to P.

The second confusion plaguing alethic postmodernists concerns the identity of the truth-bearer. As we have already seen, the informed correspondence theorist will say that propositions are truth-bearers. What is a proposition? Minimally, it is the content of declarative sentences/statements and thoughts/beliefs that is true or false. Beyond that philosophers are in disagreement, but most would agree that a proposition

1. is not located in space or time;
2. is not identical to the linguistic entities that may be used to express it;
3. is not sense perceptible;
4. is such that the same proposition may be in more than one mind at once;
5. need not be grasped by any (at least finite) person to exist and be what it is;
6. may itself be an object of thought when, for example, one is thinking about the content of one's own thought processes;
7. is in no sense a physical entity.

By contrast, a sentence is a linguistic type or token consisting in a sense-perceptible string of markings formed according to a culturally arbitrary set of syntactical rules. A statement is a sequence of sounds or body movements employed by a speaker to assert a sentence on a specific occasion. So understood, neither sentences nor statements are good candidates for the basic truth-bearer.

It is pretty easy to show that having or using a sentence (or any other piece of language) is neither necessary nor sufficient for thinking or having propositional content. First, it's not necessary. Children think prior to their acquisition of language—how else could they thoughtfully learn language—and, indeed, we all think without language regularly. Moreover, the same propositional content may be expressed by a potentially infinite number of pieces of language and, thus, that content is not identical to any linguistic entity. This alone does not show that language is not necessary for having propositional content. But when one attends to the content that is being held constant as arbitrary linguistic expressions are selected to express it, that content may easily be seen to satisfy the nonlinguistic traits of a proposition listed above.

Second, it's not sufficient. If erosion carved an authorless linguistic scribble in a hillside, for example, "I'm eroding," then strictly speaking it would have no meaning or content, though it would be empirically equivalent to another token of this type that would express a proposition were it the result of authorial intention.

Postmodernists attack a straw man when they focus on the alleged inadequacies of linguistic objects to do the work required of them in a correspondence theory of truth. Speaking for himself and other postmodernists, Joseph Natoli claims, "No one representation, or narrative, can reliably represent the world because language/pictures/sounds (signifiers) are not permanent labels attached to the things of the world nor do the things of the world dwell inside such signifiers."[4] Unfortunately, even granting the fact that language (and certain sensations) is problematic if taken to represent things in the world (e.g., that the language/world hookup is arbitrary), it follows that human subjects cannot accurately represent the world only if we grant the further erroneous claim that representational entities are limited to language (and certain sensations). But this is precisely what the sophisticated correspondence theorist denies.

Again, Richard Rorty says, "To say that truth is not out there is simply to say that where there are no sentences there is not truth, that sentences are elements of human language, and that human languages are human creations. Truth cannot be out there—cannot exist independently of the human mind—because sentences cannot so exist, or be out there. . . . Only descriptions . . . can be true and false."[5] It should be obvious that

---

[4] Joseph P. Natoli, *Primer to Postmodernity* (Oxford: Blackwell, 1997), 18.
[5] Richard Rorty, *Contingency, Irony and Solidarity* (New York: Cambridge University Press, 1989), 4–5.

Rorty attacks a straw man and that his argument goes through only if we grant that sentences are the fundamental truth-bearers.

Epistemic Postmodernism

Epistemic postmodernists do not target reality or truth; rather, the object of their rejection is reason (allegedly construed along modernist lines) and "objective rationality." The notion of objective rationality that they reject includes two components: the ability of a knowing, believing subject to have (1) objective justification for his beliefs and (2) direct, cognitive access to the objects of knowledge in the external world. Let us analyze these components in this order.

The Impossibility of Objectivity?

Postmodernists reject the notion that rationality is objective on the grounds that no one approaches life in a totally objective way without bias. Thus, objectivity is impossible, and observations, beliefs, and entire narratives are theory-laden. There is no neutral standpoint from which to approach the world. Therefore, observations, beliefs, and so forth are perspectival constructions that reflect the viewpoint implicit in one's own web of beliefs. For example, Stanley Grenz claims that postmodernism rejects the alleged modernist view of reason, which "entails a claim to dispassionate knowledge, a person's ability to view reality not as a conditioned participant but as an unconditioned observer—to peer at the world from a vantage point outside the flux of history."[6]

Regarding knowledge, postmodernists believe that there is no point of view from which one can define knowledge itself without begging the question in favor of one's own view. "Knowledge" is a construction of one's social, linguistic structures, not a justified, truthful representation of reality by one's mental states. For example, knowledge amounts to what is deemed to be appropriate according to the professional certification practices of various professional associations. As such, knowledge is a construction that expresses the social, linguistic structures of those associations, nothing more, nothing less.

---

[6] Stanley Grenz, *Revisioning Evangelical Theology* (Downers Grove, IL: InterVarsity Press, 1993), 15.

These postmodernist claims represent very deep confusion about the notion of objectivity. As a first step toward clearing away this confusion, we need to draw a distinction between psychological and rational objectivity. It is clear from the quotation above that Grenz's confused understanding of objectivity is at least partly rooted in his mistaken conflation of these two senses. Psychological objectivity is detachment, the absence of bias, a lack of commitment either way on a topic.

Do people ever have psychological objectivity? Yes, they do, typically in areas in which they have no interest or about which they know little or nothing. Note carefully two things about psychological objectivity. For one thing, it is not necessarily a virtue. It is if one has not thought deeply about an issue and has no convictions regarding it. But as one develops thoughtful, intelligent convictions about a topic, it would be wrong to remain "unbiased," that is, uncommitted regarding it. Otherwise, what role would study and evidence play in the development of one's approach to life? Should one remain "unbiased" that cancer is a disease, that rape is wrong, that the New Testament was written in the first century, or that there is design in the universe, if one has discovered good reasons for each belief? No, one should not.

For another thing, while it is possible to be psychologically objective in some cases, most people are not psychologically objective regarding the vast majority of the things they believe. In these cases, it is crucial to observe that a lack of psychological objectivity does not matter, nor does it cut one off from knowing or seeing the world directly the way it is, or from presenting and arguing for one's convictions. Why? *Because a lack of psychological objectivity does not imply a lack of rational objectivity and it is the latter that matters most, not the former.*

To understand this, we need to get clear on the notion of rational objectivity. Rational objectivity is the state of having accurate epistemic access to the thing itself. This entails that if one has rational objectivity regarding some topic, then one can discern the difference between genuinely good and bad reasons/evidence for a belief about that topic and one can hold the belief for genuinely good reasons/evidence. The important thing here is that bias does not stand between a knowing subject and an intentional object, nor does it eliminate a person's ability to assess the reasons for something. Bias may make it more difficult but not impossible. If bias made rational objectivity impossible, then no teacher—including the postmodernist herself—could responsibly teach any view the teacher believed on any subject! Nor could the teacher teach opposing viewpoints because she would be biased against them!

Grenz exhibits the twin confusions, so common among postmodernists, of failing to assess properly the nature and value of psychological objectivity and of failing to distinguish and properly assess the relationship between psychological and rational objectivity.

So much for objectivity.

No Direct Cognitive Access to Objects of Consciousness?

The second component of epistemic postmodernism is the denial of direct cognitive access to the objects of consciousness. Postmodernists adopt a highly contentious model of perception and intentionality, often without argument, and they seem to enjoin serious consideration of a (prima facie) more plausible model. The result is that postmodernists are far too pessimistic about the prospects of human epistemic success.

Postmodernists adopt a linguistic version of René Descartes's idea theory of perception (and intentionality generally). To understand the idea theory and the postmodern adaptation of it, a good place to start is with a commonsense, critical realist view of perception. According to critical realism, when a subject is looking at a red object such as an apple, the object itself is the direct object of the sensory state. What one sees directly is the apple itself. True, one must have a sensation of red to apprehend the apple, but on the critical realist view, the sensation of red is to be understood as a case of being-appeared-to-redly and analyzed as a *self-presenting property*. What is a self-presenting property? If some property F is a self-presenting one, then it is by means of F that a relevant external object is presented directly to a person, and F presents itself directly to the person as well. Thus, F presents its object mediately though directly, and itself immediately.

This is not as hard to understand as it first may appear. Sensations, such as being-appeared-to-redly, are an important class of self-presenting properties. If Jones is having a sensation of red while looking at an apple, then having the property of being-appeared-to-redly as part of his consciousness modifies his substantial self. When Jones has this sensation, it is a tool that presents the red apple mediately to him, and the sensation also presents itself to Jones. What does it mean to say that the sensation presents the apple to him mediately? Simply this: it is in virtue of or by means of the sensation that Jones directly sees the apple itself.

Moreover, by having the sensation of red, Jones is directly aware both of the apple and of his own awareness of the apple. For the critical realist, the sensation of red may, indeed, be a tool or means that Jones uses to become aware of the apple, but he is thereby directly aware of the apple. His awareness of the apple is direct in that nothing stands between Jones and the apple, not even his sensation of the apple. That sensation presents the apple directly, though as a tool, Jones must have the sensation as a necessary condition for seeing the apple. On the critical realist view, a knowing subject is not trapped behind or within anything, including a viewpoint, a narrative, a historical-linguistic perspective. To have an entity in the external world as an object of intentionality is to already be "out there"; there is no need to escape anything. One is not trapped behind one's eyeballs or anything else. It is a basic fallacy of logic to infer that one sees a point-of-viewed-object from the fact that one sees an object from a point of view.

Before leaving the critical realist view, it is important to say that the theory does not limit self-presenting properties to those associated with the five senses and, therefore, does not limit the objects of direct awareness to ordinary sensory objects. The critical realist will say that a knowing subject is capable of direct acquaintance with a host of non-sense-perceptible objects—one's own ego and its mental states, various abstract objects such as the laws of mathematics or logic, and spirit beings, including God.

By contrast, for Descartes's idea theory, one's ideas (in this case, sensations) stand between the subject and the object of perception. Jones is directly aware of his own sensation of the apple and indirectly aware of the apple in the sense that it is what causes the sensation to happen. On the idea theory, a perceiving subject is trapped behind his own sensations and cannot get outside them to the external world in order to compare his sensations to their objects to see whether those sensations are accurate.

Now, in a certain sense, postmodernists believe that people are trapped behind something in the attempt to get to the external world. However, for them the wall between people and reality is not composed of sensations as it was for Descartes; rather, it is constituted by one's community and its linguistic categories and practices. One's language serves as a sort of distorting and, indeed, creative filter. One cannot get outside one's language to see whether one's talk about the world is the way the world is. Thus, Grenz advocates a new outlook, allegedly representing some sort of consensus in the human sciences, that expresses "a more profound understanding of epistemology. Recent thinking has helped us see that the process of knowing, and to some extent even the process of experiencing the world, can occur only within a conceptual framework, a framework mediated by the social community in which we participate."[7]

It has been noted repeatedly that such assertions are self-refuting. For if we are all trapped behind a framework such that simple, direct seeing is impossible, then no amount of recent thinking can help us see anything; all it could do would be to invite us to see something *as* such and such from within a conceptual framework. Given the self-refuting nature of such claims, and given the fact that we all experience regularly the activity of comparing our conceptions of an entity with the entity itself as a way of adjusting those conceptions, it is hard to see why anyone, especially a Christian, would adopt the postmodern view. In any case, I have seldom seen the realist perspective seriously considered by postmodern thinkers, and until it is, statements like Grenz's will be taken as mere mantras by many of us.

Axiological (Religious, Nonempirical) Postmodernism

It is possible, indeed, it is widely believed that the physical world and only the physical world studied by the hard sciences employing empirical means is real, that those sciences and only those sciences furnish truth or approximate truth regarding the domain of entities within their proper domain, and that objective rationality is achieved in and only in those sciences. Underwritten by some form of empiricism, this view eschews

---

[7] Grenz, *Revisioning Evangelical Theology*, 73–74.

postmodernism as an approach to the hard sciences while employing it everywhere else. Technically, this grade of postmodern involvement should be called *nonempirical postmodernism*, but I have adopted the somewhat less accurate label *axiological postmodernism* because of the main impact of this view in contemporary life. Axiological postmodernism treats religious, ethical, political, and aesthetic claims in a postmodernist way.

Folk Empiricism

Standing behind axiological postmodernism, at least in popular culture, is an implicit epistemology that we may call *folk empiricism*, which holds that *for any belief P, P is reasonable to believe and assert if and only if P can be and has been adequately tested with one's five senses.* Let's name this claim FE. The point of FE is to limit what we can reasonably believe and assert to what can be "appropriately" tested with the five senses, and the hard sciences are taken to be the ideal exemplars of this epistemic standpoint. When many people make claims consistent with axiological postmodernism, they are assuming something like FE whether they know it or not. So we need to ask, how do things stand with respect to FE? How should we assess it?

First, in a certain sense, FE is self-refuting. As we shall see shortly, FE is, in fact, false. But it is arguably the case that FE could have been true. It is not necessarily false like "2+3=17." Rather, it is like "Cuba is a state in the United States." While false, under certain circumstances, this sentence would have been true. Similarly, arguably, FE could have been true even though it is false. By contrast and strictly speaking, self-refuting statements, for example, "No sentence of English is longer than three words," are necessarily false—they could not under any circumstances be true.

It follows, then, that, strictly speaking, FE itself is not self-refuting. But that should be of small comfort to people who assume FE. Why? Because all an advocate of FE can do is merely to shout FE and leave it at that. One cannot give any evidence that FE itself is a reasonable belief because this claim about FE's rationality *would* be self-refuting. It would amount to this assertion: It is reasonable to believe (and, thus, we all ought to believe) that "for any belief P, P is reasonable to believe and assert if and only if P can be and has been appropriately tested with one's five senses." Once one claims that FE is itself reasonable to accept, that claim is self-refuting because there is no sense experience to which one can appeal to justify belief in FE.

To clarify, suppose one claimed that there was an apple on the table. It is very clear what sensory experiences could verify or falsify that claim. But no such sensory experiences can be given to justify FE itself. Thus, FE cannot be recommended as something one should reasonably believe, and for those of us who want reasonable beliefs, that's enough for us to dismiss FE from further consideration. And if someone claims that FE is itself reasonable, his or her assertion is self-refuting.

Either adequate reasons can be given for FE or they cannot. If they cannot, then there are not adequate reasons to believe it. If there are, then FE is self-refuting and there are not adequate reasons to believe it. Either way, FE's adequacy as a viewpoint is in trouble. Not only are there no adequate reasons for believing FE; there *can* be no such reasons! So much for FE as an adequate, reasonable guide for life decisions!

But there's more. Not only can there be no adequate reasons for accepting FE, but FE fails to account for many of the things we actually know or believe on the basis of adequate reasons. Let me give some examples. For brevity, let us use seeing as a shorthand way of speaking about testing something with all five senses and not just sight.

First, truth (correspondence with reality) is not something one can see; so if we are limited to our five senses, no one could have a grasp of truth itself. If I believe that a particular book I ordered is at the bookstore waiting to be picked up, and if I go to the bookstore and see the book, I also know that my thought that the book was there is true. I can see the book, but I cannot see *my thought* that the book is there nor can I have a sense experience that the situation in the bookstore (my book being there) accurately corresponds with my thought. In a case where my wife tells me I am angry and I am not sure she's correct, I can introspect to decide the matter. If I take the thought *I am angry* and use it to search my inner feelings, then when I experience my own anger, I come to know that my wife's claim is true. But I cannot see my thought (*I am angry*), I cannot see the emotional state of anger itself, and I cannot see the true correspondence between the thought and my feeling of anger. Truth itself is not sense perceptible.

Second, adequate notions of what knowledge is, what counts as a good explanation, what makes a piece of evidence a good piece of evidence are not matters one can know or have a reasonable view about if one is limited to one's five senses. Take knowledge. Many have understood knowledge to be justified true belief. If I actually know that I had breakfast this morning, then (1) I believe I had breakfast, (2) it is actually true that I had breakfast, and (3) I must have adequate reasons (perhaps, from memory) that I had breakfast (I can't just have a lucky guess about breakfast). Some people think that this definition of knowledge is close but not entirely adequate to capture what knowledge itself is. Now, how in the world are we going to evaluate this definition of knowledge and definitions offered by detractors? How are we going to come to know what knowledge itself is if we are limited to what we can test with the five senses? Exactly to what sensation could a proponent or critic of this definition appeal to make his or her case? These questions make evident (and making something evident is not something we can recognize by our senses!) how absurd FE really is as a guide for knowledge.

We know a host of other things that are not justifiable by our five senses. We do not know our own states of consciousness (our thoughts, feelings, desires, beliefs, whether we chose to do something or did it passively out of habit), and we do not know our own selves by sensation. We don't even know which sensations in a room filled with people are ours as opposed to which belong to others by our five senses! We don't gain normative knowledge by our senses, knowledge of what we should and should not believe (rational normativity), what we should and should not do (moral normativity), or what is beautiful or ugly (aesthetic normativity). And we do have this sort of knowledge. I should rationally believe there are such things as birds or that 2+2=4, I should morally recognize that kindness and honesty are virtues not vices, and I should aesthetically recognize that a sunset viewed from Maui over a turquoise ocean is beautiful.

Even some things studied in the hard sciences cannot be known by the five senses. For example, one cannot see, touch, feel, hear, or smell a magnetic field, but we know there are such things. One can see or feel the effects of such a field, say the iron filings falling into a particular pattern, but one cannot see the field itself. We infer that there must be such a field to explain the effects.

At the end of the day, FE is an inadequate guide for living a rational life, no matter how many people believe it. To the degree that axiological postmodernism is justified by FE, then it must be rejected as well.

In this essay I have sought to clarify and distinguish four different forms of postmodernism. I have ranked them in order of their strength and, along the way, I have criticized different versions, though I admit that my critiques are brief and need further development. In so doing, I hope I have clarified the relationship between postmodernism and pluralism in their various forms.

Chapter 3

APOLOGETICALLY BLONDE
The Struggle of Women to Defend Their Faith and What They Should Do about It

Toni Allen

For the last eight years, it has been my joy to teach and encourage young people both on college campuses and in the church to pursue what I call a *well-formed thought life*. My main purpose with nonbelievers has been to discover and help clear away intellectual barriers to the truth of Jesus Christ, and to assist them in the maturation of their reasoning skills so that when true ideas present themselves, they are more easily recognized. My goal with Christians has been not only to equip them to accomplish the aforementioned, but also to see them embrace and grow in their desire to love God with all of their faculties, which vitally includes their minds.

The reason I pursue this endeavor is the same as it has always been—namely, that it is still true that "false ideas are the greatest obstacles to the reception of the gospel."[1] This oft-quoted famous and iconic declaration by J. Gresham Machen continues to bear witness and, sadly, affects the church almost as equally as the public square. For while it certainly is the case that the god of this world (Satan) has worked diligently to deceive those outside the church[2] in efforts to keep them from Christ, we also regretfully see a variety of convoluted ideas continuing to grow

---

[1] J. Gresham Machen, "Christianity and Culture," *Princeton Theological Review* 11 (1913): 7.
[2] See 2 Cor 4:4.

within the church. It is equally sad that Christians are still profusely ill-equipped to dislodge them. The need for modern believers to learn to love God with their minds has never been more pressing.

Over the past 18 months, my focus has been primarily on work-ing with Christian women with a view to encouraging them to become better equipped to defend their faith. I call this process "loving God noetically." The idea comes from the Greek concept of *noéō*, meaning "perceive, think, or understand with the *nous* or mind."[3] Thus, to love God noetically simply means to love God with the mind. This is more than just studying theology and learning Christian doctrine (although these are absolutely essential); rather, loving God noetically includes learning to reason well and with precision in order to explore ideas, both true and false, which are vital to God's kingdom.

Further, it is also crucial to develop the ability to articulate those ideas gracefully. I believe this to be of strategic importance in becom-ing a skilled apologist. This is because loving God with our minds is not some intellectual enterprise that simply makes us *smart* Christians; rather, it is the graced understanding that makes us faithful disciples.[4]

My goal with women has been to help them develop competent rea-soning skills and combine them with veridical evidence for the Christian faith. Through the development of such a well-formed thought life, we not only become equipped to give others a solid defense of Christianity, but we also guard our own minds against many of the false ideas that believers regularly encounter in the secular milieu of our culture. I do not make the distinction between sharing my faith and defending it, as I believe anytime we offer any truth of Christ to a nonbeliever, this should always be combined with supportive evidence for it. Even when sharing the love of Christ with someone who is hurting, I provide reasons for *why* Christ loves them, and not just statements that He does. Thus, I often use the phrases "sharing faith" and "defending faith" synonymously.

To this end, I have been blessed to work with some tenacious women who have committed themselves to the growth and development of their noetic capacities. In so doing, I have also identified several key issues

---

[3] *The New Testament Greek Lexicon*, accessed May 2010, http://www.searchgodsword.org/lex/grk/view.cgi?number=3539.

[4] Darren C. Marks, "The Mind under Grace," *Christianity Today*, March 12, 2010, 23.

that I believe consistently hinder women in defending the Christian faith. I consider women who struggle with these issues to be *apologetically challenged*, and I believe this has little to do with their intellectual acumen. Thus, my purpose herein is to bring attention to these areas and offer some helpful suggestions regarding their improvement, as I truly believe any woman—regardless of hair color—can do.

Before I illustrate my observations, it's important that I clarify that my intention is in no way to construct a false dichotomy between men and women in this essay. Men can also be apologetically challenged (and indeed, I believe many are), and some of the issues I outline could apply to them as well (though perhaps from a different angle). I also recognize that developing a well-formed thought life is by no means formulaic, and individuals have different interests and aptitudes when it comes to philosophical reasoning and apologetics. While I believe both genders are held to the same standard with respect to Christ's command in Matt 22:37, I want to be clear that in this essay, I am simply talking to women. I speak to them as one of them, and given my training in philosophy and my background of witnessing to many of my students as a college professor, I am blessed to be able to offer my insights and hope they will be helpful.

Conflict

The first issue I've observed that seems to hinder many women in defending their faith is their natural inclination to avoid conflict. I have had hundreds of women over the years tell me that one reason they do not readily share Christ with a coworker or nonbelieving friend is fear of either causing strife in the relationship or inciting unfriendly dialogue. This is understandable because women tend to be natural peacekeepers. In fact, we are on average 20 times less aggressive than men, and thus simply far more inclined to take precautions not to provoke conflict and to avoid it whenever possible.[5] The proverbial "butterflies" which instinctively flutter inside us when facing a possibly tense discussion can be a strong deterrent, making it difficult for women to be motivated to enter

---

[5] See Anne Campbell, "Aggression," in *The Handbook of Evolutionary Psychology*, ed. David M. Buss (Hoboken, NJ: Wiley, 2005), 628–52.

into those situations that may result in discord or unpleasant interactions with others. Further, a women's aversion to conflict is significantly stronger than a man's.[6] Studies show that when a conflict breaks out in a game, females will usually decide to stop playing, while most males do not.[7] This is because it is part of the female's design to endeavor to preserve social harmony. Women are naturally wired to forge communicative and emotional connection, create community, and protect their relationships.[8] Conflict with others simply undermines this.

Our fear of conflict wouldn't factor into our struggle to defend our faith if defending our faith wasn't perceived to be a conflict-oriented enterprise. In fact, I believe our concern that attempts to share our faith may provoke conflict is not at all misplaced. This is not only because there are times when the gospel will genuinely offend people, but also because we unfortunately live in a culture where few understand the notion of true tolerance. True tolerance is the idea that disagreement in the public square should occur amiably and without conflict. We respectfully disagree with the ideas of others, and they are free to do the same. However, in our modern culture, true tolerance has been replaced with the notion that to tolerate opposing ideas in more prejudicial areas generally means that we should abstain from public disagreement. This is especially true with respect to religious and ethical ideas, which are frequently considered to be subjectively based rather than objectively grounded. Therefore, it is often thought that they should remain a private matter. As a result, expressing disagreement, especially in these controversial areas, is regarded by many to be disrespectful and intolerant. No wonder we find ourselves anxious in those discussions with nonbelievers. They so easily misunderstand our desire for them to know the truth of Christ to be merely a desire for them to believe as we do, and thus our assertions are frequently misperceived as arrogance.

However, while this understanding may validate our strong desire to avoid conflict with others, which is a noble endeavor, it should not dissuade us from the higher calling of sharing reasons with nonbelievers to trust in the person of Christ. I believe it is apologetic knowledge

---

[6] Eleanor E. Maccoby, *The Two Sexes: Growing Up Apart, Coming Together* (Cambridge, MA: Harvard University Press, 1998), 36.

[7] Ibid.

[8] Louann Brizendine, *The Female Brain* (London: Bantam Books, 2007), 7.

combined with the art of tactful communication that can assist us in learning to overcome progressively our fear and anxiety. When we know *what* we're talking about and *how* to share it with others tactfully, our confidence grows and we naturally become less concerned about being caught off guard by questions or provocative statements. When we've taken measures to equip ourselves with solid evidence for the truth of the gospel, we can relax knowing we've done well before the Lord. This serves to strengthen our own confidence and promotes a calmer inner disposition when sharing the truth of Christ. This confidence is readily perceived by others and can serve to create an inviting atmosphere for dialogue. In fact, I find a relaxed and confident demeanor to be a vital element. In my experience, when this is combined with the offer of well-reasoned arguments for the truth of Christianity, it actually serves to help avoid acrimony. (Remember, *arguments* are not attempts to quarrel; they are tools in logic and evidence that, when constructed properly, are designed to demonstrate the truth of an idea.) Thus, on many occasions I've found that when I confidently provide genuinely satisfying explanations, nonbelievers will begin to ask more questions with less irritation.

I remember one student with whom I recently met over coffee (my preferred method) whose whole family was from India and deeply Hindu. She told me she had learned to come to terms with some difficult events in her life through her guru's teaching that free will was illusory and that fate had determined these things to make her stronger. After I listened to her story and empathized with what had happened to her, I began to explain that the concepts implied in the notion of determination are not compatible with the idea of an impersonal force such as fate. She began asking questions, and as I continued calmly to explain these concepts, the student was able eventually to admit that perhaps her guru might be mistaken about a few things.

Finally, it's good to remember that women have unique gender-based abilities that I believe God desires to use in reaching nonbelievers. Our natural inclination to avoid conflict predisposes us to keep exchanges with others peaceful, and this can be used to our advantage. When we combine this with our intuition and an articulate understanding of our faith, we can be incredibly effective in fulfilling the calling to provide an *apologia* to anyone who asks us for the hope that is within, with gentleness and respect.[9]

Spiritual Experience and Emotion

The other issue that I believe contributes to the difficulty for many women struggling to defend their faith is the one I actually believe to be the most common. That is, I find that women often depend on their experience and emotional connection with God as the primary *justification* for the beliefs they hold. In other words, women tend to perceive meaningful experiences and their corresponding emotions to be validation that what they believe is accurate. Yes, the gospel is for the whole person, and this includes existential reasons (including personal experience as well as our deepest emotions and longings)[10] and even the testimony of Christian love as the greatest apologetic of all (John 13:34). However, a well-rounded defense of the gospel will include rational reasons and evidences. Doing so will be important for three reasons.

First, when believers are overly dependent on their phenomenal experience and emotions as justification for their faith, this can severely dampen their motivation to pursue a deeper understanding of its evidential support. Second, while our experience may play an important role when sharing Christ with nonbelievers, it may not provide the cogent force necessary to overcome intellectual barriers to faith. Third, primarily depending on experience and feelings as affirmation of an idea's accuracy can lead to errors in judgment. Let me explain.

In my discussions with women about the lack of motivation to pursue well-reasoned support for their faith, the feedback I've received is very consistent. Women tend to be very satisfied with the experiential aspects of their faith. They simply don't see the need to learn to defend their faith because they already know it's true, and thus their motivation to pursue its evidential support is greatly diminished. As such, spiritual experience becomes their primary focus in confirming what they believe. One girl with whom I recently spoke stated emphatically

---

[9] See 1 Pet 3:15.

[10] C. S. Lewis, for example, presented an "argument from desire." See Clifford Williams, *Existential Reasons for Belief in God: A Defense of Desires and Emotions for Faith* (Downers Grove, IL: InterVarsity Press, 2011), 49.

that she simply preferred the emotional elements of her walk with God, and she believed that pursuing an arguable defense for her faith would detract from this. She just did not think arguing with nonbelievers communicated God's love in a robust way. Another young woman asserted that her emotional connection to God was the main reason she was passionate to serve Him, and she thought that the problem with the church in the past was that Christians were way too much in their heads, and not enough into their "hearts."

Now as a Christian, I can easily understand how believers could come to rely on their personal experience and emotional connection to God as validation of their faith. The inner testimony of the Holy Spirit does confirm to us that we are children of God and that our faith in Christ is accurately placed. Further, our experience in fellowship with God is often very satisfying, both psychologically and emotionally. Experiencing the Holy Spirit in our worship—indeed, in our day-to-day lives—leaves believers with both the confirmation and satisfaction that God truly is present in our lives. However, when publicly defending Christianity, we must realize that appeals to religious experience typically do not function as a decisive apologetic.

This is primarily because appealing to religious experience when sharing with nonbelievers is not often persuasive enough to demonstrate the truthful nature of Christianity. For one, it is very difficult to perceive the phenomenal character of another person's experience. Nonbelievers are challenged to understand the convictions of conscience, the joy of forgiveness, and the sweetness of personal fellowship with Christ that believers experience. These simply have highly nuanced qualities that prove very difficult to ascertain apart from the experience of them. Further, religious experience is not held to be that persuasive within modern culture, and it is a real struggle for many nonbelievers to understand how it is ontologically grounded. Thus, religious experience is regarded as more likely stemming from a variety of our subjective desires and emotions, and these are not generally persuasive. Finally, because of the many false ideas pervasive in secular culture, our experience is not often sufficient to break through many of the intellectual barriers that these false ideas present. When we are not able to provide evidential support, our personal testimony (as it is often called) is usually all we have left to offer. Unfortunately for many in our pluralistic society, this simply is not enough.

Finally, while it is the case that women are naturally more cognizant of their emotions, nevertheless, depending on them as the primary validation for our beliefs directly affects our judgment. This often occurs when women affirm or deny the truth of an idea based on how they feel about the idea. For example, when presenting arguments from cosmology for reasons to believe in a personal creator, on occasion I notice a negative reaction when I discuss the theory of the "Big Bang." From the feedback I've received, this largely seems the result of an unfavorable association that some mistake Big Bang Cosmology (BBC) to have with Darwinian (naturalistic) evolution, in addition to some confusion about BBC's compatibility with the creation account in Genesis. Although I clearly illustrate the argumentative support the theory provides in favor of Christianity, still I find that women take longer to overcome their negative feelings about it. In fact, in mentoring many women over the years, I have found it very common that rather than evaluate an idea on its merits, they are instead more reluctant to adopt an idea if it actuates negative feelings, or more eager to accept it because of positive ones.

The idea that emotion affects cognition is by no means a recent one in history. Aristotle himself believed that emotions had the power to rival, weaken, or bypass reason. He taught that emotion challenged reason in all three of these ways, and that our feelings often compete with our reason for control over our actions. Indeed, Aristotle believed that our emotions rob our faculty of reason of its full acuity, thus leaving us *noetically handicapped*. Further, he thought that our passions made us impetuous: "the impetuous person does not go through a process of deliberation and does not make a reasoned choice; he simply acts under the influence of a passion."[11] For Aristotle, this meant that the influence of our emotive faculties over our cognitive ones is such that there are times when our reasoning process does not enter into conscious reflection until it is too late to influence our decisions.[12]

---

[11] Cited in "Aristotle's Ethics," in the *Stanford Encyclopedia of Philosophy* (2009 ed.), accessed April 11, 2010, http://plato.stanford.edu/entries/aristotle-ethics/.
[12] Ibid.

Do not misunderstand: I am not advocating beliefs without emotion or repudiating the role of personal experience in our faith. I wholeheartedly believe that our experience and our feelings function well to passionately fuel our God-given desires to serve Him. But God designed our faculties for functioning in an integrated, holistic function.

Nevertheless, I want to be clear that experience and emotion alone tend to make for a poor defense of the Christian faith, and moreover, God never intended them to fill this role. Therefore, in our endeavor to learn to use apologetics successfully, it is vital that we strive to become aware of those times when we adopt beliefs based solely on our experience, zeal, or inclination. Adopting ideas as true or false without attempting to appraise their evidential support or philosophical soundness is poor thinking, and women must become acutely aware of this tendency and work diligently to overcome it.

Some Helpful Suggestions

At this point, I have several suggestions I want to offer to give basic direction on overcoming the struggle to defend our faith for any of the reasons I've outlined. The suggestions I offer here are not meant to be the total solution to address these issues; however, I believe they are good starting points.

First, it is important to gain *understanding*. As I've mentioned, confidence stems from understanding what you believe and why you believe it, and so it's important to take inventory of your knowledge of Christianity. I've outlined some very basic questions at the end of this essay which I hope will be of assistance in identifying those areas of faith and doctrine which generally need better understanding and evidential support. I recommend using a journal and working through each question slowly. Then go over your answers carefully and ask yourself how your answers would sound in conversation and whether the evidence you have provided would seem convincing if you were sharing it with a nonbeliever. Then identify which areas need additional work (and actually work on them).

Second, I know this must seem painfully obvious, but it's vital to *read widely*. Most importantly, find a basic primer in logic and thinking skills that is accessible at your level, and take notes while you read it. Practice using what you learn with a friend or family member. Further, read books by well-known and respected authors in philosophy and apologetics. Go through a good introduction to systematic theology. The Internet also has a wealth of resources; just do a little research to make sure they are reputable. Subscribe to the RSS feeds of apologetic web sites and to the newsletters of apologetic ministries. Scour the blogs of well-known teachers of apologetics and try to summarize their points in your own words. If you are consistently on the go, then get an e-reader, load it up and utilize it at lunch or afternoon coffee between appointments or activities. Further, it's very helpful to always be slowly working through some material that is just a bit difficult to digest. This naturally stretches our intellectual capacities and leads to wonderful growth.

Third, it's important to work on developing some rhetorical skill. After all, ladies, talking is one of the things we were designed to do! Developing conversational skills will pay great dividends in the effort to share Christ reasonably. One very effective way I have found to learn this is to *role play* consistently. Role playing with others greatly helps to identify weaknesses in conversational skills that are not readily apparent and that you want to overcome *before* you engage. Gaining knowledge is obviously primary, but then we must learn to share our knowledge successfully with others, and, for many, this is an acquired skill. Role playing will also serve to assist in overcoming that pesky nervousness that can be so persistent when taking new ideas out for a drive. After you've driven them around a bit through role play, you become more familiar with them and more confident in the ability to use them well. I suggest scheduling a regular time to meet with one or more fellow apologetics enthusiasts who will commit to growing together in this area.

In addition, I have found the following tips to be very helpful in drawing others into a productive conversation. Learning to create a noncombative atmosphere that invites dialog is not difficult, and you don't have to become a dexterous communicator to do so. The first and most important thing I do when I am entering into a conversation with someone is to attempt to avoid creating an obvious dichotomy between my ideas and theirs. This is because I do not want others to misperceive my desire for dialog to be a desire merely to win an argument with them (which can lead to conflict). Further, I ask questions with a cheerful and kind tone, and I show sincere interest in their answers. Second, I always avoid showing nonverbal skepticism, such as frowning or shaking my head, about anything they share (no matter how odd it may seem to me). My face says it all. I nod my head consistently to show that I'm listening, and what's more, I smile! I find that this often encourages them to relax and open up. Third, one of the most effective techniques I use is to try to find points in their answers that I can genuinely affirm and discuss with enthusiasm. While they are explaining their views, I interject affirmations whenever I can. This helps to demonstrate early on that I am an ally in what I consider to be a mutual search for truth. After I've questioned, listened, and then affirmed any points that I can, I casually offer my views as if naturally adding to the conversation. I find that they usually listen and often are provoked to ask questions, and this gives me the opportunity to share with conviction and influence.

The last suggestion I have is one that I have found vital in my own life. This is prayerfully to pursue personal growth through spiritual formation and character development to help identify areas that may contribute to your personal struggle to defend the faith. Underlying causes of fear and anxiety often go unidentified for many years. These issues in our lives greatly affect our ability to overcome these two troublesome bedfellows, no matter how much apologetic knowledge we gain. There is a multitude of fine Christian authors whose books can assist in areas that might need healing or expose areas previously unrecognized in our character needing our attention.

Keep in mind that a fear of conflict and even the tendency to depend overly on experience may have roots in more than one area of our lives. Personality type, upbringing, and cultural influence can contribute to these issues. Sins of pride, bitterness, or even laziness can diminish our motivation to learn to articulate the truth of Christ in a reasonable way. Spiritual formation is a vital ingredient to our Christian growth, and you may be surprised how much your ability to defend your faith grows with you as you submit your character to the work of the Holy Spirit.

As women, we should welcome the challenge of defending our faith, even if this pushes us out of our comfort zone. Positive change begins through recognizing that our natural aversion to conflict can affect our witness and through realizing that our overdependence on our spiritual experience can prevent deeper doctrinal study. As we are transformed, we will increasingly become the salt of the earth and the light of the world God desires us to be.

Basic Inventory Questions

As I previously mentioned, it is important to take personal inventory of our beliefs regarding the essential basics of the Christian faith. Answer the following questions and support your answers by providing any reasons you can for them. If you don't know an answer or cannot support an answer, then identify and do further study in these areas.

The World

1. Did the universe have a beginning?
2. Was the universe created? If so, how/by whom?
3. Is there good reason to think the physical world is all that exists?
4. If not, what types of nonphysical things exist?

The Bible

1. Is the Bible divinely inspired? What does this mean?
2. Is the Bible consistent and historically reliable? Why or why not?
3. How many books are in the Bible?
4. How did we get our Bible?
5. The Bible was originally written in which languages?
6. Do we have the original texts? If not, what do we have?

God

1. What is the nature of the Christian God?
2. Is the Christian God personal? What does this mean?
3. What does it mean to say that God is triune?

4. How does the Christian understanding of God differ from that of Islam, Mormonism, Hinduism, and other religions?
5. What are some of the evidences for God's existence?
6. According to the Christian faith, what are the human problem and its solution? How does this differ from other philosophical or religious perspectives?

Jesus Christ

1. Who was Jesus of Nazareth? Is there historical evidence for His existence?
2. What do you believe about the nature of Jesus?
   a. Was He really both God and man?
   b. Was Jesus a "sinner"?
   c. Should we worship Jesus?
   d. Is Jesus the only way to God?
3. What do you believe about the death of Jesus?
   a. How did it happen?
   b. What was its purpose?
4. What do you believe about the bodily resurrection of Jesus?
   a. Did Jesus rise from the dead?
   b. If so, how is this possible?

The Holy Spirit

1. Who is the Holy Spirit?
2. What is the role of the Holy Spirit?
   a. In the lives of believers?
   b. In the lives of nonbelievers?
   c. In the world?

Miracles

1. Are supernatural events (miracles) possible?
2. If so, what causes them to happen?
3. Did Jesus do miracles?
4. Can miracles happen today?

The Afterlife

1. Is it possible for humans to survive bodily death?
2. How would you describe the final state(s) of human beings?
3. How does one come to enjoy God's presence?
4. What does it mean to experience God's absence?

Part 2

THE GOD QUESTION

Chapter 4

OBJECTIONS SO BAD I COULDN'T HAVE MADE THEM UP
(or, the World's 10 Worst Objections to the Kalam Cosmological Argument)
William Lane Craig

"We must in my opinion begin by distinguishing between that which always is and never becomes from that which is always becoming and never is. . . . Everything that becomes or changes must do so owing to some cause; for nothing can come to be without a cause. . . .

"As for the world—call it that or 'cosmos' or any other name acceptable to it—we must ask about it the question one is bound to ask to begin with about anything: whether it has always existed and had no beginning, or whether it has come into existence and started from some beginning. The answer is that it has come into being. . . . And what comes into being or changes must do so, we said, owing to some cause." (Plato, *Timaeus* 27–28)

Introduction

In my published work on the *kalam* cosmological argument, I always try to anticipate and respond to objections that might be raised against the argument, so that readers might be equipped to deal with them should someone bring them up in conversation.[1] I figured that I'd dealt with virtually all the objections that critics might raise and that any further debate would be over the adequacy of my responses.

Alas, however, I discovered that I've been unsuccessful in covering the bases! For what I've come to realize is that some objections are so bad, indeed so off the wall, that I never could have anticipated them. These criticisms are not to be found in scholarly publications. Instead, they're put forward in popular critiques of the argument on the Internet and YouTube. Up to now, I've focused on the scholarly critiques of the argument and just ignored such popular criticisms because they were so misguided that there seemed no point in responding to them. But now I've chosen to use this opportunity to address the worst of them.

Now you might be thinking, *If these objections are really that bad, then why waste time responding to them?* Well, there are several reasons for doing so.

First, these objections are both widespread and influential. Infidel websites and YouTube are replete with these criticisms. They reach thousands of people and are confidently touted by many as delivering crushing refutations of the *kalam* cosmological argument.

Second, the average layman, not being trained in logic and philosophy, may not know how to answer these objections. I frequently receive e-mails from visitors to our website, www.ReasonableFaith.org, including a link to some video or website and asking for help in dealing with these objections. Unable to discern where the fallacy lies, people find themselves at a loss for words when confronting these objections in conversation and may even find these criticisms to be quite persuasive.

Finally, answering these objections usually yields some positive insight that is valuable. We can, for example, clarify and so come to a better understanding of certain fallacies that are alleged against the argument or gain a deeper insight into certain crucial concepts that play a role in the argument. So the time taken to answer these objections will prove to be time well spent.

---

[1] See, e.g., William Lane Craig, *On Guard: Defending Your Faith with Reason and Precision* (Colorado Springs: David C. Cook, 2010), 73–104; and *idem, Reasonable Faith,* 3rd ed. rev. (Wheaton, IL: Crossway, 2008), 111–56.

Now I had thought to arrange our world's worst objections into a sort of "Top Ten" list, climaxing with the all-time worst of the worst. But the problem is that the worst of the worst is not necessarily the most entertaining, so that our list would reach something of an anticlimax. So rather than rank the objections in this way, I've decided instead to arrange them according to the steps in the argument, grouping together objections to the general form of the argument, followed by objections to each of the argument's two premises respectively, and wrapping up with objections to the argument's conclusion.

Now for those unfamiliar with the *kalam* cosmological argument, I'll provide a brief summary of it. The argument is a simple syllogism:

1. Everything that begins to exist has a cause.
2. The universe began to exist.
3. Therefore, the universe has a cause.

The crucial second premise is supported both by philosophical arguments against the infinitude of the past and by scientific evidence for the beginning of the universe. Having arrived at the conclusion, one may then do a conceptual analysis of what properties a cause of the universe must have. One is thereby brought to conclude that an uncaused, beginningless, changeless, timeless, spaceless, immaterial, enormously powerful, personal Creator of the universe exists. For the intriguing details see the previously noted works. With this summary of the argument in hand, let's go to our objections!

Objections to the Form of the Argument

Objection #1: Craig says that he believes in God on the basis of the self-authenticating witness of the Holy Spirit in his heart, not on the basis of the *kalam* cosmological argument. In fact, he says that even if the argument were refuted, he would still believe in God. This is blatant hypocrisy on Craig's part.

Response to #1: The problem with this objection is that even if I were a hypocrite, there is just no relationship between the soundness of an argument and the psychological state of the person propounding it. The objector is thus guilty of putting forward a textbook example of an argument *ad hominem*, that is, trying to invalidate a position by attacking the character of the person who defends it.

So what makes for a sound deductive argument? The answer is: true premises and valid logic. An argument is sound if the premises of the argument are true and the conclusion follows from the premises by the rules of logic. The soundness of the *kalam* cosmological argument is thus entirely independent of me. The argument was, after all, defended by the medieval Muslim theologian al-Ghazali almost 900 years before I was even born. If the argument is sound, it was sound then. It was sound during the Jurassic period, before anyone had propounded it. My alleged hypocrisy just has nothing to do with the soundness of the argument.

Now to be a good argument, an argument must, admittedly, be more than merely sound. If the premises of an argument are true, but we have no evidence for the truth of those premises, then the argument will not be a good one. It may (unbeknown to us) be sound, but in the absence of any evidence for its premises it won't, or at least shouldn't, convince anyone. The premises have to have some sort of epistemic warrant for us in order for a sound argument to be a good one. I've argued that what is needed is that the premises be not only true but more plausible than their opposites or negations. If it is more plausible that a premise is, in light of the evidence, true rather than false, then we should believe the premise.[2]

Now plausibility is to a certain degree person-relative. Some people may find a premise more plausible than its opposite, while others may not. In that sense the goodness of an argument is not wholly

---

[2] I trust that this clears up the gross misunderstanding propagated in a YouTube video that when I say that the premises of a good argument must be more plausibly true than their negations, I am positing a range of additional truth values between true and false. No, I presume the classical Principle of Bivalence, according to which there are only two truth values, *True* and *False*. There are different degrees of plausibility, not of truth, given the varying amounts of evidence in support of one's premises. The question we must ask is: which is more plausible, that the premise is true or that it is false? Notice, too, that in a valid deductive argument like the *kalam* cosmological argument, if the premises are true, then it follows necessarily that the conclusion is true, period. It is logically fallacious to multiply the probabilities of the premises to try to calculate the probability of the conclusion. In a sound deductive argument the most we can say about the probability of the argument's conclusion is that it cannot be less than some lower bound, but it could be as high as 100 percent. The kid who posted these criticisms on YouTube, if he continues his study of philosophy, is going to look back someday on this smug video with real embarrassment.

independent of persons' psychological states. In the case of the *kalam* cosmological argument, I do find the premises more plausible than their opposites, and so I am convinced that it is a good argument.

I just don't regard the argument as the basis for my belief in God. I've been quite candid about that. My belief in God is a properly basic belief grounded in the inner witness of God's Holy Spirit. It's odd that rather than being commended for my candor, I'm accused of hypocrisy.

I've elsewhere defended the proper basicality of belief in God on the basis of the Spirit's witness,[3] but that's quite unnecessary here. For even if I were entirely mistaken about that, it would have no bearing on the worth of the *kalam* cosmological argument. To illustrate, suppose I believe that Abraham Lincoln was one of the greatest of American presidents, and in order to convince you of this, I present to you the testimony of expert historians along with a detailed account of Lincoln's amazing accomplishments. But suppose that the real reason I think Lincoln was so great is that he had a beard, and, having been once bearded myself, I am prejudiced in favor of bearded presidents. Obviously, my personal prejudice would have no bearing whatsoever upon the worth of the evidence for Lincoln's greatness.

Similarly, whatever reason I may have personally for believing in God, whether it's the witness of the Holy Spirit or the ontological argument or the teleological argument or divine revelation, or whatever, that just has no relation to the soundness or worth of the *kalam* cosmological argument. The skeptic may not *like* my taking belief in God as properly basic, but that's not a criticism of the *kalam* cosmological argument. That's at best a rejection of the proper basicality of belief in God, which has no bearing on the worth of the *kalam* argument.

Objection #2: The *kalam* cosmological argument is question-begging. For the truth of the first premise presupposes the truth of the conclusion. Therefore the argument is an example of reasoning in a circle.

Response to #2: All the objector has done is describe the nature of a deductive argument. In a deductive argument, the conclusion is implicit in the premises, waiting to be derived by the rules of logical inference. A classic illustration of a deductive argument is:

---

[3] Craig, *Reasonable Faith,* 43–51.

1. All men are mortal.
2. Socrates is a man.
3. Therefore, Socrates is mortal.

This argument has the same form as the *kalam* cosmological argument. The logical rule governing this form is called *modus ponens*. Symbolically,

$$p \supset q$$
$$p$$
$$\overline{}$$
$$\therefore q$$

It is one of the most basic of logically valid argument forms. Incredibly, I have even seen claims by Internet critics that the classic argument above is also question-begging!

This raises the question of what it means for an argument to be question-begging. Technically, arguments don't beg the question; people do. One is guilty of begging the question if one's only reason for believing in a premise is that one already believes in the conclusion. For example, suppose you were to present the following argument for the existence of God:

1. Either God exists or the moon is made of green cheese.
2. The moon is not made of green cheese.
3. Therefore, God exists.

This is a sound argument for God's existence: its premises are both true, and the conclusion follows from the premises by the rules of logic (specifically, disjunctive syllogism). Nevertheless, the argument is not any good because the only reason for believing the first premise to be true is that you already believe that God exists (a disjunction is true if one of the disjuncts is true). But that is the argument's conclusion! Therefore, in putting forward this argument you are reasoning in a circle or begging the question. The only reason you believe (1) is because you believe (3).

Now neither the argument for Socrates' mortality nor the *kalam* argument is like this. In each case reasons are given for believing the first premise that are quite independent of the argument's conclusion.

Biological and medical evidence may be marshaled on behalf of the premise that all men are mortal, and I have presented arguments (to be reviewed shortly) for the truth of the premise that everything that begins to exist has a cause. Therefore, I have not begged the question. The objector has made the elementary mistake of confusing a deductive argument with a question-begging argument.

Objection #3: The argument commits the fallacy of equivocation. In the first premise "cause" means "material cause," while in the conclusion it does not.

Response to #3: This objection raises the question of what it is to commit the fallacy of equivocation. This fallacy is using a word in the same context to mean two different things. For example, suppose some-one were to reason:

1. Socrates was Greek.
2. Greek is a language.
3. Therefore, Socrates is a language.

The untoward conclusion results from equivocating on the meaning of "Greek," using it first to denote an ethnicity or nationality and later a language.

In formulating the *kalam* cosmological argument, I intended to speak of what Aristotle called efficient causes. Aristotle distinguished between efficient causes and material causes. An efficient cause is what produces an effect in being, while a material cause is the stuff out of which a thing is made. For example, Michelangelo was the efficient cause of the statue *David*, and the material cause of *David* was the block of marble that Michelangelo sculpted. My claim was that whatever begins to exist has an efficient cause and therefore the universe, having begun to exist, must have an efficient cause. The charge of equivocation immediately evaporates.

These first three objections to the *kalam* cosmological argument, while not very scintillating, are among the very worst of the worst objections. Without challenging the truth of any of its premises, they attack what is a logically impeccable argument.

Objections to the First Premise

Objection #4: The first premise is based on the fallacy of composition. It fallaciously infers that because everything in the universe has a cause, therefore the whole universe has a cause.

Response to #4: In order to understand this objection we need to understand the fallacy of composition. This is the fallacy of reasoning that because every part of a thing has a certain property, therefore the whole thing has that same property. While wholes do sometimes possess the properties of their parts (a fence, every plank of which is green, is also green), this is not always the case. For example, every little part of an elephant may be light in weight, but that does not imply that the whole elephant is light in weight.

Now I have never argued that because every part of the universe has a cause, therefore the whole universe has a cause. That would be manifestly fallacious. Rather the reasons I have offered for thinking that everything that begins to exist has a cause are these:

1. *Something cannot come from nothing.* To claim that something can come into being from nothing is worse than magic. When a magician pulls a rabbit out of a hat, at least you've got the magician, not to mention the hat! But if you deny premise 1, you've got to think that the whole universe just appeared at some point in the past for no reason whatsoever. But nobody *sincerely* believes that things, say, a horse or an Eskimo village, can just pop into being without a cause.

2. *If something can come into being from nothing, then it becomes inexplicable why just anything or everything doesn't come into being from nothing.* Think about it: why don't bicycles and Beethoven and root beer just pop into being from nothing? Why is it only universes that can come into being from nothing? What makes nothingness so discriminatory? There can't be anything about nothingness that favors universes, for nothingness doesn't have any properties. Nor can anything constrain nothingness, for there isn't anything to be constrained!

3. *Common experience and scientific evidence confirm the truth of premise 1.* Premise 1 is constantly verified and never falsified. It's hard to understand how any atheist committed to modern science could deny that premise 1 is more plausibly true than false in light of the evidence.[4]

Note well that the third reason is an appeal to inductive reasoning, not reasoning from composition. It's drawing an inductive inference about all the members of a class of things based on a sample of the class. Inductive reasoning underlies all of science and is not to be confused with reasoning by composition.

So this objection is aimed at a straw man of the objector's own construction.

Objection #5: If the universe began to exist, then it must have come from nothing. That is quite plausible, since there are no constraints on nothing, and so nothing can do anything, including producing the universe.

Response to #5: This objector seems to be hopelessly confused about the use of the word "nothing." When it is rightly said that nothing preceded the universe, one doesn't mean that something preceded it, and it was nothing. We mean that it was not preceded by anything. Reifying negative terms has been the butt of jokes as old as Homer's story of the Cyclops and Odysseus. Imagine the following dialogue between two people discussing the Second World War:

> "Nothing stopped the German advance from sweeping across
>   Belgium."
> "Oh, that's good. I'm glad they were stopped."
> "But they weren't stopped!"
> "But you said that nothing stopped them."
> "That's right."
> "So they were stopped."
> "No, nothing stopped them."
> "That's what I said. They were stopped, and it was nothing
>   which stopped them."
> "No, no, I meant they weren't stopped by anything."

---

[4] Craig, *On Guard*, 78.

"Well, why didn't you say so in the first place?"

The objector, in thinking nothing produced the universe, seems to be guilty of the same sort of mistake. Nothingness has no properties, no powers; it isn't even anything. Therefore, it is wholly misconceived to say it produced the universe.

To say the universe was caused by nothing is to say the universe had no cause; it wasn't caused by anything. That is metaphysically absurd. Out of nothing, nothing comes. As the epigram from Plato at the head of this essay illustrates, the causal principle, which is the first premise of the *kalam* cosmological argument, is one of the oldest and most widely recognized truths of metaphysics.

Objections to the Second Premise

Objection #6: Nothing ever begins to exist! For the material of which something consists precedes it. So it is not true that the universe began to exist.

Response to #6: I think this is my favorite bad objection, since the assertion that nothing ever begins to exist is so patently ridiculous. Did I exist before I was conceived? If so, where was I? What was I doing during the Jurassic period? Has the World Trade Center always existed? How come the Native Americans never noticed it?

This objection obviously confuses a thing with the matter or stuff of which the thing is made. Just because the stuff of which something was made has always existed doesn't imply the thing itself has always existed.

The objector could save himself from the embarrassment of having to say that he has always existed by adopting *mereological nihilism*, the doctrine that there are no composite objects. On this view all that exists are the fundamental particles that can be arranged in different ways. So according to this view, there literally are no chairs or tables or horses or people or palm trees. There are just fundamental particles, which may be arranged chair-wise or table-wise or people-wise and so on. The reason why chairs and other things never begin to exist is not that they have *always* existed but rather that they never *do* exist. There just are no such things.

Unfortunately for our hapless objector, in this case the cure is worse than the disease. For now the objector has to say that the reason he never began to exist is not that he has always existed but that he himself doesn't exist at all! (That might leave us wondering why we should bother responding to him, since there's nobody to whom we can respond. Indeed, on this view, *nobody* has ever raised the present objection; so why respond to it, since it hasn't been held by anybody?)

In any case, it is absurd to deny one's own existence. I'm reminded of the story of the first-year philosophy student who had been reading Descartes. He burst into his professor's office early one morning, bleary-eyed, unshaven—he'd obviously been up all night. "Professor, you've got to tell me," he implored. "*Do I exist?*" The professor looked at him a moment and then said, "Who wants to know?" If resisting the *kalam* cosmological argument requires that you deny your own existence, then the cost is far too high.

At any rate, all these mental machinations are ultimately of no avail, for we can simply rephrase the *kalam* cosmological argument to meet the scruples of the mereological nihilist:

1′. If the fundamental particles arranged universe-wise began to exist, they have a cause.
2′. The fundamental particles arranged universe-wise began to exist.
3′. Therefore, the fundamental particles arranged universe-wise have a cause.

And now we're right back to where we were before.

The serious point of this muddled objection, I think, is its presupposition that everything that begins to exist has a material cause. But that claim is irrelevant to the truth of the two premises of the *kalam* cosmological argument and requires proof in any case. It is true that in our experience material things do not begin to exist without material causes, so that we have the same sort of inductive evidence on behalf of material causation as we have for efficient causation. But if we have good arguments and evidence that the material realm had an absolute beginning preceded by nothing, this can override the inductive evidence. What we cannot reasonably say, I think, is that the universe sprang into being without either an efficient or a material cause, since being does not come from nonbeing. But there is no sort of metaphysical absurdity involved in something's having an efficient cause but no material cause.

Objection #7: The argument equivocates on "begins to exist." In (1) it means to begin "from a previous material state," but in (2) it means "not from a material state."

Answer to #7: In order to defeat the allegation of equivocation all one needs to do is provide a univocal meaning for the phrase in both its occurrences. That's easy to do. By "begins to exist" I mean "comes into being." Everything that comes into being has a cause, and the universe came into being. No equivocation here!

If we want, we can go further and provide an analysis of what it means to begin to exist. Here is one such analysis:

> x begins to exist if and only if x exists at some time t and there is no time t^* prior to t at which x exists.

This analysis is adequate for all practical purposes. It would allow even time itself to begin to exist. It would become problematic only in case someone thinks that God is timeless without creation and enters time at the first moment of creation. In such a case God would exist at a first moment of time t^0 and there would be no time $t^* < t^0$ at which God existed. It would follow from our analysis that God began to exist at t^0, which is wrong-headed, since God did not come into being at t^0. Fortunately, this problem is easily fixed by amending our analysis:

> x begins to exist if and only if x exists at some time t and there is no time t^* prior to t at which x exists and no state of affairs in the actual world in which x exists timelessly.

So amended, the analysis does not imply that God began to exist at the first moment of time if He enters time from a state of timelessness at the moment of creation.

In sum, the objections to the second premise are just as bad as the objections to the first. The second premise is certainly controversial and open to debate but not for the reasons alleged here.

Objections to the Argument's Conclusion

Objection #8: The argument is logically self-contradictory. For it says that everything has a cause yet concludes that there is a first uncaused cause.

Response to #8: Man, how do people think these things up? Premise 1 states that everything that *begins to exist* has a cause. Something cannot *come into being* without a cause. This premise does not require that something that is eternal and never had a beginning has a cause (think again of Plato's distinction between that which always is and that which comes into being). The objector has been inattentive to the formulation of the first premise.

Notice that this is not special pleading for God. The atheist has typically said that the universe itself is eternal and uncaused. Matter and energy have existed from eternity past and so have no cause of their being. Problem is: that supposition has now been rendered dubious in light of the strong arguments in support of premise 2 that the universe began to exist.

Objection #9: The cause mentioned in the argument's conclusion is not different from nothing. For timelessness, changelessness, spacelessness, etc., are all purely negative attributions which are also true of nothingness. Thus, the argument might as well be taken to prove that the universe came into being from nothing.

Response to #9: You've got to be kidding. The argument concludes to a cause of the universe. That is a positive existential affirmation: there is a cause of the universe. To say that the universe was caused by nothing, by contrast, is to affirm that it was not caused by anything, or in other words, the universe is uncaused, which is the very opposite of the argument's conclusion.

Moreover, the argument's conclusion also implies the attribution of incredible causal power to this entity that brought the universe into being without any sort of material cause. It is therefore wholly different from nothing, which has no reality, no properties, and no causal powers.

Finally, the attribution of negative predicates such as timelessness, changelessness, spacelessness, and so on to this entity is enormously informative and metaphysically significant. From its timelessness and immateriality we can deduce its personhood, as I have elsewhere argued.[5] This is a positive property of great significance and utterly unlike nothingness.

Objection #10: Our tenth and final bad objection comes courtesy of that *enfant terrible* of the New Atheism, Richard Dawkins. He doesn't dispute either premise of the *kalam* cosmological argument. Instead he just complains about the argument's conclusion:

> Even if we allow the dubious luxury of arbitrarily conjuring up a terminator to an infinite regress and giving it a name, there is absolutely no reason to endow that terminator with any of the properties normally ascribed to God: omnipotence, omniscience, goodness, creativity of design, to say nothing of such human attributes as listening to prayers, forgiving sins and reading innermost thoughts.[6]

Response to #10. Apart from the opening dig,[7] this is an amazingly concessionary statement. Dawkins doesn't deny that the argument successfully demonstrates the existence of an uncaused, beginningless, changeless, immaterial, timeless, spaceless, and unimaginably powerful, personal Creator of the universe. He merely complains that this cause hasn't been shown to be omnipotent, omniscient, good, creative of design, listening to prayers, forgiving sins, and reading innermost thoughts. So what? The argument doesn't aspire to prove such things. It would be a bizarre form of atheism—indeed, one not worth the name—that conceded that there exists an uncaused, beginningless, changeless, immaterial, timeless, spaceless, and unimaginably powerful, personal Creator of the universe, who *may*, for all we know, also possess the further properties listed by Dawkins! We needn't call the personal Creator of the universe "God" if Dawkins finds this unhelpful or misleading, but the point remains that a being such as described above must exist.[8]

---

[5] Craig, *On Guard*, 99–100; and *Reasonable Faith*, 152–54.

[6] Richard Dawkins, *The God Delusion* (New York: Houghton-Mifflin, 2006), 77.

[7] The argument's proponent doesn't arbitrarily conjure up a terminator to the infinite regress and give it a name. Rather he presents philosophical and scientific arguments that the regress must terminate in a first member, arguments that Dawkins doesn't discuss.

[8] This also serves to answer what is surely one of the most ludicrous retorts to the argument which I have heard: "Couldn't you have replaced the word 'god' with 'bigfoot' or 'unicorn'?" Hmmm, let's see. . . . Bigfoot is a creature living somewhere in Washington State, right? So do you really think that someone living in the state of Washington is the timeless, spaceless, Creator of the Big Bang?

Conclusion

So there you have them: the world's 10 all-time worst! These represent the level of discourse that pervades the Internet and YouTube. You can see how worthless they are. I hope you don't feel that I've wasted your time. For in discussing these bad objections you've gained, I hope, a better understanding of the sort of fallacies alleged against the argument along with some deeper insight into the argument itself.

Chapter 5

THE SILENCE OF GOD

Gary R. Habermas

The broader topic of religious doubt has taken on a life of its own in recent years. When I wrote two books on the subject in the 1990s,[1] there was comparatively little published material on the subject, the majority of which was written popularly.[2] However, during the last decade, it seems that more books have been published than in the previous two decades combined. Further, the more recent books include some scholarly as well as popular titles.[3]

---

[1] My two out-of-print books on this subject are both available without cost on my website (www.garyhabermas.com): *Dealing with Doubt* (Chicago: Moody, 1990); *The Thomas Factor: Using Your Doubts to Grow Closer to God* (Nashville: Broadman and Holman, 1998).

[2] Kelly James Clark, *When Faith Is Not Enough* (Grand Rapids: Eerdmans, 1997); Os Guinness, *God in the Dark: The Assurance of Faith beyond a Shadow of Doubt* (Wheaton, IL: Crossway, 1996); R. C. Sproul, ed., *Doubt and Assurance: Looking for Certainty When the Heart Doubts* (Grand Rapids: Baker, 1993); Lynn Anderson, *If I Really Believe, Why Do I Have These Doubts? Hope for Those Who Feel They Will Never Measure Up to Other Christians' Faith* (Minneapolis: Bethany, 1992); Gary E. Parker, *The Gift of Doubt: From Crisis to Authentic Faith* (San Francisco: Harper and Row, 1990); Philip Yancey, *Disappointment with God: Three Questions No One Asks Aloud* (Grand Rapids: Zondervan, 1988); John Guest, *In Search of Certainty: Answers to Doubt when Values Are Eroding and Unbelief Is Fashionable* (Ventura, CA: Regal, 1983).

[3] For examples, see Paul Moser, *The Elusive God: Reorienting Religious Epistemology* (Cambridge: Cambridge University Press, 2009); Daniel Howard-Snyder and Paul Moser, eds., *Divine Hiddenness: New Essays* (Cambridge: Cambridge University Press, 2001); Paul Moser, *Why Isn't God More Obvious? Finding the God Who Hides and Seeks* (Norcross, GA: RZIM, 2000); J. P. Moreland and Klaus Issler, *In Search of a Confident Faith: Overcoming Barriers to Trusting in God* (Downers Grove, IL: InterVarsity, 2008); John Ortberg, *Faith and Doubt* (Grand Rapids: Zondervan, 2008); Alister McGrath, *Doubting: Growing through the Uncertainties of Faith* (Downers Grove, IL: InterVarsity, 2006); Pete Greig, *God on Mute: Engaging the Silence of*

Perhaps the most common and perplexing issue of late has to do with the seeming absence of God, either in the universe as a whole or in everyday life, including some careful nuances. For example, the aspect of God's hiddenness has taken on far more sophisticated aspects of a philosophical or theological nature.[4] Often more painful in everyday life, the more personal, practical, and existential questions have to do with the believer's own perception of divine silence—that she is being ignored or even abandoned by God.

It is this latter topic—that of the personal perception of excruciating silence and even desertion by God—with which we are primarily concerned in this essay. For instance, it seems to remain a common view among some believers that God no longer acts supernaturally in our present world. This can cause a conundrum between what Scripture depicts compared with what Christians see around them in the world today. Additionally, it may seem that numerous promises in both the Old and New Testaments portray a view of God that is far different from what Christians seem to experience in their own lives. These promises depict God as being present in daily life, meeting the needs of His followers, watching over them, healing their hurts, delivering them from calamities, and comforting them during their times of need.

Further, beyond the promises themselves, the sense many have is that the actual events, especially in the New Testament, portray God as virtually always present, meeting the daily needs of believers. The overall scriptural picture is one of God's involvement and interaction with His children, whereas Christians today often concede, sometimes only in private, that this is far from matching their private experience. Perhaps the very profound suffering of Jesus Himself provides some insights here, too.

The brevity of this essay absolutely requires that we will have to move quickly through these areas, with the hope that responding to the crux of each issue is more helpful than an in-depth look at only one subtopic.

Unanswered Prayer (Ventura, CA: Regal, 2007); Graham Cooke, *When the Lights Go Out: Surprising Growth when God Is Hidden* (Grand Rapids: Baker/Chosen, 2005); James Emery White, *Embracing the Mysterious God: Loving the God We Don't Understand* (Downers Grove, IL: InterVarsity, 2003); Philip Yancey, *Reaching for the Invisible God: What Can We Expect to Find?* (Grand Rapids: Zondervan, 2000).

[4] This can be seen in the texts above, such as Moser, *The Elusive God*, and Howard-Snyder and Moser, ed., *Divine Hiddenness*.

Accordingly, we will focus chiefly on four key questions: (1) Does an overview of the subject indicate that God still *acts supernaturally* in the world today? (2) Does the general tenor of biblical *promises* present a view of God that is at odds with current Christian experience? (3) Do New Testament *events* tell us that God actually behaved differently than He does with believers today? (4) Does *Jesus' own suffering* shed any light on these subjects?

Is God Active in the World Today?

Unfortunately, this is the chief area where I must limit the discussion to the least amount of detail.[5] I will begin by stating my conviction that not only is God very active in the world today, but it could even be that He is more frequently involved than ever before. Since doubters often report two important aspects here, I will limit myself to a few comments about each. Some wonder if God still performs supernatural feats in the world today. While perhaps still being interested in this subject, others are more concerned to decipher whether God is dealing with them on a personal level, whether or not this involvement tends to be miraculous in nature. The former tend to be more interested in modern-day evidences, while the latter frequently suffer from uncertainty regarding whether they have a personal relationship with God.

One potential indicator of God's activity is the likelihood of divine healing. Over the years I have collected several special cases of spontaneous healings in the presence of prayer, either manifested immediately or discovered just a few hours later. Whether multiple sclerosis or previously confirmed cancer tumors that either disappeared almost immediately or contain absolutely no cancerous cells, contrary to previous biopsies, these situations need to be taken seriously.[6]

Another example is that of answered prayer, where the results were drawn from either a personal journal or from select double-blind

---

[5] The interested reader may consult my recent book, which provides many additional specifics as well as key sources for the discussion in this chapter. See Gary R. Habermas, *Why Is God Ignoring Me? What to Do When It Feels Like He's Giving You the Silent Treatment* (Carol Stream, IL: Tyndale, 2010), especially chaps. 1–2.

[6] For one case, see Rodney Clapp, "One Who Took up Her Bed and Walked," *Christianity Today* (December 16, 1983): 16–17.

experiments published in medical journals. In the latter cases, it was actually concluded that the results favored medical results from prayer.[7]

Two more avenues are reported sightings of angelic beings, seemingly demonic creatures, or exorcisms. Incredibly, a number of the accounts include evidential considerations.[8]

Perhaps no area of supernatural findings is more evidential than accounts of near-death experiences. In literally dozens of cases, patients report witnessing occurrences even at a distance, even while they are near death, perhaps even without heart or brain activity. Many have concluded that this is strong evidence for the existence of some sort of afterlife.[9]

Lastly, dozens of reports have emerged where seemingly miraculous circumstances occur, which serve to link up an indigenous people who reportedly were looking for a message from God with missionaries. Many of these accounts have been collected.[10]

However, other doubters are more concerned that God relate to them in a highly personal manner, whether or not the experiences are supernatural. These are more interested in a personal touch, indicating that they are children of God. Here I will simply list a number of experiences which, according to Scripture, are the very sorts of things we should expect, and which are reported regularly by Christians.

For example, C. S. Lewis's notion of joy is experienced by believers and unbelievers alike. Though very difficult to define, it generally results from a captivating experience of music, nature, or another inspirational setting, resulting in a deep longing or yearning. It lasts only for a moment and is often experienced as a heavenly "tweaking" of the heart, reminding us of eternity (Eccl 3:11).[11]

---

[7] Randolph C. Byrd, "Positive Therapeutic Effects of Intercessory Prayer in a Coronary Care Unit Population," *Southern Medical Journal* 81 (1988): 826–29.

[8] George Otis Jr., *The Twilight Labyrinth: Why Does Spiritual Darkness Linger Where It Does?* (Grand Rapids: Baker, 1997).

[9] Many evidential accounts are contained in Gary R. Habermas and J. P. Moreland, *Beyond Death: Exploring the Evidence for Immortality* (Wheaton, IL: Crossway, 1998; Eugene, OR: Wipf and Stock, 2004), chaps. 7–9.

[10] Don Richardson, *Eternity in Their Hearts* (Ventura, CA: Regal, 1981).

[11] C. S. Lewis, *Surprised by Joy: The Shape of My Early Life* (New York: Harcourt, Brace, Jovanovich, 1955), especially 16–18.

There are also many examples of other divine contacts of a highly personal nature. These include the personal conviction of sin (1 John 3:4–10,21), the administering of individual correction as an indication of one's sonship (Heb 12:5–6,10–13; cf. Jas 1:2–4), the imparting of spiritual gifts specifically to each person (1 Cor 12:4–11,27), and the internal witness of the Holy Spirit as an indication of God's presence in our lives (Rom 8:16; 1 John 3:24; 4:13). Still other indications may consist of one's personalized experiences such as those occurring in worship, specific convictions, or indications of God's will.

Believers often seem to miss these frequent, perhaps even daily occurrences. Jotting them down in a journal would be very helpful for our future reference. This is a highly effective way to remind ourselves of what God has *already* done in our lives, helping to avoid the temptation, like children, to respond so frequently, "You never do anything with me." This is the point raised in so many of these passages of Scripture: we ought to note these signs that God is actually working in our lives. We should never lose sight of the recognition that each item here is also quite personal; it is for us alone.

If we are correct, then Christians have many indications that God is alive and well both in today's world as well as in their own lives. For those who prefer supernatural clues, several varieties and examples of each are available. Personal touches occur much more commonly, although believers most often seem to ignore them. Therefore, we must acknowledge personally and put into the proper context the regular recognition of God's activity in the world today. But it is mistaken to say that God is silent—far from it. No doubt believers often wish that God would communicate with them more often, or in a different manner, but we must remind ourselves that He often acts and speaks.

What about Our Favorite Biblical Promises?

Our initial consideration is that God is far from silent but interacts often, in both events as well as persons. This is an absolutely crucial conclusion, for it undergirds everything else on this topic and provides a bedrock from which we may move forward.

Another popular question concerns the many promises contained throughout Scripture. Should we not expect even more involvement than what we see?[12] After all, a plethora of texts, directed both to God's people in the Old Testament[13] and to Christians in the New Testament,[14] seem to promise a wide variety of blessings, such as healing, general health, God's direction, and other sorts of answered prayers. One thing that may exacerbate the problem here, as difficult as this may sound, is that these are the sorts of texts that we regularly memorize and claim. What could be wrong with that? They are found in God's Word, right?

Perhaps the key issue here is that there is another side to the question that seems even more common in Scripture. Namely, there appear to be many more texts that acknowledge in a straightforward manner that God's people have had and will continue to experience all sorts of problems in their lives. Oftentimes, these situations seem to go on and on, without resolution.[15] Intriguingly for our purposes, our very problem of God's silence was raised frequently in Scripture, too, along with other occasions in which God's answer was not what the person desired.[16] These situations are not simply recent developments!

This seems to place us directly into a conundrum. How do we respond to the contrast between Scripture texts that appear, at least on the surface, to contain both myriads of wonderful promises and the utter reality of our difficult human existence? We will explore very briefly some potential responses.

Initially, several suggested solutions simply will not do. For example, it does not help to say that different writers provide varying, even contradictory, thoughts on these subjects, with some supporting one view and others arguing the opposite. The problem here is that the very same writers, such as David, Isaiah, or Paul, regularly report both the

---

[12] For further details, see Habermas, *Why Is God Ignoring Me?* chap. 3.

[13] Among the many examples are Exod 23:25; Deut 31:6,8; Pss 32:7; 34:6; 91:10–13; Isa 26:3; 32:17; 41:13; 65:24; Jer 30:17; 33:2–3.

[14] See Matt 7:7–11; 18:19–20; John 14:13–14; Rom 8:28; Phil 4:6,19; Heb 4:16; 13:5; Jas 5:14–15.

[15] The many instances include Ps 44:9–23; Lam 3:1–19; Matt 10:23; 24:9; Acts 14:21–22; Rom 8:17–18; 2 Cor 1:5; 4:10–11; Phil 1:29; 3:10–11; 2 Tim 3:12; Jas 1:2–4.

[16] See Job 19:7; 30:20; Pss 10:1; 13:1; 35:13; 39:12–13; 44:24; 74:9; 83:1; 89:46; 109:1; 119:82,84; Isa 45:15; 57:11b; Lam 3:8,44; 5:20; 2 Cor 12:7–9; 2 Tim 4:20b.

promises as well as the problems. Further, they would not be contradicting themselves when these comments are often made in the very same context; they could hardly have forgotten what they had just written only briefly before! Neither does it help to respond that we are mixing verses regarding the Jews with other texts regarding Christians. As our lists above indicate, we can either keep these texts separate or consider them together, but it changes nothing. The same sorts of mixed promises and problems remain in both. Though it is correct to note that we are combining texts from very different types of literature, such as the Law, poetry, didactic passages, apocalyptic messages, and so on, this similarly changes nothing. In each of these venues, we find a similar mix of statements.

What sorts of solutions do better? One suggestion that we will not be able to pursue here in any detail is that the promise passages are usually spoken as general encouragements to the people of God, and while these assurances do occur quite often, they don't necessarily apply to every individual case. It could be added here that the biblical writers are very well aware of this differentiation, which explains the many contrasts between promises and problems in the exact same contexts. This would seem to be a proper response on many occasions.

Another very helpful suggestion is that believers too often jump to conclusions. It appears that many of the biblical promises do not necessitate removal *from* the troublesome situations but speak, rather, of God's ongoing presence *through* them.

For example, John 14–16 contains three of the best-known promises that believers may receive whatever they ask for (14:13–14; 15:7; 16:24). Yet, Jesus was very well aware that there were indeed some very serious limitations to what sounded like open invitations, since in the exact same context there are also three statements of a very different nature, in that believers will suffer and even lose their lives (15:20; 16:2,33). We might just note that if suffering and even death[17] are to be exempted from at least some of these promises, then these are truly major exceptions!

---

[17] John 16:2 does not literally say that the disciples would be martyred for their faith, but persecution is the immediate context, and commentators think that future martyrdoms are in view. See the discussion in Raymond E. Brown, *The Gospel According to John XII–XXI*, Anchor Bible 29B (Garden City, NY: Doubleday, 1970), 690–92.

It is at least possible that a solution is to be found in the next chapter, where Jesus prays *not* that His Father would remove His followers (as well as those who will believe through their message—17:20) *from* the world, but that God would protect them while they are *in* the world (17:15). In other words, God promises to be with believers throughout their lives, both bringing incredible blessings as well as holding their hands through troublesome times, frequently without taking them away from these latter situations.

Another factor to consider is that God's dealings with Old Testament national Israel included promises of material or physical blessings for obedience to the law of Moses—and disaster, death, disease, destitution, destruction for disobedience (Leviticus 26; Deuteronomy 27–28).[18] Occasionally, though, we encounter individuals such as Job or individual psalmists who, despite their dedication to God, meet stiff challenges to their faith. In the New Testament, God's people—the interethnic church—no longer live under the strong connection between godliness and material or circumstantial prosperity as indicative of God's covenant blessing.

Though a few suggestions were made by way of some potential resolution, it should be noted carefully that our chief point here was *not* to explain ultimately the presence of both promise and problem statements in Scripture, often by the same author and in the same context. In order to pursue the theme of this essay, we do not have to understand exactly how these passages can or should be reconciled. It is sufficient for our purposes to simply point out that the mere presence of these wonderful promises throughout Scripture, including our favorite verses, is very far from arguing that therefore God should respond to our every request. The reason is that the problem verses are even more common and tend to nullify the argument that the promise texts sufficiently explain the entire matter. The next section will further confirm this conclusion.

---

[18] Gordon Fee and Douglas Stuart list six categories of blessings: life, health, prosperity, agricultural abundance, respect, and safety. They present the punishments as 10 "D"s: death, disease, drought, dearth, danger, destruction, defeat, deportation, destitution, and disgrace. *How to Read the Bible for All Its Worth*, 3rd ed. (Grand Rapids: Zondervan, 2003), 185.

What about New Testament Events?

Do biblical events indicate that God was more active than today in the lives of believers?[19] We realize that in the Old Testament, God did deliver in various ways ancient believers such as Enoch, Noah, Elijah, and Daniel, along with others, not to mention taking care of the Jewish people in many circumstances. But we also know that Old Testament history is filled with a great deal of war, disobedience, and God's judgment. Evil rulers opposed God and His prophets, and the Jews were carried away into captivity more than once where they lived in exile, some never to return to their homes. Indeed, Hebrews 11 recounts how many of God's people were persecuted and mistreated. No doubt many Christians would not long for the return of those times!

In contrast, however, believers often have at least a vague notion that in the early church, God was almost always there for the early Christians. It just seems that healings and other miracles occurred more often than not, prayers were answered positively, and life in general was much more satisfying because God was always close at hand. So when we discuss God's actions in history along with the question of God's silence, these are the times that many Christians might desire.

But does a close study of the New Testament really indicate the truth of these conclusions? I do not think that this was the case; in fact, I do not think that it is even close to being correct. Rather, such a conclusion would involve a very selective reading of the relevant sources. After all, the same texts also explain that John the Baptist was imprisoned and later beheaded (Mark 6:16–29). Stephen was stoned to death (Acts 7:54–59). James the brother of John was slain (Acts 12:1–2). Jesus' own apostles were thrown into prison and beaten more than once (Acts 4:1–3; 5:17–41). Paul recounts his imprisonments, many serious beatings, shipwrecks, along with being stoned and left for dead (Acts 14:19–20; 2 Cor 11:23–29). Most of all, Jesus Himself did not even escape this brutality; in fact, His repeated mistreatments were followed by what was arguably the worst death of all.

Further, though not recorded in the New Testament, scholars date the martyrdoms of Paul, Peter, and James the brother of Jesus to just a

---

[19] See Habermas, *Why Is God Ignoring Me?* chap. 4.

few years after these other events. Not long afterward, Jerusalem was attacked by the Romans during a lengthy war, during which thousands of Jews were crucified. How many Christians during this time experienced famine, other suffering, and perhaps even crucifixion? Moreover, persecution broke out sporadically over the next few decades, and more disciples and other Christians were harassed and killed.

Stop and think about it. If we had lived during these times and had been caught up in any of this violence, or simply lived in constant fear for our families, what would we have thought about God? Would it not be highly likely that we would raise the exact same questions regarding His silence, or even worse? What would be our response if family members had been crucified or otherwise mistreated seriously by unbelievers? What would we have thought about God's protection when, one after another, our leaders suffered torture and death? Especially since this went on for so many years, would some even wonder whether Christianity were worth it?

My point here is that, if we judge the church's "golden years" to be a period of time where everything was wonderful and God always acted the way we desired, but where little or no bad news occurred, this seems very far indeed from the picture in the New Testament. But this simply means that we need to change our faulty conceptions. Of course we would be correct that this was a very special time, but it would also be clear that the earliest church did not experience anything resembling problem-free existence. That artificial addition seems to be a modern concept that has been foisted upon our notion of God's activity, though it seems *never* to have been the case.

In fact, the picture is even less rosy than this! After I heard repeatedly what we have called the question of God's silence, I decided to survey the New Testament evidence. Did God regularly remove believers from dangerous or painful situations where, humanly speaking, such would be very convenient? What I found was very surprising. In the large majority of these passages, believers were very seldom rescued from troublesome scenarios before any negative results took place. Actually, such divine interventions occurred very infrequently.

As a brief example of how we often pick and choose or otherwise slant our texts, while lecturing on the subject, I was once asked whether the account in Acts 16:22–34 qualified as one of God's interventions. After all, Paul and Silas were thrown into prison, but God released them by an earthquake and the jailer and his family turned to the Lord. But how could this count as one of our preferred rescue scenarios when the two men had first been beaten severely (16:23)? If we were in their place, I could imagine thinking before every single lash landed that perhaps God would now rescue us before the next one hit! Then when God did not choose to exempt us, we probably would have asked why He never delivered believers, just as He did in Old Testament times!

As a last example, we should again take a look at the life of Jesus Himself. He would surely have deserved to be freed from suffering more than anyone else. Yet, in those situations where He might have been exempted, this almost never occurred. True, He was rescued as a baby, but what about all the other youngsters in Bethlehem who were killed? Then there were events such as the 40 days of temptation, and enduring the deaths of His cousin John the Baptist and His good friend Lazarus. Finally, there was the suffering in the garden of Gethsemane, followed by His severe beatings, and then His crucifixion. As we would say today, Jesus never got a break!

The case of Jesus is so remarkable that it will be treated further in the next section. For now, we will simply note that the actual New Testament writings by no means support the case that God always, almost always, or even usually removed New Testament believers before difficult or painful situations occurred. Actually, time and again, we find the opposite to be the case: divine rescues were surprisingly rare.

Our Best Example: The Suffering of Jesus

When it comes to contemplating God's silence, there are several incredible insights to be gained by meditating on the sufferings of Jesus. This is especially the case since there is a connection between His afflictions and ours. He is our Example (Heb 4:15). We should walk in His steps, even in our suffering (1 Pet 2:20b–21). Paul longed to share Jesus' sufferings (Phil 3:10; cf. 1:29)!

It is difficult to miss the point that Jesus' plea, "My God, my God, why have you forsaken me?" (Mark 15:34 NIV) is the ultimate cry of perceived abandonment. We may never know the exact meaning of these words, or the precise amount of internal suffering that the Son of God was experiencing. But it would seem fair to say that Jesus at least *felt* as if He were abandoned. As such, this is the best example of the biblical pleas regarding God's silence, both because of the depth of Jesus' suffering as well as the fact that it so often affects our feelings, as well. Even a brief overview is worthwhile.

Jesus experienced incredibly painful beatings, followed by the process of dying via crucifixion, yet God refused to rescue Him from His cross. We rightly understand this as the means of our salvation (Mark 10:45). But these experiences stand as the all-time refutation of the notion that believers either are, or should be, exempt from even incredibly painful situations, or that God promised to remove us from our hurts. How so, when the Son of God did not escape, either physically or emotionally? So how in the world can believers demand or even expect to be removed from their suffering? After all, this is precisely what Jesus told His disciples: "If they persecuted me, they will persecute you also" (John 15:20 NIV); and again: "In this world you will have trouble. But take heart! I have overcome the world" (John 16:33 NIV).

Let's look at this another way. In Heb 5:8 we are told, incredibly, that in spite of being the very Son of God, Jesus actually learned obedience through His suffering! Further, we are told more than once (Heb 2:10; 5:9) that Jesus was perfected by His suffering. That Jesus needed to learn anything at all sounds rather startling. But then, He is our Example, and we are told to walk in His steps in our suffering.

There is an amazing application here to the believer's struggles with the silence of God. These verses in Hebrews should definitely cause us to ask ourselves at least a couple of questions. If Jesus had to learn obedience through His horrible sufferings, do we *deserve* to escape serious suffering? Dare we think that we deserve to be exempted from our hurts when Jesus clearly was not? Further, do we learn *more quickly* than did our Lord? The clear answers to these two questions mean that we have no basis to assert our "rights" or demands that God should "show Himself" after contemplating what Jesus went through. As a practical tool, I know of no better or more forceful meditation to apply precisely during those times when we wonder where God is, or if He will answer or when a situation doesn't make sense to us. If He did not intervene by exempting His own Son from arguably the worst suffering ever, what gives me the right to grow frustrated with God or cite promises out of context?

Conclusion

Through even a brief look at the detailed subject of God's silence, several things should become obvious. Perhaps the most straightforward conclusion is that God is not silent. His actions may be observed many ways, both externally as well as internally. But during those times when we wonder why God is not doing more in our lives or with others, we should learn to keep other lessons before us. Treasured promises in Scripture are precious and often occur literally. But that they do not always apply to specific cases should be clear both from the many comments about undergoing personal suffering in the exact same context, as well as the fact that, in general, even biblical heroes suffered through tough circumstances far more frequently than they were exempted from them. That Jesus, our Example, suffered so incredibly in spite of calling out to His Father is a final reminder that we will not be exempt from many difficult situations. Following our Leader, we, too, need to learn and grow through our suffering.

One last subject with absolutely huge implications should be mentioned here in passing. Hundreds of recent psychological studies have proven that, contrary to what we often think, our chief pain in life comes *not* from what happens or does not happen to us. Rather, our worst pain generally occurs from *what we tell ourselves about* the things we experience. In other words, how we download and interpret life is of the utmost importance. We cannot pursue this here, but it follows in regard to God's silence that much of our worst pain is *self-inflicted*. Most likely it is derived precisely *not* from anything that God fails to do, but from our telling ourselves things like the following: "God does not care about me, refuses to act, breaks His promises, or does things for others but not for me." Thinking and voicing such misbeliefs are the lies that

can poison our lives and can serve as the direct cause of our most painful emotions. Therefore, exchanging these lies for truth can help us align
our thinking with reality and can dramatically reverse these patterns of
self-inflicted pain (Phil 4:6–9).[20]

---

[20] See the many details in William Backus and Marie Chapian, *Telling Yourself the Truth*
(Minneapolis: Bethany, 2000); David Stoop, *You Are What You Think* (Grand Rapids: Revell,
1996).

Chapter 6

THE INSUFFICIENCY OF NATURALISM
A Worldview Critique
Robert B. Stewart

I intend in this essay to critique the worldview of naturalism.[1] In order to do this, I will evaluate naturalism according to some of the criteria that I would use to assess any other worldview. These criteria are (1) coherence, (2) correlation, (3) comprehensiveness, (4) consistency, and (5) commitment.[2]

Overview of the Criteria

Coherence is a vital ingredient of worldview analysis. By coherence I mean freedom from contradiction. Contradictory statements cannot both be true. If one is true, then the other is false, and vice versa. But bare logical consistency in and of itself is not enough for a worldview to be considered true. The world we find in *The Lord of the Rings* novels seems to me to be a coherent one, but I do not for a minute think that

---

[1] By "naturalism," I mean metaphysical naturalism. Metaphysical naturalism is not to be confused with environmental naturalism, which refers to an individual who actively seeks to commune with and/or preserve nature. Neither is metaphysical naturalism to be confused with methodological naturalism, which is the attempt on the part of a scientist or historian to state one's position without reference to supernatural beings or phenomena. A scientist or a historian may personally have a supernatural worldview but choose as a scholar to operate as a methodological naturalist.

[2] These are not the only criteria that can be used to assess a worldview, but in my view they are necessary criteria for critiquing any worldview. For more on worldview analysis, see www. nobtsapologetics.com/worldviews.

either hobbits or orcs actually exist. In other words, although coherence is necessary for a worldview to be considered adequate, coherence is not sufficient in and of itself. Other criteria are needed.[3]

Correlation is also a crucial component for a worldview. By correlation I mean that it matters a great deal that life actually seems to be the way that the worldview in question tells us it is.[4] The fundamental issue related to correlation is how well the worldview being considered describes life. To a certain degree we can live with a lack of correlation in our worldview, but at some point the cognitive dissonance from doing so becomes too great. All other things being equal, reason would dictate that no one should prefer a worldview that does less well in terms of correlation to one that does better.

Comprehensiveness deals with the question of how well the worldview does in explaining *all of life*. Coherence is much more easily attained if one leaves out certain bits of problematic data. But those problematic details cry out for attention and often are indications that something is amiss. Worldviews that don't address all areas of life are partial and incomplete. Therefore worldviews that effectively address more areas of life are preferable to those that address fewer.

Consistency addresses the question of how livable a worldview is. In many ways consistency is the truth serum of a worldview. If one has to live as though his worldview were false to get on with daily life, that does not bode well for his worldview. In fact, doing so constitutes a *performative contradiction*. A performative contradiction is when the proposition one affirms is contradicted by the action one performs, i.e., how one lives. The crucial issue is this: Does the worldview prescribe a

---

[3] In actually assessing competing worldviews it may be the case that all the worldviews being assessed appear in some sense to be incoherent. Or it may be the case that we reach a point where we are unable to know whether a worldview is truly coherent or incoherent. In such cases I suggest that the worldview that *seems* less incoherent, or about which we are less dubious in this regard, is preferable to the one that seems more incoherent or one about which we are more in doubt. My point is that matters are not always simple in worldview analysis, and thus we may have to be satisfied with assessing worldviews relative to one another, i.e., in terms of degree.

[4] Though I hold to a correspondence theory of truth, I intentionally steer away from saying "correspondence" in order not to import too much epistemological baggage into this analysis. It is enough to say that it counts strongly against a worldview that it doesn't seem to tell us how the world actually is. Similarly it counts strongly in favor of a worldview that seems to do a better job of telling us how the world actually is.

way of life that can actually be lived out consistently or must one live otherwise?

Commitment is the final criterion to be considered. Is the way of life dictated by the worldview existentially fulfilling? Can you commit yourself to it wholeheartedly? Camus put it thus: "Judging whether life is or is not worth living amounts to answering the fundamental question of philosophy."[5] Again, all things being equal, a worldview that offers more existential value is preferable to one that offers less.

These five criteria are not the only criteria by which a worldview may be judged, but they are central. They will necessarily be judged according to the standards of abductive reasoning (i.e., inference to the best explanation) rather than formal logic, on pragmatic bases rather than deductive or mathematical bases.[6]

An Examination of Each Criterion

Having given a general sketch of the criteria, here I give a more detailed explanation of why metaphysical naturalism fails to live up to these fundamental criteria for assessing any worldview.

Coherence

Naturalism holds within it a great contradiction. If all causes are material in nature—and the vast majority of naturalists believe that all causes are material—then what is the source of human rationality? Concerning this dilemma J. B. S. Haldane wrote, "If my mental processes are determined wholly by the motions of atoms in my brain, I have no reason to suppose that my beliefs are true. . . . And hence I have no reason for supposing my brain to be composed of atoms."[7]

---

[5] Albert Camus, *The Myth of Sisyphus and Other Essays*, trans. Justin O'Brien (New York: Knopf, 1955), 3. Ironically, a worldview that doesn't offer one a way of life worth dying for doesn't offer one a way of life as much worth living as one that does.

[6] For more on abductive reasoning, see Louis Pojman, *Philosophy: The Quest for Truth*, 4th ed. (Belmont, CA: Wadsworth, 1999), 29; and Umberto Eco and Thomas A. Sebeok, *The Sign of Three: Dupin, Holmes, Peirce* (Bloomington, IN: Indiana University Press, 1988).

[7] J. B. S. Haldane, "When I Am Dead," in *Possible Worlds*, ed. Carl A. Price (New Brunswick: Transaction, 2002), 209. In fact, Haldane also states that he thinks it "immensely unlikely that mind is a mere by-product of matter. . . . I am compelled to believe that mind is not wholly conditioned by matter" (ibid). On this, see C. S. Lewis, *Miracles: A Preliminary Study* (San Francisco: HarperCollins, 2001), 22.

Naturalists want to believe that they are being rational. We see this in
the titles they assign to themselves and their publications: "freethinkers,"
"free inquiry," etc. But in fact their beliefs serve to undermine our confidence in our own rationality. Atheist Patricia Churchland puts it thus:

> Boiled down to essentials, a nervous system enables the organ-
> ism to succeed in the four F's: feeding, fleeing, fighting and
> reproducing. The principal chore of nervous systems is to get
> the body parts where they should be in order that the organism
> may survive. . . . Improvements in sensorimotor control con-
> fer an evolutionary advantage: a fancier style of representing is
> advantageous *so long as it is geared to the organism's way of life*
> *and enhances the organism's chances of survival.* Truth, whatever
> that is, definitely takes the hindmost.[8]

The late atheist philosopher Richard Rorty echoes Churchland's
analysis of the implications of Darwinian theory: "The idea that one
species of organism is, unlike all the others, oriented not just toward
its own uncreated prosperity but toward Truth, is as un-Darwinian as
the idea that every human being has a built-in moral compass—a conscience that swings free of both social history and individual luck."[9]

It seems then that, on naturalism, what really matters is not whether
or not our beliefs are true but that they serve the right function. So long
as our beliefs work for survival, it doesn't matter whether they are true or
not. But are you reading this essay because you want to decide whether
Christianity is useful or because you want to know whether Christianity
is true?

Another contradiction we see is that naturalists generally work from
the presupposition that scientific knowledge is superior to any other

---

[8] Patricia Smith Churchland, "Epistemology in the Age of Neuroscience," *Journal of Philosophy*
84 (1987): 548–49. Alvin Plantinga has formulated a much-discussed argument against naturalism in which the probability of our minds producing rational beliefs is either low or inscru-
table given the conjunction of naturalism and evolution precisely because natural selection
prefers beliefs that are advantageous to those which are true. Alvin Plantinga, *Warrant and
Proper Function* (New York: Oxford University Press, 1993), 216–37. For a thorough discussion
of this argument, involving both theists and nontheists, see James Beilby, *Naturalism Defeated?
Essays on Plantinga's Evolutionary Argument against Naturalism* (Ithaca, NY: Cornell University
Press, 2002). Victor Reppert further develops this basic idea in his *C. S. Lewis's Dangerous Idea:
In Defense of the Argument from Reason* (Downers Grove, IL: InterVarsity, 2003).
[9] Richard Rorty, "Untruth and Consequences," *The New Republic*, July 31, 1995, 32–36.

sort of knowledge. But this belief cannot be supported by science. How would one construct an experiment to prove that scientific knowledge was superior to philosophical or religious knowledge? It can't be done. And it hasn't been done. What is one to make of a worldview wherein some of its most fundamental assertions lead to contradictions of the worldview itself? Certainly such a worldview does not score well in terms of coherence.

Correlation

We generally think that we can trust our mental faculties to provide us with reliable beliefs. We know that sometimes we are mistaken, but for the most part we trust our minds to guide us reliably upon reflection. Yet if naturalism is true, why should we do this? The simplest explanation is that we perceive that our beliefs are generally true. Consider the following questions:

1. Do you believe that you are reading this essay because you freely chose to do so, that you could have chosen differently, and that if you had, you would be reading—or doing—something else right now?

2. Do you believe that you are capable of thinking matters through and making a rational decision on questions such as should I get married, or should I read this essay, or should I believe that God exists?

3. Do you believe that people who eat their neighbors or abuse innocent children for their own amusement or self-gratification should be held responsible for their behavior?

4. Do you believe that *you* are consciously thinking about and answering these questions as *you* think best—that it is not simply a matter of your body through a physical process producing answers to these questions?

5. How strongly do you believe that you are a free, rational, and morally responsible person consciously thinking through these matters? What sort of evidence would it take to convince you that you are not?

I suspect that you are highly confident if not absolutely certain that at least most of the time you are free, rational, morally responsible, and conscious. One can easily see that human freedom, rationality, morality, and consciousness are not tangential or inconsequential issues; they are fundamental to what it means to be human.

But if naturalism is true, then you are very likely wrong on all these counts. This is not simply my opinion; notable naturalists themselves have made these same assertions. Consider this statement from the atheist philosopher of mind, John Searle:

> Physical events can have only physical explanations, and consciousness is not physical, so consciousness plays no explanatory role whatsoever. If, for example, you think you ate because you were consciously hungry, or got married because you were consciously in love with your prospective spouse, or withdrew your hand from the flame because you consciously felt a pain, or spoke up at a meeting because you consciously disagreed with the main speaker, you are mistaken in every case. In each case the effect was a physical event and therefore must have an entirely physical explanation.[10]

Significant issues are at stake if you believe that you are free. Consider the following from the website naturalism.org, which has many noted atheists, such as Daniel Dennett and Susan Blackmore, on its advisory board.

> From a naturalistic perspective . . . [h]uman beings act the way they do because of the various influences that shape them, whether these be biological or social, genetic or environmental. We do not have the capacity to act outside the causal connections that link us in every respect to the rest of the world. This means we do not have what many people think of as *free will*, being able to cause our behavior without our being fully caused in turn.[11]

---

[10] John Searle, *The Mystery of Consciousness* (New York: New York Review of Books, 1997), 154.

[11] "Tenets of Naturalism," accessed March 10, 2008, http://www.naturalism.org/tenetsof.htm.

Not being free has devastating implications for other important areas of life, such as ethics. Below is another naturalistic "tenet" found at naturalism.org.

> From a naturalistic perspective, behavior arises out of the inter-action between individuals and their environment, not from a freely willing self. . . . Therefore individuals don't bear ultimate originative responsibility for their actions, in the sense of being their first cause. Given the circumstances both inside and out-side the body, they couldn't have done other than what they did. Nevertheless, we must still hold individuals responsible, in the sense of applying rewards and sanctions, so that their behavior stays more or less within the range of what we deem acceptable. This is, partially, how people learn to act ethically.[12]

The question is: How can we hold individuals responsible if they aren't responsible for their actions and "couldn't have done other than what they did"? If it is true that "they couldn't have done other than what they did," then why do we call Francis of Assisi a saint and Jeffrey Dahmer a monster? Why do we lock one up and celebrate the sacrifice of the other? In fact, if we cannot do other than what we do, then theists and atheists are on equal footing—we're all determined to believe what we do. We can't do otherwise. So why write books like *The God Delusion*, which are specifically intended to change people's worldviews?[13]

Lacking freedom also has huge implications for our *human rela-tionships*. Just how do we make sense of this thing we call love? If our actions are the result of physical forces, then why does your husband or wife, boyfriend or girlfriend, love you? Why do you love your signifi-cant other? Does he or she do so freely? Do you? It is hard to see how in a naturalist world. Love, it would seem, is simply a byproduct of our biology and upbringing. In a very real sense, then, in a naturalist world we can say that love is the fruit of our genes and our experiences—but so is mental illness. How then are we to distinguish between love and psychosis?

What it boils down to is that naturalism leads to the denial of the independent existence of the self. Here is another tenet of naturalism:

---

[12] Ibid.

[13] See Richard Dawkins, *The God Delusion* (New York: Houghton Mifflin, 2006), 5.

As strictly physical beings, we don't exist as immaterial selves, either mental or spiritual, that control behavior. Thought, desires, intentions, feelings, and actions all arise on their own without the benefit of a supervisory self, and they are all the products of a physical system, the brain and the body. The self is *constituted* by more or less consistent sets of personal characteristics, beliefs, and actions; it doesn't exist apart from those complex physical processes that make up the individual. It may strongly seem as if there is a self sitting behind experience, witnessing it, and behind behavior, controlling it, but this impression is strongly disconfirmed by a scientific understanding of human behavior.[14]

What should be clear at this point is that naturalism leads to the denial of some truths that seem obvious to most people, truths such as that I can choose my actions, that I can reason through issues, that I am morally accountability for my actions, and that *I* have consciously reached these conclusions. It is thus apparent that naturalism is lacking significantly in terms of correlation.

A few months ago I was discussing some of this with some atheists, and one said that I was appealing to emotion. I think he said so because most of us would prefer being free to being determined, being rational to being nonrational, being conscious to being nonconscious automatons. But I was not then nor am I now appealing to emotion or to desire. I don't think that simply wanting something to be true will make it true.[15] So what am I appealing to here? I am appealing to *perception*, a time-honored source of knowledge. I am not saying that everything that "seems" to be so is so. Perception is not a perfect guide to truth. But when we perceive every day of our lives that we are freely choosing certain actions over other actions, that we are reasoning our way to many of our beliefs, that we and others are accountable for our actions, we ought not abandon these beliefs without extremely strong evidence to the contrary. How strong does the evidence need to be to cause us

---

[14] Ibid.

[15] I do think, however, that a strong argument for God's existence can be made on the basis of human desire. For an example of this sort of argument, see C. S. Lewis, "The Weight of Glory," in *The Weight of Glory and Other Addresses* (San Francisco: HarperSanFrancisco, 2001), 25–46.

to abandon belief in the reality of the self, of human freedom, and of human rationality? I cannot quantify my answer—nobody can—but at the very least I would say that the evidence needs to be enormous. And given the implications of naturalism related to these issues, naturalism cannot score well in terms of correlation.

One way that naturalists will try to show that we are physically determined is to show that we can track certain types of reactions in the brain scientifically. None of what I've stated means that our thoughts are not *processed* by the brain, or that a scientist working in the field of neurobiology or neuropsychology could not (at least theoretically) with the right equipment map the brain in such a way that he can know what portions of the brain are involved in mental activities such as anger, fear, memory, abstract thought, mystical states, worship, sexual arousal, and so forth. But what cannot be observed without some reference to the world beyond one's brain is the *specific content* of that mental activity. He might be able to identify the part of the brain that is involved in meditation or prayer, but he cannot discern what the individual is praying for—or to whom. This is because the *content of thought* is not to be found in the brain but in the mind. You can look in my laptop and find the data that translate to the words of this essay, but you will not find the thoughts behind the words in my computer because those thoughts are in my mind, not the instrument that I use to communicate those thoughts. I repeat, naturalism seems to be woefully deficient in terms of correlation.

Comprehensiveness

There are fundamental areas of life that naturalism cannot adequately explain.[16] One of them is consciousness. Another is purpose. Let's see what some leading naturalists have to say about consciousness. Richard Dawkins says this:

> There are aspects of human subjective consciousness that are deeply mysterious. Neither Steve Pinker nor I can explain

---

[16] I need to be very clear here that I am not attempting any sort of a "God of the gaps" move here. I am not saying that anything that cannot be explained now must be attributed to God. I am saying, though, that worldviews that can make sense of more rather than less data are, all things being equal, to be preferred over their competitors.

human subjective consciousness—what philosophers call qua-
lia. In *How the Mind Works* Steve elegantly sets out the problem
of subjective consciousness, and asks where it comes from and
what's the explanation? Then he's honest enough to say, "Beats
the heck out of me." That is an honest thing to say, and I echo
it. We don't know. We don't understand it.[17]

Consider what naturalist Ned Block has to say concerning consciousness: "We have no conception of our physical or functional nature that
allows us to understand how it could explain our subjective experience.
. . . But in the case of consciousness we have nothing—zilch—worthy of
being called a research programme, nor are there any substantive propos-
als about how to go about starting one. . . . Researchers are stumped."[18]

Some have argued that purpose is simply an illusion, and that we
simply impose purpose upon actions because we need purpose—or
because it is useful to believe that our actions have purposes. But this
is just confused. If it were true that purpose is just a figment of our
imaginations, then there would be no possibility of demonstrating that
purpose is required. But consider a simple question: Why did my fingers
move as they did when I typed out these pages? One naturalist answer
to this sort of question would be that my fingers moved because of the
contraction of muscles, stimulated by my nerves, and other physical
processes, such as chemical changes in my brain. Most people find this
sort of *instrumental* answer incomplete and unsatisfying in the extreme.
It might answer the "how" question—but it would never be able to
answer the "why" question. More importantly, the question includes
those three little words: "as they did." Why did my physical motions
render *those letters* in *that order*? Why do those letters make *words*—and
not just words but *English words*, and not just a series of English words
but *sentences*, and not disconnected sentences but sentences that fit
together and make pretty good sense? Surely we can't believe the result is
simply because of a random series of biological events. And certainly it
makes no sense to say we just impose meaning upon the product of my

---

[17] Richard Dawkins and Steven Pinker, "Is Science Killing the Soul?" accessed March 5,
2008, http://www.edge.org/3rd_culture/dawkins_pinker/debate_p4.html.
[18] Ned Block, "Consciousness," in *A Companion to the Philosophy of Mind*, ed. Samuel
Guttenplan, Blackwell Companions to Philosophy (Oxford and Malden: Blackwell, 1998),
211.

fingers moving where there is no real purpose or end. But this is what it seems we must affirm in a naturalist world. Naturalism therefore comes up short in terms of comprehensiveness.

Consistency

Naturalism is unlivable. In saying that naturalism is unlivable, I mean that the naturalist has to live in a way that contradicts his stated beliefs in any number of areas. Consider the following from naturalists Michael Ruse and E. O. Wilson:

> Human beings function better if they are deceived by their genes into thinking that there is a disinterested objective morality binding upon them, which all should obey. We help others because it is "right" to help them and because we know that they are inwardly compelled to reciprocate in equal measure. What Darwinian evolutionary theory shows is that this sense of "right" and the corresponding sense of "wrong," feelings we take to be above individual desire and in some fashion outside biology, are in fact brought about by ultimate biological processes.[19]

So Ruse and Wilson recommend that we fake it and live as though there were objective moral standards even though we know there aren't any objective moral standards. Along the same lines, Richard Dawkins has this to say:

> As an academic scientist, I am a passionate Darwinian, believing that natural selection is, if not the only driving force in evolution, certainly the only known force capable of producing the illusion of purpose which so strikes all who contemplate nature. But at the same time as I support Darwinism as a scientist, I am a passionate anti-Darwinian when it comes to politics and how we should conduct our human affairs.[20]

---

[19] Michael Ruse and E. O. Wilson, "Moral Philosophy as Applied Science," *Philosophy* 61 (1986): 179.

[20] Richard Dawkins, *A Devil's Chaplain: Reflections on Hope, Lies, Science, and Love* (New York: Houghton Mifflin, 2003), 10–11.

Perhaps the most controversial feature of contemporary atheism is the concept of a meme. Richard Dawkins introduced the concept in his book *The Selfish Gene*. Simply put, a meme is a cultural replicator. Suggested examples of memes include such disparate things as thoughts, ideas, theories, practices, habits, songs, dances, and languages. Accordingly, memes propagate themselves and can move through a culture in a manner similar to the behavior of a virus and influence behavior similarly to a gene. In coining the term, Dawkins wrote:

> We need a name for the new replicator, a noun that conveys the idea of a unit of cultural transmission, or a unit of *imitation*. "Mimeme" comes from a suitable Greek root, but I want a monosyllable that sounds a bit like "gene." I hope my classicist friends will forgive me if I abbreviate mimeme to *meme*. If it is any consolation, it could alternatively be thought of as being related to "memory" or to the French word *même*. It should be pronounced to rhyme with "cream."[21]

Several challenges arise in connection to memetic theory. One is to show how memetics is truly an empirical discipline. Simon Conway Morris, professor of evolutionary palaeobiology at Cambridge University, holds that memes seem to have no place in serious scientific reflection. "Memes are trivial, to be banished by simple mental exercises. In any wider context, they are hopelessly, if not hilariously, simplistic."[22]

Another issue is that memes can frequently appear to be nothing more than an ad hoc solution, i.e., they are not so much an explanation discovered as a solution created to solve an intractable problem. When asked to give evidence for memes at the 2007 Greer-Heard Point-Counterpoint Forum in Faith and Culture, Daniel Dennett responded that it was an accepted scientific belief and offered his article in the *Encyclopedia of Evolution* as supporting his position.[23] But what kind of evidence is this? It certainly is not the sort of evidence brought forward in support of general Darwinian theory, such as the fossil record,

---

[21] Richard Dawkins, *The Selfish Gene* (New York: Oxford University Press, 1976), 11.

[22] Simon Conway Morris, *Life's Solution: Inevitable Humans in a Lonely Universe* (Cambridge: Cambridge University Press, 2003), 324.

[23] Daniel Dennett, "Evolution," in *Encyclopedia of Evolution*, ed. Mark Pagel (Oxford: Oxford University Press, 2002). The article is reprinted in Daniel Dennett, *Breaking the Spell: Religion as a Natural Phenomenon* (New York: Viking, 2006), 341–57.

vestigial organs, embryology, geographic distribution of species, and so on. In fact, if this is a legitimate response, I see no reason why I shouldn't be allowed to hold that there is good evidence for the resurrection of Jesus because I wrote the article on the resurrection of Jesus in *The Cambridge Dictionary of Christianity*.[24] If an article with the imprint of a prestigious university press is all that's required to prove the reality of a hypothesis, then the matter seems settled. Frankly, I am advocating no such thing; it seems to be a category mistake. Simply put, while encyclopedia articles are generally sufficient to explain a theory on some basic level, they are not sufficient to establish a scientific theory—and with good reason.

Alister McGrath, an Oxford University-trained scientist and theologian and a former atheist, holds that there is no way to prove the existence of memes scientifically. This leads him to comment concerning Dennett's presentation of memes in *Breaking the Spell*, "This book, in my view, makes a critique of religion dependent on a hypothetical, unobserved entity, which can be dispensed with in order to make sense of what we observe. Isn't that actually a core atheist critique of God—an unobserved hypothesis that can be dispensed with easily? The evidence for belief in God is far better, in my view, than the evidence for belief in memes."[25]

One must remember that the concept of memes is based on an analogy between genes and ideas. An analogy is a type of supposal, a way of likening one thing to another; analogies are not evidence that *something is so* but rather illustrations of how *something could be so*. Analogies are tremendously useful things in philosophy, science, and history. Positing them often allows us to make progress. Unfortunately, analogies can also distort our view of reality and lead us down many dead-end paths. Remember that scientists in the late nineteenth century routinely posited the luminiferous ether—the hypothetical substance that was rigid in relationship to electromagnetic waves but completely permeable to matter—based on the supposed analogy between light and sound. The

---

[24] Robert B. Stewart, "Resurrection (the) of Jesus," in *The Cambridge Dictionary of Christianity*, ed. Daniel Patte (New York: Cambridge University Press, 2010).

[25] Alister McGrath, "The Future of Atheism: A Dialogue," in *The Future of Atheism: Alister McGrath and Daniel Dennett in Dialogue*, ed. Robert B. Stewart (Minneapolis: Fortress, 2008), 31.

idea was analogically plausible but mistaken. Worse, the idea of ether actually held back scientific progress. Fortunately, Einstein built on the work of Michelson and Morley and disproved it in his special theory of relativity. Dawkins believes that memes are merely waiting for scientific confirmation.[26] I concur with McGrath who thinks they are merely waiting for their Michelson and Morley to deliver the death blow to an unsatisfactory and unnecessary theory, of questionable relevance to our debate about God.[27]

What sort of score can naturalism receive in terms of consistency if even its most ardent supporters refuse to live according to their stated beliefs and must resort to creating explanations dependent on hypothetical, unobserved, immaterial entities?

Commitment

How does naturalism fare existentially? Naturalism with its commitment to biological and social determinism seems to offer no reason to stand for human freedom and against tyranny, or to praise Mother Teresa for her sacrifice and condemn Hitler for his genocidal agenda. In fairness to naturalists, many naturalists do stand for freedom, praise altruism, and even live altruistic lives. My critique is not that a naturalist *cannot* do these things. It is rather that someone who accepts naturalism's tenets has no intrinsic reason to do so. So when the naturalist makes such an existential commitment, he is living on borrowed capital, i.e., living according to values that flow from another worldview. C. S. Lewis, reflecting on his own past atheism, put it this way:

> My argument against God was that the universe seemed so cruel and unjust. But how had I got this idea of *just* and *unjust*? A man does not call a line crooked unless he has some idea of a straight line. What was I comparing this universe with when I called it unjust? If the whole show was bad and senseless from A to Z, so to speak, why did I, who was supposed to be part of the show, find myself in such violent reaction against it? . . . Of course I could have given up my idea of justice by saying it was nothing but a private idea of my own. But if I did that,

---

[26] Dawkins, *A Devil's Chaplain*, 124.
[27] McGrath, "The Future of Atheism: A Dialogue," 32.

then my argument against God collapsed too—for the argument depended on saying that the world was really unjust, not simply that it did not happen to please my private fancies. Thus in the very act of trying to prove that God did not exist—in other words, that the whole of reality was senseless—I found I was forced to assume that one part of reality—namely my idea of justice—was full of sense. Consequently atheism turns out to be too simple. If the whole universe has no meaning, we should never have found out that it has no meaning: just as, if there were no light in the universe and therefore no creatures with eyes, we should never know it was dark. *Dark* would be a word without meaning.[28]

On the other hand, naturalists often say that a world without religion would be a better world because religious belief leads people to do evil. Nobel Prize-winning physicist Steven Weinberg puts it thus: "Good people will do good things and bad people will do bad things, but for good people to do bad things—that takes religion."[29] But surely this criticism is misguided. Thomas Crean argues that even if the charge were true, it would not prove the naturalist position.

Insofar as this is true, it has no tendency to show that religion is itself a bad thing, or that its message is false. Love causes people to do evil things; so does patriotism. The love of a man and a woman can lead to unfaithfulness, to the destruction of families and even to murder. Patriotism can lead to hatred and to the indiscriminate bombing of cities. None of this means that either love or patriotism is a bad thing. It simply means that the weakness of human nature is such that any great object or cause may stir our emotions as to lead us to act against our better judgment. If religion occasions evil as well as good, this is no sign of its falsity, but simply of its power of attraction over human nature. That in the name of religion good men may do

---

[28] C. S. Lewis, *Mere Christianity* (San Francisco: Harper, 2001), 38–39.
[29] Steven Weinberg, *Facing Up: Science and Its Cultural Adversaries* (Cambridge: Harvard University Press, 2001), 242.

bad things is no argument against religion, unless crimes of passion are arguments against human love.[30]

How well can naturalism fare in terms of existential commitment if even the attempts of naturalists to build a world of peace and nonviolence depend on oversimplification and cannot be drawn out logically from the worldview itself? The existential cost of naturalism is indeed high, too high.

Conclusion

Some may object that all worldviews have their problems. This is true; all worldviews have their challenges. I think Christianity fares better than naturalism in terms of coherence, correlation, comprehensiveness, consistency, and commitment. I have tried to be fair in my assessment of naturalism by focusing on core tenets of naturalism and the implications of those tenets. I have also tried to support my critique by citing naturalists themselves, thus showing that at least some significant naturalist thinkers agree with me as to what naturalism entails. As with all worldviews, readers will have to judge for themselves whether or not naturalism is sufficient. I am of the opinion that it is not.

---

[30] Thomas Crean, *God Is No Delusion: A Refutation of Richard Dawkins* (San Francisco: Ignatius, 2007), 118–19.

Part 3

THE HISTORICAL
JESUS AND
NEW TESTAMENT
RELIABILITY

Chapter 7

GOSPEL TRUTH
The Historical Reliability of the Gospels
Craig S. Keener

H istorical information about individuals is normally preserved especially by the circles that value it; thus our best sources for ancient sages come from their disciples, for Muhammad from his followers, and for Jesus from His disciples. What we know about Jesus historically can be only as accurate as our sources. The most complete of these sources, from within a generation or two of Jesus' time, are the Gospels. How reliable are they? If scholars examine the Gospels in light of contemporary sources from their own period, instead of accumulated theories of skeptical scholarship, they should regard them as very useful sources for understanding the Jesus who lived in history. I rehearse below some key principles from my recent *Historical Jesus of the Gospels*.[1]

The Controversy

How reliable are the Gospels? Most readers are aware of some skeptical voices in the media. One very public voice is the Jesus Seminar, which has gained notoriety by using marbles to vote on which sayings of Jesus were "authentic." This self-selected group is no more a cross-section of all biblical scholars than a self-selected group of conservative scholars would be. The actual range of scholarly views is considerable

[1] Craig Keener, *The Historical Jesus of the Gospels* (Grand Rapids: Eerdmans, 2009), where I provide much more detailed documentation for the arguments offered here. Also my "Assumptions in Historical Jesus Research," *Journal for the Study of the Historical Jesus* 9 (2011): 26–58.

(with the center to the right of the Jesus Seminar and to the left of most conservative scholars), but some have marketed more skeptical scholars as the voice of scholarship in some media circles.

More generally, sectors of academia have harbored a prejudice against the miraculous, hence against documents such as the Gospels, since the radical Enlightenment. Segments of New Testament scholarship have built theory upon theory to explain away the possibility of eyewitness claims of miracles or divine activity in history, and hence have argued against the possibility of significant eyewitness material in the Gospels. Other scholars (growing in number today) instead support eyewitness material. Majority opinions among scholars shift back and forth on many points with new publications so simply taking a head count cannot settle much; instead we will look briefly at some evidence.

If we examined the Gospels by comparison with analogous works from their period, what would we gather? Are the Gospels mere works of propagandistic fiction, or do they recount a true story? No one doubts that they "preach," but the best evidence shows that the "text" from which they preached was the genuine life of Jesus.

The Gospels as Ancient Biography

Like readers through most of history, ancient readers assumed that the Gospels were "lives" (*bioi*), biographies of Jesus. The genre of biography—a work about a historical person—existed well before Jesus' ministry and was popular in the period of the Gospels. In the early twentieth century, however, some scholars noticed that the Gospels were not like modern biography, and hence decided that they were not genuine biographies. In time, however, dissenting voices chipped away at that consensus, and in the past two decades scholars favoring the category "biography" for the Gospels have become a strong majority.[2] Why is this the case?

Scholars arguing that the Gospels were not biographies were partly right in terms of what they meant: the Gospels are not *modern* biographies. The Gospels do, however, fit the character of *ancient* biographies—that

[2] See esp. Richard A. Burridge, *What Are the Gospels? A Comparison with Graeco-Roman Biography*, Society for New Testament Studies Monograph Series 70 (Cambridge: Cambridge University, 1992; 2nd ed., Grand Rapids: Eerdmans; Dearborn, MI: Dove Booksellers, 2004).

is, they are written the way biographies were written in their era. Modern biographers normally arrange their material chronologically, but while ancient biographers sometimes did this, they usually arranged their material topically (as, for example, Matthew appears to do). Modern biographies normally start from their subject's birth; while ancient biographies sometimes did so (as in the case of Matthew and Luke), they often simply opened with their public careers (as in the cases of many philosophers and politicians, and as we have in the case of Mark).

The cost of papyrus and limitations of ancient publishing required biographers to be selective in what they included; they often thus focused on those points that would teach the audience valuable lessons. They could focus at length on their subjects' deaths (as in the Gospels) when these were particularly significant (e.g., martyrs). Jesus differs from other biographic subjects, but that is a difference in Jesus, not in the genre; biographies were works about historical persons.

Ancient Biographies as Essentially Historical Works

Ancient biography was a form of historical writing.[3] A second-century critic wrote that good biographers avoided flattery that falsified events,[4] and that only bad historians invent data.[5] A later statesman who was alive during the time that the Gospels were written allowed historians to show off their literary skills *provided* they stuck to facts; this was what was distinctive about history, in contrast to some other genres.[6] A few centuries earlier, the Greek philosopher Aristotle also insisted that the fundamental characteristic of history was that it must address what actually happened.[7]

---

[3] See George A. Kennedy, "Classical and Christian Source Criticism," in *The Relationships Among the Gospels: An Interdisciplinary Dialogue*, ed. William O. Walker Jr. (San Antonio: Trinity University Press, 1978), 136 (125–55); for the close relationship, see also Benedetto Bravo, "Antiquarianism and History," in *A Companion to Greek and Roman Historiography*, ed. John Marincola, 2 vols. Blackwell Companions to the Ancient World (Malden, MA; Oxford: Blackwell, 2007), 1:516 (515–27); Philip Stadter, "Biography and History," in ibid., 528 (528–40).

[4] Lucian, *How to Write History*, 12.

[5] Ibid., 24–25.

[6] Pliny, *Epistles* 7.17.3; 8.4.1.

[7] Aristotle, *Poetics* 9.2–3, 1451b.

Biographers had perspectives, often including personal interest in and feelings about those concerning whom they wrote. Nevertheless, they and historians were supposed to try to report people's character accurately, without bias.[8] Sometimes this commitment compelled them even to report information unflattering toward persons they genuinely respected.[9] While not all biographers lived up to this standard, accuracy remained the ideal. In contrast to those writing about politicians, Jesus' followers had no reasons to "flatter" Him; if they did not believe that their story was true, they had no reason even to risk their security by following Him.

Some complain that the Gospels are engaging, like novels. Because most historians and biographers wanted to write in such a way as to keep their audiences interested, however, their works are usually engaging, often reading like stories. The difference between such works and novels is not that the former were boring and the latter were entertaining, but that the former were *also* meant to be *informative*. Moreover, historians and biographers (far more often than novelists) sometimes recounted their historical information specifically to provide moral, political, or theological lessons for their audiences (less an interest of novels). Unlike biographies, novels lacked historical prologues (such as we find in Luke 1:1–4) and usually lacked clear sources. Novels were never about recent persons and usually not about historical characters at all; they reflected little interest in communicating much historical information. Though some biographers took more liberties than others, they were clearly not writing novels.

Biographies of much earlier characters could draw on legend, but biographies of figures from the previous generation or two (like the Gospels) depended on a vast amount of historical information.[10] For example, Tacitus, writing about his father-in-law, and Suetonius, writing about recent emperors, stick very close to their sources. Josephus wrote both history and autobiography; despite his slant on some points, archaeology often confirms his substantial information. When writing about an emperor just half a century earlier, biographers and historians

---

[8] Polybius 34.4.2; see also, e.g., Dionysius of Halicarnassus, *Thucydides* 8; Tacitus, *History* 1.1. For further discussion, see Keener, *Historical Jesus*, chaps. 7–8.

[9] E.g., Philostratus, *Lives of the Sophists* 2.21.603 (of his own teacher, 2.21.602); the biographer Eunapius, *Lives* 461 (of Iamblichus, whom Eunapius considered supernatural, 459–61).

[10] Ancients themselves recognized that they could speak more certainly about recent than earlier figures; cf. e.g., Thucydides 1.21.1; Diodorus Siculus 1.6.2; 1.9.2; 4.1.1; 4.8.3–5.

overlap on a vast number of points.[11] If people concede that such biographies were even *mostly* historical (and they were), they should concede enough about Jesus in the Gospels to consider His message.

How Historical Are the Gospels?

How do we evaluate *particular* cases of ancient biography? Two factors merit special consideration. First, historians and biographers writing about the fairly recent past (including Thucydides, Polybius, and often Tacitus and Suetonius) were much more apt to have genuine information to convey than those writing about the distant past. Second, we must ask how closely particular historians stuck to their sources (which we can sometimes reconstruct by comparing earlier historians). Everyone allowed ancient historians to put their material in their own words, which results in some variation, but some closely followed their sources.

Where do the Gospels fall by these standards? The latest of the four extant first-century Gospels, John, was written perhaps 65 years after Jesus' death, and the earliest (probably Mark) within a generation of Jesus' death—when some eyewitnesses presumably remained alive (see discussion below). Among ancient biographies, then, the Gospels would be, by purely historical standards, among the more dependable sources for reconstructing the life of their subject.

How closely do they stick to their sources? While we cannot test every source, we should assume that the places where we *can* test them are representative; after all, the Gospel writers could not have known which sources would survive two millennia for later readers to test! Although scholars disagree on the exact relationship among the Gospels, the majority of scholars believe that Matthew and Luke used both Mark and another source that they shared in common. If we compare these sources, we see that, apart from variations in wording that were fairly minimal by ancient standards, the Gospels, where we can test them, stuck quite closely to their sources.

When we apply the standards of historiography to ancient biographies in general, therefore, the Gospels appear to be among the most

---

[11] See Craig Keener, "Otho: A Targeted Comparison of Suetonius' Biography and Tacitus' History, with Implications for the Gospels' Historical Reliability," *Bulletin for Biblical Research*, vol. 21, no. 3 (2011): 331–55.

rather than the least accurate. On purely historical grounds, then, even a person with no theological commitments can look to the Gospels to learn about Jesus.

Luke Reveals His Historical Method

Whereas the Gospels, taken by themselves, are biographies, Luke's Gospel is part of a two-volume work that scholars generally consider a historical monograph. Historians sometimes devoted a volume of their work to an individual figure, so that the Gospel of Luke is a biographic segment of Luke's larger history. Whereas the other Gospels do not tell us much about their method, Luke, writing history, provides information useful for learning his method even in the beginning of his volume.

Like many historians, Luke includes a historical preface, addressing the "events that have been fulfilled among us" (Luke 1:1 HCSB). Because his work is brief compared with multivolume histories, he has a correspondingly brief preface, which we find in Luke 1:1–4. This preface reveals Luke's sources, his probable research, and his purpose of confirming what Theophilus (and presumably others like him) knew about these "events that have been fulfilled among us." By studying his prologue, we learn about written sources available in his day (1:1), oral sources going back to eyewitnesses (1:2), his thorough knowledge (1:3), and the wide circulation of the accounts already by the time he wrote (1:4).[12]

Written Sources (Luke 1:1)

The vast majority of scholars date Luke somewhere between the years 62 and 90. While earlier dates might work better for our purposes than later ones, even the latest date in this range (which I think is unwarranted) places Luke within 60 years of Jesus' crucifixion. This is quite recent by ancient biographic standards. In any case, Luke notes that "many" had already written gospels before him; at least some had achieved a measure of prominence (see comments on Mark below). This means that written sources were already proliferating in the lifetime of some of the eyewitnesses, even at a time when the Christian movement was experiencing a phenomenal rate of expansion, carrying its stories

[12] Treated in my *Historical Jesus*, chaps. 6, 9–10.

about Jesus with it. Most historians would be delighted if more of our Greek and Roman biographies derived from a period so close to the subjects of the biographies.

Most scholars who compare the Gospels argue that at least one of Luke's earlier sources was Mark's Gospel, which most scholars date to around AD 70 or somewhat before (many conservative scholars, including myself, prefer a date of about 64, but the difference is negligible for our purposes). According to early second-century traditions, Mark's Gospel achieved prominence, despite its less-sophisticated style, because it was based on the memoirs of Peter. While I think this tradition likely,[13] it is enough for our purposes here to point out that this Gospel stems from within four decades after Jesus' public ministry.

Are the events of four decades before us shrouded in amnesia? Even if we lacked publications and videotapes, most of us, regardless of our age, know eyewitnesses who lived through events four decades ago. If doubt arose as to the nature of the events sufficient to concern us, we would go to the eyewitnesses. Ancient historical writers likewise consulted eyewitnesses as their ideal sources.[14]

Oral Sources (1:2)

Luke notes that his accounts were handed down from the original eyewitnesses of Jesus' ministry. The term he uses for "handing down" had several meanings, but in contexts involving oral tradition often suggested careful transmission. How accurate could this transmission be? To answer this question we must consider memory and memorization in antiquity, especially in school settings, where some even took notes; afterward we will return to the question of eyewitnesses. No one expected verbatim recall in normal settings, but remembering the substance of the information was very important.

Like other societies with a heavy emphasis on orality (which could coexist with written sources), Mediterranean society prized memory in a way that often astonishes Westerners accustomed to sound bites and

---

[13] For arguments that the early church would have correctly preserved the authors of the Gospels, see Martin Hengel, *Studies in the Gospel of Mark*, trans. John Bowden (Philadelphia: Fortress, 1985). Rarely were such large works transmitted anonymously.

[14] See here especially Samuel Byrskog, *Story as History—History as Story: The Gospel Tradition in the Context of Ancient Oral History* (Boston, Leiden: Brill Academic Publishers, 2002).

information overload. Bards, despised by the elite as uneducated, could recite the entire epics of Homer from memory; Jewish people could likewise retell lengthy stories and recall large segments of Scripture. Of course, "oral performers" could vary their wording at times, but the substance remained.[15] One of the five basic tasks of oratory was memorization of one's speech, which could often be two hours in length.

Once people began valuing and training memory, exceptional feats were possible. Seneca the Elder, father of the famous philosopher by that name, notes that in his younger days he could repeat back 2,000 names in exactly the sequence in which he had just heard them. After apologizing that his memory was no longer so strong in his old age, he proceeds to repeat parts of over 100 practice speeches he heard when he was in a school that trained speakers. He also tells of others who could memorize poems as they heard them or repeat back an entire day's sales at an auction from memory.[16] Even if we allow for some exaggeration, ancient Mediterranean culture valued, hence emphasized, memory to a degree modern Western readers consider extraordinary.

Memorization was at the heart of basic education, often involving memorizing the sayings of famous teachers; Jewish boys memorized especially Torah. More relevant to Jesus' disciples is discipleship, a form of advanced education usually beginning in the mid-teens. Greeks had two main disciplines for advanced education, rhetoric (professional public speaking) and philosophy. In both cases, students learned by heart their teachers' teachings, which they were responsible to represent accurately even if they later came to disagree with them. Memorization and propagation of the founder's teachings was even more relevant in philosophic schools. We may take as an extreme illustration the Pythagoreans, who were said to arise from bed in the morning only after they had recited the previous day's learning.

What was true of the Mediterranean world in general was also true of Jewish disciples. Our sources suggest that Jewish disciples were even more

---

[15] On oral tradition, see also discussions in James D. G. Dunn, *A New Perspective on Jesus: What the Quest for the Historical Jesus Missed* (Grand Rapids: Baker, 2005); Paul Rhodes Eddy and Gregory A. Boyd, *The Jesus Legend: A Case for the Historical Reliability of the Synoptic Jesus Tradition* (Grand Rapids: Baker Academic, 2007).

[16] E.g., Seneca, *Controversia* 1.pref.2, 19; cf. Philostratus, *Lives of the Sophists* 1.11.495; Pliny, *Epistles* 2.3.3.

rigorous in preserving and transmitting the teachings of their teachers, although many of these teachings proved to be common property of the sages.[17] Students were also interested in their teachers' example, and rabbis often appealed to earlier rabbis' actions to establish legal precedents, often assuming that their behavior would have been honorable.

Virtually everyone agrees that Jesus was a teacher and had disciples. Based on the above observations, should we not assume that Jesus' disciples, like those of other teachers, would seek to preserve and promote their teacher's teachings? Students could eventually articulate their own views, but they did not normally attribute these new views to their teachers. For some critics to treat Jesus' followers as singularly unreliable, against the normal expectation for other ancient disciples, is to reveal the critics' specific prejudice against Jesus and His movement. It is not those who defend the reliability of the Gospels who engage in special pleading on this point but those who deny it.

Students often took notes. Quintilian's rhetorical students took such careful notes that they published a book in his name without his knowledge; though wishing that they had first consulted him, he attests that they accurately presented his content.[18] Arrian took careful notes on his philosophic teacher Epictetus, duplicating even his rambling style (which is not Arrian's own). Rabbis emphasized memorization more than note taking, but some cases of note taking are known even in those circles, and the literacy of Palestinian Jews was, if anything, higher than average in the Empire. This does not prove that any of Jesus' disciples took notes at the time, but we cannot rule the possibility out. Some may have been literate, but even illiterate bards displayed feats of memory.

Because the disciples continued as a group, they could prod and correct one another's memories rather than depending only on an individual's recollections. We know that in the mid-first century, shortly before Mark wrote his Gospel, key witnesses remained in the chief positions of leadership in the church (Gal 1:18–19; 2:9) and were known to all the churches (cf. 1 Cor 15:5–7). Those whose reports would be most respected were the sources and continuing guarantors of the tradition

---

[17] Although our sources before AD 70 are limited, we do read of early disciples of Jewish teachers and have no reason to think that they were wholly different from post-70 Jewish disciples or from philosophers' disciples.

[18] Quintilian, *Institutes of Oratory* 1.pref. 7–8.

during the period when written sources began to emerge. W. D. Davies noted that only a single lifespan "separates Jesus from the last New Testament document. And the tradition in the Gospels is not strictly a folk tradition, derived from long stretches of time, but a tradition preserved by believing communities who were guided by responsible leaders, many of whom were eyewitnesses of the ministry of Jesus."[19]

Many of the witnesses—fishermen, tax collectors, and women— were not among the most respected classes whose testimony ancient society valued; no one would have invented such witnesses, about whom aristocratic pagans later complained. Yet what limited sources we have about them indicate that these witnesses were prepared to die for their testimony, and none of them renounced their claims even under duress (a situation that would have invited a defensive response).[20]

Luke's "Thorough Knowledge" (1:3)

Luke claims "thorough knowledge" of the matters about which he writes. Where could he have acquired such "thorough knowledge"? Luke's first-person pronoun resurfaces in his second volume, in particular scenes in Acts 16–28. Unwilling to grant that Luke traveled with Paul, critics sometimes contend that his "we" is a fictitious literary device; but why would a *fictitious* "we" appear mostly in minor travel scenes rather than at significant occasions such as Pentecost? The "we" leaves off in Philippi (Acts 16:16) and picks up there later (20:6). Moreover, fictitious "we's" are almost entirely limited to fictitious genres. As Harvard classicist Arthur Darby Nock pointed out, use of the first person in historical narratives is almost always a genuine claim to have been present; abundant evidence confirms (and most scholars recognize) that Luke was writing history, not a novel. Nor is it likely that Luke inadvertently simply retained another witness's "we," since he does not do this with any of his other material.

---

[19] W. D. Davies, *Invitation to the New Testament: A Guide to Its Main Witnesses* (Garden City, NY: Doubleday, 1966), 115–16; cf. similarly E. P. Sanders, *The Tendencies of the Synoptic Tradition* (SNTSMS 9; Cambridge: Cambridge University Press, 1969), 28.

[20] For the argument that the Gospels reflect eyewitness tradition, see especially now Richard J. Bauckham, *Jesus and the Eyewitnesses: The Gospels as Eyewitness Testimony* (Grand Rapids: Eerdmans, 2006).

The "we" was with Paul in Judea for as much as two years (Acts 21:17; 24:27; 27:1–2). That means that Luke had plenty of time to consult with eyewitnesses and those who knew the traditions directly from them. Luke was able to do what any historian today would do if he or she could: consult the eyewitnesses to corroborate the information already available.

Luke Appeals to Common Knowledge (1:4)

Luke writes to confirm what Theophilus had already been taught (Luke 1:4). This appeal indicates that the information Luke recounts was already widely known; Luke would hardly appeal to Theophilus's knowledge and then contradict it by making up something completely new![21] When Luke notes that he is confirming what Theophilus has already been taught, he is confirming that the message about Jesus circulating a generation after Jesus' public ministry matches with what was reported by the eyewitnesses and their circle in Jewish Palestine. The Gospels connect us with the very information about Jesus already circulating within a generation of His ministry.

Other Evidence

Although the later church debated many issues such as circumcising Gentiles, the Gospel writers did not read their views back into the collection of Jesus' teachings. The Gospels apply Jesus' teachings to their time, but they do not feel free to invent new ones attributed to Him. Indeed, if they were simply inventing stories about Jesus freely, we would not have so much overlap, especially among the "Synoptic" Gospels. Paul felt free to qualify Jesus' teaching for a new situation, but distinguished between his own teaching and "the Lord's" when he did so (1 Cor 7:10–16). His letters incidentally attest other teachings of Jesus (e.g., 1 Thess 4:15–5:4), including about the heart of his mission (1 Cor 11:23–25), circulating before our Gospels were written.

Jesus probably spoke primarily Aramaic in Galilee, and many of His sayings in the Gospels preserve Aramaic figures of speech (not least the

---

[21] Compare Paul's appeal to the Corinthians' eyewitness experience with miracles (2 Cor 12:12) and the availability of witnesses for the resurrection (1 Cor 15:6).

repeated "Son of man," which is good Aramaic but absurd Greek). Yet the bilingual Jerusalem church must have shifted quickly to Greek so that its "Hellenist" members could participate fully; the early church in urban Antioch would also have spoken Greek. Although they sometimes translated into colloquial Greek, echoes even of Jesus' Aramaic style often come through in the Gospels, and these surely come from the earliest bilingual churches.

Not only Aramaisms but the abundance of rural, Galilean characteristics fit Jesus' actual background far better than they fit the movement soon after His departure because the center of the movement quickly became urban both in Judea and throughout the Empire. Various images fit Jesus' Palestinian Jewish milieu better than that of the later church, as one may illustrate with examples like the following:[22]

- the first half of the Lord's Prayer closely resembles standard Jewish prayers, especially the Kaddish;[23]
- the Pharisees' divorce question reflects a debate among Pharisaic schools from Jesus' day;[24]
- the warning that it would be "measured" to one as one measured to others (Matt 7:2//Luke 6:38);[25]
- removing the beam from one's eye before trying to remove the chip from another's (Matt 7:3–5//Luke 6:41–42);[26]
- Jewish sages often used the phrase, "To what then should I compare?" (Matt 11:16//Luke 7:31 HCSB), especially to introduce parables;[27]
- they often used the phrase, "So-and-so is like" (Matt 11:16; 13:24; 25:1; cf. also Mark 4:26,31; 13:34; Luke 6:48–49);[28]

[22] See Keener, *Historical Jesus*, chaps. 11–22; for the examples here, see *idem, The Gospel of Matthew: A Socio-Rhetorical Commentary* (Grand Rapids: Eerdmans, 2009), passim.

[23] See, e.g., Morton Smith, *Tannaitic Parallels to the Gospels* (Philadelphia: Society of Biblical Literature, 1951), 136.

[24] Cf. *mishnah Gittin* 9:10; *Sipre Deuteronomy* 269.1.1.

[25] See *mishnah Sota* 1:7; more fully, Smith, *Tannaitic Parallels*, 135; Gustaf Dalman, *Jesus-Jeshua: Studies in the Gospels* (New York: Macmillan, 1929), 225.

[26] See Geza Vermes, *The Religion of Jesus the Jew* (Minneapolis: Augsburg Fortress, 1993), 80.

[27] See *Abot* 3:17; *mishnah Sukkoth* 2:10; *tosefta Berakoth* 1:11; 6:18; *Baba Kamma* 7:2–4; *Hagigah* 2:5; *Sanhedrin* 1:2; 8:9; *Sipra Shemini Mekhilta deMiluim* 99.2.5; *Behuqotai* pq. 2.262.1.9; *Sipre Numbers* 84.2.1; 93.1.3; *Sipre Deuteronomy* 1.9.2; 1.10.1; 308.2.1; 308.3.1; 309.1.1; 309.2.1.

[28] See, e.g., *tosefta Sukkoth* 2:6; *Sipra Shemini Mekhilta deMiluim* 99.2.2; *Behuqotai*

- "moving mountains" may have been a Jewish metaphor for accomplishing what was difficult or virtually impossible (though rabbis, who preserve it, apply it especially to labor in Torah);[29]
- later Jewish teachers, not likely influenced by Jesus, could depict what was impossible or close to impossible as a large animal "passing through a needle's eye";[30] and
- current Pharisaic debates about purity with respect to the inside or outside of cups.[31]

Objections Raised

Detractors raise various objections to the Gospels. Some contend that we should weigh other "gospels" as heavily as the Gospels we have mentioned above.[32] I cannot imagine any scholar who would not be delighted if some other first-century historical sources about Jesus (such as are mentioned in Luke 1:1) would be discovered. Unfortunately, none of the other so-called "gospels" that remain today are this early; none stems from within living memory of the eyewitnesses, and many are centuries later than Jesus' century. The earliest, the Gospel of Thomas, is usually dated to around AD 140, and some now date it a generation later. The gnostic gospels are not "lives" of Jesus but collections of sayings attributed to Jesus, with so many gnostic and non-Palestinian elements that we cannot rely on their claims.

The apocryphal gospels similarly lack first-century Palestinian Jewish traits found in the four Gospels accepted by the church as authentic. They reflect their own time, do not reflect the sort of dependence on early sources found in Matthew and Luke, and fit the form of novels.

---

pq.3.263.1.5, 8; *Sipre Numbers* 84.1.1; 86.1.1; 89.4.2; *Sipre Deuteronomy* 3.1.1; 11.1.2; 26.3.1; 28.1.1; 29.4.1.

[29] E.g., *Abot de Rabbi Nathan* 6A; 12, §29B; *Babylonian Talmud Berakoth* 63b; *Sanhedrin* 24a.

[30] Israel Abrahams, *Studies in Pharisaism and the Gospels* (2nd ser.; Cambridge: Cambridge University Press, 1924), 2:208; Dalman, *Jesus-Jeshua*, 230.

[31] Jacob Neusner, "'First Cleanse the Inside,'" *New Testament Studies* 22 (1976): 486–95 (here 492–94).

[32] See discussion in *Historical Jesus*, chap. 4, and other sources (esp. Craig Evans and Nicholas Perrin).

The apocryphal gospels in fact stem from the heyday of novels, starting in the late second century.

A major reason some scholars doubted the Gospels to begin with was that they report miracles, which modern Western critics felt could not be attributed to eyewitnesses. Whether or not one believes that miracles are genuine, however, one cannot doubt that millions of eyewitnesses even today claim to have experienced or witnessed them (including cures of blindness and the raising of the dead). However one explains unusual events, it is not possible for knowledgeable persons to deny that people witness events that they understand in such terms. Moreover, the philosophic argument against the possibility of any unexpected cures being genuine miracles rests largely on the case of Hume, whose argument against miracles is entirely circular. Simply dismissing miracle claims without consideration is to work from a bias ultimately grounded philosophically in dogmatic atheism or deism.[33]

Conclusion

The Gospels are our best sources for Jesus, and by the criteria that we use to evaluate historical sources from antiquity, they are quite good ones. They are biographies from within a generation or two after the events they describe, depend on earlier sources, and, where we can test them, follow those sources carefully. Moreover, their sources arose in a time when people looked to the eyewitnesses for leadership and memories about Jesus. These eyewitnesses were disciples, who would normally be the very people trusted to preserve a sage's message. The Gospels did not invent new sayings of Jesus to address the crises of their day but used material already available. In contrast with what we would expect for fabricated sayings, they reflect early rural Galilean traditions that were no longer the setting of the Gospels' primary audiences. In short, those who reject the Gospels' witness concerning Jesus effectively are treating these works in an eccentric way that differs from how we would treat comparable historical reports from antiquity.

---

[33] See at much greater length my *Miracles: The Credibility of the New Testament Accounts* (Grand Rapids: Baker Academic, 2011); see also my article, "A Reassessment of Hume's Case Against Miracles in Light of Testimony from the Majority World Today," *Perspectives in Religious Studies* 38, no.3 (Fall 2011): forthcoming.

Chapter 8

WILL THE REAL AUTHOR PLEASE STAND UP?
The Author in Greco-Roman Letter Writing

E. Randolph Richards

S cholars today discuss whether the letters in the New Testament bearing Paul's name were in fact written by Paul. Actually, by the word "written" they mean "authored," not who actually penned the words onto paper.[1] We are discussing whether Paul was really the author of all the letters bearing his name in the New Testament or if some of them were forgeries.[2] The four so-called *Hauptbriefe* (chief letters),[3] Romans, 1–2 Corinthians, and Galatians, are considered so "Pauline" that few have ever questioned them.[4] Philippians, Philemon, and 1 Thessalonians

---

[1] Most scholars acknowledged the use of secretaries (see Rom 16:22). Incidentally, the first draft of a letter was not on paper, likely not even on papyrus but rather a wax tablet or perhaps the newly fashionable (reusable) parchment notebooks or (wood) leaf notebooks.

[2] So the book published by Bart D. Ehrman, *Forged: Writing in the Name of God—Why the Bible's Authors Are Not Who We Think They Are* (New York: HarperOne, 2011).

[3] A common term in scholarship, originally coined by Ferdinand Christian Baur, *Paul the Apostle of Jesus Christ: His Life and Works, His Epistles and Teachings*, repr. ed., 2 vols in 1 (Peabody, MA: Hendrickson, 2003 [1845]).

[4] It may be noted this is a circular argument. "Pauline" themes are the ones we find in these four letters. Hence, these four letters are the most Pauline. The prominence of "justification by faith" in the Reformation placed these letters on a pedestal, from which no one wishes to knock them. While the typical argumentation for these letters as "particularly Pauline" is questionable, nonetheless, the authenticity of the *Hauptbriefe* (the so-called Tübingen Four) remains undisputed.

are widely viewed as from the pen of Paul.[5] Second Thessalonians and often Colossians remain suspect for some but are accepted by many Pauline scholars as genuine.

Ephesians is commonly rejected as Pauline for at least three reasons.[6] The letter is very general, addressing no issues seemingly specific to Ephesus,[7] and lacks any words of greeting. Yet, according to Acts, Paul had his longest and perhaps most fruitful ministry in Ephesus. Second, the style of the letter has been called "un-Pauline." Last, Ephesians is strikingly similar to Colossians, even verbatim in one place. Clearly, it is argued, such reuse of material is the fingerprint of a forger. For nearly a hundred years, it has been argued that a "later disciple" of Paul wrote Ephesians as a general introduction to a collection of Paul's letters.[8]

---

[5] Hilgenfeld (1875) and H. J. Holtzmann (1885) expanded Baur's four by adding these three to make a rarely disputed list of seven letters. So even Ehrman, *Forged*, 92–93.

[6] Werner Georg Kümmel, *Introduction to the New Testament*, trans. Howard Clark Kee (Nashville: Abingdon, 1996), 351–66, summarizes the arguments. The list below shows my (biased) arrangement of his arguments:

  1. Ephesians is too similar to Colossians. Ephesians copies (in his view) 73 verses from Colossians: e.g., Eph 4:1–2 = Col 3:12–13; Eph 5:19–2 = Col 3:16–17; Eph 6:21–22 = Col 4:7–8. Ephesians copies (in his view) several pivotal ideas from Colossians: e.g., saints of God, mystery, wisdom, word of truth. Both letters have multiple long complex sentences, e.g., 1:3–14; 1:15–23; 3:1–7; 4:11–16; 6:14–20.

  2. Ephesians is too different from Colossians. Ephesians has 40 new words, including "heavenly places" (1:3 NKJV); four different words for "power" (1:19 NKJV); a different word for "reconcile" (2:16 NKJV).

  3. Ephesians (and sometimes Colossians) uses ideas from authentic letters of Paul but not exactly the same way. For example, word of God, gospel, reconciliation, resurrection, glorification, and the church seem "more concrete" and less abstract in Ephesians (and Colossians).

  4. Ephesians adds ideas not found in other letters of Paul (except Colossians), such as the church as a powerful, universal church and not merely independent house churches. (In the eyes of Kümmel and others, the reference to the church as the body of Christ is a different metaphor.)

  5. Ephesians doesn't have ideas, such as spiritual gifts, that are common in other letters of Paul.

[7] In fact, the words "in Ephesus" are missing from some early manuscripts.

[8] See, e.g., E. J. Goodspeed, *The Key to Ephesians* (Chicago: University of Chicago Press, 1956). Perhaps as early as the seventeenth century, James Ussher used these same factors to suggest Paul composed Ephesians as a "circular letter" that he sent to several churches, including Ephesus and Laodicea, explaining the lack of personal greetings and specific details. Thus, Paul deliberately reused (repurposed) Colossians into a more general letter. The parallel commendations of the letter carrier (Eph 6:21 and Col 4:7–8) is the very type of material one recycled, as Ignatius did (Ign., *Phld* 11:2 and *Smyrn* 12:1).

While the authenticity of Ephesians is debated, the majority[9] of scholars agree in pronouncing the so-called "Pastoral Letters," 1–2 Timothy and Titus, as inauthentic, or to use a more pejorative (but accurate) term, forgeries.[10] These three letters are seriously doubted as Pauline, even by more conservative scholars such as Bruce Metzger and I. Howard Marshall. Again, three reasons commonly appear. These letters are perceived as having a more formal "tone." Second, the theology is accused of being "rather pedestrian."[11] For example, these letters commend a seemingly more ecclesiastical rather than pneumatic form of leadership and appeal more to "traditions" than to apostolic authority. Last, the "writing style" of the Pastorals is considered non-Pauline.

As we examine the arguments, we quickly note that the issue of "writing style" was the initial as well as formative element. A "more formal" tone is scarcely a definitive argument. Any of us would allow for a change in tone in our own writings over a span of 15 years, a change in status from a free-ranging missionary (from enjoying the protections of Rome and expecting soon his new king, Christ, to appear) to a prisoner, expecting his own imminent demise. Such could also easily explain why Paul would think a shift was needed in how leadership/authority was handled. It could even explain a shift in theology.[12] Ultimately, it is the

---

[9] Those who doubt the Pastoral Epistles are still the overwhelming majority of New Testament scholars, although many of us believe the pendulum is swinging, perhaps as evidenced by the 1–2 Timothy volume in the Anchor Bible (by Luke Timothy Johnson), which argued for Pauline authorship, or even I. Howard Marshall's (untenable) argument for quasi-Pauline authorship. Ehrman himself notes the arguments against 2 Timothy being non-Pauline are weak: "For about a year or so before I started writing this book, I myself began to be increasingly inclined to take this view [2 Tim as authentically Pauline]" (97). Since 1 and 2 Timothy are so similar and since Ehrman is convinced 1 Timothy is a forgery, he ultimately throws 2 Timothy into the forged stack (rather than vice versa). See the stylometric conclusions of Anthony Kenny below. Ehrman is correct, however, in arguing that the so-called Pastoral Letters are the pivotal issue in any authenticity debate (*Forged*, 93–103).

[10] Ehrman is correct that *if* these letters were not authored by Paul, then they are forgeries. Ellis has long argued against the concept of innocent apostolic pseudepigrapha: *Prophecy and Hermeneutic in Early Christianity*, Wissenschaftliche Untersuchungen zum Neuen Testament (WUNT) 18 (Tübingen: Mohr, 1978), 3–22. I argue the Pastoral Letters are not forgeries; they were authored by Paul—in the ancient sense of authorship.

[11] So summarized by Richard Longenecker, *Biblical Exegesis in the Apostolic Period*, 2nd ed. (Grand Rapids: Eerdmans, 1999), 90–91.

[12] For example, Ehrman notes (as have others) that Paul had argued for Christians to remain single (1 Corinthians 7), yet the Pastorals insist that elders be married (99–100). I suspect that such differences would not have resulted in rejecting the Pastorals were it not for the differences in writing style. Note the very distinctive (and dramatic) shift in Pauline eschatological

issue of writing style that precipitated and still sustains the arguments against the authenticity of the Pastoral Letters.[13]

Unquestionably, the Pastoral Letters have a vocabulary not common to the other Pauline Letters. Here's the tricky step. In today's modern world where I actually pen (or type) my own books and articles, if you see unusual vocabulary and a shift in writing style from my other writings, you should be suspicious of plagiarism or forgery. This brings up the question of how "authorship" today differs from ancient authorship.

Modern Western Authorship

Initially we might wonder how authorship could differ. After all, writing is writing. Scholars of modern *literature* pointed out how we were reading our authorship model backward.[14]

The Birth of the Modern Author

In a movement cleverly called the Death of the Author,[15] scholars in the field of literary theory argue writing was collaborative until the 1600s. What drove the need to distinguish one particular person as the "author" were practical matters, largely political and economic. For example, a king needed to know whom to arrest for the newly printed

---

language—from the very Jewish-sounding 1 Corinthians 15 (with its day of Yahweh and the archangel's trumpet sound) to the more Greek-sounding 2 Corinthians 5 (of the soul's disembodiment). No one chooses to reconcile the differences (which I think can be done) by arguing that either letter is a forgery.

[13] See P. N. Harrison, *The Problem of the Pastorals* (London: Oxford University Press, 1921), and W. Michaelis, "Pastoralbriefe und Wortstatistik," *Zeitschrift für neutestamentliche Wissenschaft* 28 (1929): 69–76. Ehrman also notes this is the pivotal issue (*Forged,* 96–98). Ehrman summarizes well the vocabulary issue in 1–2 Timothy: "whoever wrote the one letter had his favorite terms and used them in the other letters as well. It's just that those terms were not terms used by Paul." Ehrman means "terms used in other letters of Paul."

[14] How this applies to Pauline authorship is discussed more in depth in my *Paul and First-Century Letter Writing: Secretaries, Composition and Collection* (Downers Grove, IL: InterVarsity Press, 2004).

[15] The expression is usually credited to Roland Barthes's 1977 essay. It has since been argued that it was premature to declare the author dead, as noted by Stephen Donovan, Danuta Fjellestad, and Rolf Lundén, "Introduction: Author, Authorship, Authority, and Other Matters," in *Authority Matters: Rethinking the Theory and Practice of Authorship,* DQR Studies in Literature 43 (Amsterdam: Rodopi, 2008), 13: "In fact, the author continues to thrive with undiminished if not unchallenged power in many areas of literary studies. . . ."

slanderous pamphlet against his reign.[16] As is often the case, though, it wasn't politics but money that actually sealed the deal.

Publishing Houses: The primary drive likely came from the newly emerging publishing business, courtesy of Gutenberg.[17] Publishers needed to designate this book or that pamphlet as *belonging to them*.[18] Otherwise, anyone with a printing press could steal the fruit of their hard labor and investment.[19]

Western Individualism: At the same time, Western culture was shifting its emphasis from "us" to "me." Most of the world (including the ancient world) is "dyadic." The insightful works of Malherbe, Neyrey, Rohrbaugh, Malina, and other sociological exegetes provide multiple examples of how the first-century Mediterranean worldview differed from the modern, Western worldview.[20] While we are an individualist culture, the New Testament reflects a collective (dyadic) culture[21]: "It is clear that the cultures of the Hebrew Bible and the NT were much closer to a dyadic culture (embedded and interrelated culture) than to the present-day dominant Western cultural view in both theory and practice."[22]

The Academy: Obviously the academy cannot be deemed a disinterested party in this discussion, since most members are authors who wish to protect their material from theft. Much of the modern concept of

---

[16] British history provides rich examples. Publishing has always been risky business, but at times it was far more dangerous. Works were often anonymous in order to protect the person(s) involved.

[17] So Donovan, Fjellestad, and Lundén, "Introduction," 13.

[18] See Stephen Dobranski, "The Birth of the Author: the Origins of Early Modern Printed Authority," in Donovan, Fjellestad, and Lundén, *Authority Matters,* 37.

[19] The advent of a new publishing technology (the Internet) is re-creating this same challenge for publishers.

[20] See, for example, Glenn S. Sunshine, *Why You Think the Way You Do: The Story of Western Worldviews from Rome to Home* (Grand Rapids: Zondervan, 2009), especially the way he marks the historical shifts: "worldview of ancient Rome" to "Christianity" to "Medieval Worldview" on to "Enlightenment," concluding with the "decay of modernity." Worldview assumptions creep in even among scholars sensitized to it; see Zeba Crook, "Honor, Shame, and Social Status Revisited," *Journal of Biblical Literature* 128 (2009): 591–611.

[21] See, e.g., the table in K. C. Hanson, "Sin, Purification, and Group Process," in *Problems in Biblical Theology: Essays in Honor of Rolf Knierim*, ed. Henry T. C. Sun and Keith L. Eades (Grand Rapids: Eerdmans, 1997), 170–71.

[22] Gerald Klingbeil, "Between 'I' and 'We': The Anthropology of the Hebrew Bible and Its Importance for a 21st-Century Ecclesiology," *Bulletin for Biblical Research* 19 (2009): 338.

"author" is tied to the modern convention of copyright. What is mine is mine.

Modern Authorial "Sins"

Certain practices by authors have commonly been argued (in modern times) to be vices: plagiarism, ghost writing, and forgery. Some practices are very serious vices, some moderately serious, and some deemed merely in poor taste. In antiquity, these practices were viewed differently.

Plagiarism: Plagiarism is condemned by modern Western society (and laws). Generally, plagiarism is policed by academic institutions and publishing houses. Ancients who had neither formal academies nor publishing houses[23] had a different view of what moderns call plagiarism. Using someone else's material without documenting it was apparently acceptable practice, as for example we see Psalm 70 reusing Ps 40:13–17.[24] Like most aristocrats, Pliny the Elder had a slave (a *lector*) to read aloud from works, but his nephew (Pliny the Younger) tells us the slave also had notebooks on which to write down any parts his uncle wished extracted.[25] When an ancient reused material, he may or may not have indicated his source.[26] There were no copyrights. There was no wrongdoing in this. It appears 1 Peter is reusing Jude, reducing the number of biblical examples, reorganizing them into canonical order and applying them to his context.[27] In fact, some documents

---

[23] There were "academies" in the Greco-Roman world, centered on one charismatic teacher. (Many academics trace the modern academy back to the Greeks.) Students, however, were encouraged to sound as much as possible like their teacher. Arrian seems to have recorded the lectures of his teacher, Epictetus, likely paying a shorthand writer to record them. There were also publishing houses, but only marginally similar to ours today.

[24] The recent and excellent work by Karel van der Toorn (*Scribal Culture and the Making of the Hebrew Bible* [Cambridge, MA: Harvard University Press, 2009]) documents well the practices of ancient Near Eastern scribes (esp. see 109–41).

[25] Pliny, *Ep.* 3.5.15–16. "After a short repast at noon . . . he would frequently in the summer . . . repose himself in the sun; during which time some author was read to him from whence he made extracts and observations, as indeed this was his constant method whatever book he read." For other examples of using a *notarius* to record notes from reading, see also Pliny, *Epp.* 9.29.2; 36.2. For a fuller description, see also A. N. Sherwin-White, *Letters of Pliny* (Oxford: Oxford University Press, 1985), 224–25n.

[26] On occasion, Pliny the Younger noted his source (6.20.5), but this seems more the exception.

[27] I think 1 Peter is by Peter. Likewise, I think Peter repurposes Jeremiah 29 for his own letter to exiles (1 Peter); see E. Randolph Richards, "The General Epistles and Hebrews: In Exile but on the Brink of Restoration," in C. Marvin Pate, et al., *The Story of Israel: A Biblical Theology*

were clearly collections of material from multiple sources. In the case of Proverbs, some are from Solomon, others from Agur, and other proverbs from only God knows whom.

Unnamed Collaborators: Named coauthors were and still are honorable practitioners. The question here is where a book claims *one* author but someone in the background assisted in the composition—what today we call a "ghost writer." Do we really think a retired president wrote his own memoirs without assistance? As long as the named author is the source and has given her blessing on the content, we view the author as the author, recognizing "wink-wink" that there was a helper. While we may see this as undesirable or perhaps even a shadowy practice today, it was quite acceptable in antiquity. Josephus specifically refers to his "helpers." The improved Greek of those writings is commonly credited to his assistants.[28]

Forgery: While ancient authors were more gracious toward "borrowed" material and unnamed collaborators, they took a firm line against forgery. Then, as now, forgery was considered fraudulent.[29] Bart Ehrman offers a good, standard definition: "My definition of a *forgery,* then, is a writing that claims to be written by someone (a known figure) who did not in fact write it." He accurately adds that "forgery was widely condemned."[30] Against Paulinists who argue that writing under a false name was acceptable practice,[31] Ehrman declares: "Some scholars

---

(Downers Grove, IL: InterVarsity Press, 2004), 232–54.

[28] Henry St. John Thackeray notes: "The immense debt which he [Josephus] owes to these admirable collaborators [the *synergoi*] is apparent on almost every page of the work." "Introduction," in *The Life, Against Apion, and the Jewish War [Bellum Judaicum],* 3 vols., Loeb Classical Library, Greek Series (Cambridge: Harvard University Press, 1976), 1: xv.

[29] Ehrman uses stronger language:

Both of these terms [used to refer to this practice] are negative, not neutral, and they show what ancients thought about the practice of forgery. An author who produces a writing in the name of someone else has produced a "false writing," "a lie," "an illegitimate child," or "a bastard." Similar words are used by Latin writers for the act of forgery, for example, words that mean "to lie," "to falsify," "to fabricate," "to adulterate," "to counterfeit" (*Forged,* 38).

[30] Ibid., 24–25. He correctly notes that writing under a "stage name" (my term) is not a forgery. Iamblichus wrote under the pseudonym Abammon. Likewise, Ehrman clarifies (correctly) that works wrongly ascribed to someone are not forgeries.

[31] It is common to cite Iamblichus's comment about Pythagoras and his disciples: "If it be agreed that some writings now circulated are by Pythagoras, but others were composed on the basis of his lectures, and on this account the authors did not give their own names, but attributed them to Pythagoras as his work" (*Vit. Pyth.* 158). This seems to me to be a case of

have argued, strenuously, but without much evidence, that it was common and accepted practice in schools of philosophy to write a philosophical treatise and sign your master's name to it (Plato, Pythagoras, etc.), rather than your own, and that no one looked askance at the practice."[32]

As Ehrman notes, the evidence is scant. Why write under a false name if everyone knew? The purpose clearly was deceit.[33] It was condemned then and it still is now.[34] Ehrman is correct that *if* any New

---

giving credit where credit is due and not a case of forgery. Iamblichus also seemed to believe Pythagoras deserved the credit: "It was a fine custom of theirs [his disciples] also to ascribe and assign everything to Pythagoras . . ." (*Vit. Pyth.* 198). I do not believe the situation with Pythagoras is analogous to Paul at all for at least these reasons:

1. Pythagoras did not write anything himself. According to Olympiodorus, this was deliberate by Pythagoras who felt his disciples were better than "lifeless writings" which cannot defend themselves; so Mark Kiley, *Colossians as Pseudepigraphy,* Biblical Seminar 4 (Sheffield: JSOT, 1987), 22–23.

2. The so-called Pythagorean letters were clearly "public essays" to propagate doctrine (of Pythagoras) and not to be construed as true correspondence. Most of us think Deissmann over-differentiated between "literary epistles" and occasioned papyrus letters. See Adolf Deissmann, *Light from the Ancient East,* trans. L. R. M. Strachan (London: Hodder & Stoughton, 1912), esp. 290–301. Nonetheless, Hans-Josef Klauck in his magisterial work on ancient letter writing has reminded us that while the line may be fuzzy, Deissmann's distinctions are not to be dismissed (*Ancient Letters and the New Testament* [Waco, TX: Baylor University Press, 2006], 70). Paul's letters are not to be compared to these epistles; see also Stanley K. Stowers, *Letter Writing in Greco-Roman Antiquity,* Library of Early Christianity (Philadelphia: Westminster, 1986), esp. 34–35.

For more on the subject, see the Aberdeen dissertation: Terry Wilder, *Pseudonymity, the New Testament, and Deception: An Inquiry into Intention and Reception* (Lanham, MD: University Press of America, 2004).

[32] Ehrman, *Forged,* 37. *Pace* Klauck, *Ancient Letters,* 120–25, who discusses both authentic and inauthentic letters casually together. He even suggests at least one double deception: "Probably the pseudepigraphy that is certainly present in all the Pythagorean letters was taken a step further in these letters between women; the real authors or 'authoresses' could actually have been men who used these letters to propagate their own ideal of women devoted to modesty and domesticity . . . " (123). It is unclear if Klauck would agree with Ehrman's view that pseudepigraphy was universally negative.

[33] Christians can play word games with "lying," but the lines are not as fuzzy as some imply. See, e.g., E. Randolph Richards, "Stop Lying," *Biblical Illustrator* (Spring 1999): 77–80. Ehrman is correct in his critique of Kurt Aland's (unconvincing) argument that the Holy Spirit inspired these pseudepigrapha (*Forged,* 123–25). Likewise, some argue the forger of an apocalypse felt justified because God was the author. For a strong rebuttal of this argument, see Armin Baum, "Revelatory Experience and Pseudepigraphal Attribution in Early Jewish Apocalypses," *Bulletin of Biblical Research* 22 (2011): 65–92.

[34] Ehrman cites Norbert Brox and Wolfgang Speyer in building his consensus that scholars on forgery conclude it was in order to *deceive* (*Forged,* 123).

Testament documents were forgeries, then they should be condemned. (I don't believe any of them is.)

Postmodern Authorship

It is of course too early into postmodernity to make predictions, but early indicators suggest authorship is becoming (again) more collaborative. I coauthor books fairly often; my old professor never did. My students are *very* collaborative—often to my dismay. Authorship in the future is likely to move beyond named collaboration. Who's the author of a Wikipedia® article? The Logos Bible Software company is developing an online Bible encyclopedia. Potentially, it could be a Wikipedia®-style encyclopedia where evangelical scholars contribute. Who would be the author?[35] This type of interactive, live (constantly morphing) collaboration may be the new model—I don't know how we'll footnote it! Such a new model would in many ways be a return to the ancient model.

Composing an Ancient Document

As a youngster, I remember handwriting letters. When I reached the end, I signed my name, folded the pages, and sealed the envelope. The first draft was the dispatched draft. Writing in antiquity took longer and involved more people—probably like everything else in antiquity.

Using Sources

Ancient writers did not feel compelled to begin from scratch, any more than we do. They used outside material. The most obvious such materials in the New Testament are passages from the Old Testament, many of which are not explicitly cited as such (Rom 9:20; Gal 3:6).[36]

Borrowed Material: Ancients commonly borrowed material from others, sometimes indicating the source and sometimes not. This material has come to be called "preformed." I am to blame for this awkward

---

[35] Thus the author is not "dead" but "s/he" may be turning into a "we."

[36] Hays makes a compelling argument for the rich tapestry of images and allusions as well as quotations from the Old Testament in Paul's letters; Richard B. Hays, *Echoes of Scripture in the Letters of Paul* (New Haven: Yale University Press, 1993).

term, coined in a graduate paper in 1985 and then institutionalized by my old professor, E. Earle Ellis.[37] We are referring to material that was composed sometime prior to the rest of the text, either by the author himself or by another.[38] No one doubts the existence of such material in the New Testament, particularly in the letters of Paul.[39] Several passages are universally recognized as such—as much as any topic can be in Pauline studies: Rom 10:9; 1 Cor 15:3b–5; and Phil 2:6–11. The very nature of preformed material, however, is that the author usually *expects* the recipients to recognize the material and therefore does little (or nothing) to explicitly distinguish it.[40] Paul's purpose for quoting the material was often to bring the reader into the context of the citation, including the perception of the material as "generally received" or "well accepted" and not some quirky idea by Paul. As scholars were starting to note "traditional material" in Paul, three writers made preliminary attempts to establish ways to detect these.[41] I subsequently suggested six criteria related to content and three related to form.[42] Interest has not waned.[43]

Named Sources: Obviously, writers in the New Testament quoted material and indicated the source. First Corinthians 6–7 provides ample examples of Paul using the Old Testament (6:16) as well as Jesus tradition (7:10).

---

[37] E. E. Ellis, *The Making of the New Testament Documents* (Leiden: Brill, 2002), esp. 116.

[38] E. Randolph Richards, *The Secretary in the Letters of Paul,* WUNT 2/42 (Tübingen: Mohr/Siebeck, 1991), 158.

[39] W. D. Davies first brought these to my attention in a graduate class. He had been calling these "fragments of kerygma." *Paul and Rabbinic Judaism,* 4th ed. (Philadelphia: Fortress, 1980), 136–41.

[40] I am still convinced Rom 14:7–9 is preformed, although perhaps Pauline; see Richards, *Letter Writing,* 111, esp. n5.

[41] Markus Barth, "Traditions in Ephesians," *New Testament Studies* (*NTS*) 30 (1984): 10; Robert Jewett, "The Redaction and Use of an Early Christian Confession in Romans 1:3–4," in *The Living Text: Essays in Honor of Ernest W. Saunders,* ed. Dennis E. Groh and Robert Jewett (Lanham, MD: University Press of America, 1985), 100–102; and in an unpublished work: Clark Lyndon Palmer, "The Use of Traditional Materials in Hebrews, James, and 1 Peter" (Ph.D. diss., Southwestern Baptist Theological Seminary, 1985), 6–8.

[42] Richards, *Letter Writing,* 97–99.

[43] Note, for example, recently Mark M. Yarbrough, *Paul's Utilization of Preformed Traditions in 1 Timothy: An Evaluation of the Apostle's Literary, Rhetorical, and Theological Tactics,* LNTS 417 (New York: T&T Clark, 2009), who creates a modified list of criteria (esp. 17–57). Yarbrough argues 12 passages from 1 Timothy are preformed: 1:8–10,15,17; 2:5–6a; 3:1,16; 4:8,9–10b; 5:24–25; 6:7,10a,11–16 (following Ellis but rejecting seven others that Ellis had selected).

Unnamed Sources:[44] We likewise find references and allusions from Second Temple literature (2 Tim 3:8; 1 Pet 3:6; Jude 9), hymn fragments, Christian formulae, as well as what appear to be quotations of "slogans" from opponents (1 Cor 6:12).[45] Using material without citing the source was not viewed as plagiarism in antiquity.

Reused (Repurposed) Material: Cicero used the same clever piece of prose on the assassination of Caesar in two different letters.[46] He also used the same preface in at least two different works.[47] His nephew wrote an account to Cicero of some adventure and then reused the material in a letter to Atticus.[48] Ignatius reused his commendation of Burrhus, the letter carrier, in two different letters.[49] This reuse of material, even verbatim, was not viewed negatively, even when both recipients knew the material was recycled.[50] In none of these examples do scholars argue that one of the letters was a forgery because the material was taken from another of the author's letters. When Paul reuses his commendation of Tychicus in Colossians and Ephesians, it should not be argued that this makes one or both a forgery.

Using a Secretary

The use of secretaries is not disputed.[51] Letter senders usually hired secretaries because they were illiterate.

Illiteracy: How much of the ancient world could read is not easily determined. While a few have contended the world of Paul had a

---

[44] Obviously, we had to recognize it as somehow borrowed from another.

[45] It is not always clear. Some excellent work on identifying these slogans has been done by Jay Smith; see, e.g., "The Roots of a 'Libertine' Slogan in 1 Corinthians 6:18," *Journal of Theological Studies* 59 (2008): 63–95.

[46] Cic., *Fam.* 12.4.1 and *Fam.* 10.28.1.

[47] Cic., *Att.* 16.6.

[48] Cic., *Att.* 13.29.

[49] Ign., *Phld* 11:2; *Smyrn* 12:1. The parallels to Ephesians and Colossians here are striking.

[50] Richards, *Letter Writing,* 160.

[51] Francis X. J. Exler, *The Form of the Ancient Greek Letter: A Study of Greek Epistolography* (Washington, DC: Catholic University of America, 1922), noted:

It is remarkable, also, how well most letters are written . . . . One of the reasons . . . [is] the employment of professional scribes. Not a few papyri have been found which were written in the same hand yet addressed by and to entirely different persons. In purely personal letters the scribe or whoever wrote the letter did not need to declare that he, and not the person whose name was found on the document, was the writer [meaning the one writing it down] (126).

relatively high literacy rate, archaeological finds indicate otherwise.[52] When ancient letters are discovered, we often see the letter written in "a practiced hand," not from the letter sender.[53] If the "author" was able to write at all, he added something, even if merely a "goodbye," abbreviated *err.*[54] In more official letters, there was a formula, such as "Written for him because he does not know letters."[55] Although illiteracy was widespread, there were plenty of literate folks.

Literacy as Reading but Writing as Calligraphy: Literacy has traditionally been described as the ability to read and write. We moderns mistakenly presume reading and writing are two sides of the same coin.[56] One should not assume that if someone can read, then she can write. It might surprise some that literate letter writers used secretaries; yet, just a few decades ago, those in business often used secretaries to prepare letters because most couldn't type. Literacy didn't include typing, even though we could *read* something that was typed. In the first-century world, literacy meant the ability to *read*, not the ability to write, which is a practiced skill. How well do you write with your opposite hand? As for me, it is slow and with large, clumsy letters, not because I am illiterate, but because I rarely write with my left hand. Most ancient people rarely practiced writing. Paul makes a similar comment: "See what large letters I use as I write to you with my own hand!" (Gal 6:11 NIV). Paul

---

[52] Coinage was a common means of Roman propaganda for the illiterate and thus the common image of the three goddesses, Peace, Security, and Prosperity together.

[53] This point is not disputed. The lack of an illiteracy formula in a private letter is not evidence the sender wrote the letter himself; see John White, "Greek Documentary Letter Tradition," *Semeia* 22 (1981):95. See Exler, *Form of the Ancient Greek Letter.*

[54] One author wanted to write in his own hand but feared his skills inadequate and so he merely copied again the last line written by the secretary. So the phrase "I wish you farewell, sister" is repeated twice; the second one is in a different handwriting; POxy 1491.

[55] See Deissmann for this example of an illiteracy formula: "Written for him hath Eumelus the son of Herma . . . being desired so to do for that he writeth somewhat slowly" (*Light,* 166–67).

[56] Historian Harvey Graff noted that Swedish church law in 1686 required literacy of all people, and by the end of the eighteenth century, literacy (meaning the ability to read) was close to 100 percent. Yet, as marriage licenses demonstrated, many Swedes, especially women, could not write. Graff demonstrates that one can be literate without being able to write. Harvey J. Graff, *The Literacy Myth: Cultural Integration and Social Structure in the Nineteenth Century* (Edison, NJ: Transaction Publishers, 1991), xxii–xxvi. Nicholas Ostler suggested the ability to write was a professional trade secret of scribes, but he is referring to the retention of a language once it has fallen out of use. *Empires of the Word: A Language History of the World* (New York: Harper Perennial, 2006), e.g., 61.

was quite literate. Yet, writing down a letter was considered a specialized skill. A secretary needed to know how to cut and glue papyrus, cut and sharpen pens, mix ink, prick and line the sheets, write neatly, and most importantly how to use the correct forms and phrases for that specific letter situation.[57]

Secretarial Skills: They also knew the proper formatting and language (formulae and content) for various contexts. Greco-Roman letters were far more stereotyped than our letters, even the old "Dear Bob, How are you? We're fine. Sincerely, Sam" of a previous generation. Also, and perhaps more importantly, a secretary could produce a nice script on good paper for important occasions. Modern pens allow us to write quickly and smoothly; yet, even we have trouble writing as fast as a person talks— a complaint I often hear from my students! Papyrus was not as smooth; pens required redipping in the ink. Ancients just could not write as fast.[58] However, this was not the larger problem. A letter to a church, to be read publicly as Paul intended (Col 4:16), could not be scratched messily across some sheet. Ancients had a sense of propriety. Important letters should be prepared neatly on good quality papyrus.[59] Paul intended his letters for public (congregational) use (Col 4:16).[60] The quickly scrawled first draft was not suitable for sending to a church. What would Corinth think of Paul who cared so little as to send such a rag?

Since ancient letter writers used secretaries, how did that work? In other places I have outlined how ancient secretaries (*amanuenses*) plied their trade.[61] When secretaries took dictation, it meant *slow* dictation,

---

[57] See Ben Witherington, *The Paul Quest: The Renewed Search for the Jew of Tarsus* (Downers Grove, IL: InterVarsity Press, 1998), 99.

[58] Greek shorthand writers existed in the time of Paul, but they were not common. It is unlikely Paul had access to one. Romans is the only letter where I think it is possible Paul had the services of a more talented scribe, *perhaps* a shorthand writer. See the discussion in Richards, *Secretary,* 26–43; and *Letter Writing,* 67–74.

[59] For an important letter, Cicero had the final copy prepared on fine, large sheets of papyrus (*macrocolla*) in careful script (see Cic., *Att.* 13.25; 13.21a). He jests with his brother, "For this letter I shall use a good pen, well-mixed ink, and ivory-polished paper too" (Cic., *QFr* 2.15b.1). See the discussion in Richards, *Secretary,* 99–100.

[60] Luke Timothy Johnson is likely correct that 1 Timothy was intended to be read in the presence of Timothy *and* the Ephesian congregation as an "installment" of Timothy as Paul's delegate; certainly this would merit a more formal letter in both content and appearance. *The First and Second Letters to Timothy: A New Translation with Introduction and Commentary,* Anchor Yale Bible (New Haven: Anchor Bible, 2001).

[61] Initially in Richards, *The Secretary in the Letters of Paul* (1991), and then I refined the matter further in a section of Richards, *Paul and First-Century Letter Writing* (2004).

often syllable by syllable. Seneca noted a stammerer was ridiculed for talking as if he were giving dictation.[62] To dictate 1 Corinthians all the way through would have required about 10 hours of continuous slow dictation.[63] Secretaries also commonly took notes, scribbling on wax tablets.[64]

From the secretary's transcription or notes,[65] the secretary would prepare a rough draft, still on these reusable materials. The author would make changes and additions and send the secretary back to prepare another draft. Careful thought and composition were essential. Ancient writers thoughtfully pondered their drafts, weighing each phrase. Cicero was known to debate over which preposition was best to use (Cic., *Att.* 7.3.). Paul's letters were not hastily or carelessly written.[66] They were also *much* longer than even long letters. Paul's letters were expensive[67] and time-consuming efforts.

Having Assistance

Ancients did not aggrandize flying solo. I do not suggest that Paul thought to himself, *For this letter I am going to work alone.* Working

---

[62] Sen., *Ep.* 40.10.

[63] See Richards, *Letter Writing,* 92.

[64] Or washable notebooks of parchment or on notebooks made of very thinly cut wood (leaf notebooks). For good first-century examples of these leaf notebooks, see the materials from Roman Vindolanda in Britain.

[65] Previously, I mentioned that secretaries were on occasion used to compose a letter freely on behalf of the letter sender. For this, I have been severely criticized, most recently by Ehrman (*Forged,* 138–39). He quotes me when I said: "Nowhere was there *any* indication that an ordinary secretary was asked, much less presumed, to compose a letter for the author" (*Secretary,* 110). He argues I then maintain it was a secretarial role. This is misleading. In an exhaustive, scholarly work on secretaries, I listed all options, including what I deemed unlikely (this role). I later concluded (*Letter Writing,* 92) concerning a secretary freely composing in the sender's name:

   1. This was not a common practice and not ever done (as far as we can tell) by an ordinary secretary.
   2. It was used when the author did not care about the letter's contents.
   3. It was used (in the few examples we have) to deceive.

[66] See Ben Witherington, *Grace in Galatia* (Grand Rapids: Eerdmans, 1998), 442; and Hans Dieter Betz, *Galatians,* Hermeneia (Minneapolis: Fortress, 1979), 312.

[67] I conservatively estimated a letter such as Romans or 1 Corinthians to cost, in today's dollars, well over $2,000 each, plus the expense of sending someone to deliver it (Richards, *Letter Writing,* 165–70).

alone would not have occurred to him or any other.[68] Why would he exclude his own team members?

Co-authors: In at least six letters, including undisputed letters such as 1 Corinthians, Paul lists another person in the letter address where the sender/author is listed. I suggest these are co-authors—a rare but not unknown practice. Why is this so surprising? Paul's letters deviate from the norm in just about every other way.[69] Nonetheless, most scholars say the inclusion of someone such as Timothy in the letter opening of 2 Cor 1:1 is "largely a matter of courtesy."[70] As I have argued elsewhere, why is Timothy not then listed in the letter opening of Romans? He was there, as his greeting indicates in Rom 16:21. I suggest that there is *something* different about the role Timothy played in 2 Corinthians and Romans.[71] Citing another in the letter opening was the exception to custom,[72] and therefore we should not assume it was merely literary convention. It meant *something*, even if it doesn't mean coauthorship as I suggest.

Interpolations: As William Walker defines, "An interpolation is foreign material inserted deliberately and directly into the text of a document."[73] Obviously, Old Testament quotations, Christian formulae and other preformed material qualify. What most scholars mean, though, is that someone has inserted material into a letter, such as

---

[68] One could suggest the very aristocratic elite, who considered themselves above all others, preferred to work alone. While their written remarks suggest this, an examination of their letters demonstrates they also used secretaries (Cic., *Att.* 5.20, where he mentions both his and Atticus's secretaries by name), had language assistance (Cic., *Fam.* 16.4.3), allowed editing (Cic., *Fam.* 16.4.3), reused material (Cic., *Att.* 13.29), and were otherwise collaborative.

[69] In the most stereotyped aspect of Paul's letters, the letter prescript, I recently argued that Paul deviates in every single element from the norm; see Richards, "Pauline Prescripts and Greco-Roman Epistolary Convention," in *Christian Origins and Classical Culture: Social and Literary Contexts for the New Testament,* ed. Stanley Porter and Andrew Pitts, Texts and Editions for New Testament Study 1 (Leiden: Brill, 2011).

[70] To use Leon Morris's words; *The First and Second Epistles to the Thessalonians,* NICNT (Grand Rapids: Eerdmans, 1959), 47.

[71] I suppose one could suggest that Timothy was falling out of favor in Romans and was "demoted" from the letter opening to the letter closing. This scarcely seems plausible, and we have no evidence for such a practice.

[72] Luther Stirewalt suggests the practice reflects official correspondence. He is correct that those letters did list multiple individuals (those who shared the grievance or claim) in the letter to the official. I do not think Paul's letters are as analogous to these as Stirewalt argues in *Paul the Letter Writer* (Grand Rapids: Eerdmans, 2003).

[73] William Walker, *Interpolations in the Pauline Letters,* JSNTS 213 (New York: Sheffield Academic Press, 2001), 23.

1 Corinthians, *after* Paul had sent it and therefore it was "unauthorized." When that happens, it should show in the manuscript evidence.[74] As I have argued elsewhere,[75] we should also allow for the other option: predispatch and authorized insertions in the text. Someone suggests a comment or material that Paul agrees should be inserted. This could be done at that moment as a verbal insertion[76] or could be added in the next draft by giving the secretary the material in written form. In either case, three important effects are felt. First, the material would be non-Pauline; he didn't compose it. Second, the material would not be un-Pauline; he approves its insertion. Last, such material would dilute any style analysis. The existence of such predispatch, approved interpolations should not surprise us because writers used material from others and because their culture was dyadic.

Editing

Last, we must note that ancients did not carelessly compose significant writings. Ancient writing (of any significance) also went through a process of notes, drafts, edits, and final copies.[77] Ancient writers carefully chose their words too.[78] We would not argue New Testament writers were as persnickety as Cicero, but we should not assume they were careless. Unlike today, the paper (papyrus) was about twice the cost of the labor.[79] A secretary employed reusable material until the author was satisfied, then a final draft was prepared for dispatch.

---

[74] Such insertions did happen, as was done in Rom 8:1.

[75] Richards, *Letter Writing*, 99–108.

[76] In Cicero's case, it was a juicy bit of political gossip: "What's this? Curio is defending Caesar." Cic. *Fam.* 2.13.3.

[77] In addition to my work on letter writing, see the comment by Betz, *Galatians*, 312. Comments like 1 Cor 1:16 are likely rhetorical to emphasize how little it matters who baptized whom.

[78] Cic., *Att.* 7.3. Robert Yerlverton Tyrrell and Louis Claude Purser, *The Correspondence of M. Tullius Cicero,* 7 vols., 3rd rev. ed. (London: Longmans, Green, 1901–33), 1:76 note: "Every adjective is set down with as careful a pen as was ever plied by a masterhand." When Seneca calls a letter "carelessly written," Richard Bummere, the LCL editor, cautions us not to take Seneca literally (LCL 1:x).

[79] Richards, *Letter Writing,* 165–69.

Modern Efforts to Identify an Ancient "Author"

Biblical scholars may be critiqued for overemphasizing singular authorship.[80] The most common complaint I hear regarding my work on first-century letter writing revolves around my suggestion of coauthorship in some of Paul's letters. Readers want to know which sections were from Paul. Who is the "real" author?

Modern Presuppositions

It seems self-evident to us that plagiarism and "borrowing" material from other sources is wrong. Ancients, *especially* Christians, likely saw it otherwise in light of biblical admonitions to share with those in need and not to seek glory for oneself. Clearly, it was also not viewed as wrong, "sin," or deception to use other people's material.

The Need to Identify the Sole or Primary Author: We appear to superimpose negative values if we don't find a solitary author. We view co-authorship as a poor second option only used when unavoidable. The possibility that Paul's cosenders were coauthors is usually summarily dismissed rather than evaluated.

Modern Prejudice against Anonymous Works: A letter like Hebrews is clearly anonymous. Efforts are still made, however, to identify the author. It seems that we today would feel better if we could identify the author. Convincing ourselves that some disciple named John wrote the Fourth Gospel sounds more appealing than merely attributing it to a disciple of Jesus who saw those things (John 21:20–24). Perhaps we are reading from our European history, where certain authors chose anonymity because they were slandering or otherwise needing to hide their identity. Could there be a motive of merely not wanting to bring any attention to themselves?

A Presumed Lack of Plagiarism or Assistance: Probably the critiques are correct that we have applied the modern concept of "authorship" (filtered through publishers protecting their copyrights) to ancient composition, making a poor fit. One of the more glaring differences is the matter of "plagiarism." Modern academic standards label plagiarism a

---

[80] See the discussion of how authorship was more coauthorship until post-seventeenth century; Dobranski, "The Birth of the Author," esp. 37. Witherington, *Paul Quest,* 114, notes: "We cannot assume that Paul was much like a modern individualist."

vice, sin, or even a crime. To make a biblical case against plagiarism, we must typically connect it to dishonesty (clearly a biblical vice), even if the perceived dishonesty is only in the eyes of an evaluator. Since plagiarism is now considered a "sin" (and many of us believe the Bible to be without such things), then logically there can be no plagiarism, even though we know there is, as noted by even a casual reader of Psalms 40 and 70. For example, a common reason for rejecting 2 Thessalonians as Pauline is the *similarity* with 1 Thessalonians; notably 2 Thess 3:8 is almost identical to 1 Thess 2:9—a mark of forgery, we are told.[81]

Peter is commonly rejected as the author of 1 Peter[82] for the reasons Ehrman cites:

> Whoever wrote 1 Peter, for example, was a highly educated Greek-speaking Christian who understood how to use Greek rhetorical devices and could cite the Greek Old Testament with flair and nuance. That does not apply to the uneducated, illiterate, Aramaic-speaking fisherman from rural Galilee. . . .[83]

These are the very same reasons I use to argue that Peter[84] took someone else's material (Jeremiah 29) and with the help of a secretary and perhaps other assistants reworked it into a new letter to exiles.[85] Ehrman dismisses any influence from a secretary (and presumably others):

---

[81] Ironically, others argue 2 Thessalonians is a forgery because of *dissimilarity*. Udo Schnelle, for example, argued the narrow and tame theology of 2 Thessalonians was too different from the lively, constantly shifting style of Paul: *Apostle Paul: His Life and Theology*, trans. M. Eugene Boring (Grand Rapids: Baker, 2005). The argument that these letters are too similar and too different was done quite recently; see the blog: accessed on April 30, 2011, http://debunking-christianity.blogspot.com/2009/06/anchor-bible-dictionary-on-authorship.html.

[82] Peter is commonly rejected as the author of 2 Peter but for different reasons. The Greek of 2 Peter was not beyond his skill set. Usually, two reasons are cited. First, 2 Peter refers to a seeming collection of Paul's letters (3:16). Second, 2 Peter is an example of a "Testament." I have responded to the first elsewhere; E. Randolph Richards, "The Codex and the Early Collection of Paul's Letters," *BBR* 8 (1998): 151–66. Second, if 2 Peter is an example of the Testament genre, it was a lousy one. See most recently, Mark Matthews, "The Genre of 2 Peter: a Comparison with Jewish and Early Christian Testaments," *BBR* 21 (2011): 51–64, who argues 2 Peter lacks "significant elements" of the genre.

[83] Ehrman, *Forged*, 138–39.

[84] If Peter were so untrained in writing, why would he write at all? Perhaps there was some peer pressure: Paul and James were writing letters. There are actually many possible explanations. What is clear is that many ancients did, despite being uneducated, illiterate commoners.

[85] Richards, in Pate et al., *The Story of Israel*, 232–54.

And it does not seem possible that Peter gave the general gist of what he wanted to say and that a secretary then created the letter for him in his name, since, first, then the secretary rather than Peter would be the *real author* of the letter, and second, and even more important, we don't seem to have any analogy for a procedure like this from the ancient world.[86]

Ehrman is mistaken on both accounts. First, he is confusing singular authorship with authority. No one disputes that Josephus wrote both *Antiquities* and *The Jewish Wars*, even though the Greek in the latter was beyond his skills, as the Loeb editor, H. St. John Thackeray, noted.[87] Josephus acquired collaborators (*sunergoi*) for exactly the purpose of turning a first-century, Aramaic-speaking Jew (Josephus) into the author of a finely written Greek document. Why is that not possible for Peter? Josephus remains the author; he was the one who inspired, directed, and then checked and signed off on the work. Cicero notes about a letter of Pompey: "I have never seen anything more Sestian in its style."[88] Nonetheless Cicero still considers the letter to be from Pompey, not Sestius. Pompey was responsible for the content no matter how much assistance he was provided. Second, Ehrman claims there is no analogy for using a secretary this way, but there are, for instance, many, many examples of well-written Greek letters from common Egyptian soldiers and farmers.[89] In fact, this assistance was a good reason for hiring a secretary.

Since we don't acknowledge repurposed material, we don't allow it to impact authorship discussions. Modern authors paraphrase—that is, we put the repurposed material into our own words—and we presume ancient authors did also. In our mind, borrowed material should reflect the new author's style.[90] Thus, we feel justified in including all

---

[86] Ehrman, *Forged*, 139 (italics mine).

[87] H. St. John Thackeray, "Introduction," LCL, xv, notes the lack of skill in *Ant.* and then the admirable Greek in the *B.J.* (*Bella judaica* = *Jewish Wars*). Josephus elsewhere admits to having "assistants for the sake of the Greek" (Jos. *Ap.* 1.50.).

[88] Cic., *Att.* 15.3.

[89] See Exler's comments, n51 above, and the many examples in the Michigan Papyri, esp. book 8. I also cite many examples of secretaries having an editorial and/or contributing role in Richards, *Letter Writing*, 74–77.

[90] And in the case of students, it is improper if it does not.

the material in a letter of Paul in any vocabulary or style analysis.[91] It is far more likely, particularly when a secretary was pulling from a written source, that the reused material was *not* reworked into the author's idiosyncratic vocabulary and style (unless he felt it necessary).

Verifying Ancient Authorship Claims

This is not to say that ancients were unconcerned about authorship. It was—then and now—a question of authenticity and thus often authority. Ancients were on the lookout for forgery.

More Reliable Methods: There were several ways to detect a forgery. Some methods were more reliable than others.

(a) "Signatures" and Seals. Once the final draft was prepared and the writer had secured someone to carry it, the letter was ready to be signed and sealed for dispatch. A person's handwriting was known to his friends and family. We today in the West commonly write our name in cursive as a "signature"—an odd custom. In the East, writers often have a highly stylized and very distinctive way of writing their name; it is usually scarcely legible, but it is very identifiable. In antiquity, they did neither. They wrote a little something in their own handwriting, even as little as a few letters. Less commonly, the writer would add quite a bit in his own handwriting. In any case, if the sender had any ability to write at all, he would append something at the end in his own handwriting.[92] In fact, a common phrase was used: "I am writing this in my own hand." Paul's comment is quite normal: "I, Paul, am writing this with my own hand" (Phlm 19 NIV).

Typical letters were folded (accordion-style), then folded in half. (Longer letters were merely rolled into a scroll.) A string, usually just pulled from the edge of the papyrus sheet, was tied around it. A blob of clay (or wax) was squeezed over the knot. The wealthier and/or official senders of letters had a seal to press. During a time of Roman intrigue,

---

[91] Obviously, this method is vulnerable to accusation of being a circular argument: one omits non-Pauline material and *voilà!*—the rest is Pauline. If however the material isn't from Paul, then it shouldn't be included in a style analysis.

[92] These subscriptions or postscripts were used for multiple other purposes in addition to adding a personal or validating touch. A writer would summarize the salient points, add some new detail learned since the final draft was written, or append some secretive or sensitive information. See Richards, *Letter Writing,* 171–87.

Cicero wished to hide his identity and so he did not write any part in his own hand and did not use his seal.[93] So we see that for most people, handwritten signatures and seals were usually adequate protection.[94] Unfortunately, this method works only for originals.

(b) Content and Argumentation: During this same time of Roman political upheaval, forgeries were a tool. Cicero received a copy of a letter of Caesar. He comments to a friend: "For it is grudgingly written, and raises great suspicion that it was not by Caesar; I expect you noticed that too."[95] Cicero doesn't argue that the vocabulary or grammar is un-Caesar. Rather, it is out of character. Likewise, Tyrrell and Purser, the great scholars of Cicero, reject as a forgery a letter from Cicero to Octavian because of its content and argumentation: "the complete lack of dignity, the feeble impotent abuse, and the utter aimlessness."[96] Similarly, Paul appeals to *content* as a means of distinguishing his genuine letters (2 Thess 2:2–3) as well as of course his signature (3:17).

Less Reliable Methods: Other methods can assist in determining authorship; they are less effective but can be part of a holistic argument.

(a) Authorship Claims: Obviously, forgers also did this. Nonetheless, one should begin with the claim of authorship and then see how ancients responded to it. They were very aware of the presence of forgeries. They rejected 3 Corinthians, as they did the supposed letters between Paul and Seneca. We should not uncritically accept all claims—ancients didn't—but we shouldn't hypercritically reject all claims. Like those of Paul's day, we should look for marks of authenticity.

(b) Stylometry: The statistical measure of writing style has been applied to Pauline letters first by P. N. Harrison (1921). The method was applied thoroughly by A. Q. Morton and James McLeman (1972), when better tools were available.[97] These early methods relied

---

[93] Cic., *Att.* 2.20.

[94] One might think these methods would be completely reliable, but we must not underestimate the ingenuity of thieves especially when significant money was involved. After the death of Caesar, his secretary, Dolabella, was paid (or forced) to alter documents to benefit Faberius (Cic., *Att.* 14.18). There were also individuals adept at forging handwriting; see Suet., *Tit.* 3.2; *Vesp.* 6.4; Jos. *B.J.* 1.26.3.

[95] Cic., *Att.* 11.16.

[96] Tyrrell and Purser, *Cicero,* 5:338–39.

[97] Best seen in Sidney Michaelson and Andrew Q. Morton, "Last Words: A Test of Authorship for Greek Writers," *NTS* 18 (1972): 192–208. Although objections have been

primarily on the frequency of unusual words—what is now seen as a poor method. Newer techniques, such as Type-Token-Ratio analysis, use better measures, such as sentence length, distribution of "and" (*kai*), word position, and other factors not influenced by subject matter. The most recent thorough analysis was by Anthony Kenny (1986), using what appears to be the best methodology. Scholars on all sides of the debate were dissatisfied with his results. His data indicated a great deal of diversity among all 13 letters; yet they all contain about the same amount of commonality:

> There is no support given by [the data] to the idea that a single group of Epistles (say the four major Tübingen Epistles) stand out as uniquely comfortable with one another; or that a single group (such as the Pastoral Epistles) stand out as uniquely diverse from the surrounding context.[98]

The quest for a useful stylometric analysis continues with equally frustrating results.[99] Luke Timothy Johnson has argued well that grouping the so-called Pastoral Letters together has also skewed the data, obscuring similarities, among others, between 2 Timothy and Philippians (noted earlier by Kenny)[100] and between 1 Timothy and 1 Corinthians.[101] I suggest that the role of the secretary and other assistants (contributors, teammates, possibly coauthors) dilutes the Pauline

---

raised previously (e.g., Yule in 1944), see P. F. Johnson, "The Use of Statistics in the Analysis of the Characteristics of Pauline Writing," *NTS* 20 (1973): 92–100.

[98] Anthony Kenny, *A Stylometric Study of the New Testament* (Oxford: Clarendon, 1986), 99–100.

[99] More recently, Armin Baum, "Semantic Variation within the *Corpus Paulinum:* Linguistic Considerations Concerning the Richer Vocabulary of the Pastoral Epistles," *Tyndale Bulletin* 59 (2008): 271–92. Baum concludes the Pastorals have a more diverse vocabulary—these letters are shorter than Paul's other letters but have more vocabulary (different words). Baum then concludes Paul was more careful in writing the Pastorals, since he wrote them down rather than dictated them—a point Ehrman rightly critiques as "special pleading" and then (oddly to me) concludes: "Baum doesn't cite any evidence to suggest the Pastorals were composed in writing by Paul rather than dictated, by Paul or anyone else" (*Forged,* 278n14). Since Ehrman is allowing here for secretarial mediation, why isn't "a more literate secretary" an option? This seems as or more likely to explain a richer vocabulary. It seems unjustified by the evidence to suggest "dictation" meant word-for-word dictation, as I have argued previously (Richards, *Letter Writing,* 29–31).

[100] Kenny, *Stylometric,* 100.

[101] See, for example, Luke Timothy Johnson, *The Writings of the New Testament,* 3rd ed. (Philadelphia: Fortress, 2010), 242, 378.

style enough so that no statistical method works. While Paul is responsible for every word in his letters, when a draft returned with a different but acceptable phrase than he may have chosen, he did not bother to change it.[102] Authority and (singular) authorship are closely related but are not synonymous; responsibility is the connector.

The Arrogance of the Modern Scholar

Can we better assess authorship 2,000 years later than could those scholars of the earlier day? While such may on occasion be true, we should require some sort of new evidence rather than merely reconsidering what has always been there. The task remains the same: Which historical reconstruction best explains the evidence? I suggest that the practices of ancient authorship explain better the letters we have than suggesting *everyone* has been duped by a forger. As Bauckham and others have noted, it would be a far more difficult challenge to forge New Testament documents than Bart Ehrman has implied. I find myself in agreement with Ben Witherington, in his online critique of Ehrman's book:

> My view would be there are no forgeries in the NT at all, no pseudonymous documents, but that does not mean that all documents in the NT mean a modern way of looking at authorship, which is what Bart is applying to the NT documents . . . in addition to that, the varied practices of scribes writing or copying on behalf of others must be taken into account.[103]

Conclusion

Ancient authorship was not like modern authorship. Thus, we cannot apply the same standards.[104] Ancient authors borrowed material,

---

[102] It is better argued that the *document* is inspired, not the author; see Richards, *Letter Writing*, 224–29.

[103] Ben Witherington, "Forged: Chapter Four—Alternatives to Forgery," accessed on April 30, 2011, http://www.patheos.com/community/bibleandculture/2011/04/07/forged -chapter-four-alternatives-to-forgery.

[104] Ibid. Witherington notes specifically of Ehrman: "This frankly seems to be because he [Ehrman] is assuming an all too modern notion about authorship, and is ignoring the evidence

reused their own, accepted input, and collaborated in ways not commonly acceptable today. Furthermore, the writing process included a secretary who rarely took dictation. His own verbiage and style would inevitably find its way into the various drafts. During the editing process, I am confident Paul would have corrected any wording he did not like—he was responsible for the letter. Nonetheless, we cannot assume synonyms, stylistic preferences, and other minor differences—the kind that show up in style analyses—are indications of forgery. Such differences were inevitable in the ancient writing process. When analyzing the letters of Trajan to Pliny, Sherwin-White concludes: "The hand of Trajan cannot easily be detected by formal stylistic analysis";[105] yet the letters are not forgeries. Likewise Tyrrell and Purser, the undisputed authorities on Cicero's letters, noted some of Cicero's letters are stylistically more like the letters of *other* writers than like his own.[106] Yet, those letters are not pronounced forgeries. In ancient writing, minor stylistic differences abound. Yet, Trajan's, Cicero's, or Josephus's divergent works are not declared forgeries. Ancient authorship was different. We ask: Will the real author please stand up? When we ask the wrong question, we are unlikely to get the right answer. Trajan, Cicero, and Paul "wrote" letters but not like we do.

---

of the way ancient scribes worked, compiling ancient documents. In other words, he too quickly rules out whole ranges of possibilities that experts in ancient oral and scribal cultures have provided copious evidence for."

[105] Sherwin-White, *Letters of Pliny,* 541. There has been no more thorough examination of Pliny's letters.

[106] Tyrrell and Purser, *Cicero,* 2:lxix-lxx. His speeches and formal letters have enough stylistic similarity, e.g., the celebrated "law of clause endings" detected by T. Zieliński, while his letters to friends do not; 2:lxvi-lxvii n.

Chapter 9

FISH TALES
Bart Ehrman's Red Herrings and the Resurrection of Jesus

Michael Licona

M ost people in North America who are interested in the discussion of the historical evidence for Jesus' resurrection are familiar with a scholar named Bart Ehrman. Ehrman made his name in the field of textual criticism and is a former student of the late prominent Princeton professor, Bruce Metzger. However, Ehrman has also published extensively in the fields of the New Testament, the historical Jesus, and early Christianities. Many of his books have been best sellers, including *Misquoting Jesus* and *Jesus, Interrupted*. His book *The New Testament: A Historical Introduction to the Early Christian Writings* is a widely used textbook. Ehrman, once an evangelical, abandoned his Christian faith and now regards himself as a "happy agnostic." While his thinking is hardly original, as his positions are those largely embraced by mainstream skeptical scholarship, he is a gifted communicator with the ability to present complex positions in a lay-friendly manner.

I have had the opportunity to debate Bart Ehrman on two occasions. Ehrman and I have shared a few meals together and have corresponded numerous times via e-mail. I have found him to be a nice guy and regard him as a friend. However, being nice does not necessarily assist one in producing good arguments.

Both of our debates focused on the topic, "Can historians prove that Jesus rose from the dead?" Ehrman insisted on phrasing the question from this angle. His position is that there are a number of insurmountable challenges faced by historians that prohibit them from assessing a miracle claim. Accordingly, it is not even necessary for an agnostic like Ehrman to argue that Jesus was not raised. For him, a historical investigation of the matter is stopped in its tracks before it can get started.

Since I have a strong interest in matters related to the philosophy of history and historical method, I happily agreed to Ehrman's demand that the question to be debated be phrased in the manner he requested.[1] In both debates, I laid out a carefully defined historical method I would follow.[2] Regarding the historical facts I would submit to historical method, I chose only three, all of which Ehrman has granted in his writings:

1. Jesus' death by crucifixion;
2. His disciples having experiences that they interpreted as the risen Jesus who had appeared to them in both individual and group settings;
3. a skeptic named Paul having an experience he interpreted as the risen Jesus who had appeared to him.

I wanted to make it easy to focus on the debate topic we had chosen. The facts would not be disputed, since both of us agreed on the facts I presented. Instead, we could focus on the method I used to arrive at the conclusion that Jesus had been raised from the dead. If my historical method could withstand Ehrman's scrutiny, then the conclusion followed that historians can prove that Jesus rose from the dead.

In Ehrman's opening statement, he devoted all but a fraction of his time to attacking the Gospels as historically reliable sources. At first look, this may appear to be a valid approach. After all, if the Gospels are not historically reliable sources, then it would appear to be a difficult task to

---

[1] Elsewhere, I have written extensively on the topic of historians and miracle claims. See chap. 2 in Michael R. Licona, *The Resurrection of Jesus: A New Historiographical Approach* (Downers Grove, IL: IVP Academic, 2010).

[2] The first of these two debates took place at Midwestern Baptist Theological Seminary on February 28, 2008, and may be viewed online at www.4truth.net/debate1. I had lost my voice the day of that debate and, consequently, am difficult to understand at times. Viewers may be more interested in our second debate which took place at Southern Evangelical Seminary on April 2, 2009, and may be viewed at www.4truth.net/debate. The second debate may also be viewed at http://www.youtube.com/watch?v=zyHA3K_6H0g.

establish that historians could prove that Jesus had been raised from the dead. On a closer look, however, Ehrman's case completely falls apart.

In logic, there is a fallacy known as a "red herring." The term is borrowed from the sport of fox hunting in which a dried, smoked herring—red in color—is dragged across the fox's path and into the woods in an attempt to divert the attention of the dogs. In debate, a red herring is an argument that is irrelevant to the debate at hand. However, it is of interest. And therein lay the danger. For if the debaters and audience members are not careful, they will be drawn by the red herring into a different debate than the one agreed upon.

Most of Ehrman's objections to the resurrection of Jesus focused on attacking the Gospels and are red herrings for at least two major reasons. First, the New Testament literature is comprised of 27 books and letters, only four of which are the Gospels. The three facts that I presented can be established using only literature written prior to the Gospels, such as Paul's letters. So, Ehrman's objections to the Gospels are irrelevant. The second reason is of even greater interest. Despite Ehrman's hesitations toward the Gospels, in his books he still grants as historical the three facts I presented. Therefore, his objections to the historical reliability of the Gospels are all red herrings when it comes to the question of whether historians can prove that Jesus was raised from the dead.

Unfortunately, a number of the audience members took Ehrman's bait and followed him off the path we had agreed to follow beforehand. Although he lost the debate on Jesus' resurrection, Ehrman was effective in placing doubts about the Gospels in the minds of a number of the Christians present. Since Christians are rightly concerned with whether the Gospels are reliable sources on Jesus and the debate on Jesus' resurrection was not the place to answer Ehrman's red herrings, I would like to address them in what follows. To that end, I intend to answer *Bart Ehrman's four major objections to the historical reliability of the Gospels.*

Challenge #1: The Problem of Authorship: Who Wrote the Gospels?

Ehrman claims that the traditional authorship of the New Testament Gospels (i.e., Matthew, Mark, Luke, and John) is mistaken, since the original manuscripts did not contain the titles now prominent in our New Testaments (e.g., "The Gospel According to Matthew"). Therefore, Ehrman refers to the Gospels as "forgeries."[3] In fact, in his book *Jesus, Interrupted*, Ehrman contends that of the current 27 books and letters in the NT, all but eight are "forgeries." This is a colossal overstatement intended to shock his readers. Scholarship has not confirmed such a conclusion. (See the previous chapter for a more detailed critique of Ehrman on this.)

So who wrote the Gospels? Ehrman may be correct that the originals—which we do not have—did not contain the titles found in our New Testaments. Of course, we cannot know for certain, since, as just stated, we do not have the originals. But even if the titles were absent on the originals, this is not nearly as big a problem as Ehrman imagines.

It was not unusual for ancient authors to leave their names out of their works. Plutarch was a Greek author who penned more than 50 known biographies during the late first to early second centuries. Plutarch's name is absent from all of them. It is the tradition that has been passed down through the centuries that gives us information pertaining to who wrote these biographies. And no one questions that Plutarch is the author.

So, what ancient traditions inform us concerning the authorship of the canonical Gospels? The very first is a Christian leader named Papias who wrote c. AD 120 and perhaps earlier. Papias may have known the apostle John or another Christian leader who was close to the apostles.[4] He was the first to report that Matthew and John had been members of the 12 disciples of Jesus and penned the Gospels attributed to them. He also reported that Mark wrote what had been relayed to him by the apostle Peter, another of the Twelve. A few decades later, another Christian leader named Justin (c. AD 150) reported that Luke, who had been a traveling companion of Paul, wrote the Gospel of Luke. Shortly thereafter, still another Christian leader named Irenaeus (c. AD 170),

---

[3] Bart D. Ehrman, *Jesus, Interrupted: Revealing the Hidden Contradictions in the Bible (and Why We Don't Know About Them)* (San Francisco: HarperOne, 2009), 136. Also see Bart D. Ehrman, *Forged: Writing in the Name of God—Why the Bible's Authors Are Not Who We Think They Are* (San Francisco: HarperOne, 2011).

[4] Papias, *Fragments* 1:4; 3:1–4, 7; 11; 15; 16:1.

who had probably heard one of the followers of the apostle John named Polycarp, reiterated Papias's tradition about the Gospels' authorship.

Historians are faced with the challenge of determining the extent to which these reports are reliable. For some time, they have debated whether the traditional authorship of the Gospels is accurate, and many, like Ehrman, have opted to reject it. However, many hold to the traditional authorship of all four Gospels and especially to that of Mark and Luke.[5] A number of scholars hold to the traditional authorship of John, although today's majority contends that a minor disciple who was not one of the Twelve but who had traveled with Jesus and was an eyewitness to his ministry is the source behind John's Gospel. These scholars think that one or two of the unnamed disciple's pupils wrote what they had heard from him, perhaps even under his close guidance. In this case, we still would have eyewitness testimony from one of Jesus' disciples who had traveled with him. The authorship of Matthew is the most heavily contested of the four Gospels. Yet there are a number of impressive scholars who maintain its traditional authorship.[6] I am not contending here for a particular position. Instead, I am making the point that in spite of the ongoing debate—one that is far from settled—the evidence in support of the traditional authorship of all four Gospels is strong enough to render it a reasonable position.

So, what about Ehrman's claim that the New Testament Gospels are "forgeries"? This is a statement intended to shock the reader. If an evangelical scholar were to argue that the traditional authorship of the Gospels is established beyond doubt, Ehrman would probably say that he has every right to believe that the evidence supports traditional authorship but that "established beyond doubt" is more than the evidence can bear. In a similar way, Ehrman has a right to believe that the traditional authors did not actually pen the Gospels and that their actual authorship is unknown. But to say that the New Testament Gospels were of a certainty not written by their traditional authors is

[5] Robert H. Gundry, "Trimming the Debate," in *Jesus' Resurrection: Fact or Figment? A Debate Between William Lane Craig and Gerd Lüdemann*, ed. Paul Copan and Ronald K. Tacelli (Downers Grove, IL: InterVarsity Press, 2000), 117 (n15).

[6] Robert H. Gundry, *Matthew: A Commentary on His Handbook for a Mixed Church Under Persecution*, 2nd ed. (Grand Rapids: Eerdmans, 1994), 609–20; Andreas J. Köstenberger, L. Scott Kellum, and Charles L. Quarles, *The Cradle, the Cross, and the Crown: An Introduction to the New Testament* (Nashville: B&H Academic, 2009), 180–84.

an overstatement. While no rock-solid evidence exists pertaining to the authorship of the Gospels, the ancient testimony supporting traditional authorship is good, although not beyond question. The fact that our earliest manuscripts do not include the traditional titles that appear in our Bibles does not mean that we have no idea who wrote the Gospels. As the Gospels began to circulate, and more were written and also circulated, it could be that it was at this time that the titles were added in order to avoid confusion.[7]

In summary, a reasonable case can be made for the traditional authorship of the Gospels. Although the matter is debated, it is certainly misleading to assert that we have no idea who wrote them. Most importantly, modern scholars, including Ehrman, mine the Gospels for historical nuggets and find numerous historical facts that can be known about Jesus. And they do this apart from the issue of authorship.

Challenge #2: The Problem of Dating: When Were the Gospels Written?

In agreement with most biblical scholars, Ehrman states that the New Testament Gospels were written 35–65 years after the events they purport to describe. He regards this time gap as being too wide for purposes of historical reliability, and asserts that historians desire sources written much closer to the events. He adds that this time gap between the events and when they are reported in the Gospels is similar to the distance in time between WWII and now. While that may be true of John's Gospel, the gap between Jesus and the Synoptics (i.e., Matthew, Mark, and Luke) is closer to the gap in time between us and the Vietnam War. Is this also too wide a time gap for Ehrman? If the History Channel interviewed three Vietnam veterans concerning their combat experiences in 1974, we would express no pause concerning the time distance between the events and their interview. Even the 65 years for John is not that long when eyewitnesses are involved. If Ehrman truly believes what he is saying, he should notify the History Channel

---

[7] See also Martin Hengel, *Studies,* 64–84, cited by Robert H. Gundry, *Mark: A Commentary on His Apology for the Cross* (Grand Rapids: Eerdmans, 1993), 1041.

that all documentaries including recent interviews of WWII veterans are unreliable.

It can forthrightly be granted that recollections of the past can become fuzzy and inaccurate as time progresses. Our brains can redact memories to conform to how we may wish that the events may have turned out or adapt our responses to be more positive or powerful than they actually were. However, this sort of redaction usually has its limits, and this is especially true while other eyewitness testimony is available. Moreover, I may have a less accurate recollection of the content of my dinner discussion of one week ago while maintaining near pinpoint accuracy of a major and unique event that occurred in my life 40 years ago.

Let's now consider an ancient example. Caesar Augustus is regarded as Rome's greatest emperor and was ruling the empire when Jesus was born. Historians rely on six chief sources to learn about Augustus's adulthood: a funerary inscription that is nearly 4,000 words in length, Plutarch who wrote around 90 years after Augustus's death, and four others writing 100–200 years after his death.[8] When we consider that this is what we have for the greatest Roman emperor, four biographies of Jesus written within 35–65 years of His death is pretty good!

The error of Ehrman's historical thinking does not stop here. He further claims that the stories about Jesus in the Gospels were carelessly passed from one Christian to another, as in the modern game of telephone, in which an elementary school teacher whispers a sentence to a student who then whispers the same statement to the student next to him and so forth until the last student hears it. The result, of course, is a final statement that is a significantly distorted rendition of the original. Ehrman suggests that the stories about Jesus became grossly distorted over the several decades that followed Jesus' death before they were reported in written form in the Gospels. This is surprising and reveals a naiveté on Ehrman's part pertaining to how Jewish tradition was transmitted in antiquity.

---

[8] Suetonius, Tacitus, Appian, and Dio Cassius. Additional sources that mention Augustus exist just as there are other sources in the early Christian literature that mention Jesus. For example, Paterculus wrote within 20 years of Augustus just as Paul penned his first letter within 20 years of Jesus and before the Gospels were written. However, these six sources that mention Augustus are the major sources used by historians given the breadth of knowledge they contain, just as the Gospels are the major sources on Jesus for the same reason.

For well over a decade I trained in the Korean martial art of tae-kwondo, earning a second-degree black belt. From 1986 to 1989, I ran a martial arts school where I trained a number of students through the black belt level. One of the most important components of traditional martial arts training is "the form," which is a series of movements simulating a fight against multiple opponents. Generally speaking, martial arts forms are very old, having been passed from instructor to student for centuries. Students are carefully trained to perfect the forms of their particular art in order to master various techniques. In the mid-1980s, I learned forms from an eighth-degree black belt who had received instruction from General Choi Hong Hi, who had founded the art of taekwondo in 1955. Given the emphasis on passing along the same form, I was confident that my instructor had passed along to me the same form he had received from General Choi, although it had been three decades since the forms had been created. I, in turn, passed along the same form to my students that I had received from my instructor.

In antiquity, much learning occurred by means of oral tradition, since only about 10 percent of the general population could read. When Paul communicated apostolic tradition concerning Jesus, he did not take liberties to alter it. And we can actually test him on the matter. In 1 Corinthians 7, Paul gives his nonbinding opinion, followed by a teaching of Jesus (i.e., Jesus tradition) which was binding, followed by Paul's apostolic ruling which was also binding. What is noteworthy is Paul did not do what numerous scholars often accuse the early Christians of doing: attribute a teaching to Jesus in order to answer a present situation he had not actually addressed. We observe in 1 Corinthians 7 that Paul refused to pass off his teachings as though they were from Jesus. The Jesus tradition had been passed along to him most likely by the Jerusalem apostles and was to be entrusted to others unaltered. For this reason, nonnarrative tradition was preserved in formulas, creeds, and hymns for easy memorization. Paul wrote, "I delivered to you as of first importance what I also received" (1 Cor 15:3 RSV). Accordingly, it is demonstrable that, at least for Paul, the practice of passing along the Jesus tradition more closely resembled the passing along of the forms in the martial arts than it did the game of telephone.

Paul had learned the Jesus tradition from those who had known Him. His letters contain oral traditions that are even earlier than the Gospels, and in some cases much earlier. Although Paul does not write a biography of Jesus, his letters reveal his familiarity with a number of details pertaining to the life of Jesus that had been communicated to him by Jesus' disciples and their colleagues. In Gal 1:18, a letter certainly written by Paul, he tells us that he visited with the apostle Peter for 15 days. Noteworthy is the Greek term Paul uses for "visited," *historēsai*, from which we get the English term "history." Paul had met with Peter and had inquired of him about the life of Jesus. So, Paul provides us with a few details about Jesus he had received from those who had known Jesus very well. We observe such traditions in 1 Cor 11:23–25 and 15:3–7 in which details are reported pertaining to the Last Supper as well as Jesus' death and resurrection. There are about a dozen references to Jesus' teachings in Paul's letters and about 30 additional possible echoes. Because Paul was well acquainted with the life of Jesus, he is able to instruct the Corinthian believers: "Imitate me, just as I also imitate Christ" (1 Cor 11:1 NKJV). How could Paul imitate Christ if he knew nothing about Him? Therefore, to the extent that the Gospels reflect Pauline teachings concerning Jesus, they probably reflect the teachings of the Jerusalem apostles, most of whom had walked with Jesus.

In summary, although Ehrman contends that the New Testament Gospels were written too long after the events they purport to describe to be regarded as reliable accounts, we observed that this is simply not so. Moreover, his contention that the tradition about Jesus was changed dramatically during the 35- to 65-year period before it was put into writing is based on an inaccurate understanding of how oral tradition was preserved and passed along to others in the early Christian church.

Challenge #3: The Problem of Differences: Do the Gospels Contradict One Another?

Ehrman contends that the New Testament Gospels are not reliable because they contain differences between them when reporting the same

event. Pertaining to Jesus' death, Ehrman asks whether Jesus was crucified on the day of the Passover meal or the day after it, at 9:00 a.m. or
just after noon, whether he or Simon of Cyrene carried His cross, and
whether one or both thieves with whom He was crucified cursed Him.
Regarding Jesus' resurrection, Ehrman asks how many women went to
the tomb, what were their names, whether one angel, two angels, or a
young man appeared at the tomb, whether the women reported the
empty tomb to the male disciples or remained silent, whether Jesus first
appeared to His disciples in Jerusalem or Galilee, and whether Jesus
ascended on Easter or weeks later. To all of these questions Ehrman
answers, "It depends which Gospel you read."[9]

Bracketing for the moment the question of whether these differences can be reconciled, how important are they, historically speaking?
Differences among accounts are of interest to historians. However, they
are not usually as toxic to historical investigation as Ehrman suggests.
You may be surprised to learn that survivors of the *Titanic* contradicted
one another pertaining to whether the ship broke in two prior to sink-
ing or went down intact. We may wonder how some of the eyewitnesses
could have been so mistaken when they were right there. And yet, no
one concluded that the *Titanic* did not sink. The only conclusion was
that a question mark remained pertaining to this peripheral detail.

Let's consider an example from antiquity. In July of AD 64, the city
of Rome caught fire and burned. The event is reported by three primary
sources: Tacitus (c. AD 112), Suetonius (c. AD 115), and Dio Cassius
(c. AD 200), none of whom are ideal sources. Tacitus has an aristocratic bias and invents speeches. Suetonius is indiscriminate in his use of
sources, and Dio contradicts himself. None were eyewitnesses to many,
if any, of the first-century events they report. And their accounts of the
fire of Rome contain differences. Did Nero send men openly to torch
the city (*Suetonius*), or did he do it in secret (*Dio*), or was he probably
not responsible for the fire (*Tacitus*)? It depends whom you read. Did
Nero watch the blaze from the tower of Maecenas (*Suetonius*) or from
his palace rooftop (*Dio*), or was he 35 miles away in Antium (*Tacitus*)?
It depends whom you read. We may never have certainty pertaining to

---

[9] See Ehrman in our debates at www.4truth.net/debate and www.4truth.net/debate1.

some of the peripheral details related to the fire. But these sources are good enough to conclude that Rome burned.

The same historical principle applies to the Gospels, and Ehrman knows it. While he contends that the Gospels are biased, not written by eyewitnesses, and contain differences, he still agrees with nearly every other New Testament scholar that they are reliable enough to provide historians with a substantial collection of facts that can be known about Jesus. Ehrman writes: "How is it possible to use such sources to find out what really happened historically? In fact, there are ways. Scholars have devised some methodological principles that, if followed closely and rigorously, can give us some indications of who Jesus really was."[10]

My point is that, even prior to a discussion over whether the differences among the Gospels can be resolved, it is noteworthy that differences in the Gospels often cited involve relatively minor details that are of limited importance. They do not disqualify the sources in which they are found as containing relatively reliable historical recollections.

So, what about the differences cited by Ehrman? Many of them can be easily resolved without having to engage in hermeneutical gymnastics. For example, having been severely scourged, Jesus could have carried His cross a portion of the way but soon had to be assisted, resulting in Simon of Cyrene's enlistment to complete the task. All historians are selective in the material they preserve, and John simply may not have found the story of Simon to be necessary for inclusion in his Gospel. A contradiction would exist only if John had clearly stated that Jesus was alone in carrying His cross the entire way. Without difficulty, we may imagine both thieves cursing Jesus and one later becoming repentant after seeing how Jesus suffered righteously and without bitterness toward His enemies.

Pertaining to Jesus' resurrection, much confusion has occurred over a quick reading of the beginning of John 20. Matthew, Mark, and Luke report that multiple women went to the tomb while John appears to report that Mary went alone. However, a careful reading of John 20:1–2 reveals that John was only showcasing the woman who was talking, since Mary reported to the disciples, "They have taken away the Lord out of the tomb, and *we* do not know where they have laid Him" (NKJV).

---

[10] Ehrman, *Jesus, Interrupted*, 151.

Luke makes a similar move in reference to the disciples who went to the tomb upon hearing the women's report, first mentioning Peter only later to note that several had gone to the tomb (Luke 24:12,24). This observation can also account for the differences in reports pertaining to whether there were one or two angels at the tomb.

Did the first group appearance of the risen Jesus to His disciples occur in Jerusalem or Galilee, and did Jesus ascend on Easter or weeks later? Much of the confusion results from Luke's account where Jesus' resurrection, all of the appearances, and the ascension occur in Jerusalem on Easter, whereas the appearances and ascension are spread over a period of locations and time in the other Gospels. This, too, is easily resolved when we consider the literary device of *time compression*. Perhaps for purposes of economy, Luke compressed all of the events into one day. However, he was certainly aware that they had occurred over a longer period, since in Acts 1:3 he reports that the risen Jesus had appeared to His disciples over a period of 40 days. Ehrman's indictment of the Gospels as unreliable for reporting different locations and durations simply reveals that he has not spent enough time carefully considering these texts in the context of ancient literary conventions.

Not all differences in the Gospels are so easily addressed. But it is important to note that most of these impact little. Again, Ehrman knows this. For despite the hesitations he expresses toward the Gospels' reports of Jesus' death, he still concludes, "One of the most certain facts of history is that Jesus was crucified on orders of the Roman prefect of Judea, Pontius Pilate."[11] Regarding the resurrection appearances to Jesus' disciples, he writes, "Why, then, did some of the disciples claim to see Jesus alive after His crucifixion? I don't doubt at all that some disciples claimed this."[12]

So, differences in the Gospels are clearly red herrings when Ehrman employs them in reference to the question of whether Jesus rose from the dead.

---

[11] Bart D. Ehrman, *The Historical Jesus: Lecture Transcript and Course Guidebook*, Part 2 of 2 (Chantilly, VA: The Teaching Company, 2000), 162; cf. Bart D. Ehrman, *The New Testament: A Historical Introduction to the Early Christian Writings*, 4th ed. (New York: Oxford, 2008), 261–62.

[12] Ehrman, *Jesus, Interrupted*, 177.

Challenge #4: The Problem of Selection:

Why Were the Four Gospels Included in Our New Testaments Selected and Not the Other Gospels That Were Floating Around in Antiquity?

The answer to this question is far more involved than can be fairly discussed here. One important criterion for the early church was that the book or letter had either been written by an apostle or one of their close colleagues. While other Gospels claimed to have been written by Thomas, Peter, Philip, Mary, Judas, and others, scholars are virtually unanimous in concluding that these Gospels were actual forgeries written sometime in the second and third centuries. The lone possible exception is Thomas, which some scholars believe was written in the latter part of the first century, although the evidence now suggests the end of the second century may be more likely.[13]

For Ehrman, the 27 books and letters in our present New Testament are there because at the end of the canon debates, the winners got to write the past, or at least determine which accounts of the past would be preserved. Ehrman is correct to an extent. But sometimes the winners deserve to win. Ehrman would do well to consider the comments of a prominent scholar on the subject of these "other Gospels" who writes,

> [T]hese other accounts are interesting in the extreme and well worth reading. But they do not, as a rule, provide us with reliable historical information. They are all later than the Gospels of the New Testament and are filled with legendary, though intriguing, stories of the Son of God. . . . [I]f we want to know about the life of the historical Jesus, we are more or less restricted to using the four Gospels of Matthew, Mark, Luke, and John.

Interestingly, the scholar who wrote this statement is Bart Ehrman.[14]

When we look at the decisions pertaining to which Gospels to include in the New Testament, we observe that the ancient church got it right.

---

[13] Nicholas Perrin, *Thomas: The Other Gospel* (Louisville: Westminster John Knox, 2007), 73–106, esp. 106; Craig A. Evans, *Fabricating Jesus: How Modern Scholars Distort the Gospels* (Downers Grove, IL: InterVarsity, 2006), 67–77, esp. 77.

[14] Ehrman, *Jesus, Interrupted*, 151.

This particular attack by Ehrman differs little from the others we have observed. They grab our attention on very important topics. However, in the end we learn that his ultimate conclusions consist mainly of smoke and mirrors rather than the findings of scholars. Ehrman's shock statements and excellent writing skills sell a lot of books. This is good for Ehrman and for his publishers. It is unfortunate, however, that many sincere people have been and will continue to be misled by them. On a positive side, Ehrman's books create opportunities for Christians to become educated on the issues upon which he touches and improve our ability to discuss the credibility of our faith, which is grounded in solid historical evidence.

So, if you like a good fish fry, you will enjoy Ehrman's red herrings on the Gospels. But readers should proceed with caution, since many who have taken his bait have gone off the path and into the woods where logic and sound historical method cannot protect them—and have shipwrecked their faith as a result.

Chapter 10

DOES THE STORY OF JESUS MIMIC PAGAN MYSTERY STORIES?

Mary Jo Sharp

Three years ago, an Islamic apologist expressed interest in a public debate with me. I suggested we center the debate on the theory of the mythological origins of Christ's resurrection. His response was that since most scholars consider this a "dead subject," such a debate probably would not be very fruitful. These kinds of sentiments are not isolated. Two years prior to that exchange, while I was researching for my master's thesis on this very topic, several colleagues responded similarly: "Why are you researching this topic? No one still argues from the perspective that Jesus' story was a myth." Even more recently, biblical scholar James D. G. Dunn satirically exclaimed, "Gosh! So there are still serious scholars who put forward the view that the whole account of Jesus' doings and teachings are a later myth foisted on an unknown, obscure historical figure."[1] Dunn concludes that he cannot see much life in the argument at all. However, in surveying the most influential communication media—the Internet, television, and movies—the accusation of mythological origins is one of the most utilized arguments against belief in Jesus Christ. While not much scholarly work in the past 20 years has been focused on this argument, at the popular level the argument is alive and kicking.

---

[1] James D. G. Dunn, "Response to Robert M. Price," in *The Historical Jesus: Five Views*, ed. James K. Beilby and Paul Rhodes Eddy (Downers Grove, IL: InterVarsity Press, 2009), 94.

The Argument

Basically, the argument is this: the biblical narratives of Christ's life and teachings are mythological in nature and origin rather than actual historical accounts. Many offshoots of this overarching theme have cropped up over the years: (1) Christian dependence on mystery religions to explain baptism and the Lord's Supper, or (2) the doctrine of salvation evolving from mystery religions, or (3) Christianity as just another Hellenistic mystery religion, or (4) Christian beliefs and practices dependent on similar beliefs and practices in the mysteries.[2] However, more recent work in this area has focused on the last two arguments, in which the mystery religion stories are thought to be source material for the authors of the Gospels. Our focus will be on this more specific argument with regard to borrowing elements of the mystery religion stories. (This chapter complements the subsequent chapter, in which Mark Foreman discusses the *Zeitgeist* movie.)

First, we must understand what is meant by "pagan mystery religions." These were religious cults that were named "mysteries" because of the vow of secrecy taken by followers concerning the cult's teachings and the wisdom these teachings imparted. The late theologian and philosopher Ronald Nash explained, "The reason these mystery religions were called mystery religions is that they involved secret ceremonies known only to those initiated into the cult. The major benefit of these practices was thought to be some kind of salvation."[3]

The purpose of this chapter is not to provide a comprehensive response to each accusation related to Christianity's supposedly borrowing mythic elements, but rather to offer the reader a method of investigating these kinds of arguments and to point out some excellent resources on the topic. Most people who are impressed by the mystery-cult-influence argument have not scrutinized the claims meticulously enough, probably not going any further than watching a television show, viewing a few YouTube clips, or glancing through an article or two on random blogs. The person who lacks a solid grounding in Christian doctrine and knowledge of history can easily fall prey to confusion and

---

[2] Ronald Nash, *The Gospel and the Greeks* (Phillipsburg, NJ: P&R Publishing, 2003), 106–7.
[3] Ronald Nash, "Was the New Testament Influenced by Pagan Religions?" *Christian Research Journal* (Winter 1994): 8.

doubt induced by poor arguments left unchallenged. Thus, to avoid this predicament, I suggest three steps as a minimum guideline in considering whether or not the story of Jesus is a copy of contemporary or preexistent pagan mysteries.

Step #1: Get the Whole Story

A fundamental aspect of engaging any argument is an investigation into the credentials of the sources. While I don't commend intellectual snobbery, I do suggest challenging a person who has confused "catch phrases" with facts, preferably before these ideas begin to engender doubt. For example, one of my family members once stated that "radical Christianity is just as threatening as radical Islam." The first thing I asked was, "Where are you getting that from?" Since she couldn't remember, I told her, "You are getting that from Rosie O'Donnell. Why would you trust an actress's statement on philosophy of religion when she hasn't done any studying in this area?" O'Donnell has a right to her own opinion, but to promote her opinion as a convincing fact, she should be able to reference some relevant scholarly sources.

Asking the Right Questions

So to ascertain whether or not proponents of the copy-cat argument have attempted intellectually honest research in forming their conclusions, keep these kinds of questions in mind:

- Who is reporting the information? (*"Where are you getting that from?"*)
- Is the reporter a credentialed scholar in this area? (*"Why should I trust this person's statement as fact?"*)
- Have the arguments been published in peer-reviewed journals and/or analyzed by people of differing views within this field of research?
- What are the reporter's sources?
- Is the reporter interacting with the primary texts (such as the *Egyptian Book of the Dead*)?

- Is the reporter dealing with the actual stories as found in the original texts or the walls of pyramids or other artistic depictions?
- What are the actual stories, in their entirety?

Primary sources, the actual text or depictions, are the most important sources. A source that is farther removed should be interacting with some of the primary and secondary sources, at the very least. Through interaction with these sources, the person making the argument is more likely to have dealt with the whole story and not just a cherry-picked version which makes it appear much more like the story of Christ. As we move into the next section and read summaries of the three gods from two pagan mysteries—the Cult of Isis and Osiris and the Cult of Mithras—we will uncover the Achilles' heel of the Jesus-myth approach.

A Tale of Three Deities

1. Osiris. While some critics of Christ's story utilize the story of Osiris to demonstrate that the earliest followers of Christ copied it, these critics rarely acknowledge how we know the story of Osiris at all. The only full account of Osiris's story is from the second-century AD Greek writer, Plutarch: "Concerning Isis and Osiris."[4] The other information is found piecemeal in Egyptian and Greek sources, but a basic outline can be found in the Pyramid Texts (c. 2686-c. 2160 BC). This seems problematic when claiming that a story recorded in the *second* century influenced the New Testament accounts, which were written in the *first* century. Two other important aspects to mention are the evolving nature of the Osirian myth and the sexual nature of the worship of Osiris as noted by Plutarch. Notice how just a couple of details from the full story profoundly strain the comparison of Osiris with the life of Christ.

Who was Osiris? He was one of five offspring born of an adulterous affair between two gods—Nut, the sky-goddess, and Geb, the earth-god.[5] Because of Nut's transgression, the Sun curses her and will not allow her to give birth on any day in any month. However, the god

---

[4] Plutarch, "Concerning Isis and Osiris," in *Hellenistic Religions: The Age of Syncretism*, ed. Frederick C. Grant (Indianapolis: Liberal Arts Press, 1953), 80–95.

[5] In some depictions, Nut and Geb are married. Plutarch's account insinuates that they have committed adultery because of the anger of the Sun at Nut's transgression.

Thoth[6] also loves Nut. He secures five more days from the Moon to add to the Egyptian calendar specifically for Nut to give birth. While inside his mother's womb, Osiris falls in love with his sister, Isis. The two have intercourse inside the womb of Nut, and the resultant child is Horus.[7] Nut gives birth to all five offspring: Osiris, Horus, Set, Isis, and Nephthys.

Sometime after his birth, Osiris mistakes Nephthys, the wife of his brother Set, for his own wife and has intercourse with her. Enraged, Set plots to murder Osiris at a celebration for the gods. During the festivities, Set procures a beautiful, sweet-smelling sarcophagus, promising it as a gift to the attendee whom it might fit. Of course, this is Osiris. Once Osiris lies down in the sarcophagus, Set solders it shut and then heaves it into the Nile. There are at least two versions of Osiris's fate: (a) he suffocates in the sarcophagus as it floats down the Nile, and (b) he drowns in the sarcophagus after it is thrown into the Nile.

Grief-stricken Isis searches for and eventually recovers Osiris's corpse. While traveling in a barge down the Nile, Isis conceives a child by copulating with the dead body.[8] Upon returning to Egypt, Isis attempts to conceal the corpse from Set but fails. Still furious, Set dismembers his brother's carcass into 14 pieces, which he then scatters throughout Egypt. A temple was supposedly erected at each location where a piece of Osiris was found.

Isis retrieves all but one of the pieces, his phallus. The body is mummified with a model made of the missing phallus. In Plutarch's account of this part of the story, he noted that the Egyptians "presently hold a festival" in honor of this sexual organ.[9] Following magical incantations, Osiris is raised in the netherworld to reign as king of the dead in the land of the dead. In *The Riddle of Resurrection: Dying and Rising Gods in the Ancient Near East*, T. N. D. Mettinger states: "He both died and rose. But, and this is most important, he rose to continued life in the

---

[6] Plutarch refers to Thoth as Hermes in "Concerning Isis and Osiris."

[7] Plutarch's "Concerning Isis and Osiris" appears to be the only account with this story of Horus's birth.

[8] This aspect of the story, which was a variation of Horus's conception story, is depicted in a drawing from the Osiris temple in Dendara.

[9] Plutarch, "Concerning Isis and Osiris," 87.

Netherworld, and the general connotations are that he was a god of the dead."[10] Mettinger quotes Egyptologist Henri Frankfort:

> Osiris, in fact, was not a dying god at all but a dead god. He never returned among the living; he was not liberated from the world of the dead, . . . on the contrary, Osiris altogether belonged to the world of the dead; it was from there that he bestowed his blessings upon Egypt. He was always depicted as a mummy, a dead king.[11]

This presents a very different picture from the resurrection of Jesus, which was reported as a return to physical life.

2. Horus. Horus's story is a bit difficult to decipher for two main reasons. Generally, his story lacks the amount of information for other gods, such as Osiris. Also, there are two stories concerning Horus that develop and then merge throughout Egyptian history: Horus the Sun-god, and Horus the child of Isis and Osiris. The major texts for Horus's story are the Pyramid Texts, Coffin Texts, the Book of the Dead, Plutarch, and Apuleius—all of which reflect the story of Horus as the child of Isis and Osiris.[12] The story is routinely found wherever the story of Osiris is found.

Who was Horus? He was the child of Isis and Osiris. His birth has several explanations as mentioned in Isis and Osiris's story: (1) the result of the intercourse between Isis and Osiris in Nut's womb; (2) conceived by Isis's sexual intercourse with Osiris's dead body; (3) Isis is impregnated by Osiris after his death and after the loss of his phallus; or (4) Isis is impregnated by a flash of lightning.[13] To protect Horus from his uncle's rage against his father, Isis hides the child in the Delta swamps. While

---

[10] T. N. D. Mettinger, *The Riddle of Resurrection: Dying and Rising Gods in the Ancient Near East* (Stockholm: Almqvist & Wiksell, 2001), 175.

[11] Henri Frankfort, *Kingship and the Gods: A Study of Ancient Near Eastern Religion as the Integration of Society and Nature* (Chicago: Oriental Institute of the University of Chicago, 1962), 289; cf. 185; cited in Mettinger, *Riddle of Resurrection*, 172.

[12] For the purposes of this chapter, I use the following sources and translations: E. A. Wallis Budge's translation of the *Book of the Dead*; Plutarch's "Concerning Isis and Osiris"; Joseph Campbell's piecing together of the story in *The Mythic Image*; as well as other noted interpretations of the story.

[13] The latter two versions of Horus's birth can be found in Rodney Stark, *Discovering God: The Origins of the Great Religions and the Evolution of Belief* (New York: Harper Collins, 2007), 204. However, Stark does not reference the source for these birth stories.

he is hiding, a scorpion stings him, and Isis returns to find his body lifeless. (In Margaret Murray's account in *The Splendor That Was Egypt*, there is no death story here, but simply a poisoned child.) Isis prays to the god Ra to restore her son. Ra sends Thoth, another Egyptian god, to impart magical spells to Isis for the removal of the poison. Thus, Isis restores Horus to life. The lesson for worshippers of Isis is that prayers made to her will protect their children from harm and illness. Notice the outworking of this story is certainly not a hope for resurrection to new life, in which death is vanquished forever as is held by followers of Jesus.[14] Despite this strain on the argument, some still insist that Horus's scorpion poisoning is akin to the death and resurrection of Jesus.

In a variation of Horus's story, he matures into adulthood at an accelerated rate and sets out to avenge his father's death. In an epic battle with his uncle Set, Horus loses his left eye, and his uncle suffers the loss of one part of his genitalia. The sacrifice of Horus's eye, when given as an offering before the mummified Osiris, is what brings Osiris new life in the underworld.[15] Horus's duties included arranging the burial rites of his dead father, avenging Osiris's death, offering sacrifice as the Royal Sacrificer, and introducing recently deceased persons to Osiris in the netherworld as depicted in the Hunefer Papyrus (1317–1301 BC). One aspect of Horus's duties as avenger was to strike down the foes of Osiris. This was ritualized through human sacrifice in the first dynasty, and then, eventually, animal sacrifice by the eighteenth dynasty. In the *Book of the Dead* we read of Osiris, "Behold this god, great of slaughter, great of fear! He washes in your blood, he bathes in your gore!"[16] So Horus, in the role of Royal Sacrificer, bought his own life from this Osiris by sacrificing the life of others. There is no similarity here to the sacrificial death of Jesus.

3. Mithras. There are no substantive accounts of Mithras's story, but rather a pieced-together story from inscriptions, depictions, and surviving Mithraea (man-made caverns of worship). According to Rodney Stark, professor of social sciences at Baylor University, an immense amount of "nonsense" has been inspired by modern writers seeking to "decode

---

[14] The development of Isis's worship as a protector of children is a result of this instance; Margaret A. Murray, *The Splendor That Was Egypt*, rev. ed. (Mineola: Dover, 2004), 106.

[15] Joseph Campbell, *The Mythic Image* (Princeton, NJ: Princeton University Press, 1974), 29, 450.

[16] Murray, *The Splendor That Was Egypt*, 103.

the Mithraic mysteries."[17] The reality is we know very little about the mystery of Mithras or its doctrines because of the secrecy of the cult initiates. Another problematic aspect is the attempt to trace the Roman military god, Mithras, back to the earlier Persian god, Mithra, and to the even earlier Indo-Iranian god, Mitra. While it is plausible that the latest form of Mithraic worship was based on antecedent Indo-Iranian traditions, the mystery religion that is compared to the story of Christ was a "genuinely new creation."[18] Currently, some popular authors utilize the Roman god's story from around the second century along with the Iranian god's dates of appearance (c. 1500–1400 BC).

This is the sort of poor scholarship employed in popular renditions of Mithras, such as in *Zeitgeist: The Movie*. For the purpose of summary, we will utilize the basic aspects of the myth as found in Franz Cumont's writing and note variations, keeping in mind that many Mithraic scholars question Cumont, as well as one another, as to interpretations and aspects of the story.[19] Thus, we will begin with Cumont's outline.

Who was Mithra? He was born of a "generative rock," next to a river bank, under the shade of a sacred tree. He emerged holding a dagger in one hand and a torch in the other to illumine the depths from which he came. In one variation of his story, after Mithra's emergence from the rock, he clothed himself in fig leaves and then began to test his strength by subjugating the previously existent creatures of the world. Mithra's first activity was to battle the Sun, whom he eventually befriended. His next activity was to battle the first living creature, a bull created by Ormazd (Ahura Mazda). Mithra slew the bull, and from its body, spine, and blood came all useful herbs and plants. The seed of the bull, gathered by the Moon, produced all the useful animals. It is through this first sacrifice of the first bull that beneficent life came into being, including human life. According to some traditions, this slaying took place in a cave, which allegedly explains the cave-like Mithraea.[20]

---

[17] Stark, *Discovering God*, 141.

[18] Roger Beck, "The Mysteries of Mithras: A New Account of Their Genesis," *Journal of Roman Studies* 88 (1998): 123.

[19] Roger Beck, M. J. Vermaseren, David Ulansey, N. M. Swerdlow, Bruce Lincoln, John R. Hinnells, and Reinhold Merkelbach, for example.

[20] More contemporary Mithraic scholars have pointed to the lack of a bull-slaying story in the Iranian version of Mithra's story: "there is no evidence the Iranian god ever had anything to do with a bull-slaying." David Ulansey, *The Origins of the Mithraic Mysteries* (New York:

Mit(h)ra's name meant "contract" or "compact."[21] He was known in the Avesta—the Zoroastrian sacred texts—as the god with a hundred ears and a hundred eyes who sees, hears, and knows all. Mit(h)ra upheld agreements and defended truth. He was often invoked in solemn oaths that pledged the fulfillment of contracts and which promised his wrath should a person commit perjury. In the Zoroastrian tradition, Mithra was one of many minor deities (*yazatas*) created by Ahura Mazda, the supreme deity. He was the being who existed between the good Ahura Mazda and the evil Angra Mainyu—the being who exists between light and darkness and mediates between the two. Though he was considered a lesser deity to Ahura Mazda, he was still the "most potent and most glorious of the yazata."[22]

The Roman version of this deity (Mithras) identified him with the light and sun. However, the god was not depicted as one with the sun, rather as sitting next to the sun in the communal meal. Again, Mithras was seen as a friend of the sun. This is important to note, as a later Roman inscription (c. AD 376) touted him as "Father of Fathers" and "the Invincible Sun God Mithras."[23] Mithras was proclaimed as invincible because he never died and because he was completely victorious in all his battles. These aspects made him an attractive god for soldiers of the Roman army, who were his chief followers. Pockets of archaeological evidence from the outermost parts of the Roman Empire reinforce this assumption. Obviously, some problems arise in comparing Mithras to Christ, even at this level of simply comparing stories. Mithras lacks a death and therefore also lacks a resurrection.

Oxford University Press, 1989), 8; see Bruce Lincoln, "Mitra, Mithra, Mithras: Problems of a Multiform Deity," review of John R. Hinnells, *Mithraic Studies: Proceedings of the First International Congress of Mithraic Studies,* in *History of Religions* 17 (1977): 202–3. For an interpretation of the slaying of the bull as a cosmic event, see Luther H. Martin, "Roman Mithraism and Christianity," *Numen* 36 (1989): 8.

[21] "For the god is clearly and sufficiently defined by his name. 'Mitra' means 'con-tract', as Meillet established long ago and D. [Professor G. Dumézi] knows but keeps forgetting." Ilya Gershevitch, review of *Mitra and Aryaman* and *The Western Response to Zoroaster,* in the *Bulletin of the School of Oriental and African Studies* 22 (1959): 154. See Paul Thieme, "Remarks on the Avestan Hymn to Mithra," *Bulletin of the School of Oriental and African Studies* 23 (1960): 273.

[22] Franz Cumont, *The Mysteries of Mithra: The Origins of Mithraism* (1903). Accessed on May 3, 2008, http://www.sacred-texts.com/cla/mom/index.htm.

[23] *Corpus Inscriptionum Latinarum* VI. 510; H. Dessau, *Inscriptiones Latinae Selectae* II. 1 (1902), No. 4152, as quoted in Grant, *Hellenistic Religions,* 147. This inscription was found at Rome, dated August 13, AD 376. Notice the late date of this title for Mithras—well after Christianity was firmly established in Rome.

Now that we have a more comprehensive view of the stories, it is quite easy to discern the vast difference between the story of Jesus and even the basic story lines of the commonly compared pagan mystery gods. One must only use the very limited, general aspects of the stories to make the accusation of borrowing, while ignoring the numerous aspects having nothing in common with Jesus' story, such as missing body parts, sibling sexual intercourse inside the womb of a goddess-mother, and being born from a rock. This is why it is important to get the whole story. The supposed similarities are quite flimsy in the fuller context.

Step #2: Take the Parallels Head to Head

It is necessary when encountering this argument to take a detailed look at the parallels in question. The suggested parallels between the story of Christ and the stories of Osiris, Horus, and Mithras are built on superficial comparisons and logical fallacies. First, some of the similarities are those that are common to most religions, such as belief in the afterlife or in salvation for mankind.[24] These are not incredible new insights discovered by modern scholars, nor were scholars throughout history afraid to mention them or make conclusions because of mere religious "taboo."[25] In reality, the similarities have been noted for years in the study of comparative religions and in studies of human nature.[26] Second, proponents have committed the logical fallacy of special pleading by ignoring aspects of the story that do not support their position. Let's look at some examples.

Payam Nabarz, author of *The Mysteries of Mithras,* writes that Mithras and Jesus were both "born of a virgin," even while noting that the Roman Mithras's birth involved springing forth from the underworld by way of a rock; no human female virgin gave birth to him. Nabarz's second explanation for Mithra's birth comes from the Zoroastrian goddess, Anahita, who conceived Mithra (the Persian version of the

---

[24] J. Ed Komoszewski, M. James Sawyer, and Daniel B. Wallace, *Reinventing Jesus: How Contemporary Skeptics Miss the Real Jesus and Mislead Popular Culture* (Grand Rapids: Kregel, 2006), 236.

[25] Timothy Freke and Peter Gandy, *The Jesus Mysteries: Was the "Original Jesus" a Pagan God?* (New York: Three Rivers Press, 1999), 2.

[26] These aspects are discussed by ancient Greek philosophers, early Christian writers, medieval philosophers, and Enlightenment and post-Enlightenment philosophers.

name) with the seed of Zoroaster as preserved in Lake Humum, Iran.[27] Nabarz quotes one inscription at a dedicatory temple in Iran from 200 BC: "Anahita, the Immaculate Virgin Mother Goddess of the Lord Mithra." However, he fails to show which Anahita traditions resemble the human virgin Mary, the mother of Christ. Also, Mithra was not only her child but became her loving partner in Zoroastrian tradition: Mithra was the god who presided over wide pastures, and Anahita was the goddess who presided over the waters.

Nabarz states that both Mithras and Jesus were savior gods. Two problematic aspects of this comparison present themselves. First, Nabarz does not explain in what sense Mithras was considered a "savior"—an important subject since the earliest stories of Mithra (Mithras's Persian antecedent) provide no such title.[28] Second, Nabarz does not include the historical dating of Mithras's association with the terms "savior" or "salvation"; both are found only in later first-century to second-century Mithraic dedicatory and monumental records—again, after the influence of Christianity on the Roman Empire.[29] In addition to cherry-picking, Nabarz does not explain what exactly is *similar* about the "virgin birth" or "savior" stories. For example, being born out of a rock, being born of a goddess with the seed of a man, and being born of a virgin human female are *not similar* births. This is an important detail to include. Further, Mithras's bull-slaying said to have "saved us by blood shed"[30] is not comparable to Jesus' sacrifice of Himself as payment for the sin of all mankind.

In *The Jesus Mysteries,* Timothy Freke and Peter Gandy also use special pleading in their comparison of the resurrection stories of Jesus and of Osiris: "After his death, Jesus descends to hell, then resurrects on the third day. Plutarch tells us that Osiris, likewise, is said to have descended to hell and then arisen from the dead on the third day."[31]

---

[27] Payam Nabarz, *The Mysteries of Mithras: The Pagan Beliefs That Shaped the Christian World* (Rochester: Inner Traditions, 2005), 19.

[28] Ibid., 48.

[29] Beck, "The Mysteries of Mithras: A New Account of Their Genesis," 123. "The great innovation, the primary 'invention' of the Mysteries, was the bull-killing of Mithras construed as a mighty act of 'salvation.'" In a footnote, Beck writes: "The reason that we hear no hint of a bull-killing Mithras prior to the late first century A.D. is, *quite simply, that he did not exist until shortly before that time*" (n153, my emphasis).

[30] Roger Beck, "Merkelbach's Mithras," *Phoenix* 41 (Autumn 1987): 301.

[31] Freke and Gandy, *The Jesus Mysteries*, 56.

Again, we encounter several problems with such parallels. First, the argument is anachronistic, in that Freke and Gandy use a second-century Greek magical papyrus of the same time frame as Plutarch's *Concerning Isis and Osiris* in order to obtain the language similar to the creed of the Christians concerning the rising on the third day.[32]

Second, no attention is given to what exactly the term "resurrection" meant to the hearers. The "resurrection" was a renewal of the spirit life, the KHU and the SEKHEM, in the place where Osiris ruled as king of the dead—not a renewal of the KHAT, or physical body.[33] Plus, the Egyptian believer hoped Osiris would give him a place of permanence in the netherworld, as evidenced in the *Book of the Dead*: "Grant thou [Osiris] to me a place in the nether-world, near the lords of right and truth, my estate may it be permanent in Sekhet-hetep."[34] Also, Freke and Gandy completely leave out ancient Egyptian concepts of the body, spirit, and soul. Budge comments on this:

> We may then say that a man consisted of body, soul, and spirit. But did all three rise, and live in the world beyond the grave? The Egyptian texts answer this question definitely; the soul and the spirit of the righteous passed from the body and lived with the beatified and the gods in heaven; but the physical body did not rise again, and it was believed never to leave the tomb. . . . Already in the [fifth] dynasty, about B.C. 3400, it is stated definitely:—"The soul to heaven, the body to earth"; and three thousand years later the Egyptian writer declared the same thing, but in different words, when he wrote:—"Heaven hath thy soul, and earth thy body."[35]

---

[32] Ibid., 270. At n251, they write: "Plutarch, op.cit. 39 and 42. A Greek magical papyri of the same period records: 'At the port of Bousiris I'll cry the name of him who remained three days and three nights in the river, Osiris the drowned one,' see Linday, J. (1970), 172."

[33] For resurrection as a netherworldly event, see Campbell, *The Mythic Image*, 41; Mettinger, *The Riddle of Resurrection*, 172–73. Also, The "Khu" as labeled by Budge can also be called the "Akh." The Khat is also the "Kha." Also, the KHAT was thought to be tied to certain spiritual bodies of a man, and these spirit bodies would not survive without the KHAT.

[34] *The Egyptian Book of the Dead*, trans. E. A. Wallis Budge (New York: Barnes & Noble, 2005 [1895]), 74.

[35] E. A. Wallis Budge, *Egyptian Religion* (1899; repr., New York: Arkana, 1987), 167. Budge mentions that there were "no doubt" ignorant Egyptian people who believed in the resurrection of the corruptible body, which would entail an afterlife that was very much a continuation of the current life. However, he states that the people who were following the teaching

Third, in the story of Osiris, the deceased must pass judgment, based on the merit of his own earthly works, before he can be introduced to Osiris and receive the hope of spiritual renewal in the netherworld (or the place of the dead).[36] Contrarily, "resurrection" in the story of Christ meant bodily resurrection—a transformed physicality—as evidenced in the physical nature of the appearances of Jesus (1 Cor 15:35–49).[37] In addition, the hope for an individual Christian's resurrection to new life is not based on judgment of his earthly works but in the work of Jesus Christ.

Thus, we find that the similarities offered as proof positive of Christian borrowing are irreparably strained. By the same fallacious methodology, anyone can nearly equate almost anything with anything else. Everything in the universe has at least one property in common with everything else in the universe. If nothing else, there is the property that I can conceive of them both in my mind. Vague similarities accomplish nothing to show causal historical influences. Note the alleged parallels in the chart on the next page:

Step #3: Set Everything in Context

After a thorough look at the stories and a comparison of any parallels, the next step is to go deeper into the historical-cultural and linguistic context of each story. We must understand what the terms and stories meant to the people receiving them rather than basing interpretations of the stories on a modern perspective. Terminology such as "resurrection" should be set strictly within the cultural conception of the term for the time and place in which it was utilized. As noted earlier, the Egyptian conception of Osiris's rising from the dead was an entirely spiritual conception. The Egyptians did not plan to return to physical life; neither did the Greeks. Ante-Nicene church father Athanasius makes this clear: "For although the

---

of the sacred Egyptian writings knew that these beliefs were inconsistent "with the views of their priests and of educated people in general." He then goes on to demonstrate the generally accepted Egyptian view of the soul and body as stated above. Since my case is built on comparing available texts, I must use the textual evidence available, not an indefinite reference to a group of people who "no doubt" existed. Budge's references for his quotations are: *Recueil de Travaux*, tom. iv. P.71 (l. 582); and Horrack, *Lamentations d'Isis* (Paris, 1866), 6.

[36] John H. Taylor, *Death and the Afterlife in Ancient Egypt* (London: The British Museum Press, 2001), 36, figure 17.

[37] See N. T. Wright, *The Resurrection of the Son of God* (Minneapolis: Fortress, 2003).

Greeks have told all manner of false tales, yet they were not able to feign a Resurrection of their idols,—for it never crossed their mind, whether it be at all possible for the body again to exist after death."[38] They wanted to be free of the flesh and unite with their god in a spiritual land.

Four Alleged Parallels Compared

	Osiris	Horus	Mithras	Jesus
Virgin Birth	Adulterous affair between gods	Isis & Osiris: (1) Two unborn gods had intercourse in their mother's womb; (2) Isis has intercourse with Osiris's dead body; (3) Isis impregnated by Osiris after his death and the loss of his phallus; (4) Isis impregnated by a flash of lightning	(1) Sprang forth from a rock near a riverbed (2) Born of a goddess and the seed of Zoroaster	Born of a human female who had not had sexual intercourse before Jesus' birth
Death	Killed by being lured into a sarcophagus	(1) Doesn't die; (2) Death by scorpion sting in the swamps or in Sekhet-An	Doesn't die	Lays down His own life in accordance with His own prediction
Resurrection	Raised to the land of the dead to rule as king of the dead	Revived by the magical incantations of another god after a scorpion sting	No death; so no resurrection	Rose from the grave to new, transformed physical life
Title of "Savior"	Hope for salvation is the release from the fleshly body to be with god in the spirit realm; Osiris does nothing to secure this position for a person	Horus introduces those who have passed through judgment to the dead king, Osiris	(1) Hope for victory in this life; (2) Bull-slaying act as "sacrificial"	Salvific act was for the sin of all humankind in order that man may be declared righteous before a righteous God (Rom 4:25)

---

[38] Athanasius, "On the Incarnation," in *The Nicene and Post-Nicene Fathers Second Series,* vol. IV, *Athanasius: Selected Works and Letters,* ed. Philip Schaff (Oak Harbor, WA: Logos Research Systems, 1997), S. 64.

N. T. Wright explains that the Christian view of resurrection was different from the pagan view of the afterlife in *The Resurrection of the Son of God*:

> "Resurrection" denoted a new embodied life which would follow whatever "life after death" there might be. "Resurrection" was, by definition, not the existence into which someone might (or might not) go immediately upon death; it was not a disembodied "heavenly" life; it was a further stage, out beyond all that. It was not a redescription or redefinition of death. It was death's reversal.[39]

In the ancient pagan world, death was a one-way street.

It is misguided to say, therefore, that the early Christians borrowed the idea of resurrection from pagan stories. These Christians did not end up with a view of resurrection consistent with the pagan view. To the contrary, Paul's teaching on the resurrection of Jesus was considered a foreign concept by the Gentiles to whom he preached. According to Acts 17:18,

> Some of the Epicurean and Stoic philosophers also conversed with him. And some said, "What does this babbler wish to say?" Others said, "He seems to be a preacher of foreign divinities"—because he was preaching Jesus and the resurrection. (ESV)

Paul was teaching resurrection as transformative, as something that would not leave a corpse behind (cf. 1 Cor 15:51; Phil 3:21).[40] This teaching struck the pagans and Gentile philosophers in Athens as odd since it did not match their own conception of death and the afterlife.[41] Such problematic modern analyses that read Christian concepts back into the texts and stories of pagan writers and artists must be addressed in every area—including salvation, virgin birth, judgment, death, afterlife, communal meals, baptism, and sacrifice. All of these allegedly borrowed aspects of the Christian story have been addressed thoroughly in

---

[39] Wright, *The Resurrection of the Son of God*, 83.

[40] Craig S. Keener, *The Historical Jesus of the Gospels* (Cambridge: Eerdmans, 2009), 346.

[41] See Acts 17:20; cf. 19:23–41 on the pagan reaction to Paul's teaching in Ephesus. However, financial motives, at least in part, are factors in their response.

the refutations by twentieth-century scholars, whose work should be considered before coming to any conclusions.[42]

The pagan mysteries we have investigated offer precious little to ground their stories in history—a marked contrast with what we find in the New Testament. The story of Jesus includes many historical dates, places, people, and events. For example, Luke 3:1–2 reads:

> In the fifteenth year of the reign of Tiberius Caesar—when Pontius Pilate was governor of Judea, Herod tetrarch of Galilee, his brother Philip tetrarch of Iturea and Traconitis, and Lysanias tetrarch of Abilene—during the high priesthood of Annas and Caiaphas, the word of God came to John son of Zechariah in the desert. (NIV)

These two verses offer a specific time and place in history that can be utilized to verify the historicity of the events. Do we find the same type of material in the two pagan mystery stories? No. The Roman mystery cult of Mithras has no substantive written record; therefore there is no way of checking for accuracy of dates, people, places, events, and such. The Osirian myths do mention the Nile River, some cities in Egypt, and a few persons, but most of the events have no date and most of the characters in the stories are gods. A comparative analysis of New Testament dates, locations, places, people, and events with the same material available from the pagan mysteries will show a cavernous gap in the amount of historical grounding. The mysteries are not solidly placed in human history. Instead, they are cosmic epics in heavenly realms. The stories reference earthly places infrequently, if at all, and with indifference to historical setting. While not arguing here for the historical validity of the New Testament claims, there is a marked difference from the pagan mysteries.

Finally, while some may argue that the chronology of the stories proves Jesus' story is a copy, and therefore untrue, this argument cannot stand alone. First, some of the arguments from chronology are

---

[42] Cf. Ronald Nash, *The Gospel and the Greeks: Did the New Testament Borrow from Pagan Thought?* (Phillipsburg, NJ:P&R, 2003); Arthur Darby Nock, "Introduction," in William James, *The Varieties of Religious Experience: A Study in Human Nature* (1902; repr., London: Fontana, 1971); Gunter Wagner, *Pauline Baptism and the Pagan Mysteries* (Edinburgh: Oliver & Boyd, 1967). Also see, in addition to works cited in this chapter, the work of Bruce Metzger, Edwin Yamauchi, and J. Gresham Machen.

counterproductive because of not only the previously mentioned problems of context but also because of the actual order of appearance of the terminology. For example, it is claimed that Mithras was called a savior, but this title is known from an inscription dating later than the early Christian testimony to Jesus as "Savior." Hence, when faced with the chronology argument, it is wise to go back to the question of sources and ask, "Where are you getting this from?" This practice will clear up poor scholarship such as that found in *Zeitgiest: The Movie.*

Second, chronology does not establish genealogy. The chronology of the stories cannot be the sole consideration for influence on the development of the Christian story. Such an argument amounts to nothing more than a *post hoc ergo propter hoc* fallacy: assuming one event caused another event simply because the second event followed the first—and not taking other factors into account that may rule out the connection. Other possible influences require at least as much investigation as the chronology of the stories: (1) Christianity as developed within first-century Jewish monotheism, (2) the effect of the failed Hellenization of the Jews by Antiochus IV Epiphanes in the second century BC, and (3) the beliefs of the earliest Christian authors, such as Paul, as evidenced in their own writings. Larry Hurtado in *One God, One Lord: Early Christian Devotion and Ancient Jewish Monotheism* offers: "early Christian devotion did not result from a clumsy crossbreeding of Jewish monotheism and pagan polytheism under the influence of gentile Christians too ill-informed about the Jewish heritage to preserve its character."[43]

Conclusion

Does the story of Jesus imitate pagan mystery stories? No. There is too much left untouched in this assertion to conclude reasonably that Christianity is another pagan mystery religion. As we have seen, the argument superficially relates one story to the others without consideration of comprehensiveness or context. The proponents read context back into the stories rather than appeal to the actual historical context of the mystery religions themselves. To respond to the problematic

---

[43] Larry Hurtado, *One God, One Lord: Early Christian Devotion and Ancient Jewish Monotheism* (New York: Continuum, 1998), 100.

paralleling of the Jesus story and the pagan mystery stories, take three important steps: (1) get the whole story, (2) take the parallels head to head, and (3) set everything in context. In so doing, we can show how merely *asserting* a claim is inadequate; it must be substantiated. Because of the popularity of such false claims in the media, we should be prepared to offer a well-researched, thoughtful, and scholarly response.

Chapter 11

CHALLENGING THE *ZEITGEIST* MOVIE
Parallelomania on Steroids
Mark W. Foreman

A few semesters back, a student approached me after class and wanted to know whether he could meet with me. He was having some doubts about his faith because of a movie he had seen on the Internet called *Zeitgeist* (pronounced "***tzaiyt-gaiyst***"). He shared with me how this movie had made claims that Christianity was a total fiction—that it was completely made up from a combination of other religious claims—and that all world religions were just different expressions of sun worship. He blurted out, "They really backed up their claims with all sorts of evidence, Dr. Foreman. I don't know what to believe anymore. Is it true? Is all this stuff I was taught in church just a big hoax?" I had not seen the film at the time, but I had heard there was something out there on the web and decided to investigate it. What I found was a very polished film that might come across to the uninformed at first glance as well argued but actually was full of fallacious arguments and false claims. In fact, they weren't even *new* bad arguments. Some of them go back to the late nineteenth century.

In this essay, I want to briefly examine some of the arguments and claims of *Zeitgeist*. My purpose will be to show that these arguments are replete with poor reasoning and that the argument that Christianity is just a rehash of old pagan myths does not hold up under close scrutiny.

The *Zeitgeist* Movie

Zeitgeist (a German word meaning "spirit of the age") was produced and written by Peter Joseph and was released online in June of 2007. The film is a two-hour documentary conspiracy theory that attempts to show a connection among three supposed frauds: Christianity, the terrorist attacks of 9/11, and the domination of world events by international bankers. The film is made up of three parts, each part dedicated to one of these three supposed frauds. For purposes of this essay, we will only discuss the claims from part 1 about Christianity.

This first portion of the film is divided into two main arguments: (1) Christianity is a myth based on teachings from earlier pagan myths; (2) all these myths, including Christianity, are in essence astrologically based—a view called "astrotheology." Because of space constraints, I shall examine only the first argument. The basic thesis of this argument is well stated in *The Companion Guide to* Zeitgeist*: Part 1*. The book was written by Acharya S, the periodic pen name of Dorothy M. Murdock, who was a primary consultant for the film and whose book, *The Christ Conspiracy: The Greatest Story Ever Sold*, was one of the main sources for many of the claims in the film. She writes: .

> Indeed, it is my contention and that of others deemed "Jesus mythicists" that the creators of the gospel tale picked various themes and motifs from the pre-Christian religions and myths, including and especially the Egyptian, and wove them together, using also the Jewish scriptures, to produce a unique version of the "mythos and ritual." In other words, the creators of the Christ myth did not simply take an already formed story, scratch out the name Osiris or Horus and replace it with Jesus. They chose their motifs carefully, out of the most popular religious symbols, myths and rituals, making sure they fit to some degree with the Jewish "messianic scriptures" as they are termed, and created a new story that hundreds of millions since have been led to believe really and truly took place in history. . . . In other words, we are convinced that "Jesus Christ"

is a *fictional character* created out of older myths, rituals and symbols.[1]

The idea that the early church of the first century borrowed its beliefs from other pagan religions is often referred to as the copycat theory. The main tactic employed in supporting this claim is to cite parallels between the pagan religions and Christianity. Here is an example from the film:

> Broadly speaking, the story of Horus is as follows: Horus was born on December 25th of the virgin Isis-Meri. His birth was accompanied by a star in the east, which in turn, three kings followed to locate and adorn the new-born savior. At the age of 12, he was a prodigal child teacher, and at the age of 30 he was baptized by a figure known as Anup and thus began his ministry. Horus had 12 disciples he traveled about with, performing miracles such as healing the sick and walking on water. Horus was known by many gestural names such as The Truth, The Light, God's Anointed Son, The Good Shepherd, The Lamb of God, and many others. After being betrayed by Typhon, Horus was crucified, buried for 3 days, and thus, resurrected.
>
> These attributes of Horus, whether original or not, seem to permeate in many cultures of the world, for many other gods are found to have the same general mythological structure.
>
> Attis, of Phrygia, born of the virgin Nana on December 25th, crucified, placed in a tomb and after 3 days, was resurrected.
>
> Krishna, of India, born of the virgin Devaki with a star in the east signaling his coming, performed miracles with his disciples, and upon his death was resurrected.
>
> Dionysus of Greece, born of a virgin on December 25th, was a traveling teacher who performed miracles such as turning water into wine, he was referred to as the "King of Kings,"

---

[1] Acharya S, *The Companion to* Zeitgeist: *Part 1* (Seattle, WA: Stellar House Publishing, 2009), 8 (emphasis hers).

"God's Only Begotten Son," "The Alpha and Omega," and
many others, and upon his death, he was resurrected.

Mithra, of Persia, born of a virgin on December 25th, he had
12 disciples and performed miracles, and upon his death was
buried for 3 days and thus resurrected, he was also referred to as
"The Truth," "The Light," and many others. Interestingly, the
sacred day of worship of Mithra was Sunday.[2]

This tactic of citing parallels is not new. In fact, in a 1962 article in
the *Journal of Biblical Literature*, Samuel Sandmel referred to such sloppy
scholarship as "parallelomania," which he defined as "that extravagance
among scholars which first overdoes the supposed similarity in passages
and then proceeds to describe source and derivation as if implying literary connection flowing in an inevitable or predetermined direction."[3]
Zeitgeist is parallelomania on steroids.

In addressing the copycat charge, I do not intend to examine every
parallel being claimed, though I will comment on some of them.[4] Instead,
my approach is to look at the overall method used in making the arguments in the film and by other supporters of the copycat theory. I will
argue that these arguments are baseless, and poorly argued, and most of
them are rejected by all but a tiny percentage of scholars in the field.

Assessing the Copycat Theory

Before examining the specific fallacies involved in the copycat theory,
I need to make some general comments. First, while the ideas portrayed
in *Zeitgeist* may be new to many viewers, the basic charge is an old one.
The copycat theory emerged in the mid-nineteenth century and was
popularized mostly through James Frazer's *The Golden Bough* (1890).
It continued until the early twentieth century, when its methods and

---

[2] Peter Joseph, *Zeitgeist: The Movie*. Online Transcript (2007). Accessed Sept. 23, 2011,
http://en.wikiversity.org/wiki/Zeitgeist_the_movie/Transcript.

[3] Samuel Sandmel, "Parallelomania," *Journal of Biblical Literature* 81 (1962): 1. Sandmel
admits that he did not originate the term "parallelomania" but does not remember where he
first came across it.

[4] Unfortunately, space does not allow me to do more than offer a short overview of the main
problems of the copycat theory. I encourage the reader to seek out the sources cited in this article (especially Rahner, Metzger, Nash, and Komoszewski et al.) for a more thorough treatment.

conclusions were rejected by critical scholars.[5] In fact, the vast majority of sources cited in the online *Zeitgeist* transcript to support its claims come either from these late-nineteenth- and early-twentieth-century authors or from more recent writings that depend heavily on these sources.[6] While the copycat theory is largely ignored by critical scholars, the movement has gained some new momentum more recently, in part owing to films such as this.[7] While the view is regaining popularity, however, no new evidence has been presented in its support. The same old sources are just being dusted off and repackaged as slickly produced films like *Zeitgeist*. Arguments don't stop being bad simply because of their upgraded, flashy attire.

Another point to note is that certain similarities between pagan religions and Christianity are inevitable. The simple fact that we categorize them under the same term—"religion"—means that they will have some things in common. Many religions believe in and worship a godlike figure, have rites and ceremonies that express this belief, and deal with the universal struggles of the human condition. These are often conveyed in a shared language and analogous symbols.[8] Ronald Nash comments, "After all, religious rituals can assume only a limited number of forms,

---

[5] The *Religionsgeschichtliche Schule*, or history of religions school, coming out of Germany, was one of the instigators of this line of thinking, but was abandoned by the early 1930s because of its radical methodology and approach. See Kurt Rudolph, "*Religionsgeschichtliche Schule*," *The Encyclopedia of Religion*, ed. Mircea Eliade (New York: Macmillan, 1987), 12:293–96.

[6] Forty percent of the citations offered come from only three sources: Gerald Massey, a nineteenth-century amateur Egyptologist, author of *The Historical Jesus and the Mythical Christ* (1886); Thomas Doane, *Bible Myths and Their Parallels in Other Religions* (1882); and James Frazer, *The Golden Bough* (1890). My argument is not that age makes a work necessarily inferior. It is simply to point out that this is an old theory that has been abandoned by all but a tiny handful of scholars, a fact of which viewers of the film are likely to be unaware.

[7] One writer suggests that much of the resurgence is because of a "ready access to unfiltered information via the internet and the influential power of this medium. The result is junk food for the mind—a pseudointellectual meal that is as easy to swallow as it is devoid of substance." J. Ed Komoszewski, M. James Sawyer, and Daniel B. Wallace, *Reinventing Jesus: How Contemporary Skeptics Miss the Real Jesus and Mislead Popular Culture* (Grand Rapids: Kregel, 2006), 221–22.

[8] Hugo Rahner writes, "A vast number of ideas, words, rites, which formerly were designated offhand as 'borrowings' of Christianity from the mysteries, grew to life in the early church from a root that has indeed no bearing on a historical-genetic dependence, but that did spring from the universal depths of man, from the psychological nature common to heathen and Christian alike—'from below,' as we have said. Every religion forms sensory images of spiritual truths: we call them symbols." Hugo Rahner, "The Christian Mystery and the Pagan Mysteries," in *Pagan and Christian Mysteries: Papers from the Eranos Yearbooks*, ed. Joseph Campbell (New York: Harper Torchbooks, 1955), 171–72.

and they naturally relate to important or common aspects of human life. Alleged similarities might reflect only common features of a time or culture, rather than genetic dependence."[9]

Similarity, we see, does not imply dependence. In order to better understand this, we need to make "a clear distinction between dependence in the genetic sense and the dependence of 'adaptation.'"[10] A "genetic" dependence is one where we can trace an idea or belief back to an original earlier source. A dependence of "adaptation" occurs when one borrows words, symbols, or concepts to convey an idea or belief, the substance of which does not originate in another religion. For example, the apostle Paul adapts the Athenians' belief in an unknown God in the speech on Mars Hill to talk about the Christian God. The church father Clement of Rome (d. AD 110) does the same thing when he says, "Come, I shall show you the Logos, and the mysteries of the Logos, and I shall explain them to you in images that are known to you."[11] The adaptation sense of dependence is still used today by Christian missionaries to communicate the gospel message in foreign cultures.

Is there any evidence of genetic dependence of Christian beliefs on pagan religions? Yes and no. There is strong evidence that the pagan religions did have some influence over certain beliefs and practices of the Christian church. However, as biblical scholar Bruce Metzger comments, "A distinction must be made between the faith and practice of the earliest Christians and that of the Church during subsequent centuries. One cannot deny that post-Constantinian Christianity [fourth and fifth centuries AD], both Eastern and Western, adopted not a few pagan rites and practices."[12] For example, mystery religions may well have

---

[9] Ronald H. Nash, *The Gospel and the Greeks: Did the New Testament Borrow from Pagan Thought?* (Phillipsburg, NJ: P&R Publishing, 2003), 140.

[10] Rahner, "Christian Mystery," 152; Nash, *Gospel*, 8–9; and Komoszewski, et al., *Reinventing Jesus*, 227–28, refer to this distinction as strong (genetic) and weak (adaptation) dependence.

[11] Clement, *Protrepticus* 12.119.1, cited in Rahner, "Christian Mystery," 146. Much has been made about Justin Martyr's defense of the virgin birth of Jesus by referencing the belief in the virgin birth of Perseus. However, the "adaptation" concept of dependence accounts for what Justin is doing here. He is not affirming Perseus's virgin birth but just using this widespread belief to communicate his message.

[12] Bruce M. Metzger, "Methodology in the Study of the Mystery Religions and Early Christianity," *Historical and Literary Studies: Pagan, Jewish, and Christian* (Grand Rapids: Eerdmans, 1968), 4. Every student interested in this topic should read Metzger's and Rahner's essays.

influenced the selection of December 25 as the celebration of the birth of Christ, but this date was not widely observed until the fourth century.[13] We do not deny such late influences. What is missing, though, is evidence to suggest that any pagan religion influenced basic Christian teaching or the Gospel accounts of Jesus written in the first century. There are two reasons for this. First, there is no evidence of pagan mystery religions existing in Palestine in the first century.[14] Second, Judaism was an extremely exclusive monotheistic religion and would not have tolerated the syncretism of the mystery religions. Christianity was even more exclusivistic and has often been referred to as the "anti-mystery" religion.[15]

A third point has to do with the overall fallacy behind these arguments: *post hoc, ergo propter hoc*—a form of the fallacy of the false cause. It is committed when a causal connection is drawn between two events or ideas without adequate evidence of such a connection. While *Zeitgeist* is full of individual examples of *post hoc* fallacies,[16] my point

---

[13] *Zeitgeist* makes the point of claiming that all of the pagan gods were born on December 25. Of course, this is moot when it comes to Jesus, as the New Testament makes no mention of the date of his birth. Acharya S is aware of this response and states:

"Nevertheless it has been argued that this comparison is erroneous because Jesus Christ was *not* born on December 25th, an assertion in itself that would come as a surprise to many, since up until just a few years ago only a miniscule percentage of people knew such a fact. In any event, this argument constitutes a logical fallacy, because over the centuries since the holiday was implemented by Christian authorities, *hundreds of millions of people* have celebrated Jesus' birthday on December 25th, or *Christmas*, so named after *Christ*. Moreover, hundreds of millions continue to celebrate the 25th of December as the birth of Jesus Christ, completely oblivious to the notion that this date does not represent the 'real' birthday of the Jewish son of God" (Acharya S, *Companion*, 24, emphasis hers).

I am not sure how this strengthens the parallel or where the "logical fallacy" is. Just because Christians have celebrated the birth of Jesus on December 25 has nothing to do with the origin of the belief and, hence, the parallel.

[14] According to Metzger, "Unlike other countries bordering the Mediterranean Sea, Palestine has been extremely barren in yielding archaeological remains of the paraphernalia and places of worship connected with Mysteries" (Metzger, "Methodology," 8). He cites one second-century source that contains a detailed list of places where Isis was worshipped: 67 in Egypt and 55 outside Egypt, only one of which is in Palestine—namely, Strato's Tower in Caesarea, which was built by the wicked king Herod.

[15] "In the matter of intolerance Christianity differed from all pagan religions, and surpassed Judaism; in that respect it stood in direct opposition to the spirit of that age. . . . It frowned upon the hospitality of the competing cults. The rites of pagans were in her eyes performed to devils; pagan worship was founded by demons and maintained in the interest of demons." Samuel Angus, *The Mystery Religions: A Study in the Early Religious Background of Early Christianity* (New York: Dover Publications, 1975 [1928]), 279.

[16] To offer just one example: "The Virgin Mary is the constellation Virgo, also known as

is that the entire argument based on parallels is one flagrant *post hoc* fallacy. For even if it is true that these parallels between pagan religions and Christianity exist, that fact alone does not constitute evidence that Christianity was influenced or based on these pagan mystery religions. While one might speculate and assert a causal connection, speculation and assertion are not evidence of a causal connection between the two.[17] Correlation does not entail causation.

Finally, *Zeitgeist* makes clear that its producers believe the entire story of Jesus is fictional: "Once the evidence is weighed, there are very high odds that the figure known as Jesus, did not even exist. . . . The reality is, Jesus was the Solar Deity of the Gnostic Christian sect, and like all other Pagan gods, he was a mythical figure."[18] The nonexistence of Jesus is essential to the theory behind the *Zeitgeist* movie, for it wants to argue that every major aspect in the life of Jesus—his birth, teachings, baptism, followers, miracles, crucifixion, and resurrection—is based not on real historical events but on previous pagan religious myths that were around long before the time of Jesus. Before one can reasonably make that case, however, one must address something more basic: There are a massive number of New Testament critical historical scholars, holding a wide range of theological perspectives, still confidently affirming the historicity of Jesus. The film simply ignores this scholarship. It is outside the scope of this article to present such evidence, but it can be categorically stated that, while there are certainly widely divergent views

---

Virgo the Virgin. Virgo in Latin means virgin. The ancient glyph for Virgo is the altered 'm.' This is why Mary along with other virgin mothers, such as Adonis's mother Myrrha or Buddha's mother Maya, begin [sic] with an M" (*Zeitgeist* transcript).

The film is suggesting a causal connection between the astrological symbol for the constellation Virgo and the names of the mothers of pagan gods as if the symbol is the cause of the names. However, there is no evidence for such a connection.

[17] In the *Companion to Zeitgeist: Part 1,* Acharya S offers this as an explanation for the parallels:

"In essence, when studying this situation, the scenario that reveals itself is that the creators of the gospel story in large part appear to have been scouring the vast Library of Alexandria in Egypt and elsewhere, such as Antioch and Rome, and picking out various attributes of the pre-Christian religion to be used in their creation of a cohesive Christian mythical tale that was later fallaciously set into history and presented to the gullible masses as a 'true story'" (*Companion*, 16).

No evidence is offered for this charge of calculated and intentional deception on the part of the early church, and the inherent implausibility of the stipulated scenario strains the credulity of the most gullible indeed.

[18] *Zeitgeist* transcript.

concerning certain specific events in the life of Jesus, the vast majority of critical scholars acknowledge the existence of the historical Jesus and most of the major aspects of His life in some form.[19] The historical evidence for Jesus is a major argument against the whole theory behind *Zeitgeist*.[20]

Zeitgeist Fallacies

Space constraints preclude a discussion of all but a few of the many specific fallacies *Zeitgeist* commits. One of the most blatant is the *terminology fallacy*. That is, events in the lives of the mythical gods, for example, are expressed using Christian terminology in order subtly to manipulate viewers into accepting that the same events in the life of Jesus also happened in the lives of mythical gods. We are told, for instance, that Horus, Krishna, Dionysius, and others were "baptized," "born of a virgin," "crucified," and "resurrected"—just to mention a few. Examples of such locutions, however, involve assertions with no evidence, are ripped out of their Christian context, or are obtained from post-first-century sources. Nash observes: "One frequently encounters scholars who first use Christian terminology to describe pagan beliefs and practices and then marvel at the awesome parallels that they think they have discovered."[21] A few examples will suffice.

It is claimed that Horus was "born of the virgin Isis-Meri."[22] In the most common version of the Osiris-Isis-Horus myth, Osiris has been

---

[19] John Dominic Crossan, certainly no conservative scholar, comments on the crucifixion of Jesus: "That he was crucified is sure as anything historical can ever be." John Dominic Crossan, *Jesus: A Revolutionary Biography* (San Francisco: HarperCollins), 145.

[20] Among the plethora of scholars affirming the historicity of Jesus are N. T. Wright, *Jesus and the Victory of God* (Minneapolis: Augsburg/Fortress Press, 1997); E. P. Sanders, *The Historical Person of Jesus* (New York: Penguin, 1996); John P. Meier, *A Marginal Jew: Rethinking the Historical Jesus*, 4 vols., Anchor Bible Reference Library (New York: Doubleday, 1991–2009); Craig Keener, *The Historical Jesus of the Gospels* (Grand Rapids: Eerdmans, 2009). This list barely scratches the surface.

[21] Nash, *Gospel*, 116.

[22] The term "Isis-Meri" is specifically used to associate Isis with Mary the mother of Jesus. Actually the term "meri" is used of almost all of the gods of Egypt, as Acharya S herself admits: "In reality, the epithet meri/mery [meaning 'beloved'] was so commonly used in regards to numerous figures in ancient Egypt, such as gods, kings, priests, government officials and others that we could not list here all the instances in which it appears." So the term has no substantive connection with Isis.

murdered by Set and cut into 14 pieces. Isis, his wife (so we can assume she is not a virgin), retrieves all but one of the pieces and reconstructs Osiris. She cannot find the fourteenth piece (his sexual organ); so she fashions one out of wood and then has sexual relations with him. She later gives birth to Horus. Here are other alleged "virgin births." Attis is conceived when Zeus spilled his seed on the side of a mountain which eventually became a pomegranate tree. Nana, mother of Attis, is sitting under the tree when a pomegranate falls in her lap and she becomes pregnant with the child of Zeus. Devaki, the mother of Krishna, had seven children before Krishna.[23] Dionysius's mother, Semele, was impregnated by Zeus. In fact, none of the mythical gods experienced a "virginal" conception even close to the manner that Scripture claims of Jesus.[24]

What of the claim that these figures were "crucified"? Krishna was shot in the foot with an arrow and died from his wounds. Attis castrated himself in a jealous rage, fled into the wilderness, and died. Depending on which version of the myth one reads, Horus either (1) did not die, (2) was merely stung by a scorpion, or (3) his death is conflated with the death of Osiris.[25] Adonis was gored by a wild boar. Yet, Acharya S justifies the use of the term "crucify" to describe the death of Horus as follows:

> When it is asserted that Horus (or Osiris) was "crucified" it should be kept in mind that it was not part of the Horus/Osiris myth that the murdered god was held down and nailed on a cross, as we perceive the meaning of "crucified" to be, based on the drama we believe allegedly took place during Christ's purported passion. Rather in one myth Osiris is *torn to pieces*

---

[23] I read one online post that claimed: "In the Krishna tale we are not talking about real people but about myths. In the world of mythology, gods and goddesses can have a number of children and still be considered 'chaste' and 'virginal.'" If one can use language so equivocally, I suppose one can claim just about anything.

[24] New Testament scholar Raymond Brown comments, "These 'parallels' consistently involve a type of *hieros gamos* where a divine male, in human or other form, impregnates a woman, either through normal sexual intercourse or through some substitute form of penetration. They are not really similar to the non-sexual virginal conception that is at the core of the infancy narratives, a conception where there is no male deity or element to impregnate." Raymond E. Brown, *The Virginal Conception and Bodily Resurrection of Jesus* (New York: Paulist Press, 2003), 64.

[25] It is common in the development of Egyptian myth to conflate the gods. This is a major way copycats draw many of the parallels with Horus/Osiris.

before being raised from the dead, while Horus is *stung by a scorpion* prior to his resurrection. However, Egyptian deities, including Horus, *were* depicted in cruciform with arms extended or outstretched, as in various images that are comparable to *crucifixes*.[26]

So, according to Murdock, anytime deities are depicted with arms outstretched, we are justified in claiming they were crucified.

A final example is the claim that all of these gods were "resurrected" from the dead. While the idea that the resurrection of Jesus was borrowed from the "dying and rising gods" of the pagan mystery religions was very popular at one time, almost all scholars have abandoned this view today. Jonathan Z. Smith writes:

> All of the deities that have been identified as belonging to the class of dying and rising deities can be subsumed under the two larger classes of disappearing deities or dying deities. In the first case, the deities return but have not died; in the second case, the gods die but do not return. *There is no unambiguous instance in the history of religions of a dying and rising deity.*[27]

The best known example of a resurrection claim is the Horus/Osiris myth, but Osiris did not rise from the dead and return to this world as

---

[26] D. M. Murdock, *Christ in Egypt: The Jesus-Horus Connection* (Seattle: Stellar House, 2009), 335. It is interesting to note that even Murdock states that there are other reasons gods are depicted with arms outstretched: "The god Ptah is the very ancient Father-Creator who in 'suspending the sky' resembles other Egyptian deities such as Isis and Horus with arms outstretched in the vault of heaven, as well as the Greek god Atlas supporting the world on his shoulders" (*Companion*, 32).

[27] Jonathan Z. Smith, "Dying and Rising Gods," in *Encyclopedia of Religion*, ed. Eliade, 1:522 (emphasis mine). Until recently this view was close to unanimous by critical scholars. In 2001, T. N. D. Mettinger published a monograph titled *The Riddle of the Resurrection: Dying and Rising Gods in the Ancient Near East* (Stockholm: Almquist & Wiksell International, 2001); in it he argued that there is some evidence of at least three cases of pre-Christian belief in dying and rising gods (none of whom are those highlighted in *Zeitgeist*). Copycat supporters have made much of Mettinger's book, but (1) his evidence is largely circumstantial; (2) he is the only scholar who supports the view (a point he concedes); and (3) he does not believe such ancient belief led to the early church's proclamation of Jesus' resurrection. He writes, "There is, as far as I am aware, no *prima facie* evidence that the death and resurrection of Jesus is a mythological construct, drawing on the myths and rites of the dying and rising gods of the surrounding world. While studied with profit against the background of Jewish resurrection belief, the faith in the death and resurrection of Jesus retains its unique character in the history of religions" (Mettinger, *Riddle*, 221).

did Jesus. Instead, he was made king of the underworld.[28] After his death, Attis eventually turns into a pine tree. Many sources claiming resurrections were written long after the first-century sources for Christianity and therefore could not have influenced the Gospel accounts or Paul's teaching in letters such as 1 Corinthians. A second-century source tells us of the resurrection of Adonis. Claims of Krishna's resurrection do not emerge until the sixth or seventh century.[29] Older tradition holds he simply entered the spirit world where he is always present. This is not a resurrection in the manner in which the Gospels claim Jesus rose from the dead.

A second fallacy is the *nonbiblical fallacy*. This is where a parallel is claimed about some aspect of Jesus that is not even reported in the Gospel accounts. One example is where *Zeitgeist* claims a parallel between the three stars in the belt of Orion called the "three kings" and the three kings who visited the baby Jesus. The problem is that the Gospels never call them kings and never state how many there are.[30] Another example, mentioned above, is the oft-claimed parallel of the birth date of all these deities, December 25, with the birth date of Christ.

A third fallacy is the *chronological fallacy*. In order for the copycat charge of borrowing to succeed, one needs to provide evidence that the parallel preceded the writing of the Gospel accounts and the letters of Paul—all written in the first century. However, this simply is not the case. First, as mentioned above, there is no evidence that there was any pagan mystery influence in first-century Palestine.[31] Second, the

---

[28] "Whether this can be rightly called a resurrection is questionable, especially since, according to Plutarch, it was the pious desire of devotees to be buried in the same ground where, according to local tradition, the body of Osiris was still lying" (Metzger, "Methodology," 21).

[29] A number of scholars point to evidence that these late sources may actually have borrowed from Christianity rather than the other way around. Rahner comments, "As modern scholars have become more objective in this field, they have turned with increasing interest to another aspect, namely the possible influence of Christianity on the Greek mysteries" (Rahner, "Christian Mystery," 176). See also Metzger, "Methodology," 11; Nash, *Gospel*, 187; and Komoszewski, et al., *Reinventing Jesus*, 232–33.

[30] In fact, the film states that the three stars have been called the "three kings" from ancient times but offers no ancient text naming them so. It could very well be that they received this nickname from the Christian nonbiblical tradition of the three kings and not the other way around.

[31] "There is no evidence whatever, that I know of, that the mystery religions had any influence in Palestine in the early decades of the first century"; Norman Anderson, *Christianity and World Religions* (Downers Grove, IL: InterVarsity, 1984), 53–54.

mystery religions evolved over time, and as they did, their beliefs and narratives changed. This results in several versions of the various pagan myths. Most of the evidence we have of their narratives comes from sources dated in the second and third centuries, a time when they were experiencing the peak of their influence in the Mediterranean world. We have little evidence of the beliefs of these religions from the first century. Nash comments:

> Far too many writers on the subject use the available sources to form the plausible reconstructions of the third-century mystery experience and then uncritically reason back to what they think must have been the earlier nature of the cults. We have plenty of information about the mystery religions of the third century. But important differences exist between these religions and earlier expressions of the mystery experience (for which adequate information is extremely slim).[32]

A fourth fallacy closely connected with this last one is the *source fallacy*. One of the comments often made in praise of *Zeitgeist* is how well the claims are documented. It is true that, in the transcript of the movie, many of the claims are documented; some by multiple sources. The brief section quoted above has 44 citations from 11 different sources to support its claims. At first glance this may seem impressive. As scholars will insist, however, it is not the number of sources that matter but their quality—and the quality of these sources is highly questionable. Not one of them is a primary source of the religion under discussion. They are all secondary, and most of them are the older, discredited sources that have been abandoned by most critical scholars. These sources often make undocumented assertions, speculate on causal relationships, and offer selective interpretations of some texts (of which there is much unrevealed disagreement). Often the authors are not experts in the field of religion, or they are experts in a related field (such as Egyptology), neither of which is a qualification over which to drape a cloak of scholarship. What inevitably results is rabid and unprincipled speculation on the origin of Christianity.

---

[32] Nash, *Gospel*, 116.

One reason why primary sources are not relevant is that they are not as conclusive as copycat theorists would lead one to believe. Because these ancient religions evolved over time, often no one authoritative story exists to which one may appeal. For example, the story of Horus in *Zeitgeist* is pieced together from a number of sources, some of which conflict. It is like playing "connect the dots," but interpreting how to connect those dots is a slippery, unscholarly enterprise. These writers seem to use the life of Jesus as a guide for how to connect the dots for the life of Horus and then proclaim that the story of Jesus is based on Horus—when actually it is the other way around! Other religions don't fare much better. For example, there is no text for Mithraism; everything we know about the religion comes either from interpreting reliefs and statues or from brief comments by other ancient writers, almost all of whom are post-first century. Metzger comments, "It goes without saying that alleged parallels which are discovered by pursuing such methodology evaporate when they are confronted with the original texts. In a word, one must beware of what have been called 'parallels made plausible by selective description.'"[33]

The final fallacy to mention is the *difference fallacy*, which is committed by an overemphasis on (supposed) similarities between two things while ignoring the vast and relevant differences between them. Again, Metzger observes, "In arriving at a just estimate of the relation of the Mysteries to Christianity as reflected in the New Testament, attention must be given to their differences as well as resemblances."[34] The differences between Christianity and the pagan religions are enormous, and yet *Zeitgeist* ignores them.

Here are a few examples. First, whereas all of the mystery religions are tied into the vegetative cycle of birth-death-rebirth and continue to follow this cycle year after year *ad infinitum*, Christianity is linear, viewing all of history as headed on a trajectory culminating in God's transforming this world into a renewed creation—the new heaven and new earth. Second, mystery religions are secretive. One has to go through secret initiation rites to become a member. They are full of secret knowledge, available only to some, which is one reason we don't know a lot

---

[33] Metzger, "Methodology," 9.
[34] Ibid., 12.

about them. By contrast, Christianity is open to all to scrutinize and to embrace. It is a "mystery of revelation."[35] Third, doctrine and beliefs are totally unimportant in pagan mystery religions. In fact, a characteristic hallmark is their syncretism: you can hold almost any belief and still become a member of their religion. They emphasize feeling and experience over doctrine and belief.[36] In diametric contrast, doctrine and beliefs are the heart and soul of Christianity, which is highly exclusivistic. That is one of the major reasons Christians were so persecuted in the Roman Empire. They held that there was only one way to God. Fourth, the pagan mystery religions are almost completely void of almost any ethical element. Rahner comments:

> At no stage [of their development] do the mysteries bear comparison with the ethical commandments of the new Testaments and their realization in early Christianity. The two terms are truly incommensurable—and this is not the foregone conclusion of apologists but results from an unbiased examination of the sources by scholars who cannot be accused of denominational commitment.[37]

Fifth, even if one accepts the "dying and rising gods" concept, the meaning of the death of Christ is completely different. Christ died for the sins of mankind; none of the pagan gods died for someone else. Pagan gods died under compulsion, but Jesus died willingly. Jesus died and was raised once; the pagan gods die cyclically. Jesus' death was not tragic or a defeat; it was a victory. Pagans mourn and lament the death of their gods.[38] Finally, and most importantly, the view of the church from the very beginning is that Jesus was a real person who lived in history. His death and resurrection were actual events of history. Metzger states, "Unlike the deities of the Mysteries, who were nebulous figures of an imaginary past, the Divine being whom the Christian worshipped as Lord was known as a real Person on earth only a short time before

---

[35] Rahner, "Christian Mystery," 167.

[36] "They are a religion of feeling. They do not address themselves to the perplexed intellect of man, they are no 'doctrine' or 'dogma,' and the cult legend with its thousands of variations has no bearing upon religious action." Ibid., 159.

[37] Ibid., 169.

[38] See Nash, *Gospel*, 160–61, for a further development of the contrasts.

the earliest documents of the New Testament were written."[39] It is the historicity of Jesus' life, death, and resurrection that makes Christianity the true anti-mystery.

Conclusion

Imagine we are 2,000 years in the future. Through some sort of cataclysmic event only a handful of documents of the history of the United States are available, and these are just fragments. After sifting through these fragments, a small group of historical enthusiasts come to a radical conclusion: The myth of President John F. Kennedy is based on the earlier myth of Abraham Lincoln. Their reason for such a conclusion: "Just look at all the parallels!"

- Lincoln was elected to Congress in 1846; Kennedy was elected to Congress in 1946.
- Lincoln was elected president in 1860; Kennedy was elected President in 1960.
- "Lincoln" and "Kennedy" each have seven letters in their names.
- Lincoln had a secretary named Kennedy; Kennedy had a secretary named Lincoln.[40]
- Both married, in their thirties, a 24-year-old socially prominent girl who could speak fluent French.
- Both presidents dealt with civil rights movements for African-Americans.
- Both presidents were assassinated on a Friday, in the back of the head, before a major holiday, while sitting next to their wives.
- Both their assassins were known by three names consisting of 15 letters (John Wilkes Booth, Lee Harvey Oswald).

---

[39] Metzger, "Methodology," 13. He then quotes Plutarch, "Whenever you hear the traditional tales which the Egyptians tell about the gods, their wanderings, dismemberments, and many experiences of this sort, . . . you must not think any of these tales actually happened in the manner in which they are related" (Plutarch, *De Isede at Osiride*, trans. Frank Cole Babbitt, Loeb Classical Library [Cambridge, MA: Harvard University Press, 1936], 11).

[40] While this is often asserted, there is absolutely no evidence that Lincoln had a secretary named "Kennedy."

- Oswald shot Kennedy from a warehouse and was captured in a theater; Booth shot Lincoln in a theater and was captured in a warehouse.[41]

- Both assassins were shot and killed with a Colt revolver days after they assassinated the president and before they could be brought to trial.

- Both presidents were succeeded by vice presidents named Johnson, from the South, born in 1808 and 1908 respectively.[42]

This example shows that insignificant, spurious, false, and misleading parallels can be used to argue just about anything.

When one considers the fallacies that permeate the "parallelomania" of *Zeitgeist*, one is left agreeing with Rahner: "It is and remains a riddle how in the period of unrestricted 'comparative religion' scholars should even have ventured a comparison, not to speak of trying to derive the basic doctrines of Christ from the mystery religions."[43] But it is Adolf von Harnack, writing in 1911, who deserves the last word here:

> We must reject the comparative mythology which finds a causal connection between everything and everything else, which tears down solid barriers, bridges chasms as though it were child's play, and spins combinations from superficial similarities. . . . By such methods one can turn Christ into a sun god in the twinkling of an eye, or transform the Apostles into the twelve months; in connection with Christ's nativity one can bring up the legends attending the birth of every conceivable god or one can catch all sorts of mythological doves to keep company with the baptismal dove; and find any number of celebrated asses to follow the ass on which Jesus rode into Jerusalem; and thus with the magic wand of "comparative religion," triumphantly eliminate every spontaneous trait in any religion.[44]

---

[41] Well, not really. Booth was actually captured in a barn. "But it's kind of a warehouse."

[42] These parallels are available from a number of sources and have become part of our American folklore even though they prove absolutely nothing.

[43] Rahner, "Christian Mystery," 168.

[44] Translated by and cited in Rahner, "Christian Mystery," 153. From Adolf von Harnack, *Wissenschaft und Leben* (Giessen, Germany: Töplemann, 1911) 2:191.

Part 4

ANCIENT ISRAEL AND OTHER RELIGIONS

Chapter 12

DID YAHWEH HAVE A WIFE?
Iron Age Religion in Israel and Its Neighbors
Richard S. Hess

Importance of the Study of Israelite Religion

The study of Israelite religion has enjoyed a renaissance in the past generation.[1] Several factors have contributed to this development. Following the so-called end of the biblical theology movement around the middle of the twentieth century, scholars became dissatisfied with traditional approaches to Old Testament theology and disenchanted with the pursuit of a single unifying theological principle. They reacted by identifying a plurality of theologies with contradictory approaches and interpretations somehow grouped together within the collection of literature known as the Hebrew Bible.

This approach meant that there would be a radical disjunction between an idealized and late final edition of the Old Testament and the recoverable earlier multiplicity of parties and contentious views regarding worship and religious beliefs. From such a milieu, Israelite religion strengthened itself as a discipline independent of Old Testament theology. Those who studied it sought a path between the Scylla of a "flattened out" Old Testament with no acknowledgment of its multiple

[1] For more details see my book-length study, *Israelite Religions: An Archaeological and Biblical Survey* (Grand Rapids: Baker, 2007).

voices and the Charybdis of an agnosticism that could not know anything about the history of early Israel and its religion.

Thus the study of this subject turned away from a fundamentally literary task aimed at distilling the principal teachings of the Old Testament
for faith, and life, and, especially in Christian contexts, for a connection
with the New Testament and Jesus Christ. In place of this, it focused
on the growing body of textual and archaeological evidence addressing
the subject of ancient Israel's life. This result is the second factor contributing to general interest in the religion of Israel. The analysis of cult
centers and burials in Palestine emerged with the astonishingly intensive
archaeological explorations and excavations of the region throughout
the past century. Such cult centers, whether mere assemblages of cultic
materials and altars or larger architectural structures, led to questions as
to how they relate to the inhabitants of the land, and especially to Israel.
The same was true of the burials where complements of eating utensils
and cultic paraphernalia raised questions about a cult of the dead.

With an increasing accumulation of data there also emerged refined
methods for the investigation and typological classification of these two
phenomena. Hand in hand with the material cultural there appeared
significant new inscriptional evidence. While written texts continue to
be studied and published from all periods, there is no question but the
evidence from ancient Palestine and its immediate neighbors has created
the greatest interest.

Above all, those ninth-eighth-century inscriptions from the northern Sinai site of Kuntillet 'Ajrud, commonly understood as mentioning
"Yahweh and his Asherah," have provided what is arguably the major
catalyst for a revolution in the understanding of the beliefs of Israelites
during the monarchy. The inscriptions that mention this blessing, while
not limited to the Sinai caravansary or cult center (which one it was
depends on one's interpretation of the architecture and location), provide the centerpiece for discussion of the role of a goddess or cult symbol and its relationship to Yahweh. It is, in fact, no longer possible to
accept a simple division between those who worshipped Yahweh as a
single and unique deity, on the one hand, and those who served Baal
and a pantheon of deities, on the other. Yahweh has now become a
member of the pantheon of Iron Age Palestine.

A third and final factor in the emergence of the study of Israelite religion has been the methodological and cultural impact of a cluster of philosophies and worldviews that may be grouped under the general term of postmodernism. Its wide-scale rejection of traditional authoritarian forms and its acceptance of particular types of pluralism have driven the discipline and its interpretation of the extrabiblical evidence in a specific direction. Thus scholars of Israelite religion in the past generation have directed their research away from assumptions of a single authoritarian faith with a single deity.

Instead, more inviting and inherently more probable from this perspective is the presence of multiple religions standing side by side in ancient Israel. These beliefs remained continually in a state of flux and transformation as they were affected by political, economic, and cultural forces from outside and from within the society. Far from an aberration in a dominant Yahwistic society, the "Yahweh and (his) Asherah" material at Kuntillet 'Ajrud and Khirbet el-Qom represent the majority perspective of ancient Israel. There is a prevalence of multiple deities. Therefore, the Hebrew Scriptures must be penetrated behind the Deuteronomist and priestly redactors to find evidence of this religious pluralism.

How then should the question of the influence of postmodernism and prevailing philosophies on the study of Israelite religion be considered? Some have sought to examine it directly in terms of the philosophical rationale itself. That task, however essential it might be, lies beyond the scope of this study. Others would emphasize again the role of biblical theology as a legitimate enterprise. This too holds much promise but is not the direction of the present chapter.

Rather, this study proposes to reexamine the extrabiblical evidence for the religions of the southern Levant in the Iron Age and to locate features that might be distinctive in terms of the religions of Israelites and Judeans. If it succeeds at all, it will at best serve as an initial body of data that can be used for the study of Israelite religion. It will not directly answer the more profound questions of the influence of philosophies on the current models, but will rather address that which remains anomalous on the landscape of ancient religion and that which may best be interpreted by reaching beyond the context of ancient Near Eastern history and culture.

Definitions

Up to this point I have begged the question as to the definition of my terms, particularly "religion." As this has been largely a review of current trends, it has not been necessary to identify this term. However, the selection of evidence that will proceed from here must consider this basic question. And it must be considered in the light of archaeology and epigraphy, not merely as an abstract theological construct. Philosopher Paul Griffiths defines *religion* along these lines: "a form of life that seems to those who inhabit it to be comprehensive, incapable of abandonment, and of central importance."[2] In other words, religion is no mere add-on but is a comprehensive, identity-shaping worldview and way of life. *Webster's New Collegiate Dictionary* (7th edition) provides for us a heuristic definition of *religion*: "the service and worship of the divine or supernatural through a system of attitudes, beliefs, and practices."

The limitations of the present study require that it be selective. Further, this chapter will seek to avoid, as much as possible, the influence of the Bible and of the diverse and contradictory assumptions used in the evaluation of the biblical sources. It will do this by largely bracketing these biblical sources out of consideration. Of course, any successful synthesis of the religion and history of ancient Israel must deal with those sources.

The decision to set this material aside is a provisional one, designed to allow a separate evaluation of the extrabiblical material before adding on the biblical element with its own history of interpretive issues and critical methods. It is methodologically indefensible in terms of any final statement on Israelite religion that must take into account all the evidence. However, it is possible because the nature of the contemporary extrabiblical evidence remains separate from the Bible. Further, this

---

[2] Paul J. Griffiths, *Problems of Religious Diversity* (Oxford: Blackwell, 2001), 7; see also 2–12.

may permit a fresh evaluation of these important sources without using them to secure assumptions about the history of the biblical sources.[3]

In addition to a definition of religion, it is also appropriate to consider the significance of the "Israelite" in Israelite religion. Spatial and temporal parameters form the strictures here. The spatial position for ancient Israel must place it in the highlands of Canaan to the west and perhaps east of the Jordan River. Near the beginning of the Iron Age, in the last decade of the thirteenth century, the victory stele of Pharaoh Merneptah records Israel as a people group alongside a list of three fortified cities: Ashkelon, Gezer, and Yanoam. Assuming a location of Yanoam to the east of Pella in modern north Jordan and a geographical proximity for all four named entities, then Israel's location could be somewhere in Palestine or immediately east of the Jordan River.

Because Israel is not previously mentioned in Egyptian records until one of the last pharaohs of the era to wage war in Asia, it is reasonable to assume that Israel may be a new group on the scene of western Asia. This, combined with the sudden appearance of more than 300 village sites at the beginning of the twelfth century in the highlands of Palestine, provides a positive correlation for the identification of Israel with some or most of these settlements in highland Canaan, west of the Jordan River. A distinctive cultural connection between these settlements and those Iron Age I settlements to the east of the Jordan River and Dead Sea suggest Israel's habitation of this region. The dramatic demographic shift of the highlands settlement pattern, joined with the initial appearance of the name Israel in the final decades of Egypt's New Kingdom presence in Canaan, suggest a significant historical marker at c. 1200 BC.

The question of ethnicity cannot be answered here. The definition of Israel in Iron Age I will remain a geographical one, rather than an ethnic one. This is because it is difficult to determine an ethnic difference between the Israelites of the highlands of Palestine and those other groups (Canaanites, Amorites, etc.) that may have inhabited the

---

[3] For this reason there will be no discussion of the two distinctive characteristics that Mark S. Smith finds in Israelite religion that have no antecedent or comparison in Canaanite religion: Yahweh's southern sanctuary in Sinai (or other mountains) and the exodus tradition from Egypt. See his *The Early History of God: Yahweh and the Other Deities in Ancient Israel,* 2nd ed. (Grand Rapids: Eerdmans, 2003), 25.

same region.[4] Thus it remains true that without the biblical evidence these highland and Transjordanian cultures cannot be further defined as Israelite, Canaanite, or whatever. However, despite evidence for cultural continuity with the preceding Late Bronze Age and an awareness of a mixture of people groups in this region, religious distinctives may yet emerge. Their connection with later, more clearly defined territories of Israel and Judah may assist in identifying that which was Israelite even in Iron Age I.

At the other end of the period, the invasions of the Babylonian army led by Nebuchadnezzar culminate in the events of 587 and 586. Of particular interest for this study is the period before the latter part of the seventh century. After this there is more general agreement as to the emergence of a distinctive monotheistic belief fostered by Josiah and his allies.

By this time the spatial coordinates of Israel, including both the earlier northern kingdom of Israel as well as the southern kingdom of Judah, have been recognized textually in the Moabite, Aramean, and Assyrian accounts of battles and conquest in this area. They may be positioned as far north as Dan and as far south as the area west of the Dead Sea. Their eastern borders at times reach beyond the Jordan River into territories disputed with Moab and Ammon. The western borders tend to be defined by the strength of lowland rivals such as Philistia and its cities, as well as city-states such as Dor, Acco, and even Tyre when it extends its influence southward.

Distinctive Elements of Israelite Religion

Within this context it is appropriate to consider whether Israelite religion possesses any distinctives when compared with its neighbors. In

---

[4] Cf. Judg 2:9–12 and Elizabeth Bloch-Smith, "Israelite Ethnicity in Iron I: Archaeology Preserves What Is Remembered and What Is Forgotten in Israel's History," *Journal of Biblical Literature* 122 (2003): 401–25. Bloch-Smith's attempt to identify cultural distinctives to Israelites in relation to the Philistines uses boundary distinctions in a method not unlike that applied here. Among the many discussions of ethnicity and ancient people groups, see Steven Grosby, *Biblical Ideas of Nationality: Ancient and Modern* (Winona Lake, IN: Eisenbrauns, 2002), 13–68. He does not identify a nation (national identity) to Israel before the United Monarchy. Alternatively, see William G. Dever, *What Did the Biblical Writers Know and When Did They Know It? What Archaeology Can Tell Us about the Reality of Ancient Israel* (Grand Rapids: Eerdmans, 2001), for an attempt to identify specific cultural forms that distinguish the Canaanites from Israelites in the Iron Age I.

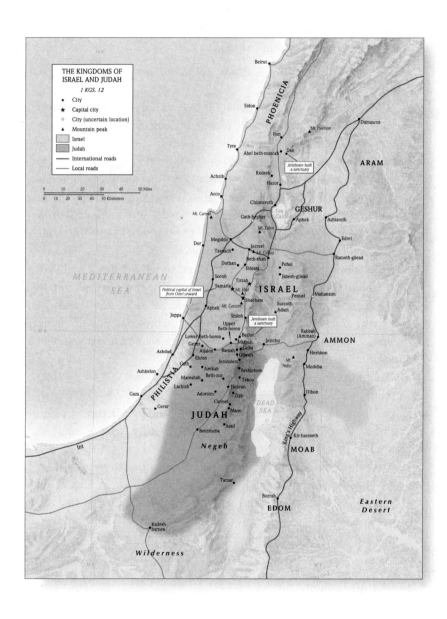

THE KINGDOMS OF
ISRAEL AND JUDAH
1 KGS. 12

- ● City
- ★ Capital city
- ○ City (uncertain location)
- ▲ Mountain peak
- ▢ Israel
- ▢ Judah
- —— International roads
- —— Local roads

order to do this, four areas of extrabiblical evidence will be summarized in terms of their major distinctive elements: cult centers and burials, iconography, epigraphy, and onomastics.

Cult Centers and Burials

The Iron Age I period (1200–1000 BC) includes the emergence of several hundred villages in the highlands of Palestine and the areas east of the Jordan during the first part of the twelfth century. At least some of the inhabitants of these villages may be identified as recently settled Israel, as suggested above. The unusual aspect of these villages, in terms of religion, is their minimalization of objects related to worship.

Using the traditional means to identify cult centers, the early Iron Age cult sites are virtually free of any of the expected objects or architecture that customarily identify religious centers. There are almost no figurines, nor are there any distinctive altars or temple/shrine architecture. Unlike the large fortress temple at Shechem, for example, village sites at Dan, Ai, Khirbet Raddana, Tell Irbid, Tell es-Sa'idiyeh, and Tell el-'Umeiri contained evidence of cultic structures that stood among domestic structures. One finds at these sites an occasional standing stone, offering bench, or distinctive vessel.[5]

This is in contrast with the evidence from occupied sites of the same hill country region in the preceding Late Bronze Age (1550–1200 BC). Thus Alpert Nakhai identifies six sites west of the Jordan and four sites east of the Jordan that are within the region of early Israel or immediately adjacent to it where excavations have revealed distinctive architecture or cultic objects indicating material elements that suggest religious activities.[6] These sites are also often characterized as larger population centers, whereas those highland settlements of the Iron Age I period were villages.

---

[5] Beth Alpert Nakhai, *Archaeology and the Religions of Canaan and Israel* (Boston: Americans Schools of Oriental Research, 2001), 170–76. Villages at Hazor and Megiddo contained more elaborate remains, but these may have included forms from the Bronze Age. Tel Qiri, located near the ancient sacred area of Mt. Carmel and close to the Canaanite passes into the Megiddo Plain, contains materials that may reflect its situation close by important international trade routes.

[6] Ibid., 120, 136–52, lists Beth Shean, Shechem, Aphek, Shiloh, Gezer, and Jerusalem west of the Jordan; and Pella, Tell Abu al-Kharaz, Tell Deir Alla, and Tel Safut east of the river.

The finds at these village sites have revealed little or no distinctions in terms of any specialized architectural constructions or any prestige objects such as jewelry or cult items. The people of this society simply did not manufacture or use the same sorts of objects for worship as the evidence of their settled predecessors suggests. While some sites such as Shechem and Shiloh continue to exhibit special cultic buildings and objects into the Iron Age I, others such as Tell el-'Umeiri developed defenses with cultic installations. However, the highland villages of Iron Age I did not follow this pattern.

There remain two exceptions to this generalization: the Bull site east of Dothan and the anomalous structure on Mt. Ebal. The former, the Bull site, includes an oval-shaped open sanctuary marked by a ring of stones. One stone that may be a standing stone (or *mazzebah*) was found inside, as well as a figurine of a bull. This latter image resembles those of bulls from north of Israel. A similar one appears at Bronze Age Hazor and represents a southern extension of northern cultural and religious activities.

Although this site occurs within the area of the early Iron Age villages in the hill country, it appears to be unique. The small size of the cultic site and the immediately surrounding area do not support a view that this was a center for many worshippers. Rather, it appears to have been local to the village or villages near which it was found. Further, given the comparisons already noted, there remains nothing distinctive about this site. Finally, there is a question about the dating, so that some would reassign it to the Middle Bronze Age.[7]

The same cannot be said of the Mt. Ebal site. Mt. Ebal is the highest mountain in Samaria. Mt. Gerazim, its counterpart situated immediately to the south, is slightly smaller. They form the sides of the valley of Shechem that lies between them. Adam Zertal led the Israeli survey of this region. On Mt. Ebal he found nothing from the Bronze or Iron Ages I and II, except for this installation.

The site occurs some feet away from the ridge that forms the third highest peak on the mountain. It is surrounded by a stone wall.[8] Two

---

[7] Israel Finkelstein, "Two Notes on Northern Samaria: The 'Einun Pottery and the Date of the Bull Site," *Palestine Exploration Quarterly* 130 (1998): 94–98.

[8] The outer enclosure wall encompasses some 14,380 square meters. No building was found in the outer court. There is an inner enclosure wall, encompassing some 3,850 square meters of the higher northern side of the area. There are three steps at the entrance to this part.

levels were found. The earlier is dated by two Egyptian scarabs (small replicas of dung beetles) to the second half of the thirteenth century BC.[9] The site opens up on an area that would make it possible for many people to gather and view it.

Excavations revealed a central complex, a low western wall with an entrance, and an outer enclosure wall. In the central complex were found two layers of ash with some 2,800 bones, representing a variety of animals.[10] West of the altar were two areas identified as courtyards. The major concentration of animal bones was found at the central structure. The upper, later layer is mainly that of cattle bones. The bones are burnt and have cut marks. In contrast with lowland sites from the same time period, where analysis revealed bones of dogs and donkeys, there are none here. Bones of gazelles and pigs were found elsewhere, especially Philistia, but not here. Horwitz suggests we have here "a pastoral economy based primarily on caprovine [i.e., sheep and goat] herding and to a lesser extent cattle."[11] The area seems not to have been a food-producing place. No sickle blades were found similar to those in contemporary domestic sites.

The earlier thirteenth-century level included a round installation with ashes and bones found at the center of the twelfth-century structure, in addition to a fill of earth and stones. At the east side of the altar was found a chalice of volcanic stone. At about 1200 BC, with no indication of a violent disruption or break, apparently the same people built the larger structure that the excavator identified as an altar. This level of occupation lasted for about 50 years, according to ceramic evidence, and then it was abandoned without any indication of what happened. No figurines were found. The north courtyard contains what may be a "ramp" going up to center of the stone structure. Zertal identified a veranda around the top.[12]

---

[9] James Weinstein, "Exodus and Archaeological Reality," in *Exodus: The Egyptian Evidence*, ed. Ernest S. Frerichs and Leonard H. Lesko (Winona Lake, IN: Eisenbrauns, 1997), 88–89, argues that this is insufficient evidence to date this structure. He prefers a twelfth-century date but does not explain why.

[10] The bones included sheep, goats, cattle, and fallow deer predominantly, but also hedgehogs, doe, porcupine, and lizards in much smaller quantities.

[11] Liora Kolska Horwitz, "Faunal Remains from the Early Iron Age Site on Mount Ebal," *Tel Aviv* 13–14 (1986–87): 173–89.

[12] Ziony Zevit, *The Religions of Ancient Israel: A Synthesis of Parallactic Approaches* (London

Although the dominant pottery type changed somewhat between the two occupation levels and although there are three times as much pottery in the later phase, the material culture does not otherwise appear different. The excavator found that 20 percent of the pottery is distinct to the northern hill country area. It appears at the beginning of the thirteenth century BC and disappears at the end of the twelfth century BC. It occurs in Transjordan at sites such as Deir Alla.[13]

The excavator has suggested an identification of this altar with the Israelites, specifically with the altar of Joshua in Josh 8:30–35 and chap. 24. This interpretation has been disputed.[14] Perhaps, after all, this is merely an early farmhouse and agricultural installation.[15] Or perhaps it is a watchtower. Zertal disagrees.

The rough stones for the "altar," the area capable of handling a large public gathering, the animal bones found in the area, the lack of any sizeable wall for defense, and the position of the structure away from the peak of the ridge itself (where it would be if it were a watchtower) may suggest a cultic installation. Of course, that is not the same thing as saying it is the altar of Joshua. Nor does it seem to be an altar at all. There is no evidence of the sorts of things usually found at altars: cult figurines,

---

and New York: Continuum, 2001), 303, considers this a *yesod* as was required for certain blood sacrifices. Was it used to sprinkle blood on the four corners of the altar?

[13] Zertal argues that the Transjordanian pottery appears earlier and thus represents an east-to-west movement of the pottery. Adam Zertal, "Israel Enters Canaan—Following the Pottery Trail," *Biblical Archaeology Review* 17/5 (1991), 32–34; *idem, The Manasseh Hill Country Survey: The Eastern Valleys and the Fringes of the Desert* (Tel Aviv: University of Haifa and Ministry of Defense, 1996); *idem,* "The Iron Age I Culture in the Hill Country of Canaan—A Manassite Perspective," in *Mediterranean Peoples in Transition: Thirteenth to Early Tenth Centuries B.C.E.,* ed. Seymour Gitin, Amihay Mazar, and Ephraim Stern (Jerusalem: Israel Exploration Society, 1998 [Hebrew]), 220–38, referring to the distribution of three types of cooking pots. However, William G. Dever, "How to Tell a Canaanite from an Israelite," in *The Rise of Ancient Israel: Symposium at the Smithsonian Institution October 26, 1991,* ed. Hershel Shanks, et al. (Washington, DC: Biblical Archaeology Society, 1992), 51, disputes this as impossible to demonstrate from an archaeological standpoint. Nevertheless, ongoing publication of the ceramic data continues to support this (Zevit, *The Religions of Ancient Israel,* 102–3) as does the analysis of the genealogical data of Chronicles (Gershon Galil, *The Genealogies of the Tribes of Judah,* Ph.D. thesis, Hebrew University, Jerusalem, 1983, xxiii–xxiv).

[14] Dever, "How to Tell," 33–34; *idem, Who Were the Early Israelites and Where Did They Come From?* (Grand Rapids: Eerdmans, 2003), 89–90.

[15] Gösta W. Åhlström, *The History of Ancient Palestine from the Palaeolithic Period to Alexander's Conquest,* Journal for the Study of the Old Testament: Supplement Series 146 (Sheffield: JSOT Press, 1993), 366.

votive offerings, and standing stones. But then the biblical texts argue that such was not allowed.[16]

Methodologically, the focus of this essay removes the discussion from any consideration of whether one can associate this structure with a biblical altar. However, it is appropriate to ask whether the structure has religious significance. Bloch-Smith and Alpert Nakhai describe the site as cultic and an atypical one for Iron I sites of this region insofar as it is isolated on a hilltop and distant from any extensive agricultural land.[17]

Thus it does not fit into the typology of surrounding sites in the region from the same period. Bloch-Smith and Nakhai suggest the earlier altar may have been Canaanite and that the later structure was built on top of it by the Israelites. However, the absence of Canaanite cultic paraphernalia makes a Canaanite altar difficult to identify there in the first place. Further, the continuity of culture between the phases suggests the same people who used the earlier one may also have used the later one.

The bull site and the Mt. Ebal site are the only two possible cult centers identified in the hill country villages. The bull site does demonstrate continuity with the surrounding Canaanite culture. However, the Mt. Ebal site does not. It remains anomalous. Perhaps for this reason some, such as Dever, wish to remove any cultic association from it.[18] By so doing, its obvious discontinuity with the earlier cults of the surrounding areas does not require explanation.

However, no other interpretation of the site commends itself. It seems not to be well positioned for a watchtower. This would make more sense were the structure moved a distance of some feet to the peak of the ridge itself. The identification of a farmhouse requires one to explain the absence of horse, donkey, pig, and gazelle bones. As Ziony Zevit observes: "The skewed distribution of bones supports a non-domestic interpretation of the site."[19] Note also his observation that the pottery, both the

---

[16] Adam Zertal, "Three Iron Age Fortresses in the Jordan Valley and the Origin of the Ammonite Circular Towers," *Israel Exploration Journal* 45 (1995): 273, concludes that the cultic nature of the site has been generally accepted and that no convincing alternative for it has been successful. His own analysis of contemporary and later fortresses in the region concludes that they are not like the Mt. Ebal site.

[17] Elizabeth Bloch-Smith and Beth Alpert Nakhai, "A Landscape Comes to Life: The Iron Age I," *Near Eastern Archaeology* 62 (1997): 71, 77.

[18] Dever, *Who Were the Early Israelites?* 89–90.

[19] Zevit, *Religions of Ancient Israel*, 200.

types and their distribution over the site, point toward a site where at least some of the animals may have been killed for cultic purposes.

Typologically, although the site is unique, the altar resembles that of the later Israelite sanctuary in the fort at Arad. Both were built of an outer shell of uncut stones with an inner fill of dirt, stones, and (at Mt. Ebal) ash. This altar construction distinguishes them from other forms of Canaanite altars and those in surrounding cultures. The continuity of the Ebal altar for animal sacrifice with one built three or more centuries later at Arad implies a tradition of altar construction that was unique and ongoing in the religious life of ancient Israel. Finally, the single structure may imply a single deity as the focus of worship. If this site on Mt. Ebal is an altar, then the absence of images, the particular animals sacrificed, the possible connection with a later Israelite cult site, and the single altar provide a distinctive collection of elements that set it apart from other Canaanite evidence.

The Iron Age II periods of interest here extend from 1000 to 587/6 BC. As already noted, the concerns here will focus on the evidence before 650 BC. During this earlier period, the population centers shift from a dominance of unfortified village life to a larger focus on fortified towns and cities in the region. Thus the major cultic sites of interest in the north and the south are found at Tel Dan and at Tel Arad respectively. Tel Dan's large sanctuary structure has been discussed in detail elsewhere. Its contents are not unlike those found at other Iron Age sanctuaries.

Tel Arad lay in the south.[20] As at Dan, its cultic structure seems to have been located publicly and prominently in the fort, suggesting a religious shrine that conformed to state policy.[21] Despite disputes regarding the precise dating of the strata that comprise the cult center in the corner of the fort at Arad, there is general agreement that it dates to the period of Iron Age II. The tripartite structure, as well as the standing stones and the incense altars, have parallels elsewhere in Israel and Judah as well as among their neighbors. However, an altar constructed of uncut fieldstones with a core of dirt and stones is unique to this site

---

[20] Ibid., 656–57.

[21] Following the typological analysis of J. S. Holladay Jr., "Religion in Israel and Judah under the Monarchy: An Explicitly Archaeological Approach," in Patrick D. Miller Jr., Paul D. Hanson, and S. Dean McBride, eds., *Ancient Israelite Religion: Essays in Honor of Frank Moore Cross* (Philadelphia: Fortress, 1987), 249–99.

and that of Mt. Ebal. As noted above, it supports a typological connection between the two and invites the possibility that the sites represent centers of related religious practice.

Regarding burials, Bloch-Smith has shown a continuity of types of burials in the regions of Israel and Judah throughout the Iron Age.[22] While no single form is unattested elsewhere, the bench tomb seems to have gained dominance in the latter part of the period. From late in the eighth century onward, the adoption of the bench tomb overwhelmingly in Judah and almost exclusively in Jerusalem has no statistical parallel. While known and used elsewhere in the Iron Age Levant, it never dominates as it does in the highlands of Judah.[23]

However, as the number of burials does not approximate population estimates for the period, these bench tombs were likely built for special individuals and families. As elsewhere, most people were probably buried in simple cist graves. Nevertheless, the significance of the bench tomb as a dominant form of elite burial practice may have unique religious implications. In many of these tombs the body of a recently deceased person was laid out on the bench cut into the rock in the tomb. At some later point, the remaining bones were then collected and placed along with the bones of other ancestors in a recess of the tomb. As much and more than any other form of burial, this type symbolized a physical connection of the members with the rest of their family in death.

Iconography

The iconography of the Iron Age I village sites does not preserve unique forms. The major representative of this period, the bronze bull from the bull site, has already been discussed above.

1. Iron Age IIA and Taanach Cult Stands. Keel and Uehlinger observe that the tenth century saw the gradual disappearance of anthropomorphic representations of deities, especially associated with Egypt in this area, and an orientation toward the north where deities were represented with

---

[22] Elizabeth Bloch-Smith, *Judahite Burial Practices and Beliefs about the Dead,* Journal for the Study of the Old Testament: Supplement Series 123; Journal for the Study of the Old Testament/American Schools of Oriental Research Monograph 7 (Sheffield: JSOT, 1992); *idem,* "Life in Judah from the Perspective of the Dead," *Near Eastern Archaeology* 65 (2002): 120–30.

[23] Bloch-Smith, *Judahite Burial Practices,* 137, 142.

their symbols.[24] Thus the tree and lion become symbols of the goddess Asherah. The "Lord of the Ostriches" theme may point to a representation of Yahweh as God of the steppe or as an aggressive deity.

While many pictorial objects suggest religion, few provide the wealth of images found in one of the Taanach cult stands, included among the finds that Holladay associates with a cult center there.[25] Dated to the tenth century BC, this object provides a unique glimpse into something of the mythology or ideology that informed an (presumably) official religion in this town, a population center adjacent to or within the area of Israelite influence, culture, and religion.[26] As a cult stand, its assembly of artistic representations is unique. On one of the four sides of the stand there are a series of four panels, each portraying a different scene. I will number the panels from bottom (panel 1) to top (panel 4). Panels 1 and 3 are both flanked by carvings of two lions facing the viewer. On panel 1 there is the portrait of a nude female with each arm raised toward the ear of one of the lions. Two identical creatures with four legs flank panel 2. They face the viewer. These creatures have human faces, however, and their bodies, which continue along the mold of the two sides of the stand, exhibit wings. They are best identified as sphinxes or griffins. Between them is an empty space void of any molding. This space shows no sign of ever having contained anything that might have broken and fallen off. The molding around the empty space is smooth and intact. Panel 3, flanked by lions, has at its center a tree. Two identical animals flank either side of the tree, each facing the tree and standing on its back legs. The animals are either ibexes or goats.[27] Panel 4, at the

---

[24] Othmar Keel and Christoph Uehlinger, *Gods, Goddesses, and Images of God in Ancient Israel,* trans. Thomas H. Trapp (Minneapolis: Fortress, 1998), 133–75.

[25] Holladay, "Religion in Israel and Judah."

[26] In addition to the above comments regarding the shift of population to such fortified centers, the comments of Smith, *The Early History of God,* 54, are pertinent:

If the stand is dated correctly, then it might constitute evidence for Israelite religion. Judges 1:27 would suggest that the city remained at least partially Canaanite down to the monarchy. Afterwards following the rise of the Davidic dynasty, the city became Israelite. Solomon's organization of the nation lists Taanach and Megiddo in the fifth district (1 Kgs 4:12). Though politically identified as Israelite, the city may have continued its Canaanite cultic traditions, which flourished in the valleys and the coast in the Late Bronze Age. Dated to the early monarchy, the stand would appear to provide evidence for Israelite polytheism (including Asherah), continuous with earlier Canaanite traditions.

[27] Cf. Lev 17:7.

top of this side of the stand, portrays a quadruped, drawn more simply than any of the other living creatures portrayed on the four panels. The quadruped faces to the left. Over its body there hovers a disk with wavy lines extending out from either side of it. This is a winged sun disk. Voluted columns flank the animal.

There are difficulties with any interpretation of pictorial symbols such as those described here. Scholars who have studied the first and third panels and compared the scenes with other parallels in iconography and in West Semitic texts have suggested that both the woman and the tree represent the same deity, Asherah.[28] The tree represents the tree of life, also called the asherah, which appears in iconography at Kuntillet 'Ajrud and perhaps also in a blessing there (see below).

If the first and third panels represent Asherah, what do the second and fourth represent? The fourth panel displays a quadruped surmounted by a sun disk. Scholars have been inclined to identify the animal as a calf, a natural enough deduction given the known association of the calf with Canaanite worship.[29] Associations of this animal with Baal have led Ruth Hestrin to identify the fourth panel as a representation of Baal.[30]

However, J. Glen Taylor suggests that the animal portrayed in this panel is an equid. He refers to two animal biologists who have examined

---

[28] William G. Dever, "Asherah, Consort of Yahweh? New Evidence from Kuntillet 'Ajrud," *Bulletin of the American Schools of Oriental Research* 255 (1984): 33n24; Ruth Hestrin, "The Cult Stand from Ta'anach and Its Religious Background," in *Phoenicia and the East Mediterranean in the First Millennium B.C.: Proceedings of the Conference Held in Leuven from the 14th to the 16th of November 1985,* ed. Edward Lipinski, Studie Phoenicia V, Orientalia Lovaniensia Analecta 22 (Leuven: Peeters, 1987), 68–71; J. Glen Taylor, "Yahweh and Asherah at Tenth Century Taanach," *Newsletter for Ugaritic Studies* 37/38 (1987): 16–18; idem, "The Two Earliest Representations of Yahweh," in *Ascribe to the Lord: Biblical & Other Studies in Memory of Peter C. Craigie,* ed. Lyle Eslinger and J. Glen Taylor, Journal for the Study of the Old Testament: Supplement Series 67 (Sheffield: JSOT, 1988), 560. See, however, Philip J. King and Lawrence E. Stager, *Life in Biblical Israel,* Library of Ancient Israel (Louisville: Westminster, 2001), 343, who do not accept the identity with Asherah as established. Indeed, they are correct in terms of a text. Nevertheless, this is the best understanding of a female portrayed with animals.

[29] Paul W. Lapp, "The 1968 Excavations at Tell Ta'annek: The New Cultic Stand," *Bulletin of the American Schools of Oriental Research* 195 (1969): 44; Hestrin, "Cult Stand from Ta'anach," 67.

[30] Ruth Hestrin, "Canaanite Cult Stand," in *Treasures of the Holy Land: Ancient Art from the Israel Museum,* ed. John P. O'Neill (New York: Metropolitan Museum of Art, 1986), 161–63; idem, "Cult Stand from Ta'anach," 75; Philip J. King, *Amos, Hosea, Micah—An Archaeological Commentary* (Philadelphia: Westminster, 1988), 107.

this image and come to this conclusion.[31] The sun disk, the equid, and the columns (representing the temple) all fit together as a Canaanite religious expression. The winged sun disk is a common motif in iconography throughout the Ancient Near East.[32] Its possible association with horses also appears in figurines found in Palestine, including at Megiddo and at Jerusalem (Cave 1).[33]

Panel 2 represents two sphinxes on either side of an empty space. The lack of indication of anything broken off the molding around that space is clear. Taylor has proposed that the two sphinxes are cherubs and that this is a representation of an aniconic deity, whom he identifies with Yahweh.[34] Given the parallelism, if panels 1 and 3 represent Asherah, then panels 2 and 4 would also represent the same deity. If panel 2 is a (non)representation of Yahweh, then we should expect the same of panel 4, whether it is an equid or a bovine.

---

[31] J. Glen Taylor, "Two Earliest Known Representations of Yahweh," 561–66; *idem, Yahweh and the Sun: Biblical and Archaeological Evidence for Sun Worship in Ancient Israel,* Journal for the Study of the Old Testament: Supplement Series 111 (Sheffield: JSOT, 1993), 24–37; *idem*, "Was Yahweh Worshipped as the Sun?" *Biblical Archaeology Review* 20/3 (May/June 1994): 55–59. This suggestion was first made by Albert E. Glock, "Taanach," in *Encyclopedia of Archaeological Excavations in the Holy Land,* ed. Michael Avi-Yonah and Ephraim Stern (Jerusalem: Israel Exploration Society, 1978), 4:1138–47. It is followed by Judith M. Hadley, *Yahweh's Asherah in the Light of Recent Discovery,* Ph.D. thesis, Cambridge University, 1989, 219; *idem, The Cult of Asherah in Ancient Israel and Judah: Evidence for a Hebrew Goddess,* University of Cambridge Oriental Publications 57 (Cambridge: Cambridge University, 2000). Ruth Hestrin, "Understanding Asherah: Exploring Semitic Iconography," *Biblical Archaeology Review* 17/5 (Sept./Oct. 1991): 59, argues that the absence of a mane on the representation opposes the interpretation of these animals as horses. She also identifies this image with the reference in 2 Kgs 23:11 to the horses dedicated to the sun. Josiah destroyed them.

[32] See especially George E. Mendenhall, *The Tenth Generation: The Origins of the Biblical Tradition* (Baltimore and London: Johns Hopkins University, 1973), 32–56. For the appearance of this motif in the Bible, see Taylor, *Yahweh and the Sun*; Mark S. Smith, "'Seeing God' in the Psalms: The Background to the Beatific Vision in the Hebrew Bible," *Catholic Biblical Quarterly* 50 (1988): 171–83; *idem*, "The Near Eastern Background of Solar Language for Yahweh," *Journal of Biblical Literature* 109 (1990): 29–39.

[33] Herbert G. May, *Material Remains of the Megiddo Cult,* Oriental Institute Publications 26 (Chicago and London: University of Chicago, 1935); Kathleen M. Kenyon, *The Bible and Recent Archaeology* (Atlanta: John Knox, 1978), 76; Thomas A. Holland, "A Study of Palestinian Iron Age Baked Clay Figurines with Special Reference to Jerusalem Cave 1," *Levant* 9 (1977): 121–55; Hadley, *Yahweh's Asherah,* 219; *idem, Cult of Asherah;* Taylor, "Was Yahweh Worshipped," 58. Mark S. Smith, *The Early History of God: Yahweh and the Other Deities in Ancient Israel* (San Francisco: Harper & Row, 1990), 116, also indicates that these objects were discovered at Lachish and Hazor.

[34] King and Stager, *Life in Biblical Israel,* 344, argue that the cherubim themselves represent Yahweh. However, this is not clear from any biblical text.

This Canaanite representation of Yahweh may suggest an aspect of the portrayal unique to the northern kingdom. If it is a bovine, it could suggest a portrayal of the deity as a calf.[35] If it is an equid, then this deity's image may be associated with the horse figurines found elsewhere at Megiddo and Jerusalem.[36] As will be noted below, the inscription at Kuntillet 'Ajrud associates Yahweh with Asherah. The arguments of symmetry in the presentations, of the aniconic nature of panel 2, and of the evidence from Kuntillet 'Ajrud all point to an association of both panels 2 and 4 with Yahweh.[37]

Archaeologists discovered another cult stand at Taanach.[38] Judith Hadley has identified alternating rows of lions and sphinxes although earlier scholars found only lions. This suggests similar deities as are found on the first stand mentioned above. There is also a tree flanked by ibexes and architectural features on the top tier. Although more poorly made, the motifs resemble those of the first cult stand discussed. The lions and the tree may suggest that this stand also depicted Asherah.[39]

Zevit suggests that these stands represent different views of a shrine with the top register pointing toward the inner sanctum.[40] The alternating pattern created by the four panels on the first stand recalls the A-B-A'-B' parallelism found in Ugaritic and Canaanite poetry and literature.[41] Scholars have noted the use of parallelism for the purposes of

---

[35] Dated to the tenth century, it could suggest the portrayal of Yahweh that Jeroboam I intended. He erected images of calves at the cult centers of Dan and Bethel.

[36] Cf. 2 Kgs 23:11.

[37] Smith, "Near Eastern Background," 32n16, suggests that a tradition associating the calf and Baal could have persisted at Taanach and could be represented on panel 4. This is a possibility, but my present assessment of the arguments favors Taylor's identification with Yahweh. Smith does not address the question of the identification of panel 2. Hadley, *Yahweh's Asherah*, 220–21; idem, *Cult of Asherah*, accepts the identification with Yahweh and observes that neither the Ugaritic literature nor the Bible provides substantial identification of Asherah with Baal, the one other god whom scholars have identified here. Cf. Zevit, *Religions of Ancient Israel*, 324, who determines that Yahweh and Asherah are represented (maximally; minimally he suggests two deities).

[38] Ernst Sellin, *Tell Ta'annek* (Vienna: Denkschriften der Kaiserlichen Akademie der Wissenschaften, 1904), 75–76; Lapp, "The 1968 Excavations," 16–17; Glock, "Taanach," 1143–44; Hadley, *Yahweh's Asherah*, 221–22; idem, *The Cult of Asherah*.

[39] Ruth Hestrin, "A Note on the 'Lion Bowls' and the Asherah," *Israel Museum Journal* 7 (1988): 117.

[40] Zevit, *Religions of Ancient Israel*, 325.

[41] Wilfred G. E. Watson, *Classical Hebrew Poetry: A Guide to Its Techniques*, Journal for the Study of the Old Testament: Supplement Series 26 (Sheffield: JSOT, 1986), 114–22.

emphasis.[42] The same sort of emphasis of these two deities may be taking place on this cult stand, and may reflect both their association and prominence among inhabitants of Taanach in the tenth century.

2. Iron Age IIB and Kuntillet 'Ajrud. In Iron IIB (c. 925–c. 722 BC), Judah possessed few pictorial representations other than symbols of royalty adapted from Egypt, and some local motifs. The northern kingdom adapted and contributed to the flourishing Phoenician artistic and religious traditions.

At Kuntillet 'Ajrud, the presence of distinctive drawings, especially those that appear near inscriptions referring to Yahweh and asherah/Asherah, have generated some discussion. These occur on a collection of shards that form a large storage jar. There are three figures. Two on the left (from the viewer's viewpoint) are standing. They have bovine faces and feet, and are adorned with feathered headdress. They stand with their arms behind their back and linked to one another. Dots decorate the upper parts of their bodies. They suggest some form of apparel. The lower parts of their bodies do not have this decoration, suggesting possible nakedness. The projection between the legs of each figure may be a phallus or a tail. The third figure to the right sits and plays a lyre. The "dotted apparel" stretches the full length of the body. It also describes the hair. The figure faces to the right toward the lyre, unlike the two standing figures who face toward the front.

Can these figures be identified? Do they have any relationship to the inscription that occurs with them? Some have tied the identification of the figures to the inscription (see below). In that case, either the two standing figures appear as representations of Yahweh and Asherah, or the lyre player represents Asherah. Arguments for these interpretations include: the bull calf imagery of Yahweh in the Bible, formal similarities of the lyre player to figures elsewhere identified as Asherah, and the etymology of Asherah as one who follows her male consort (introducing a three-dimensional perspective into the drawing).[43] However, none of

---

[42] James L. Kugel, *The Idea of Biblical Poetry* (New Haven: Yale University, 1981), 51; cf. Robert Alter, *The Art of Biblical Poetry* (New York: Basic Books, 1985).

[43] For bull/calf imagery, cf. Michael D. Coogan, "Canaanite Origins and Lineage: Reflections on the Religion of Ancient Israel," in *Ancient Israelite Religion*, ed. Miller et al., 119; P. Kyle McCarter Jr., "Aspects of the Religion of the Israelite Monarchy: Biblical and Epigraphic Data," in ibid., 137–55. For formal comparisons with Asherah, cf. Dever, "Asherah, Consort of Yahweh?" For the etymology of Asherah as one who follows after and its association with the

these arguments can overturn the careful analysis of art historian Pirhiya Beck. She concludes that the two standing figures are both representations of Bes, the Egyptian dwarf deity who appears throughout the eastern Mediterranean in various forms.[44] The facial appearance, the nudity, the headdress, and even the accompanying lyre player are understandable in this interpretation. The artistic form is Phoenician. The lyre player cannot be a deity of superior rank because this musician would occupy an inferior role playing for the Bes figures.[45] Zevit argues that the Bes figures are symbols of deity that can apply to any god or goddess.[46] In this case he suggests that the larger one signifies Yahweh without actually portraying him. Zevit identifies Ashera(ta)h as the lyre player, pointing to such a portrayal of her in Ugaritic mythology.[47]

However, the unparalleled appearance of these types of Bes figures with Yahweh and Asherah creates doubt that there was an intentional association with the figures and the accompanying writing. Instead, it represents one more example of figures and writing found on the plastered walls and shards throughout the caravansery. This interpretation of the figures and their lack of association with the inscription is much more understandable given the noncultic nature of the structure in which they occur. If this was a cult center of some sort, arguments relating the art and inscriptions to a single ideology or theology would be more persuasive. A priestly leadership would have directed the cult and probably represented an official or state cult. However, an interpretation of the site as noncultic allows the iconography and the inscriptions to represent random expressions of popular piety, emanating from different times and different ethnic groups that might have passed through

inscription, cf. Baruch Margalit, "Some Observations on the Inscriptions and Drawing from Khirbet el-Qôm," *Vetus Testamentum* 39 (1989): 374.

[44] Pirhiya Beck, "The Drawings from Horvat Teiman (Kuntillet 'Ajrud)," *Tel Aviv* 9 (1982): fig. 4. See also Saul M. Olyan, *Asherah and the Cult of Yahweh in Israel*, Society of Biblical Literature Monograph Series 34 (Atlanta: Scholars Press, 1988), 29 nn.31, 32. Olyan refers to a similar conclusion that the figures are those of Bes, by Fritz Stolz, "Monotheismus in Israel," in *Monotheismus im alten Israel und seiner Umwelt*, ed. Othmar Keel, Biblische Beiträge 14 (Fribourg: Schweizerisches Katholisches Bibelwerk, 1980), 168. Dever, "Asherah, Consort of Yahweh?" (cf. Hadley, *Yahweh's Asherah*, 184–85; *idem, Cult of Asherah*) argues that the Bes figures were intentionally placed at the entrance to the caravansary to ward off wild animals and other dangers.

[45] Hadley, *Yahweh's Asherah*, 184, 194.

[46] Zevit, *Religions of Ancient Israel*, 387–89, 392.

[47] *Ugaritica V*, 557–58, RS 24.245, lines 5–7.

the site.[48] It is possible that this was true, at least for a short period. In such a case the figure on the votive containers in the cultic room could represent the chief deities, Yahweh and Asherah, expressed in the form of Bes figures.

3. Iron Age IIC. In Iron Age IIC (c. 722–586 BC) Assyrian centers of power in Palestine become foci for Assyrian cultural and religious influence. Keel and Uehlinger note that a lack of female deities in pictorial art except in cheaper terracottas is a feature of most of Iron Age II.[49] However, hundreds of these pillar base female figurines have been attested. They occur in homes and tombs reflecting the family piety that was expressed by earlier (Late Bronze Age and Iron I) plaque figures. In the coastal regions, but not Judah, the naked goddess plaques continue. She is identified with Astarte by Keel and Uehlinger. In fact, the pillar base figurines are prominent throughout Judah and their presence can

---

[48] Positions that argue for a state-controlled cult represented at Kuntillet 'Ajrud may turn out to be correct. However, the weight of evidence is not on their side at present. The inscriptions and drawings (with the lack of cultic artifacts) would appear to indicate that this was one of the "peripheral sites exposed to foreign influence." Cf. Jeffrey H. Tigay, *You Shall Have No Other Gods: Israelite Religion in the Light of Hebrew Inscriptions,* Harvard Semitic Series 31 (Atlanta: Scholars Press, 1986), 29; *idem,* "Israelite Religion: The Onomastic and Epigraphic Evidence," in *Ancient Israelite Religion,* ed. Miller et al., 176. Some argue that the structure in which the inscriptions and drawings were found is a government structure and that therefore the views represented must be those of the state-supported cult. Cf. Silvia Schroer, *In Israel Gab es Bilder: Nachrichten von darstellender Kunst im Alten Testament,* Orbis Biblicus et Orientalis 74 (Freiburg: Universitätsverlag; Göttingen: Vandenhoeck & Ruprecht, 1987), 32; Klaus Koch, "Aschera als Himmelskönigen in Jerusalem," *Ugarit Forschungen* 20 (1988): 99; Zevit, *Religions of Ancient Israel.* This view requires the demonstration that (1) the building was controlled by a government such as Judah or Israel, rather than a local group; (2) that government was capable and interested in exerting its control in cultic matters; and (3) that the government concerned can be identified, not an easy task given the variety of places named in the inscriptions. Zevit, *Religions of Ancient Israel,* has attempted to make the case. He argues, among other things, that (1) the topography of the site, built high above the surrounding area, would make it an unlikely spot to drag animals up to; (2) the position of some inscriptions on lintels and the professional nature of the writing suggest something more than graffiti; and (3) the benched room with the inscriptions, drawings, and pottery typologically resembles contemporary Israelite and Judean cult centers. Argument 1 is not convincing as the prominent position would be expected, whether a state fort or a caravansery. Argument 2 argues a stronger case than previously that the inscriptions were authorized rather than random. Argument 3 suggests that the room was an intentional cult site. However, this does not require the assumption that the material here necessarily represented official Judean religious policy. Nevertheless, both the witness of 2 Chron 25:14 and the relatively brief occupation of the site may suggest that for a short time this did represent a religious polytheism with which the monarchy was comfortable. It could provide background to the indictments of Isaiah and Micah a few generations later.

[49] Keel and Uehlinger, *Gods, Goddesses,* 288–372.

be used, for the most part, to define the territorial limits of Judah in the latter period of the Monarchy. Their identification with a particular goddess is in dispute. The connection with the Phoenician plaques would suggest Astarte while others connect them with Asherah.[50]

Statues of a horse with a male rider occur, numbering above 450. Although the horse and rider statues, which can appear in groups, have been associated with the host of heaven and with guardian angels, there is little in the figurines themselves to require this. The solar symbolism of the numerous rosettes in seventh-century Judah may refer directly to symbols of Yahweh. Otherwise, seals from Judah lack images in Iron IIC, including the early part, which is the period of our interest.[51] Thus this era saw an end to Egyptian influence, an increasingly Assyrian influence, and some evidence of an increasing aniconism.

Keel and Uehlinger note that there is an absence of anthropomorphic iconography of deities in the latter part of the Monarchy.[52] This is in contrast with Edom, for example, where there was a goddess portrayed alongside the chief deity, Qaus. In Judah, images disappear from seals. From panel two of the tenth-century Taanach cult stand in the north to the absence of images in Judah, especially in the later period, aniconism seems to have been a distinctive part of the religious life of this region.

Epigraphy

There are very few inscriptions from Israel or its neighbors in the period between 1200 and 900 BC, for a variety of reasons.[53] Therefore, as with the iconography, little can be said regarding this period's religion in terms of inscriptions. Yahweh as a chief deity is so identified for the first time in the ninth century. Although the name may appear as part of

---

[50] For the Astarte identification, see Smith, *Early History of God,* 111.

[51] The 211 seal motifs found in the Burnt Archive in Jerusalem include only two with solar motifs, indicating the diminution of the influence of solar imagery (and Egypt). However, this archive appears to date later than the time of Josiah and thus outside the period of our interest.

[52] Keel and Uehlinger, *Gods, Goddesses.*

[53] Richard S. Hess, "Literacy in Iron Age Israel," in *Windows into Old Testament History: Evidence, Argument, and the Crisis of "Biblical Israel,"* ed. V. Philips Long, David W. Baker, and Gordon J. Wenham (Grand Rapids: Eerdmans, 2002), 82–102.

a place name already in the fourteenth century, its occurrence as a deity is suggested in the Mesha stele and is indicated clearly in the Kuntillet 'Ajrud inscriptions.[54]

There are mentions in monumental inscriptions of national deities, such as Chemosh the god of Moab in the ninth-century Mesha stele. The same stele also describes Yahweh as god of Israel and describes his cult in a Transjordanian Israelite town in the mid-ninth century, where a key element is the *'r'l yhwh* ("altar hearth of Yahweh").[55] So understood, Yahweh is the only god associated with Omride Israel and possesses no image at the site (which would have certainly been mentioned by Mesha if it existed) but rather an object that may have been used for the burning of incense.

Deir 'Allā is an ancient cult site located in the Jordan Valley. Plaster fragments containing writing have been found in what may have been a cult center. This site may be dated to the late ninth century. The ink writing presents a text in a distinctive dialect of Aramaic, influenced by the Canaanite dialects of the area. As reconstructed from the plaster fragments, it describes a seer named Balaam son of Beor. Balaam has a vision that has been understood as a picture of the natural world turned upside down.[56] The name of the god El appears. Of interest for the question of religious distinctives is the mention of the Shaddayin, who appear as a divine council responsible for the supernatural effects. The term, Shaddayin, occurs only at this Transjordan site.[57]

---

[54] See Richard S. Hess, "The Divine Name Yahweh in Late Bronze Age Sources," *Ugarit Forschungen* 23 (1991): 181–88, for a summary of the other possible occurrences of the divine name, Yahweh, in Bronze Age sources, and a critique of some of the identifications.

[55] So Anson F. Rainey, "Syntax, Hermeneutics and History," *Israel Exploration Journal* 48 (1998): 249.

[56] Jo Ann Hackett, *The Balaam Texts from Deir 'Allā*, Harvard Semitic Monographs 31 (Chico, CA: Scholars, 1980), 29–30.

[57] For the former, see Smith, *Early History of God*, 58. For the latter, see James Robert Engle, *Pillar Figurines of the Iron Age and Asherah/Asherim*, Ph.D. diss., University of Pittsburgh, 1979, 55, 62; and Ruth Hestrin, "The Lachish Ewer and the Asherah," *Israel Exploration Journal* 37 (1987): 221–22. Cf. also Hadley, *Cult of Asherah*, 196–205; Holland, "Study of Palestinian Iron Age Baked Clay Figurines"; Raz Kletter, "Between Archaeology and Theology: The Pillar Figurines from Judah and the Asherah," in *Studies in the Archaeology of the Iron Age in Israel and Jordan*, ed. Amihai Mazar, with Ginny Mathias, Journal for the Study of the Old Testament: Supplement Series 331 (Sheffield: Sheffield Academic, 2001), 177–216; and Elizabeth C. LaRocca-Pitts, *"Of Wood and Stone": The Significance of Israelite Cultic Items in the Bible and Its Early Interpreters*, Harvard Semitic Monographs 61 (Winona Lake, IN: Eisenbrauns, 2001), 161–204.

Occupied at approximately the same time as Deir 'Allā, c. 800 BC, Kuntillet 'Ajrud, the caravansery or cult center in the northern Sinai, has yielded important inscriptions. These mention Yahweh and Asherah as deities invoked in the pronouncement of blessings upon various people. El and Baal are also mentioned in a single poem. The interpretation of these texts bristles with problems. Elsewhere, I have argued that the mention of Asherah, in conjunction with Yahweh, is not a cult symbol nor is "his Asherah" the best translation. Instead, it is preferable to render the goddess's name as Asherata, in accordance with the spelling and reading of her name everywhere outside the Bible for more than a thousand years.[58]

It is not certain who wrote all these inscriptions. In particular, the texts that mention Baal and El have been thought to have been composed by non-Israelites. The texts associate these deities with war and with theophanies. If they are Israelite, and this is increasingly more likely, they indicate that either Baal, like El, should be identified with Yahweh, or that there was a rival cult that accepted Baal as a martial deity.[59] The most frequently mentioned deity, the only one associated with Asheratah, and the one who appears in blessings formulae, is Yahweh. His name is associated with two place names that occur as Yahweh of the Teman (*htmn*) and Yahweh of Samaria (*šmrm*). (The) Teman can be identified as a desert region to the south of Judah while Samaria can be associated with the capital of the northern kingdom of Israel or, possibly, with the nation of Israel itself.

Although best identified as a caravansary with some cultic associations in my view, this site yields the following distinctives in terms of its religious inscriptions: (1) Yahweh as a deity associated both with the state of Israel and with a region outside Israel and Judah, in the southern desert; (2) Yahweh as a male deity with a female consort, Asheratah, a goddess also associated with El, the chief deity in thirteenth-century mythological texts from Ugarit; (3) Yahweh and Asheratah as powerful deities capable of blessing others.

---

[58] Richard S. Hess, "Yahweh and His Asherah? Religious Pluralism in the Old Testament World," in *One God, One Lord: Christianity in a World of Religious Pluralism*, ed. Andrew D. Clarke and Bruce W. Winter, 2nd ed. (Carlisle, UK: Paternoster; Grand Rapids: Baker, 1992), 13–42; *idem*, "Asherah or Asheratah?" *Orientalia* 65 (1996): 209–19.

[59] Smith, *Early History of God*, 73.

Some would date the paleography of the Jerusalem pomegranate to this same period, although with only a few letters the paleography is difficult to ascertain. Purchased from the black market, this small ivory pomegranate functioned as the head of a scepter. Although several of the letters for "house/temple" and "Yahweh" are missing, the most likely reconstruction allows a translation, "Belonging to the temple of Yahweh, holy to the priests."[60] This translation implies a temple and priesthood related to Yahweh in Israel. It is not possible to determine the location of the temple or the function of the scepter.

From c. 750 BC at the southern Judean site of Khirbet el-Qom (probably ancient Makkedah), a tomb inscription mentions Yahweh as a deliverer of the writer, Uriyahu, from his enemies. This deliverance is associated either with the work of Asheratah or as something done for her benefit. Thus salvation from surrounding enemies is ascribed to Yahweh. Further, Asherata is mentioned multiple times as also involved. This association of these two deities at a second site suggests that this belief was more than casual, even if the writing represents a view outside the official cult. It is not impossible that in both Judah and Israel for some time in the late ninth and eighth centuries a view of Yahweh with a consort prevailed.

To this evidence should be added the possibly eighth-century BC seal, *lmqnyhw 'bd yhwh*: "Belonging to Miqneyahu, servant of Yahweh."[61] This seal provides evidence for an active cult of Yahweh in which figures such as Miqneyahu could serve as officiants. From the time of the Monarchy, seals of Israelites and Judeans are given titles such as "the priest" and "priest of Dor."[62] The absence of any Hebrew seals with titles that mention other deities or those in service to them may be significant. Clearly, similar evidence does not exist for any deity other than Yahweh.

---

[60] André Lemaire, "Un inscription paleo-hébraïque sur grenade en ivoire," *Revue Biblique* 88 (1981): 236–39; Hess, "Yahweh and His Asherah?"; *idem*, "Asherah or Asheratah?"

[61] Graham I. Davies, *Ancient Hebrew Inscriptions. Corpus and Concordance* (Cambridge: Cambridge University, 1991), #100.172; Nahman Avigad and Benjamin Sass, *Corpus of West Semitic Stamp Seals* (Jerusalem: Israel Exploration Society, 1997), #227.

[62] Cf. Ephraim Stern, "Pagan Yahwism: The Folk Religion of Ancient Israel," *Biblical Archaeology Review* 27/3 (May/June 2001): 26. These figures are so identified on the basis of the personal names being compounded with Yahweh.

From c. 700 BC in a cave in the heights above Ein Gedi there occurs an inscription that Zevit has studied at length.[63] Although there is more than one interpretation of this inscription, all are agreed that it mentions Yahweh as blessed and associates him with lines describing his rule among the nations. Two or three lines later in the same inscription *'dny* is also blessed. Otherwise unidentified as a deity, and possessing the legitimate interpretation of "my lord," it is not unreasonable to understand this term as an epithet for Yahweh.

Khirbet Beit Lei is a cave about eight kilometers east of Lachish that includes several important inscriptions. A major question concerns the dating of the cave's epigraphy. An early paleographic study of the latter suggested a sixth-century date.[64] However, Zevit argues for an eighth- or seventh-century date, citing the tomb's contents and architecture, as well as the paleography.[65] The paleography of the inscriptions mentioning Yahweh has been dated to c. 700 by Lemaire, a date with which Naveh and Zevit agree.[66] This has become more convincing with the discovery of the above inscriptions and their dating to the time of the Monarchy. None of the texts mention any deity other than Yahweh. The most important inscriptions are those in the antechamber directly opposite the entrance. Faults in the rock surface and other marks render the two upper lines and the single lower line difficult to read. The upper inscription attests to Yahweh's sovereignty over Jerusalem and probably Judah. The lower line is a request or prayer for Yahweh's absolution.

These inscriptions describe an awareness of and worship of several deities, including Asheratah, Baal, El, and perhaps the Shaddayin in Israel and Judah. However, the dominant deity in all these inscriptions was Yahweh. Occasionally, he was also the only deity. He is mentioned exclusively in the ninth-century Mesha stele as the one deity associated with Israelite communities who had cultic objects. He appears alone in the Miqneyahu seal as well as at Ein Gedi and in the inscriptions at

---

[63] Zevit, *Religions of Ancient Israel,* 351–59.

[64] Frank M. Cross, "The Cave Inscription from Khirbet Beit Lei," in *Near Eastern Archaeology in the Twentieth Century: Essays in Honor of Nelson Glueck,* ed. James A. Sanders (Garden City: Doubleday, 1970), 299–306.

[65] Zevit, *Religions of Ancient Israel,* 405–37.

[66] Zevit, *Religions of Ancient Israel,* 420; Joseph Naveh, "Old Hebrew Inscriptions in a Cave," *Israel Exploration Journal* 13 (1963): 81–87; André Lemaire, "Priéres en temps de crise: les inscriptions de Khirbet Beit Lei," *Revue Biblique* 83 (1976): 558–65.

Khirbet Beit Lei. Thus Yahweh functions either as dominant or as sole deity. Israelites are involved in his cult. He alone is identified as "my lord." He alone is appealed to for blessing, for absolution, and for his reign over Jerusalem and his people.

Onomastics: The Personal Names[67]

Names can reveal something of the popular faith of the people. Seals and impressions (bullae) from the Iron Age give evidence of some 1,200 personal names, and the number is increasing with new evidence coming to light. What is unusual for Judah and Israel is the near absence of personal names compounded with divine names of deities other than Yahweh or the generic term for "god" (*'el*). Over 46 percent of all names are Yahwistic names, about 6 percent are *'el* names, and about 1 percent comprise personal names compounded with all other divine names that are clearly not epithets.[68] Before the Monarchy there is no clear extra-biblical evidence for names compounded with "Yahweh" or its abbreviated form.[69] Van der Toorn hypothesizes that at the earlier time the worship of Yahweh was restricted to a minority population (and later

---

[67] It is difficult to separate the place names from the biblical evidence because they are a primary source for understanding ancient Israelite toponymy. Of the 502 place names in the Bible, none are Yahwistic. However, toponyms with *b'l* are unattested in Canaanite toponyms from Egyptian sources. Therefore, some suppose that the Israelites introduced them. In the south, in Judah and Simeon in particular, some eight place names have a form of this element. This leads Zevit to conclude that Baal worship was more prevalent than might be supposed on the basis of biblical evidence alone (Zevit, *The Religions of Ancient Israel*, 606). Baal was a popular deity of the towns (ibid., 649). However, it should be noted that many of the Baal place names are not found on the well-traveled lowland routes that the Egyptians used and whose place names they more easily recorded. Nor are places with Baal names usually identified as major population centers. Thus the rarity of the Baal names in Egyptian New Kingdom sources may have more to do with the selection of regions and sites whose names were recorded in Egyptian records than with the absence of such sites altogether.

[68] Tigay, *You Shall Have No Other Gods,* identified 557 Yahwistic personal names, 44 *'el* names, and a handful of *ba'al* names. Cf. Alan R. Millard, "The History of Israel against the Background of Ancient Near Eastern History," in *From the Ancient Sites of Israel: Essays on Archaeology, History and Theology in Memory of Aareli Saarisalo (1896–1986),* ed. Timo Eskola and Eero Junkkaala, Iustitia Supplement Series (Helsinki: Theological Institute of Finland, 1998), 101–17; Smith, *Early History of God,* 35.

[69] The suggestion of an Iron Age I arrowhead with a personal name compounded with YHWH has been disputed as to its reading (personal communication, A. Lemaire, 7/2003). For the theories of De Moor that Yahweh occurs at Ugarit and in the Amarna letters from Tyre, whether as part of personal names or separately, see the problems with this interpretation in Hess, "The Divine Name Yahweh."

grew to a national religion).[70] Others note an "onomastic lag" between the introduction of deity and the use of that deity in personal names.[71] However, no explanation is certain.

In terms of the public use of personal names in society, Israel and Judah were Yahwistic worshipping communities. The one exception is the north kingdom at the capital of Samaria in the early eighth century, where a number of personal names in the ostraca found there use Baal. Even here, however, it is not the majority, and the *bʿl* element may simply refer to the common noun, "lord," an epithet of any deity, including Yahweh.

To Yahweh were ascribed the many characteristics of other deities as found in personal names. For examples, Sheharya ("Yahweh is dawn")[72] ascribes an image to the God of Israel that at Ugarit is given status as a separate deity (Shahar—"Dawn"). However, there were also distinctives among the Yahwistic theophoric names, when compared with theophoric names of surrounding nations.[73]

The distinctive nature of Yahwistic names has been studied by Fowler. Unlike neighboring onomastica, Yahweh is never described as producing offspring or involved in fertility. Yahweh is never associated with a divine consort and rarely is he depicted in the form of an animal.[74] He is not identified with architecture, cities, or astral phenomena. Unlike Mesopotamian names, no Israelite personal name suggests that the deity may harm an individual, act vengefully, or need to be appeased. The

---

[70] Karel van der Toorn, *Family Religion in Babylonia, Syria and Israel: Continuity and Change in the Forms of Religious Life,* Studies in the History and Culture of the Ancient Near East 7 (Leiden: Brill, 1996). It is a testimony to the syncretism of Judg 2:9–11.

[71] Tigay, *You Shall Have No Other Gods,* 17.

[72] Taylor, *Yahweh and the Sun,* 90.

[73] Jeaneane D. Fowler, *Theophoric Personal Names in Ancient Hebrew: A Comparative Study,* Journal for the Study of the Old Testament: Supplement Series 49 (Sheffield: JSOT, 1988), 314–18. The criticisms of the book, particularly Emerton's rebuttal to her critique of Gray's study (John A. Emerton, Review of Fowler, *Theophoric Personal Names,* in *Vetus Testamentum* 29 [1989]: 246–48), do not overturn the main conclusions of the work or its significance.

[74] There is much discussion of the Samaria ostraca's eighth-century BC name, *ʿglyw.* Although some see this as undoubtedly identifying Yahweh with a calf, others prefer the interpretation, "calf of Yahweh," noting parallels in Akkadian personal names and biblical references to young men as *ʿgl.* See Fowler, *Theophoric Personal Names,* 120; Martin Noth, *Die israelitischen Personennamen im Rahmen der gemeinsemitischen Namengebung* (Stuttgart: Kohlhammer, 1928), 150; André Lemaire, *Inscriptions hébraïques. Tome I. Les ostraca. Littératures anciennes du proche-orient* (Paris: Les editions du Cerf, 1977), 53. For the first option, see Smith, *Early History of God,* 83.

qualities of compassion, mercy, love, joy, transcendence, and perhaps salvation seem to occur to a unique degree in Israelite names in a manner that is not present in Ugaritic, Phoenician, Palmyrene, and Aramean names.[75]

Also in terms of the mention of other deities, the situation is different outside Israel, both in Canaan before the arrival of the Israelites and in the Phoenician and Aramaic names contemporary with Israel. In all cases, other divine names occur in the personal names.[76] In fourteenth-century Canaan, *Baal* and *Asherah* occur in names: *Baal* by itself (Baalumme) or with a predicate nominative (Balumehr, "Baal is a warrior") and *Asherah* in the form of "servant of Asherah" (Abdi-Ashirti).[77] In Phoenician and Punic names, Anat, Baal, Eshmun, and Melqart occur as deities, by themselves, and compounded in personal names.[78] However, these collections are not directly comparable with

---

[75] Fowler, *Theophoric Personal Names,* 315–18, observes the absence of divine compassion and mercy in Ugaritic and Phoenician names, the absence of deities as a source of joy or compassion in Aramaic names, and the absence of divine choice and compassion in Palmyrene names. She concludes that each collection of onomastica reflects a different type of "piety." Further, and importantly, she notes that the theophoric names in the epigraphical material contain the same semantic material as that found in the biblical onomastica.

[76] John Day, *Yahweh and the Gods and Goddesses of Canaan,* Journal for the Study of the Old Testament: Supplement Series 265 (Sheffield: Sheffield Academic Press, 2000), 227–28, argues against the view of Tigay that this demonstrates the worship of a single deity in Monarchic Israel. While the extreme position of total monotheism can hardly be demonstrated (neither in the Bible nor in extrabiblical inscriptions), the Yahwistic element of the personal names is significant. Day presents four arguments: (1) Yahwistic names imply not that Yahweh was the only deity but that he was the most important deity; (2) many names could be traditional; (3) Tigay's evidence is limited to late monarchic Judah; (4) the statistic ratio of the number of Yahwistic names in comparison with the number of "pagan" names is lower than suggested. The following responses to these arguments may be made. (1) The first argument is not relevant because it does not challenge the data nor does it prove the alternative. (2) Whether the names are traditional or not, it nevertheless proves that people preferred Yahwistic names. (3) Tigay's evidence includes all available onomastic data from within Palestine. Although a preponderance of the evidence originates in late Monarchic Judean contexts, the dramatic increase in the number of personal names in the decade since Tigay wrote has not changed the percentages and conclusions. (4) The error is not identified in detail by Day so it is difficult to evaluate the validity of this argument. However, the scholars cited in this section do not seem to agree with this observation.

[77] Cf. Richard S. Hess, *Amarna Personal Names,* American Schools of Oriental Research Dissertation Series 9 (Winona Lake, IN: Eisenbrauns, 1993), 235–36.

[78] Frank L. Benz, *Personal Names in the Phoenician and Punic Inscriptions,* Studia Pohl 8 (Rome: Biblical Institute Press, 1972), 233–34. Richard J. Clifford, "Phoenician Religion," *Bulletin of the American Schools of Oriental Research* 279 (1990): 55–64, has observed the multiplicity of deities worshiped in all of the Phoenician deities, arguing for a special emphasis on a triad of deities at the top.

the Israelite evidence because they derive from multiple urban centers across widely dispersed geographic regions.

But is there really a difference in the contemporary extrabiblical evidence among surrounding nations?[79] For example, Lemaire notes that, in inscriptions of Transjordanian and Aramaean peoples, the names all contain a limited number of deities, less than in Mesopotamia or Egypt.[80] Therefore, this suggests a resemblance to Israelite personal names.

Although Zevit endorses this conclusion, his own analysis of the Ammonite onomastica tells a different story.[81] There the chief deity, Milkom, occurs in only nine names.[82] *'l* occurs 150 times, lending

---

[79] There clearly seems to be a difference if the personal names in the Bible are taken into account. Zevit, *Religions of Ancient Israel*, 586–609, presents a different view of the Israelite personal names with divine name elements. He notes that the Yahweh names are the largest class of Israelite names, dominant from the United Monarchy until the exile. Yahweh is never depicted as an animal nor is he ever referred to as "Prince" (*zbl*) or "treasure" (*nks*). This is based on the 2,202 Israelite names counted in Ran Zadok, *The Pre-Hellenistic Israelite Anthroponymy and Prosopography*, Orientalia Lovaniensia Analecta 28 (Leuven: Peeters, 1988): 397–459. Zevit estimates that less than 20 percent of Israelites bore non-Yahwistic names (*Religions of Ancient Israel*, 608n95). Other deities that were worshipped include: Canaanite ˒*nt, ym, mwt*, and *ršp* (but not Asherah!); and the Egyptian '*mwn, ḥwr, bs* (Bes in *bsy*, Ezra 2:49), and *ʾs* (Isis). Given that Yahwistic names appear from the time of the United Monarchy, it is clear that the spread of Yahwism is pre-Davidic as many in David's administration bore Yahwistic names (Zevit, *Religions of Ancient Israel*, 607). If the majority of Israelites were Yahwistic, the multiple cult centers suggest no single or centralized means of worshipping. Following Dennis Pardee, "An Evaluation of the Proper Names from Ebla from a West Semitic Perspective: Pantheon Distribution according to Genre," in *Archiv reali di Ebla* 1 (Rome: Missione Archaeologica Italiana in Syria, 1988), 132, Zevit, *Religions of Ancient Israel*, 608, argues that Yahwistic names indicate little about cultic affiliation (though this is not strictly what Pardee said). First Kings 19:18 reports 7,000 who had not bowed to Baal, this out of a total population of the ninth-century north Israel of about 500,000 is less than 5 percent. On the other hand, exclusive Baal worshippers of the north in the ninth century could fill the temple of Baal, and that could be at most a few thousand (2 Kgs 10:19–21; Zevit, *Religions of Ancient Israel*, 649–50). Within Israel there was a minority who chose the names of other deities for their children, but in general the non-Yahwistic names seem to have been used by parents with Yahwistic names and vice versa (Zevit, *Religions of Ancient Israel*, 649). This suggests random choices for at least one minority group.

[80] André Lemaire, "Déesses et dieux de Syria-Palestine d'apres les inscriptions (c. 1000–500 Av. N. E.)," in *Ein Gott allein? JHWH-verehrung und biblischer Monotheismus im Kontext der Israelitischen und altorientalischen Religiongeschichte*, ed. Walter Dietrich and Martin A. Klopfenstein (Fribourg: Universitätsverlag; Göttingen: Vandenhoeck & Ruprecht, 1994), 135–45.

[81] Zevit, *Religions of Ancient Israel*, 651n75. For these purposes Zevit relies on the work of Aufrecht 1989:356–376, a collection of Ammonite inscriptions including all available data from seals and bullae.

[82] Zevit notes this fact but does not attempt to explain it.

credence to the view that this is a generic term for "god," whether in Ammon or Israel.[83] Other deities and their frequencies include: *b'l*—2; *gd*—3; *yh/yhw*—3; *mwt*—1; and *mr*—1.[84] When the earlier study of Jackson on the Ammonite names is used, similar results obtain: *'l*—48; *'nrt*—1; *bl*—1; *šm*—1; *nny*—1; *'m'*—1.[85] In contrast with Israel, where Yahwistic names have a huge dominance compared with all those compounded with other deities, in Ammon the evidence is the opposite. Ammonite personal names composed of other deities outnumber those with Milkom. Thus the situation provides a real contrast. Similar implications can be found when examining the Moabite and Philistine collections of personal names. However, all these provide considerably fewer names than the Ammonite corpus.

A challenge to the use of personal names in the study of Israelite religion has come from Callaway.[86] Using biblical and archaeological evidence, he attempts to argue that the personal names on Israelite seals and bullae describe an elite, urban population that was dominated by the reforms of Josiah and does not reflect the larger rural population. However, none of this is convincing.

First, there is much more evidence of writing in ancient Israel than his sources would suggest.[87] The eleventh-century abecedary at the village of Izbet-Sartah, the multiple attestations of writing from villages

---

[83] Walter Aufrecht, "The Religion of the Ammonites," in *Ancient Ammon*, ed. Burton MacDonald and Randall W. Younkers (Leiden: Brill, 1999), 152–62, suggests the view that El was the chief deity in Ammon, and therefore these references are not to a generic term for a deity but rather to a god named El similar to the chief deity of the Ugaritic pantheon. However, no textual evidence outside the onomastica supports this. Further, the consistent usage of *'l* as a generic term for deity in Israelite texts, as well as those of all surrounding peoples in the Iron Age, places the burden of proof on the attempt to assert that El was recognized as a specific deity in Ammon.

[84] As in Israel, goddesses such as Asherah receive little or no mention.

[85] Kent P. Jackson, "Ammonite Personal Names in the Context of West Semitic Onomasticon," in *The Word of the Lord Shall Go Forth: Essays in Honor of David Noel Freedman in Celebration of His Sixtieth Birthday*, ed. Carol L. Meyers and Michael O'Connor (Philadelphia: American Schools of Oriental Research, 1983), 518.

[86] Roger Callaway, "The Name Game: Onomastic Evidence and Archaeological Reflections on Religion in Late Judah," *Jian Dao* 2 (1999): 15–36.

[87] Cf. David W. Jamieson-Drake, *Scribes and Scribal Schools in Monarchic Judah: A Socio-Archaeological Approach*, Journal for the Study of the Old Testament: Supplement Series 109; Social World of Biblical Antiquity 9 (Sheffield: Almond, 1991). Contrast Alan R. Millard, "The Knowledge of Writing in Iron Age Palestine," *Tyndale Bulletin* 46 (1995): 207–17; Hess, "Yahweh and His Asherah?"

and rural areas in every century of the Iron Age, and the seals with written names possessed by individuals of many different classes attest to the wide use of writing. Further, the number of published seals and bullae has more than doubled since discovery of the sources that Callaway used, and there is a wide range of writing styles on these seals, reflecting both the elite and their professional scribes as well as those who were neither professional nor artistic.[88] To attribute all seals and sources of personal names to Judah's urban elite is speculation.

Second, Callaway ignores the neighboring cultures where the evidence for the personal names exists at the same time on similar sources of seals and bullae and yet reveals a completely different set of data in terms of references to foreign deities, as noted above. In this regard, a major pillar of Callaway's argument rests on what he calls standardization, in which personal names of a whole nation, or at least the elite, are changed to follow the policy of the capital.

If this is the case in Jerusalem, there is no evidence for it. There are no contemporary examples. More importantly, one would expect to see examples of names changing from non-Yahwistic forms to Yahwistic forms between generations. This does not exist. Nor can it be argued that all the seals and bullae must come from Josiah's reign and later, that is, after 650 BC. Paleography does not support this claim.

To conclude regarding the onomastic evidence, the dominant and almost sole use of the divine name Yahweh in the onomastics of ancient Israel suggest that this deity played a role in Israel distinct from how the surrounding nations regarded their chief deities. While it is certainly true that the mention of deities in the personal names does not necessarily prove the dominance of a deity in the religion of the peoples, the onomastic evidence should not be dismissed as completely irrelevant. Like all the other types of evidence, it must be taken into consideration where the totality of data is limited.[89] In the eighth and seventh

---

[88] Tigay, *You Shall Have No Other Gods*. See Aaron Demsky and Meir Bar-Ilan, "Writings in Ancient Israel and Early Judaism," in *Mikra: Text, Translation, Reading and Interpretation of the Hebrew Bible in Ancient Judaism and Early Christianity*, ed. Martin Jan Mulder (Assen/Maastricht: Van Gorcum; Philadelphia: Fortress, 1988), 15; Nahman Avigad, *Hebrew Bullae from the Time of Jeremiah* (Jerusalem: Israel Exploration Society, 1986), 121; William M. Schniedewind, "Orality and Literacy in Ancient Israel," *Religious Studies Review* 26/4 (October 2000): 328.

[89] See Pardee, "An Evaluation of Proper Names"; Callaway, "Name Game"; and Smith, *Early*

centuries, the only period of Iron Age Israel with significant onomastic evidence, the public recognition of Yahweh in Israel and Judah's naming of their children reached an exclusive level that has no parallel among the neighboring nations.[90]

Conclusions

This brief survey of selected evidence has revealed several important observations about the distinct nature of ancient Israelite religion as evident in several of the forms of the extrabiblical evidence.

First, the evidence suggests an aniconic aspect that is evident in many of the assemblages of evidence. This is true in the highland villages of Iron Age I Palestine where there is a significant absence of religious paraphernalia in contrast with predecessors and with contemporary fortified sites. If there was an altar on Mt. Ebal, then this absence of images seems to have been found in Israelite religion from the beginning. Its continuation at a major center such as Tel Arad may attest to the ongoing presence of this phenomenon. Tryggve Mettinger's careful survey of the evidence leads him to conclude an association between this imageless religion and that found in the desert to the south, a region also associated with the earliest appearance of the divine name Yahweh, as part of a place name.[91] Mettinger relates this aniconism to the unworked

---

History of God, 4–5, for the discussion of the limitations of the onomastic evidence. This is based on the Ugaritic and Punic personal names and the deities represented in them. While it is true that *ṯrt* is rare in personal names from Ugarit, it is nevertheless also true that deities such as Baal and Dagan, who are represented in the major temples and archaeological evidence from Ugarit, also occur frequently in the personal names. Furthermore, Baal (along with the other names of the storm deity, *hdd*), is second in frequency in the "principal gods of the cultic-sacrificial pantheon of Ugarit," those receiving the most offerings. On the other hand, Dagan is not mentioned among the first 17 deities. See Gregorio del Olmo Lete, *Canaanite Religion: According to the Liturgical Texts of Ugarit* (Bethesda: CDL, 1999), 71. Thus the evidence from the cultic texts does not agree with that of the archaeological data. Therefore, none of this evidence should be dismissed. Instead, it should all be taken into consideration until such a time as evidence is available that allows greater clarity.

[90] See Richard S. Hess, "Aspects of Israelite Personal Names and Pre-Exilic Israelite Religion," in *New Seals and Inscriptions: Hebrew, Idumean and Cuneiform,* ed. Meir Lubetski, Hebrew Monographs 8 (Sheffield: Sheffield Phoenix, 2007), 301–13, for a diachronic analysis of the theophoric elements in the personal names from four archives of Israel and Judah that supports the exceptionally large percentage of Yahwistic names in these states in contrast with the corresponding theophoric elements in the neighboring states.

[91] See Tryggve N. D. Mettinger, *No Graven Image? Israelite Aniconism in Its Ancient Near*

standing stones or mazzebot that occur at the bull site, at Tel Arad, and at other sites within ancient Israel. He notes the earlier presence of these sorts of mazzebot in the Negev, particularly in the Uvda and Timnah Valleys in the southern part.[92] Thus the origins of this aspect of Israelite religion and perhaps its earlier manifestation suggest that it was brought from the southern desert by groups, perhaps the Israelites themselves, at the time of their earliest appearance and settlement in Palestine.

Second, it is possible that the chief deity was at times represented in a form common to that of the leading West Semitic god, El, as a bull.[93] In addition, the leading storm god, Baal or Hadad in West Semitic tradition, could be represented as a bull or bull calf. This image is found on the Taanach cult stand, on a panel that corresponds to a vacant one, perhaps representing the imageless form and the image of the chief god. Of course the twelfth-century bull site itself produced a form of just such a creature. The other images considered here, those on the jar fragments from Kuntillet 'Ajrud c. 800 BC, suggest Bes-type figures that cannot be definitely correlated with the writing scribbled on a line beside them. These may point to deities but if so (following Zevit) the Bes forms symbolize the deity; they are not intended as a pictorial representation of Yahweh and Asherata. Elsewhere the general absence of pictorial images, which reaches a total dearth in seventh-century Judah, implies the increasing influence of the aniconic religious belief on practitioners in the southern kingdom.

Third, other deities were known in ancient Israel. Baal may occur in some personal names from eighth-century BC Samaria, though this

---

Eastern Context, Coniectanea Biblica Old Testament Series 42 (Stockholm: Amqvist & Wiksell, 1995), 174. For a compilation of the evidence, biblical and archaeological, for the origins of Yahweh worship in the south, see especially Lars E. Axelsson, *The Lord Rose Up from Seir: Studies in the History and Traditions of the Negev and Southern Judah*, Coniectanea Biblica Old Testament Series 25 (Stockholm: Amqvist & Wiksell, 1987).

[92] For this he is dependent on the seminal research of Uzi Avner, "Ancient Cult Sites in the Negev and Sinai Deserts," *Tel Aviv* 11 (1984): 115–31; *idem*, "Ancient Agricultural Settlement and Religion in the Uvda Valley in Southern Israel," *Biblical Archaeologist* 53 (1990): 125–41; *idem*, *Maççebot* Sites in the Negev and Sinai and Their Significance," in *Biblical Archaeology Today, 1990: Proceedings of the Second International Congress on Biblical Archaeology; Jerusalem, June-July 1990*, ed. Avraham Biran and Joseph Aviram (Jerusalem: Israel Exploration Society, 1993), 166–81; *idem*, "Sacred Stones in the Desert," *Biblical Archaeology Review* 27/3 (May/June 2001): 30–41.

[93] Daniel E. Fleming, "If El Is a Bull, Who Is a Calf? Reflections on Religion in Second-Millennium Syria-Palestine," *Eretz-Israel* 26 (1999): 23–27.

is disputed. He is mentioned in the Kuntillet 'Ajrud inscription. El also appears there and in the Deir 'Allā inscriptions, although their language suggests that they may have been written by non-Israelites. Like Baal, El appears in personal names. However, it is even more likely that this is a common noun "god" that describes the chief deity, and so may be used as an epithet for Yahweh. In fact, the sole deity that achieves any prominence is the goddess Asherah or Asherata.

Her appearance in Israelite religion seems to occur as early as the tenth century, if the Taanach cult stand can be considered truly Israelite and if two of the panels that center on a naked female and on a tree can be identified with her. She may also appear with Yahweh in the blessings found at Kuntillet 'Ajrud and at Khirbet el-Qom. While this interpretation is disputed, I have argued elsewhere and continue to believe that this is the most probable interpretation of the references to "Yahweh and Asheratah."[94] If she is identified with the terracotta figurines, then Asherah continues to be present in Judah right to the end of the period and the Babylonian destruction of Jerusalem.[95]

Therefore, some Israelites regarded Asherah as an important goddess and consort of Yahweh. However, this must be balanced with the absence of Asherah in the onomastica, in other inscriptions such as Ein Gedi and Khirbet Beit Lei, and with the elimination of any reference to her in the many inscriptions that date to the final decades of the Judean Monarchy. The last 60 years of this period were omitted from consideration, because of the generally recognized appearance of Yahwistic monotheism at this time. However, it is important to note that Asherah's complete absence in all the blessing formulae of letters and all other Judean references to deity is a surprise if she was a prominent figure in the immediately preceding period.

In fact, it remains to be proven that Asherah was a dominant deity even in c. 800 BC. Her absence in the onomastica and in other inscriptions, as well as the lack of association of this deity with Israel among any of the inscriptions from nearby nations, make it difficult to accept that she held any clear place in the official cult(s). Her domestic role,

---

[94] Hess, "Yahweh and His Asherah?"
[95] William G. Dever, *Did God Have a Wife? Archaeology and Folk Religion in Ancient Israel* (Grand Rapids: Eerdmans, 2005).

while emphasized by some scholars,[96] remains unclear because there is no inscriptional material to connect her to the female terracotta figurines, whose own function remains unclear.

Fourth and finally, the onomastica suggest a role for Yahweh as chief god in a manner distinct from neighboring lands. Pardee demonstrated that, in terms of the relative importance of the different deities at Ugarit, the onomastica reveal a different perspective than do the myths and other text genres.[97] However, this does not prove that the personal names reveal nothing about the relative importance of various deities. This is all the more true when a concentration of Yahwistic names exists to the near exclusion of others and when this is unique in comparison with surrounding nations. Further, this deity possesses distinctive character traits not found in the onomastica of other nations. Together, the evidence suggests that on the public level of personal names, the worship of Yahweh was somewhat exclusive in ancient Israel and virtually exclusive in Judah, especially later in time.

Thus the overall evidence is that of an ongoing contest between a special worship of Yahweh, on the one hand, and a worship of Yahweh that included other deities (especially Asherah) on the other. Although there is evidence of times when Yahweh was part of a pantheon, this deity's dominance is exceptional, and it suggests something more than a chief or national deity. To this should be added the largely aniconic nature of the worship and the distinctive confessional aspects found in some inscriptions and the personal names.

Yahweh appears sovereign over forces of nature and exhibits mercy, love, joy, and compassion. In general, he is not identified with physical objects, with animals, nor with the production of offspring. While both the names and texts are largely limited to the latter part of the period under consideration, they remain the only written evidence that we possess. Thus the Yahweh of these texts, supported by the iconography and cult sites that reach into earlier periods, all attest to a distinctive role and view of this deity that diverges from that of the other nations and their deities.

---

[96] Dever, *What Did the Biblical Writers Know*; idem, *Did God Have a Wife?*
[97] Pardee, "An Evaluation of the Proper Names."

Chapter 13

DID GOD COMMAND THE GENOCIDE OF THE CANAANITES?

Matthew Flannagan

O ne of the most perplexing issues facing Christian believers is a series of jarring texts in the Old Testament. After their liberation from slavery in Egypt, the Israelites arrived on the edge of the Promised Land. In Deuteronomy, God commanded Israel to "destroy totally" the people occupying these regions (the Canaanites); the Israelites were to "not leave alive anything that breathes" (20:16 NIV). The book of Joshua records the carrying out of this command at Jericho: "they devoted the city to the LORD and destroyed with the sword every living thing in it—men and women, young and old, cattle, sheep and donkeys" (6:21 NIV). Several chapters later, we read that throughout the region Joshua "left no survivors. He totally destroyed all who breathed, just as the LORD, the God of Israel, had commanded" (10:40; cf. 11:14). The text mentions city after city where Joshua, at God's command, puts every inhabitant "to the sword," "totally destroyed everyone," and "left no survivors" (10:28,30,33,37,39–40; 11:8).

If one takes these passages literally, one must conclude this is a record of divinely authorized commission of genocide. Critics of Christian theism often ask a rhetorical question: How could a good and loving God command the extermination of the Canaanites?[1]

---

[1] Raymond Bradley develops this objection in "A Moral Argument for Atheism," in *The Impossibility of God*, ed. Michael Martin and Ricki Monnier (Amherst, NY: Prometheus Books, 2003), 144–45. Similar arguments to Bradley's have been made by Wes Moriston, "Did God Command Genocide? A Challenge to the Biblical Inerrantist," *Philosophia Christi*

One response, which goes back to the patristic era, is to suggest that the strict, literal reading on which this rhetorical question is based is mistaken. Recently, several Protestant scholars have suggested a hyperbolic reading of the relevant passages.[2] They suggest language such as "destroy totally," "do not leave alive anything that breathes," destroy "men and women, young and old," and so on, should be understood more like how we understand what a person means who yells, in the context of watching Lennox Lewis in a boxing match: "Knock his block off! Hand him his head! Take him out!" or hopes that the All Blacks will "annihilate the Springboks" or "totally slaughter the Wallabies." Now, the sports fan does not actually want Lennox Lewis to decapitate his opponent or for the All Blacks to become mass murderers. The same could be true here: understood in a nonliteral sense, the phrases probably were hyperbolic ways of telling the Israelites to defeat and drive out the Canaanites and "were not used and are not intended literally."[3]

Nicholas Wolterstorff suggests:

> The Book of Joshua has to be read as a theologically oriented narration, stylized and hyperbolic at important points, of

---

11/1 (2009): 8–26; Randal Rauser, "Let Nothing that Breathes Remain Alive: On the Problem of Divinely Commanded Genocide," *Philosophia Christi* 11/1 (2009): 27–41; Michael Tooley, "Does God Exist?" in Michael Tooley and Alvin Plantinga, *The Knowledge of God* (Malden, MA: Blackwell Publishers, 2008), 73–77; Edwin Curley, "The God of Abraham, Isaac, and Jacob," and Evan Fales, "Satanic Verses: Moral Chaos in Holy Writ," in *Divine Evil? The Moral Character of the God of Abraham*, ed. Michael Bergmann, Michael J. Murray, and Michael C. Rea (New York: Oxford University Press, 2011), 58–78, 91–108; Louise Antony, "Atheism as Perfect Piety," and Walter Sinnott-Armstrong, "Why Traditional Theism Cannot Provide an Adequate Foundation for Morality," in *Is Goodness without God Good Enough? A Debate on Faith, Secularism, and Ethics*, ed. Robert K. Garcia and Nathan L. King (Lanham, MD: Rowman & Littlefield Publishers, 2009), 67–84, 101–16.

[2] Alvin Plantinga, "Comments on 'Satanic Verses: Moral Chaos in Holy Writ,'" in Bergmann, Murray, and Rea, *Divine Evil?* 110–11; Paul Copan, "Yahweh Wars and the Canaanites: Divinely Mandated Genocide or Corporate Capital Punishment," *Philosophia Christi* n.s. 11/1 (2009): 73–90; idem, *Is God a Moral Monster? Making Sense of the Old Testament* (Grand Rapids: Baker Books, 2011), 158–97; Christopher Wright, *The God I Don't Understand: Reflections on Tough Questions of Faith* (Grand Rapids: Zondervan, 2008), 87–88. In his latest discussion on the issue, William Lane Craig states, "I've come to appreciate that the object of God's command to the Israelis was not the slaughter of the Canaanites, as is often imagined. The command rather was primarily to drive them out of the land. The judgment upon these Canaanite kingdoms was to dispossess them of their land and thus destroy them as kingdoms." See "Question 147: Divine Command Morality and Voluntarism," accessed October 29, 2010, http://www.reasonablefaith.org/site/News2?page=NewsArticle&id=7911.

[3] Plantinga, "Comments," 111.

Israel's early skirmishes in the Promised Land, with the story of these battles being framed by descriptions of two great rit- ualized events. The story as a whole celebrates Joshua as the great leader of his people, faithful to Yahweh, worthy successor of Moses. If we strip the word "hagiography" of its negative connotations we can call it a hagiographic account of Joshua's events.[4]

In this essay I will defend Wolterstorff's position. In Part 1, I will sketch, adapt, and defend Wolterstorff's argument. In Part 2, I will argue that external evidence from comparative studies in ancient Near Eastern conquest accounts gives considerable support to Wolterstorff's position. Finally, in part 3, I will look at two implications of this position.

Wolterstorff's Argument

Wolterstorff's contention is that "a careful reading of the text in its literary context makes it implausible to interpret it as claiming that Yahweh ordered extermination." It is important to understand what he means by context. Here, it is clear that Wolterstorff is advocating a *canonical* approach. He notes that

Joshua as we have it today was intended as a component in the larger sequence consisting of Deuteronomy, Joshua, Judges, I and II Samuel, and I and II Kings. . . . I propose that we interpret the Book of Joshua as a component within this larger sequence—in particular, that we interpret it as preceded by Deuteronomy and succeeded by Judges.[5]

Joshua comes after Deuteronomy and before Judges. These books should be read as a single narrative—a connected literary unit. For example, Josh 24:28–31 mentions Joshua's death and burial place at Timnathserah "in the hill country of Ephraim" (NIV). This is deliber- ately connected to Judg 2:6–9, which mentions Joshua's death and burial place at Timnath-heres "in the hill country of Ephraim" (NIV). The first

---

[4] Nicholas Wolterstorff, "Reading Joshua," in *Divine Evil? The Moral Character of the God of Abraham*, ed. Michael Bergmann, Michael J. Murray, and Michael C. Rea (New York: Oxford University Press, 2010), 252–53.

[5] Ibid., 249.

and last consonants are switched (from *serah* to *heres*)—a Hebrew literary device. Not only this, Judges connects to 1 (and 2) Samuel (the next
book in the Hebrew canon) with its reference to "the hill country of
Ephraim."[6]

When one does read these books as a connected literary unit, several
issues are apparent. Joshua 6–11 summarizes several battles and concludes, "So Joshua took the entire land, just as the LORD had directed
Moses, and he gave it as an inheritance to Israel according to their tribal
divisions. Then the land had rest from war" (Josh 11:23 NIV).[7] Judges,
however, opens with a battle that occurs *after* Joshua's death; it states,

> After the death of Joshua, the Israelites inquired of the Lord,
> "Who shall go up first for us against the Canaanites, to fight
> against them?" The Lord said, "Judah shall go up. I hereby
> give the land into his hand." Judah said to his brother Simeon,
> "Come up with me into the territory allotted to me, that we
> may fight against the Canaanites; then I too will go with you
> into the territory allotted to you." So Simeon went with him.
> Then Judah went up and the Lord gave the Canaanites and the
> Perizzites into their hand; and they defeated ten thousand of
> them at Bezek. (Judg 1:1–4)

Taken literally, the book of Joshua states that Joshua conquered the
whole land and yet Judges states that much of the land was unconquered.

---

[6] Note this phrase "the hill country of Ephraim" in Joshua (17:15; 19:50; 20:7; 24:30,33),
then in Judges (2:9; 3:27; 4:5; 7:24; 10:1; 17:1,8; 18:2,13; 19:1,16,18), and then in 1 Samuel
(1:1; 9:4). The linkage of Judg 17:1 and 19:1 with 1 Sam 1:1 is connected by the general three-
fold pattern of (1) "There was a (certain) man . . . "; (2) "from the hill country of Ephraim";
(3) "and his name was _____."

As mentioned in the text, Josh 24:28–31 mentions Joshua's death and burial place at
Timnath-serah "in the hill country of Ephraim," and then Judg 2:6–9 refers to Joshua's death
and burial place at Timnath-heres "in the hill country of Ephraim." That is, Joshua and Judges
are literarily connected in their mention of Joshua's (1) death and (2) burial. (1) Both books
state that "Joshua son of Nun, the servant of the LORD, died" at the age of "a hundred and ten"
(Josh 24:29; Judg 2:8). (2) Then a deliberate literary connection is made on the burial place
of Joshua, using the Hebrew letter-substitution cipher known as *atbash*, in this case revers-
ing the first and last consonants of the burial place from "-*serah*" to "-*heres*." Compare "they
buried him in the territory of his inheritance in *Timnath-serah*, which is in the hill country of
Ephraim, on the north of Mount Gaash" (Josh 24:30, NASB, my emphasis) with "they buried
him in the territory of his inheritance in *Timnath-heres*, in the hill country of Ephraim, north
of Mount Gaash (Judg 2:9, NASB, my emphasis). I owe these examples to Paul Copan.

[7] All Scripture quotations are from the NIV unless otherwise stated.

Similarly, Joshua affirms that he exterminated all the Canaanites in this region; repeatedly the text states that Joshua left "no survivors" and "destroyed everything that breathed" in "the entire land" and "put all the inhabitants to the sword." Alongside these general claims, the text identifies several specific places and cities where Joshua exterminated everyone and left no survivors. These include Hebron, Debir, the hill country, the Negev, and the western foothills (Josh 10:38,40). Yet in the first chapter of Judges we are told that the Canaanites lived in the Negev, the hill country, the western foothills, Hebron, and Debir (1:9–11). Moreover, they did so in such numbers and strength that they had to be driven out by force. These are the same cities that Joshua 10 tells us Joshua had annihilated, leaving no survivors.[8]

Likewise, Josh 11:23 states that "Joshua took the entire land" and then "gave it as an inheritance to Israel according to their tribal divisions" (NIV). Note: the conquered region is the *same land* that is later divided among the Israelite tribes. Only a chapter later, when the text turns to giving an account of these tribal divisions, the allotments begin with God telling Joshua, "You are very old, and there are still very large areas of land to be taken over" (13:1 NIV). Moreover, when one examines the allotment given to Judah, we see Caleb asking permission to drive the Anakites from the hill countries (14:11), and we also hear how Caleb has to defeat Anakites living in Hebron and, after this, marches against the people "living in Debir" (15:13–19). Similarly, it is evident with several of the other allotments that the people were yet to drive out Canaanites entrenched in the area and that the Israelites were not always successful in doing so.

We read, for example, that the Ephraimites and Manassites "did not dislodge the Canaanites living in Gezer; to this day the Canaanites live among the people of Ephraim" (Josh 16:10 NIV). Similarly, in chap. 17 it states, "Yet the Manassites were not able to occupy these towns, for the Canaanites were determined to live in that region. However, when the

---

[8] In addition to these general claims about exterminating populations, Josh 11:21–22 states, "Joshua went and destroyed the Anakites from the hill country: from Hebron, Debir and Anab, from all the hill country of Judah" (NIV). This happened after Joshua is already said to have killed the inhabitants in these areas in Josh 10:30–40. Joshua 11:21 states that no *Anakites* were left living in Israeli territory after this campaign. In Judg 1:21 the text explicitly states that Anakites are in Hebron.

Israelites grew stronger, they subjected the Canaanites to forced labor but did not drive them out completely" (17:12–13 NIV). We hear that "Danites had difficulty taking possession of their territory, so they went up and attacked Leshem, took it, put it to the sword and occupied it. They settled in Leshem and named it Dan after their forefather" (19:47). Here, we see the same land said to be subdued and conquered by Joshua in battles where he exterminated and left alive nothing that breathed. This land was yet to be occupied by the tribes of Israel and is occupied by Canaanites, often heavily armed and deeply entrenched (17:17–18).[9]

Finally, the account of what God commanded differs in the two narratives. Joshua asserts: "He left no survivors. He totally destroyed all who breathed, *just as the* LORD, *the God of Israel, had commanded*" (10:40, my italics) and "exterminating them without mercy, as *the* LORD *had commanded Moses*" (11:20b, my italics). However, when this command is retroactively referred to in Judg 2:1, there is no mention of genocide or annihilation. Instead we hear of how God had promised to drive them out as well as His command to the Israelites not to make treaties with the Canaanites and to destroy their shrines. This silence is significant in

---

[9] Kenneth A. Kitchen, *On the Reliability of the Old Testament* (Grand Rapids: Eerdmans, 2003). Kitchen notes that a careful reading of the earlier chapters makes it clear that Israel did not actually conquer the areas mentioned at all. Kitchen notes that, according to Josh 4:19, after crossing the Jordan the Israelites set up camp in Gilgal on the eastern border of Jericho (161). Rather, after every battle in the next six chapters the text explicitly states that they returned to Gilgal:

> The conflict with Canaanite city-state rulers in the south part of Canaan is worth close observation. After the battle for Gibeon, we see the Hebrews advance upon six towns in order, attacking and capturing them, killing their local kings and such of the inhabitants as had not gotten clear, *and moving on, not holding on to these places*. Twice over (10:15, 43), it is clearly stated that their strike force *returned to base camp at Gilgal*. So there was no sweeping takeover and occupation of this region at this point. And *no* total destruction of the towns attacked (162).

Kitchen goes on to comment:

> What happened in the south was repeated up north. Hazor was both leader and famed center for the north Canaanite kinglets. Thus as in the south, the Hebrew strike force defeated the opposition; they captured their towns, killed rulers and less mobile inhabitants, and symbolically burned Hazor, and Hazor only, to emphasise the end of its local supremacy. Again Israel did *not* attempt to immediately hold on to Galilee; they remained *based at Gilgal* (cf. 14:6) (ibid.).

Kitchen points out that "the first indication of a *real* move in occupation outward beyond Gilgal comes in 18:4" (162). This is after the first allotment of "lands-to-be-occupied had been made," and as we saw above, the Israelites did not find occupying these allotments easy. He concludes: "these campaigns were essentially *disabling raids*: they were not territorial conquests with instant Hebrew occupation. The text is very clear about this" (ibid.).

the context. If God had commanded genocide, then it is odd that only instructions concerning treaties and shrines were mentioned.

Therefore, taken as a single narrative and taken literally, Joshua 1–11 gives a seemingly different account of events to that narrated by Judges and also to that narrated by the later chapters of Joshua itself.[10]

Wolterstorff makes a further point,

> Those whose occupation it is to try to determine the origins of these writings will suggest that the editors had contradictory records, oral traditions, and so forth to work with. No doubt this is correct. But those who edited the final version of these writings into one sequence were not mindless; they could see, as well as you and I can see, the tensions and contradictions— surface or real—that I have pointed to. So what is going on?[11]

Wolterstorff's point is that, regardless of what sources or strata of tradition are alleged behind the final form of Joshua, the editors who put these books into a single narrative would have been well aware of the obvious tensions in the passages mentioned above. Moreover, they were not mindless or stupid. They would not want to affirm that both accounts were a literal description of what occurred. Yet they chose to put in the canon, next to Joshua, a book that began with a narration at odds with a literal reading of the early chapters of Joshua. Moreover, the author of Joshua chose to juxtapose the picture of Joshua 1–11 with the later chapters I mentioned above. They cannot, therefore, be asserting that both accounts are literally true.

---

[10] In this section I am arguing that the record of Joshua *fulfilling* the command is hyperbolic. Even many evangelical scholars who believe the command was literal accept this. For example, David M. Howard Jr. argues that, on the one hand, statements claiming Joshua subdued "the whole region" (10:40) are hyperbolic assertions emphasizing that "there was indeed a sweeping victory" and that "no significant opposition remained." Such was intended "to reiterate the theological point made many times in the book that God was indeed giving Israel the entire land." On the other hand, "the author acknowledged elsewhere that the conquest was indeed not complete" and that "there was still much work to do" (*Joshua*, New American Commentary [Nashville: B&H, 1998], 259). See also Richard Hess, *Joshua: An Introduction and Commentary*, Tyndale Old Testament Commentary (Downers Grove, IL: InterVarsity, 1996), 284–86. Where I differ from them is over the implications of this conclusion. I argue below that if fulfillment is hyperbolic, then a plausible implication is that the command itself was hyperbolic.

[11] Wolterstorff, "Reading Joshua," in Bergmann et al., *Divine Evil?* 251.

I think Wolterstorff is right on this. However, his position could be strengthened on theological grounds. In *Divine Discourse: Philosophical Reflections on the Claim that God Speaks,* Wolterstorff provides an interesting and rigorous analysis of the notion that Scripture is the Word of God. Central to his analysis is that "an eminently plausible construal of the process whereby these books found their way into a single canonical text, would be that by way of that process of canonization, God was authorizing these books as together constituting a single volume of divine discourse."[12]

This understanding of Scripture provides the theological justification for reading the text as a single series. By examining what was affirmed in Judges and in later passages of Joshua, one can determine what the author of the early chapters of Joshua intended.[13] Moreover, if the primary author of Scripture is God, then obviously the primary author of the final canonical text is unlikely to have deliberately (or accidentally) authored an obviously contradictory narrative. Hence, even if the contradictions were not obvious to the authors (and I think Wolterstorff correctly infers that these apparent contradictions would have been),[14]

---

[12] Nicholas Wolterstorff, *Divine Discourse: Philosophical Reflections on the Claim that God Speaks* (Cambridge: Cambridge University Press, 1995), 295. See also "Unity behind the Canon," in *One Scripture or Many? The Canon from Biblical, Theological and Philosophical Perspectives,* ed. Christine Helmer and Christof Landmesser (New York: Oxford University Press, 2004), 217–32.

[13] Alvin Plantinga argues in *Warranted Christian Belief* (New York: Oxford University Press, 2000), 385:

> [A]n assumption of the enterprise is that the principal author of the Bible—the entire Bible—is God himself (according to Calvin, God the Holy Spirit). Of course each of the books of the Bible has a human author or authors as well; still, the principal author is God. This impels us to treat the whole more like a unified communication than a miscellany of ancient books. Scripture isn't so much a library of independent books as itself a book with many subdivisions but a central theme: the message of the gospel. By virtue of this unity, furthermore (by virtue of the fact that there is just one principal author), it is possible to "interpret Scripture with Scripture." If a given passage from one of Paul's epistles is puzzling, it is perfectly proper to try to come to clarity as to what God's teaching is in this passage by appealing not only to what Paul himself says elsewhere in other epistles but also to what is taught elsewhere in Scripture (for example, the Gospel of John).

[14] Nicholas Wolterstorff in the question-and-answers session following presentation of his paper "Reading Joshua" (presented at the "My Ways Are Not Your Ways: The Character of the God of the Hebrew Bible" conference at the Center for Philosophy of Religion, University of Notre Dame, 12 September 2009, accessed Dec. 19, 2009, <http://www.nd.edu/~cprelig/conferences/documents/HBprogram_006.pdf>, stated that the phrase "he killed all the inhabitants with the edge of the sword" occurs at least 15 times in Joshua 6–11 in close succession. This is "hammered home with emphasis." This is then followed in the next chapter by the

they would be evident to God. Given that the process whereby these books were incorporated into a "single canonical text" constitutes God authorizing them, this process cannot have involved the authorization of a text that affirms, as literally true, two contradictory accounts.

It may be contended that an appeal to divine authorship in this way begs the question, but I think this is mistaken. As I understand the objection, the skeptic who claims that God commanded genocide is offering a *reductio ad absurdum*; he starts by assuming that whatever God commands is right and that Scripture is the Word of God and then derives from these assumptions the absurd conclusion that genocide is not wrong. The question then is whether, *granting these assumptions*, such a conclusion does, in fact, follow. If Scripture is a unified divine discourse, the skeptic's conclusion need not follow, because another assumption of the skeptic—namely, that all accounts were intended to be taken as literal—is not evidently true.

At this point Wolterstorff raises a further issue about the type of literature Joshua appears to be. He notes that the early chapters of Judges, by and large, read like "down-to-earth history." However, he continues, anyone carefully reading the book of Joshua will recognize in it certain stylistic renderings—"formulaic phrasings" and "formulaic convention[s]"[15] as well as "the highly ritualized character of some of the major events described."[16]

> The book is framed by its opening narration of the ritual-
> ized crossing of the Jordan and by its closing narration of the
> equally-ritualized ceremony of blessing and cursing that took
> place at Shechem; and the conquest narrative begins with the
> ritualized destruction of Jericho.[17]

---

claim that Joshua had not conquered the whole land. In the next five chapters it is stressed repeatedly that the land is not yet conquered. This is followed by the opening chapters of Judges, which affirms eight times in a single chapter that the Israelites had failed to conquer the land or the cities, finishing with the Angel of the Lord at Bokim rebuking them for failing to do so (Judg 2:1–5). These are not subtle contrasts. They are, in Wolterstorff's words, "flamboyant"; it is unlikely that an intelligent author or editor would have missed this.

[15] Wolterstorff, "Reading Joshua," Bergmann et al. in *Divine Evil?* 251.

[16] Ibid., 252.

[17] Ibid. The ritualized nature of the narration is also stressed by Duane L Christensen, *Deuteronomy 1:1–21:9* (Nashville: Thomas Nelson, 2001).

A related ritualistic feature is "the mysterious sacral category of *being devoted to destruction*."[18] Most significant is the use of formulaic language:

> Anyone who reads the Book of Joshua in one sitting cannot fail to be struck by the prominent employment of formulaic phrasings. . . . Far more important is the formulaic clause, "struck down all the inhabitants with the edge of the sword."

> The first time one reads that Joshua struck down all the inhabitants of a city with the edge of the sword, namely, in the story of the conquest of Jericho (6:21), one makes nothing of it. But the phrasing—or close variants thereon—gets repeated, seven times in close succession in chapter 10, two more times in chapter 11, and several times in other chapters. The repetition makes it unmistakable that we are dealing here with a formulaic literary convention.[19]

Thus Joshua itself appears to be full of ritualistic, stylized, formulaic language. It therefore looks like something other than a mere literal description of what occurred. In light of these facts Wolterstorff argues that Judges should be taken literally whereas Joshua is hagiographic history, a highly stylized, exaggerated account of the events designed to teach theological and moral points rather than to describe in detail what *literally* happened. Wolterstorff provides the example of North American morality tales of the noble Puritan or Washington crossing

---

[18] Wolterstorff, "Reading Joshua," in Bergmann et al., *Divine Evil?* 252. That the word *herem*, translated as "devoted to destruction," often serves a figurative or rhetorical function is also noted by Christopher Wright in *The God I Don't Understand: Reflections on Tough Questions of Faith* (Grand Rapids: Zondervan, 2008), 87–88:

> Now we need to know that Israel's practice of *herem* was not in itself unique. Texts from other nations at the time show that such total destruction in war was practiced, or at any rate proudly claimed, elsewhere. But we must also recognize that the language of warfare had a conventional rhetoric that liked to make absolute and universal claims about total victory and completely wiping out the enemy. Such rhetoric often exceeded reality on the ground.

At the other end of the spectrum, minimalist scholar Thomas L. Thompson, writing on the use of *herem* in the Mesha Stele, notes that the "use of the ban at both Ataroth and Nebo are clearly part of the totalitarian rhetoric of holy war rather than historical considerations" ("Mesha and Questions of Historicity," *Scandinavian Journal of the Old Testament* 22/2 [2007]: 249).

[19] Wolterstorff, "Reading Joshua," in Bergmann et al., *Divine Evil?* 251.

the Delaware. These are idealized, exaggerated accounts of the past designed to teach a moral lesson; they are not intended to be taken as accurate accounts of what actually occurred.

Ancient Near Eastern Conquest Accounts

Wolterstorff's argument has, I think, considerable force. Judges and Joshua cannot both be taken literally as their accounts are at odds; given the internal evidence Wolterstorff cites, it is reasonable to contend that Joshua is the one that is nonliteral. Wolterstorff, however, limits his case to what I call internal evidence, evidence from within the text itself. I think there is some interesting external evidence, evidence of how particular terms and language were used in other ancient Near Eastern histories of conquests and battles, which could be added to Wolterstorff's argument. Here I will cite three such lines of evidence.

The first is that comparisons between the book of Joshua and other ancient Near Eastern conquest accounts from the same period demonstrate some important stylistic parallels. Various studies have documented these similarities. Commenting on the structure of the campaigns mentioned in Joshua 9–12, Kenneth Kitchen reminds us:

> This kind of report profile is familiar to readers of ancient Near Eastern military reports, not least in the second millennium. Most striking is the example of the campaign annals of Tuthmosis III of Egypt in his years 22–42 (ca. 1458–1438). . . . [T]he pharaoh there gives a very full account of his initial victory at Megiddo, by contrast with the far more summary and stylized reports of the ensuing sixteen subsequent campaigns. *Just like Joshua* against up to seven kings in south Canaan and four-plus up north.[20]

Kitchen adds,

> The Ten Year Annals of the Hittite king Mursil II (later fourteenth century) are also instructive. *Exactly like the "prefaces" in the two Joshua war reports* (10:1–4; 11:1–5), detailing hostility by a number of foreign rulers against Joshua and Israel as the

---

[20] Kitchen, *Historical Reliability*, 170 (emphasis added).

reason for the wars, so in his annals Mursil II gives us a long "preface" on the hostility of neighbouring rulers and people groups that lead to his campaigns.[21]

Kitchen offers other examples. He observes that the same formulaic style found in Joshua is also used in the Amarna letters EA 185 and EA 186.[22] Similarly, before his major campaigns,

> Joshua is commissioned by YHWH not to fear (cf. 5:13–15; 10:8; 11:6). So also by Ptah and Amun were Merenptah in Egypt, and Tuthmosis IV long before him; and likewise Mursil II of the Hittites by his gods (Ten-Year Annals, etc.), all in the second millennium, besides such kings as Assurbanipal of Assyria down to the seventh century.[23]

Similar studies have been done by John Van Seters[24] and James Hoffmeier.[25] However, the most comprehensive is that done by K. Lawson Younger. Younger notes similarities in the preface, structure, and even the way the treaty with the Gibeonites is recorded between Joshua and various ancient Near Eastern accounts.[26] Joshua follows this convention in describing numerous battles occurring in a single day or within a single campaign.[27] Ancient Near Eastern accounts also, like Joshua, repeatedly make reference to the enemy "melting with fear."[28] Even the way postbattle pursuits are set out and described shows similarities with pursuits in ancient Near Eastern literature.[29] I could mention more examples. The point is that "when the composition and rhetoric of the Joshua narratives in chaps. 9–12 are compared to the conventions of

---

[21] Ibid. (emphasis added).

[22] Ibid., 172.

[23] Ibid., 174–75.

[24] John Van Seters, "Joshua's Campaign of Canaan and Near Eastern Historiography," *Scandinavian Journal of the Old Testament* 2 (1990): 1–12.

[25] James K. Hoffmeier, "The Structure of Joshua 1–11 and the Annals of Thutmose III," in *Faith, Tradition, and History: Old Testament Historiography and Its Ancient Near Eastern Context*, ed. A. R. Millard, James K. Hoffmeier, and David W. Baker (Winona Lake, IN: Eisenbrauns, 1994), 165–81.

[26] K. Lawson Younger Jr., *Ancient Conquest Accounts: A Study in Ancient Near Eastern and Biblical History Writing* (Sheffield: Sheffield Academic Press, 1990), 200–204.

[27] Ibid., 216.

[28] Ibid., 258–60.

[29] Ibid., 220–25.

writing about conquests in Egyptian, Hittite, Akkadian, Moabite, and Aramaic texts, they are revealed to be very similar."[30]

Second, Younger notes such accounts are "highly figurative"[31] and narrate military events via a common transmission code. The literary motif of divine intervention is an example. Both *The 10 Year Annals of Mursilli* and *Sargon's Letter to the God* record a divine intervention where the god sends hailstones on the enemy.[32] Tuthmosis III has a similar story regarding a meteor.[33] Younger observes that these accounts are very similar to parallel accounts in Joshua 10. Similarly, Younger points out that in many ancient Near Eastern texts "one can discern a literary technique in which a deity is implored to maintain daylight long enough for there to be a victory,"[34] which has obvious parallels to Josh 10:13–14. Similarly, Richard Hess points to Hittite conquest accounts that describe the gods knocking down the walls of an enemy city in a manner similar to that described in the battle of Jericho.[35] The fact that similar events are narrated in multiple different accounts suggests they are "a notable ingredient of the transmission code for conquest accounts"[36]—that is, part of the common hyperbolic rhetoric of warfare rather than descriptions of what actually occurred.

Third, part of this "transmission code" is that victories are narrated in an exaggerated hyperbolic fashion in terms of total conquest, complete annihilation and destruction of the enemy, killing everyone, leaving no survivors, and so on. Kitchen offers illuminating examples:

---

[30] Ziony Zevit, *The Religions of Ancient Israel: A Synthesis of Parallactic Approaches* (London and New York: Continuum, 2001), 114.

[31] Younger states: "As the ancient historian (whether Near Eastern, biblical, or otherwise) reconstructed "historical" referents into a coherent description, he produced a figurative account, a 're-presenting representation.'" K. Lawson Younger Jr., "Judges 1 in Its Near Eastern Literary Context," in Millard et al., *Faith, Tradition, and History*, 207. He also suggests such a historian functions as "a literary artist." He adds: "Ancient Near Eastern conquest accounts are figurative in three ways: (1) the structural and ideological codes that are the apparatus for the text's production; (2) the themes or motifs that the text utilizes; and (3) the usage of rhetorical figures in the accounts" (ibid.).

[32] Younger, *Ancient Conquest Accounts*, 208–11.

[33] Ibid., 217.

[34] Ibid., 219. For further discussion of the relationship between Joshua's long day and other ancient Near Eastern texts, see John Walton, "Joshua 10:12–15 and Mesopotamian Celestial Omen Texts," in Millard et al., *Faith, Tradition, and History*, 181–90.

[35] Richard Hess, "West Semitic Texts and the Book of Joshua," *Bulletin for Biblical Research* 7 (1997): 68.

[36] Younger, *Ancient Conquest Accounts*, 211.

The type of rhetoric in question was a regular feature of military reports in the second and first millennia, as others have made very clear. . . . In the later fifteenth century Tuthmosis III could boast "the numerous army of Mitanni, was overthrown within the hour, annihilated totally, like those (now) non-existent"—whereas, in fact, the forces of Mitanni lived to fight many another day, in the fifteenth and fourteenth centuries. Some centuries later, about 840/830, Mesha king of Moab could boast that "Israel has utterly perished for always"—a rather premature judgment at that date, by over a century! And so on, ad libitum. It is in this frame of reference that the Joshua rhetoric must also be understood.[37]

Younger offers numerous other examples. Merenptah's Stele describes a skirmish with Israel as follows, "Yanoam is nonexistent; Israel is wasted, his seed is not."[38] Here a skirmish in which Egypt prevailed is described hyperbolically in terms of the total annihilation of Israel. Sennacherib uses similar hyperbole, "The soldiers of Hirimme, dangerous enemies, I cut down with the sword; and not one escaped."[39] Mursilli II records making "Mt. Asharpaya empty (of humanity)" and the "mountains of Tarikarimu empty (of humanity)."[40] Mesha (whom Kitchen cited as stating "Israel has utterly perished for always") describes victories in terms of him fighting against a town, taking it, and then killing all the inhabitants of the town.[41] Similarly, *The Bulletin of Ramses II*, a historical narrative of Egyptian military campaigns into Syria, narrates Egypt's considerably less-than-decisive victory at the battle of Kadesh with the following rhetoric:

> His majesty slew the *entire force* of the wretched foe from Hatti, together with his great chiefs and all his brothers, as well as *all* the chiefs of *all* the countries that had come with him, their infantry and their chariotry falling on their faces one upon the other. His majesty slaughtered and slew them in their

---

[37] Kitchen, *Reliability of the Old Testament*, 174.
[38] Younger, *Ancient Conquest Accounts*, 227.
[39] Ibid., 228.
[40] Ibid.
[41] Ibid., 227.

places. . . . He took no note of the *millions* of foreigners; he
regarded them as *chaff.*[42]

Numerous other examples could be provided. The hyperbolic use of
language similar to that in Joshua is strikingly evident.[43]

It is equally evident that histories of this sort are highly stylized
and often use this exaggeration for what could be called hagiographic
purposes to commend the kings as faithful servants of the gods, rather
than for giving literal descriptions of what occurred.[44] They constitute
"monumental hyperbole."[45]

Three things become evident about the book of Joshua as we study
the evidence. First, taken as a single narrative and taken literally, Joshua
1–11 gives an account of events at odds with that narrated by Judges
and also with that narrated by the later chapters of Joshua itself. Second
is that, as Wolterstorff commented, "those who edited the final version
of these writings into one sequence were not mindless," particularly
if God speaks through them. Third, while Judges reads as "down to
earth history," a careful reading of Joshua reveals it to be full of ritualistic, stylized, and formulaic language. This third point is supported

---

[42] Ibid., 245 (emphasis added).

[43] In addition, both Kitchen and Younger observe that such hyperbolic language is used in
several places within the book of Joshua itself. Joshua 10:20, for example, states that Joshua
and the sons of Israel had "finished destroying" and "completely destroyed" their enemies.
Immediately, however, the text affirms that the "survivors went to fortified cities." In this
context, the language of total destruction is clearly hyperbolic. Similarly, the account of the
battle of Ai is clearly hyperbolic. After Joshua's troops feign a retreat, the text states that "all
the men of Ai" are pressed to chase them. "Not a man remained in Ai or Bethel who did not
go after Israel. They left the city open and went in pursuit of Israel" (8:17 NIV). Joshua lures
the pursuers into a trap "so that they were caught in the middle, with Israelites on both sides.
Israel cut them down, leaving them neither survivors nor fugitives" (8:22 NIV). Then the text
immediately following states: "When Israel had finished killing all the men of Ai in the fields
and in the desert where they had chased them, and when every one of them had been put to
the sword" (8:24 NIV), they went to the city of Ai and killed all the men in it.

[44] Thomas Thompson examines several different ancient Near Eastern conquest accounts of
this type and notes they have a hagiographic function. See his "A Testimony of the Good King:
Reading the Mesha Stele," in *Ahab Agonistes: The Rise and Fall of the Omri Dynasty*, ed. Lester
L. Grabbe (Edinburgh: T&T Clark, 2007), 236–92.

[45] John Goldingay goes on to give yet another example from within the Bible itself: "While
Joshua does speak of Israel's utterly destroying the Canaanites, even these accounts can give a
misleading impression: peoples that have been annihilated have no trouble reappearing later
in the story; after Judah puts Jerusalem to the sword, its occupants are still living there 'to this
day' (Judg. 1:8, 21)." See his "City and Nation," in *Old Testament Theology*, vol. 3 (Downers
Grove, IL: InterVarsity, 2009), 570.

by research into ancient Near Eastern conquest accounts. Such studies show (1) such accounts are highly hyperbolic, hagiographic, and figurative, and follow a common transmission code; (2) comparisons between these accounts and the early chapters of Joshua suggest Joshua is written according to the same literary conventions and transmission code; and (3) part of this transmission code is to portray a victory hyperbolically in absolute terms of totally destroying the enemy or in terms of miraculous divine intervention: "such statements are rhetoric indicative of military victory,"[46] not literal descriptions of what occurred.

I think these three points, taken together, provide compelling reasons for thinking that one should interpret the text as a highly figurative and hyperbolic account of what occurred. In light of these factors, it seems sensible to conclude that the accounts of battles in Joshua 6–11 are not meant to be taken literally.

Implications

We can draw two important implications in light of what we have seen so far. First, as Wolterstorff asserts, on the assumption that Deuteronomy and Joshua are both literarily and linguistically connected and canonically sequenced,

> this interpretation of Joshua forces a back-interpretation of Deuteronomy. If "struck down all the inhabitants with the edge of the sword" is a literary convention when used to describe Joshua's exploits, then it is likewise a literary convention when similar words are used by Moses in his instructions to Israel in general and to Joshua in particular.[47]

I think Wolterstorff is correct here: this interpretation of Joshua does force a back-interpretation of Deuteronomy. Deuteronomy 7:2 states "when the LORD your God has given them up before you and you have struck them, you shall utterly destroy them." Similarly, Deut 20:16–17 commands: "do not leave alive anything that breathes. Completely

---

[46] K. Lawson Younger Jr., "Joshua," in *The IVP Bible Background Commentary: Old Testament*, ed. John H. Walton, Victor H. Matthews, and Mark W. Chavalas (Downers Grove, IL: InterVarsity Press, 2000), 227.

[47] Wolterstorff, "Reading Joshua," in Bergmann et al., *Divine Evil?* 252.

destroy them" (NIV). In Joshua 10 one sees the formulaic language of "and the LORD gave [the city]" and he/they "struck it and its king with the edge of the sword" until "there was no one remaining" (NRSV). The chapter is summarized with the phrase, "So Joshua defeated the whole land . . . ; he left no one remaining, but utterly destroyed all that breathed" (v. 40 NRSV). The similar phraseology is evident.

Moreover, the book of Joshua clearly, explicitly, and repeatedly identifies what Joshua did in these chapters with the command that Moses had given regarding the Canaanites in Deuteronomy: "He left no survivors. He totally destroyed all who breathed, *just as the* LORD, *the God of Israel, had commanded*" (Josh 10:40 NIV, emphasis added). So, if the language of "striking all the people by the sword," "leaving no survivors," "totally destroying," "striking all the inhabitants with the edge of the sword," and so on is hyperbolic (as the evidence suggests it is), then the command cannot have been intended to be taken literally.

This understanding of Deuteronomy's commands also solves some other interpretive problems. Here I will mention briefly three.

(1) What God commanded regarding the Canaanites differs in various canonical books. As noted above, in Judges 2 when the Angel of the Lord refers back to the original command, it is stated in terms of not making treaties with them, destroying their shrines, and driving them out; it is not stated in terms of literally exterminating them. Similarly, in the earlier book of Exodus the command is given in terms of not allowing the Canaanites to live in the land, again, not in terms of extermination. This is significant. "Deuteronomy" in Greek means "second law"; and throughout Deuteronomy, Moses repeats laws already laid down in the book of Exodus, sometimes expanding on them. The Decalogue, for example, which was delivered on Sinai in Exodus 20, is repeated in Deuteronomy 5. The laws about releasing an *ebed* (an indentured servant) in Exod 21:1 are repeated and expanded in Deut 15:12–18. Similarly, Deut 22:28–29 is a repetition of a law spelled out in Exod 22:15.[48] The same occurs with the law under discussion. Deuteronomy 7 repeats the same promises and commands laid down in Exod 23:20–32; however, in Deuteronomy, the language of "destroy them" replaces

---

[48] Gordon Wenham, "Bethulah: A Girl of Marriageable Age," *Vetus Testamentum* 22 (1972): 326–48.

the "do not let them live in your land" in Exodus. Wolterstorff's inter-pretation explains this.

(2) The word *herem*, which is translated "destroy" in Deut 7:2, has the primary meaning of the irrevocable giving over or devotion of some-thing to Yahweh and hence implies renunciation. The term has also developed a secondary secular meaning of "to destroy,"[49] but, a literal reading of "destroy" here does not fit the context well. The command to "destroy" the Canaanites occurs alongside several other commands, "Make no treaty with them, and show them no mercy. Do not inter-marry with them. Do not give your daughters to their sons or take their daughters for your sons" (Deut 7:2–3 NIV). However, this seems odd: killing is not an obvious antithesis to marrying or making a cov-enant; moreover, the text goes on to elaborate the command in terms of smashing idols and driving them out—in a similar vein as Judges. For this reason Christopher Wright argues *herem* should be translated as "renounce," and is a command to shun the idolatrous Canaanites.[50] This reading clashes with the parallel verse in Deut 20:17, where "*herem* is used epexegetically to verse 16, 'you shall not leave alive anything that breathes.'"[51] However, taking the word as "destroy" and understanding it hyperbolically makes sense of this.[52]

---

[49] J. P. U. Lilley, "Understanding the *Herem*," *Tyndale Bulletin* 44 (1993): 170–73.

[50] Christopher J. H. Wright, *Deuteronomy*, New International Biblical Commentary (Peabody, MA: Hendrickson, 1996), 109.

[51] Lilley, "Understanding the *Herem*," 174.

[52] Other commentators such as Duane L. Christensen and J. Gordon McConville suggest "destroy" is being used in a figurative sense. McConville, for example, states "the concept of complete annihilation of the nations is always a kind of ideal, symbolizing the need for radical loyalty to Yahweh on the part of Israel." J. Gordon McConville, *Deuteronomy*, Apollos Old Testament Commentary (Downers Grove, IL: InterVarsity, 2002), 161.

Some object that a hyperbolic interpretation does not fit the context, which draws a con-trast between sparing "the women, the children, the livestock" (v. 14) and totally destroying them (v. 16: "do not leave alive anything that breathes"). This is mistaken. First, the empha-sis in v. 14 is not on sparing noncombatants but rather on the permissibility of marrying the women of conquered enemies, adopting their children, and using their cattle. Second, the contrast is not between vv. 14 and 16, but between v. 16 and the whole set of instruc-tions regarding nations that are far away (vv. 10–15). These verses command Israel to seek to make peace treaties first and if they go to war and kill combatants they can marry the women, adopt children, and keep the livestock. In other words, as much as possible they are to seek peaceful coexistence with these nations. A command to go to war and drive them out expressed hyperbolically as "totally destroy them" and "leave nothing alive that breathes" would stand in contrast with this. A final point on this is that the crucial issue is whether the hyperbolic interpretation is more plausible than a literal one, even if a literal interpretation

(3) The hyperbolic reading addresses another apparent contradiction in the text noted by many readers of the Pentateuch. While Deut 7:2 and 20:16–17 command Israel to "utterly destroy" the Canaanites and to "not leave alive anything that breathes," numerous other texts claim the Canaanites are to be "driven out," "dispossessed," "thrust out," and so on. In fact, often the "drive out" language is juxtaposed with the language of "destroy." Taken literally, these pictures are inconsistent. If I stated that I had driven an intruder from my house, one would not assume the intruder was dead in my lounge. Similarly, if I said I had killed an intruder, one would not normally think this meant the intruder had fled. The Hebrew confirms this; the language of driving out and casting out is used elsewhere to refer to Adam and Eve being driven from Eden (Gen 3:24), Cain being driven into the wilderness (Gen 4:14), and David being driven out by Saul (1 Sam 26:19). All are cases where the meaning precludes something being literally destroyed.[53] Moreover, when the "drive out" language is used of Canaan, it often is used in a context where it does not literally mean destroyed, but rather dispossessed. In Lev 18:26–28, *in the same way* the Canaanites would be driven out, so Israel would be for violating the covenant.[54] This ultimately happened during the Babylonian exile—which was obviously not an annihilation of ethnic Jews. Furthermore, the language of destroying whole nations in several places in Deuteronomy is used in a rhetorical or hyperbolic sense, alongside references to "driving out" the nation in question or dispossessing them; it does not mean exterminating them. Hence, Wolterstorff's suggestion has ample precedent from within the text itself.[55]

---

fits Deuteronomy 20 better. Above, I have argued that a literal interpretation puts Joshua 6–11 at odds with Judges 1–2 and the later chapters of Joshua. It would be odd to reject a hyperbolic interpretation because one passage in Deuteronomy 20 does not cohere with it and instead embrace a literal interpretation, which creates an even greater incoherence in the text.

[53] I owe this point to conversations with Paul Copan. See his comments on this in *Is God a Moral Monster?* 181–82.

[54] "But you must keep my decrees and my laws. The native-born and the aliens living among you must not do any of these detestable things, for all these things were done by the people who lived in the land before you, and the land became defiled. And if you defile the land, it will vomit you out as it vomited out the nations that were before you" (NIV).

[55] Deut 2:10–12, 20–22; 4:26–30; 28:63.

A second implication of Wolterstorff's position is that Joshua does not assert that Israel engaged in divinely authorized genocide:

> . . . when a high-school basketball player says his team slaughtered the other team last night, what is he asserting? Not easy to tell. That they scored a decisive victory? Maybe. But suppose they just barely eked out a win? Was he lying? Maybe not. Maybe he was speaking with a wink-of-the-eye hyperbole.[56]

In the same way, when one realizes that Joshua is hagiographic and highly hyperbolic in its narration of what occurred, the best one can conclude from the accounts of killing everyone that breathed is this:

> Israel scored a decisive victory and once you recognize the presence of hyperbole it is not even clear how decisive the victories were. Joshua did not conquer all the cities in the land nor did he slaughter all the inhabitants in the cities he did conquer. The book of Joshua does not say that he did.[57]

Canonical factors force the same conclusion. I noted above that in Judges and Exodus the command is expressed in terms of avoiding treaties and driving the Canaanites out. In Joshua and Deuteronomy the command is expressed in the language of "utterly destroying them." The conclusion we have reached is that the latter is figurative language and the former is literal. If this is the case, then the command was to drive them out and it was not to literally exterminate them.

Conclusion

I contend that the widely held view that the book of Joshua teaches that God commanded the genocide of the Canaanites is questionable. Joshua is accepted as part of a canon. Read in this context, taking the account of total annihilation of the Canaanite populations as a literal description of what occurred contradicts what is affirmed to have literally occurred in Judges. Moreover, it conflicts with how the command is described elsewhere in Judges and Exodus. The writers

---

[56] Nicholas Wolterstorff, "Reply to Antony," in Bergmann et al., *Divine Evil?* 263.

[57] Nicholas Wolterstorff, "Reading Joshua," presented at the "My Ways Are Not Your Ways: The Character of the God of the Hebrew Bible" conference; this paragraph was in the paper presented at the conference but was omitted from the published version in *Divine Evil?*

would have known this and, not being mindless, could not have meant both accounts to be taken literally. This means one must be nonliteral. The literary conventions Joshua uses are highly stylized, figurative, and contain hyperbolic, hagiographic accounts of what occurred. The conventions in Judges are less so. Consequently, the so-called genocide in Joshua and the command to "utterly destroy" the Canaanites should not be taken literally.

Appendix: The Case of the Midianites

Wolterstorff's approach may also shed light on some other troubling texts such as the apparent genocide of the Midianites in Numbers 31. After the Israelites "fought against Midian, as the LORD commanded Moses, and killed every man" (v. 7 NIV), Moses commanded them to "kill all the boys. And kill every woman who has slept with a man, but save for yourselves every girl who has never slept with a man" (vv. 17–18 NIV). Taken in isolation, this text affirms that every Midianite was killed and only female virgins survived so they could be assimilated into the Israelite community. However, read in its literary context, as part of a single narrative—a connected literary unit—similar issues are apparent.

First, Numbers 31 is one part of a broader context; it is both part of the Pentateuch and also part of a larger canonical sequence. The Pentateuch contains the Torah or Law. Normally in the Torah when Moses utters a command on God's behalf the passage begins with "The LORD commanded Moses"; this preface is absent from the commands in Numbers 31. The passages merely state that God commanded them to make war on Midian; v. 7 states, "They fought against Midian, *as the* LORD *commanded Moses*, and killed every man." This suggests the Israelites fulfilled this command. Moses' command to kill women and children occurs after this and appears to be on his own authority.[58] If one

---

[58] Alvin Plantinga, "Comments on Satanic Verses in Holy Writ," in Bergmann et al., *Divine Evil?* 110. Plantinga is responding to Evan Fales, who based his reading on the mistaken reading of the verse "kill all the women but save for yourselves every girl who has never slept with a man" as commanding rape—a reading he also ascribes to Deuteronomy 21. In fact, a glance at the immediate context shows that the reference to a woman not sleeping with a man in the former passage was mentioned to distinguish the women in question from those who had seduced Israelite men into idolatry; it is not there to emphasize their availability for sex. Deuteronomy

reads the laws of war that are elaborated in the book of Deuteronomy, which follows Numbers, God commanded Israel not to kill noncombatants, such as women and children. He condemns the kind of conduct Moses commands here.[59]

21, in fact, protects female captives from being raped or sold as concubines. See Copan, *Is God a Moral Monster?* 118–21, 180.

[59] Some might object that God did command the killing of men, women, and children in 1 Samuel 15, where God commanded Saul to "utterly destroy [*haram*]" and "not spare" the Amalekites. God used the sweeping language of "put to death both man and woman, child and infant, ox and sheep, camel and donkey" (15:3 NASB). It is important to note that Saul carried this command out, see 1 Sam 15:7–9:

> Saul attacked the Amalekites all the way from Havilah to Shur, to the east of Egypt. He took Agag king of the Amalekites alive, and all his people he totally destroyed with the sword. But Saul and the army spared Agag and the best of the sheep and cattle, the fat calves and lambs—everything that was good. These they were unwilling to destroy completely, but everything that was despised and weak they totally destroyed. (NIV)

The language of "utterly destroy" (*haram*, and its noun cognate *herem*), the reference to cattle and sheep, and the reference to "sparing" all parallel the language of the command. So it would be difficult to justify interpreting the command as literal and the fulfilment as hyperbolic; the command and fulfilment need to be read in the same sense. Agag, the sole survivor, was executed a few verses later (15:33). So taken in isolation and read literally, this passage records a divinely commanded genocide that was carried out.

However, if when one reads this passage as part of a single narrative—a connected literary unit—then several issues are apparent. First, the narrative states quite emphatically that the Amalekites were not, in fact, literally wiped out. In 1 Sam 27:8–9 David invaded a territory full of Amalekites:

> Now David and his men went up and raided the Geshurites, the Girzites and the Amalekites. (From ancient times these peoples had lived in the land extending to Shur and Egypt.) Whenever David attacked an area, he did not leave a man or woman alive, but took sheep and cattle, donkeys and camels, and clothes. Then he returned to Achish.

Not only does this text affirm the Amalekites still exist, but the reference to Egypt and Shur states they exist in the same area that Saul attacked in the previous passages. Moreover, David killed Amalekite men and women living in his area and took sheep and cattle as plunder. However, these are the very things Saul was said in 1 Samuel 15 to have eradicated.

As we showed above, Saul was said to have killed all the Amalekites, men and women from "Havilah to Shur, to the east border of Egypt" and all the livestock had either been destroyed or taken as plunder. Further, in 1 Samuel 30, a sizeable Amalekite army attacked Ziklag (1 Sam 30:1). David pursued this army and fought a long battle with them and 400 Amalekites fled on horseback (1 Sam 30:7–17). In 2 Sam 1:8, an Amalekite took credit for killing Saul, and 1 Chron 4:43 tells us Amalekites were still around during the reign of Hezekiah. So, if you view 1 Samuel and its canonical context as a single literary unit the text cannot be sensibly claiming that 1 Samuel 15 and 27 are both literally true accounts of battles with the Amalekites. Third, the genre and style of the accounts suggest 1 Samuel 15 is the nonliteral; it appears highly hyperbolic and contains obvious rhetorical exaggeration. Saul's army was said to be 210,000 men, and thus larger than any army known at this time in antiquity. Moreover, Saul struck the Amalekites from Havila to Shur. Shur is on the edge of Egypt; Havila is in Saudi Arabia. This is an absurdly large battlefield. The text used standard hyperbolic rhetoric of exaggerated numbers and geography. Similarly, 1 Samuel 15's use of the language of "utterly destroying [*haram*]" populations "with the sword," is the same as that used hyperbolically in Joshua. Further, the language of "do not spare"

If one looks at the larger canonical sequence, the subsequent narrative states quite emphatically that the Midianites were not, in fact, literally wiped out. In Judges 6 and 7, the Midianites invade Israel in numbers said to be "like swarms of locusts. It was impossible to count the men and their camels" (Judg 6:5 NIV). Israel was so overrun with Midianites that they fled to "mountain clefts, caves and strongholds" (Judg 6:2 NIV). Unable to win in open battle, Gideon was forced to use deception to defeat them. This is not congruous with the Midianites having been "utterly destroyed."

Second, these tensions in the text are fairly obvious. As with Joshua, whoever "edited the final version of these writings into one sequence"[60] juxtaposed several accounts, which, if taken literally, describe Israel, at Moses' command, annihilating the entire population of Midian (including noncombatants); yet several other accounts affirm that God prohibits the killing of noncombatants and that the Midianites were not annihilated. Assuming this person was not "mindless," he cannot have intended to affirm both as literally true.

Third, the genre and style of the accounts suggests Numbers 31 is the nonliteral account. Numbers 31 appears highly hyperbolic; it contains obvious rhetorical exaggeration.[61] The Israelite army is said to have killed every Midianite man in battle without a single Israelite fatality (Num 31:50).[62] Moreover, the spoil from the battle is said to be 32,000 maidens and 675,000 sheep and goats—this is astronomically and absurdly large.[63] Daniel Fouts notes that exaggerated numbers are common forms of hyperbole in ancient Near Eastern battle accounts.[64]

---

the Amalekites but "put to death both man and woman, child and infant, ox and sheep, camel and donkey" appears to be stereotypical language; it is very similar to the hyperbolic description of military defeat in 1 Chron 36:16–1, where Jewish defeat and exile to Babylon were described in similar language. There are also obvious parallels between 1 Samuel 15 and the hyperbolic rhetoric of the Mesha Stele. I discuss the issue of the Amalekites in more detail in Paul Copan and Matthew Flannagan, "Some Reflections on the Ethics of Yahweh Wars," in *Old Testament 'Holy War' and Christian Morality: Perspectives and Prospects*, ed. Jeremy Evans, Heath Thomas, and Paul Copan (Downers Grove, IL: InterVarsity Press Academic, 2012).

[60] Wolterstorff, "Reading Joshua," 251.

[61] Jacob Milgrom, *Numbers: The Traditional Hebrew Text with the New JPS Translation* (Philadelphia: Jewish Publication Society of America, 1990), 490–91.

[62] Ibid., 490.

[63] Ibid.

[64] Daniel M. Fouts, "A Defense of the Hyperbolic Interpretation of Numbers in the Old Testament," *Journal of the Evangelical Theological Society* 40/3 (1997): 377–87.

Wolterstorff suggests, "These are all hyperbolic descriptions of battles that took place."[65]

So, if we read the text in the literary context of the broader canon, we again see the author juxtaposing two accounts. One claims that God prohibits killing noncombatants and that the Midianites continued to live in the land as a serious military threat; another account, using rhetoric known to be used hyperbolically in military contexts, states that Israel, at Moses' command, wiped them all out. Assuming the author was an intelligent person,[66] we are at least owed an argument as to why one should read these texts as literally claiming that God commanded genocide.[67]

---

[65] Personal correspondence between Nicholas Wolterstorff and Paul Copan (May 2, 2011).

[66] One again needs to remember the dialectical context here. The skeptic who claims that God commanded genocide is offering a *reductio ad absurdum*; she starts by assuming that whatever God commands is right and that Scripture is the Word of God, she then derives from these assumptions the absurd conclusion that genocide is not wrong. The question then is whether, *granting these assumptions*, such a conclusion does, in fact, follow; hence, one is quite entitled, in this context, to assume the author was an intelligent person.

[67] In *Divine Discourse: Philosophical Reflections on the Claim That God Speaks* (Cambridge: Cambridge University Press, 1995), Wolterstorff defends an account of how the Bible constitutes God's Word in terms of appropriation. On page 54 he writes, "All that is necessary for the whole [Bible] to be God's book is that the human discourse it contains have been appropriated by God, as one single book, for God's discourse." An implication of Wolterstorff's position is that when one reads the Bible as the Word of God one must read the canon as appropriated discourse. Citing as an example an imaginary case where he appropriates the writings of another person, Wolterstorff elucidates the principles of interpreting appropriated discourse on page 205:

> The fundamental principle, I submit, is this: the interpreter takes the stance and content of my appropriating discourse to be that of your appropriated discourse, unless there is good reason to do otherwise—such "good reason to do otherwise" consisting, at bottom, of its being improbable, on the evidence available, that by my appropriation in this situation, I would have wanted to say that and only that. At those points where the interpreter does have good reason to do otherwise, he proceeds by selecting the illocutionary stance and content which have the highest probability of being what I intended to say in this way. If the most probable of those is nonetheless improbable, then he adopts some such fall-back option as that I didn't really appropriate the discourse but only appeared to do so, that in appropriating it I said something I never intended to say, that I misunderstood the discourse I appropriated—or that he has misunderstood the appropriated discourse.

Wolterstorff suggests the same principle applies when God appropriates the "discourse by inscription" of another human being except that some of the fall-back options are excluded. "God does not unwittingly say things God never intended to say, nor does God misunderstand the discourse God appropriates!" The upshot of this is that one cannot just offer a literal reading of the relevant passages and conclude from this that the Bible is not the Word of a just and loving God. To conclude God did not appropriate the text the critic needs to contend that, given the evidence available, the most probable of all alternative interpretations is that God is literally affirming that He commanded genocide and all other alternatives are improbable so

A similar phenomenon occurs with the case of the Amalekites,[68] the Babylonian invasions,[69] and the sacking of the Jebusite city of Jerusalem.[70] In each case a battle is narrated in totalistic terms of complete destruction of all the people, yet later narration goes on to assume matter-of-factly that it did not literally occur. The fact that this happens on multiple occasions in different books rapidly diminishes the probability that these features are coincidental or careless errors. Why is it that *almost every time* a narration of "genocide" occurs, it is followed by an account that presupposes it did not happen? These facts significantly raise the probability that this is a deliberate literary construction by the authors.

---

that the only other alternative is the fall-back option that God did not really appropriate the text. Hence the critic needs to argue that the literal reading is the most plausible of all available readings and also that it is more plausible than claiming that the critic has misunderstood the appropriated discourse.

[68] See n60.

[69] Compare 2 Chron 36:17 with 36:20 and also 36:18 with 36:19.

[70] See n45.

Chapter 14

DOES THE OLD TESTAMENT ENDORSE SLAVERY?

Paul Copan

H arriet Beecher Stowe (1811–96) was the famed author of *Uncle Tom's Cabin*. When Abraham Lincoln met her when she came to the White House, he purportedly said, "So you're the little woman who wrote the book that started this great war!" Stowe described the nature of antebellum (pre-Civil War) slavery: "The legal power of the master amounts to an absolute despotism over body and soul," and "there is no protection for the slave's life."[1]

When Christians and non-Christians alike read about "slaves" or "slavery" in Israel, they often think along the lines of antebellum slavery with its slave trade and cruelties. This is a terrible misperception, and many, including the "New Atheists," have bought into this misperception. One of them, Sam Harris, writes that slaves are human beings who are capable of suffering and happiness. Yet the Old Testament regards them as "farm equipment," which is "patently evil."[2] This is, unfortunately, distortion and misrepresentation.

In my essay, I shall respond to the problem of "slavery," primarily in the Old Testament. The first two sections are devoted to servitude in the Old Testament—a general overview followed by a treatment of some problem passages. The final section will address slavery in light of the

---

[1] Harriet Beecher Stowe, *A Key to Uncle Tom's Cabin; Presenting the Facts and Documents upon which the Story is Founded, together with Corroborative Statements verifying the Truth of the Work* (Boston: John P. Jewett, 1853), I.10, 139.

[2] Sam Harris, *The End of Faith* (New York: Norton, 2004), 18.

New Testament. While I have to be brief, I go into more detail in my book, *Is God a Moral Monster? Understanding the Old Testament God*, to which I refer the reader.[3]

Hebrew Servanthood as Indentured Servitude

Hebrew debt-servanthood (many translations, unfortunately, call it "slavery") is more fairly compared to apprentice-like positions to pay off debts—much like the indentured servitude during America's founding. People would work for about seven years to pay off the debt for their passage to the New World; then they went free. In most cases, servanthood was more like a live-in *employee*, temporarily embedded within the employer's household until terms of the contract were completed. Even today, sports players get "traded" to another team, which has an "owner," and they "belong" to a franchise. This language hardly suggests slavery but rather a formal contractual agreement that has to be fulfilled—like in the Old Testament.[4]

Through failed crops or other disasters, debt tended to come to *families*, not just individuals. One would *voluntarily* enter into a contractual arrangement ("sell" himself) to work in the household of another: "one of your countrymen becomes poor and sells himself" (Lev 25:47 NIV). A wife or children could be "sold" to help sustain the family through economically unbearable times—unless kinfolk "redeemed" them (paying their debt). They would be debt-servants for six years.[5] Family land would have to be mortgaged until the year of Jubilee every 50 years.[6]

Note well: *servanthood wasn't imposed by an outsider*—as in the antebellum South.[7] Indentured servants could even be "hired from year to year" and weren't to be "rule[d] over . . . ruthlessly" (Lev 25:53–54).

---

[3] Paul Copan, *Is God a Moral Monster? Understanding the Old Testament God* (Grand Rapids: Baker, 2011). This chapter is adapted from three essays I wrote for *Enrichment Journal*.

[4] Douglas Stuart, *Exodus* (Nashville: B&H Academic, 2009), 474–75.

[5] From Tikva Frymer-Kenski, "Anatolia and the Levant: Israel," in *A History of Ancient Near East Law*, vol. 2, ed. Raymond Westbrook (Leiden: Brill, 2003).

[6] See Gregory C. Chirichigno, *Debt-Slavery in Israel and the Ancient Near East*, JSOT Supplement Series 141 (Sheffield: University of Sheffield Press, 1993), 351–54.

[7] See Gordon Wenham, "Family in the Pentateuch," in *Family in the Bible*, ed. Richard S. Hess and Daniel Carrol (Grand Rapids: Baker Academic, 2003), 21.

Rather than being excluded from Israelite society, servants were thoroughly embedded within Israelite homes.

Unavoidable lifelong servanthood was prohibited—unless someone loved the head of the household and wanted to attach himself to him (Exod 21:5). Servants were to be granted eventual release every seventh year with all debts forgiven (Lev 29:35–43). Their legal status was unique in the ancient Near East (ANE)—a dramatic improvement over ANE law codes: "Hebrew has no vocabulary of slavery, only of servanthood."[8]

So, an Israelite strapped for shekels might become an indentured servant to pay off that debt to a "boss" or "employer" (*'adon*). Calling him a "master" is often far too strong a term—just as the term *'ebed* ("servant, employee") typically shouldn't be translated "slave." John Goldingay comments that "there is nothing inherently lowly or undignified about being an *'ebed*" in Israel. Indeed, it is an honorable, dignified term.[9]

An Israelite servant's guaranteed eventual release within seven years was a *control* or *regulation* to *prevent the abuse and institutionalizing of such positions.* The release year reminded the Israelites that poverty-induced servanthood wasn't an ideal social arrangement. On the other hand, *servanthood existed in Israel precisely because poverty existed: no poverty, no servants in Israel.* And *if servants lived in Israel, this was voluntary (typically poverty-induced)—not forced.*

The Dignity of Servants in Israel

Israel's servant laws were concerned about *controlling* or *regulating*— not *idealizing*—an inferior work arrangement. Israelite servitude, we've seen, though not optimal, was entered into voluntarily. The intent of Israel's laws was to combat potential abuses, not to institutionalize servitude. *Indeed, forced slavery (kidnapping) was punishable by death,* as we shall see. Once a person was freed from his servant obligations, he had the "status of full and unencumbered citizenship."[10]

---

[8] J. A. Motyer, *The Message of Exodus* (Downers Grove, IL: InterVarsity, 2005), 239.

[9] John Goldingay, *Old Testament Theology: Israel's Life*, vol. 3 (Downers Grove, IL: InterVarsity Press, 2009), 460.

[10] John I. Durham, *Exodus* (Waco, TX: Word, 1987), 321.

Old Testament legislation sought to *prevent voluntary debt-servitude.* A good deal of Mosaic legislation was given to prevent the poor from entering even temporary, voluntary indentured service. The poor were given opportunities to glean the edges of fields or pick lingering fruit on trees from their fellow Israelites' harvest (Lev 19:9–10; 23:22; Deut 24:20–21; cf. Exod 23:10). Also, fellow Israelites were commanded to *lend freely to the poor* (Deut 15:7–8), who *weren't to be charged interest* (Exod 22:25; Lev 25:36–37). And when the poor couldn't afford high-end sacrificial animals, they could *sacrifice smaller, less-expensive ones* (Lev 5:7,11). Also, *debts were to be automatically canceled every seven years.* And when debt-servants were released, *they were to be generously provided for*—without a "grudging heart" (Deut 15:10). The bottom line: *God didn't want there to be any poverty (or servanthood) in Israel* (Deut 15:4). So, servant laws existed to *help* the poor, not *harm* them or *keep them down.*

Rather than relegating treatment of servants ("slaves") to the end of the law code (commonly done in other ANE law codes), the matter is front-and-center in Exodus 21. *For the first time in the ANE, legislation required treating servants ("slaves") as persons, not property.* No wonder: Gen 1:26–27 affirms that all human beings are God's image-bearers. Job himself declared that master and slave alike come from the mother's womb and are ultimately equals (31:13–15). As one scholar writes: "We have in the Bible the first appeals in world literature to treat slaves as human beings for their own sake and not just in the interests of their masters."[11]

Three Remarkable Provisions in Israel

A simple comparison of Israel's law code with those of the rest of the ANE reveals three remarkable differences. If these three provisions had been followed by "Bible-believing" Southerners, then antebellum slavery would not have existed or been much of an issue.

#1: Anti-Harm Laws. One marked improvement of Israel's laws over other ANE law codes is the *release* of *injured servants themselves* (Exod 21:26–27). When an employer ("master") accidentally gouged out the

---

[11] Muhammad A. Dandamayev, s.v. "Slavery (Old Testament)," in *Anchor Bible Dictionary*, vol. 6, ed. David Noel Freedman (New York: Doubleday, 1992).

eye or knocked out the tooth of his male or female servant/employee, she was to go free. No bodily abuse of servants was permitted. If an employer's disciplining his servant resulted in immediate death, that employer ("master") himself was to be put to death for murder (Exod 21:20)—unlike other ANE codes.[12] In fact, Babylon's Code of Hammurabi actually *permitted* the master to cut off his disobedient slave's ear (¶282). Typically in ANE law codes, *masters—not slaves—were merely financially compensated.* The Mosaic law, however, held masters to legal account for *their own* treatment of their own servants—not simply of *another* person's servants.

#2: Anti-Kidnapping Laws. Another unique feature of the Mosaic law was its *condemnation of kidnapping* a person to sell as a slave—an act punishable by death: "He who kidnaps a man, whether he sells him or he is found in his possession, shall surely be put to death" (Exod 21:16 NASB; cf. Deut 24:7). By contrast, of course, kidnapping is how slavery in the antebellum South got off the ground.

#3: Anti-Return Laws. Unlike the antebellum South, Israel was to *offer safe harbor to foreign runaway slaves* (Deut 23:15–16)—a marked contrast with the Southern states' Fugitive Slave Law. Hammurabi's Code demanded the death penalty for those helping runaway slaves (¶16). In other less-severe cases—in the Lipit-Ishtar (¶12), Eshunna (¶49–50), and Hittite (¶24) laws, *fines* were exacted for sheltering fugitive slaves. Some claim that this is an improvement. Well, sort of! In these "improved" scenarios, *the slave was still just property*; the ANE extradition arrangements *still* required that the slave be returned to his master. And not only this, the slave was going back to the harsh conditions that prompted him to run away in the first place![13] Even upgraded laws in first-millennium BC Babylon included, yes, compensation to the owner (or perhaps something more severe) for harboring a runaway slave. Yet the returned slaves themselves were disfigured, including

---

[12] See Christopher Wright, *Old Testament Ethics and the People of God* (Downers Grove, IL: InterVarsity Press, 2006), 292.

[13] ANE legal text references are from *The Context of Scripture: Volume II: Monumental Inscriptions from the Biblical World*, ed. William W. Hallo (Leiden: Brill, 2003); Martha T. Roth, *Law Collections from Mesopotamia and Asia Minor*, 2nd ed. (Atlanta: Scholars Press, 1997). See also Elisabeth Meier Tetlow, *Women, Crime, and Punishment in Ancient Law and Society: Volume 1: The Ancient Near East* (New York: Continuum, 2004).

slitting ears and branding.[14] This isn't the kind of improvement to publicize too widely!

Old Testament scholar Christopher Wright observes: "No other ancient near Eastern law has been found that holds a master to account for the treatment of his own slaves (as distinct from injury done to the slave of another master), and the otherwise universal law regarding runaway slaves was that they must be sent back, with severe penalties for those who failed to comply."[15]

If these three clear laws from Exodus and Deuteronomy had been followed in the American South, then "slavery" would have been a nonissue. What's more, Israel's treatment of servants ("slaves") was unparalleled in the ANE.

Examining Difficult Texts

We've looked at the general nature of Old Testament servitude. Now, let's look at three of the most challenging Old Testament servitude texts.

Beating Slaves to Death?

> "If a man strikes his male servant or his female servant with a staff so that he or she dies as a result of the blow, he will surely be punished [*naqam*]. However, if the injured servant survives one or two days, the owner will not be punished [*naqam*], for he has suffered the loss." (Exod 21:20–21 NET)

Is the servant merely property here? The Old Testament affirms each person's full dignity (e.g., Gen 1:26–27; Deut 15:1–18; Job 31:13–15), and this passage proves no exception. If the servant died after "a day or two," the master was given the benefit of the doubt that no murderous intent was involved. But the master's striking a servant so that he immediately dies means the master would be tried for capital punishment: "he shall be avenged" (ESV). This verb *naqam* always involves the death

---

[14] Raymond Westbrook, ed., s.v. "Neo-Babylonian Period," in *A History of Ancient Near Eastern Law*, ed. Raymond Westbrook, Handbook of Oriental Studies (Leiden: Brill Academic, 2003), 2: 932.

[15] Wright, *Old Testament Ethics*, 292.

penalty.[16] This theme reinforces the "life for life" theme (21:23–24), which follows the servant-beating passage. The servant was to be treated not as property, but as a dignified human being.

Leaving Wife and Children Behind?

> "If you buy a Hebrew servant, he is to serve you for six years, but in the seventh year he will go out free without paying anything. If he came in by himself he will go out by himself; if he had a wife when he came in, then his wife will go out with him. If his master gave him a wife, and she bore sons or daughters, the wife and the children will belong to her master, and he will go out by himself. But if the servant should declare, 'I love my master, my wife, and my children; I will not go out free,' then his master must bring him to the judges, and he will bring him to the door or the doorposts, and his master will pierce his ear with an awl, and he shall serve him forever." (Exod 21:2–6 NET)

Above, we noted that, out of desperation, a man might contract to hire out temporarily ("sell") his wife or children or even himself to help get the family out of debt—a *voluntary* servitude, quite unlike antebellum slavery. The man, wife, and children would have a roof over their heads with food and clothing supplied by the employer ("master"). As for this particular law, some critics complain that a woman and children are disadvantaged—even trapped—but the man gets to go free, and this reflects an anti-woman/-child bias—or it traps the man into staying with the master if he marries a fellow servant woman.

Three responses are in order. *First, we have good reason to think this passage isn't gender-specific.* This is an example of case law ("if such-and-such a scenario arises, then this is how to proceed"), and case law was typically gender-neutral. Furthermore, Israelite judges were quite capable of applying laws to male and female alike. An impoverished woman, who wasn't given by her father as a prospective wife to a (widowed or

---

[16] Chirichigno, *Debt-Slavery in Israel and the Ancient Near East*, 155–63.

divorced) man or his son (Exod 21:7–11), could perform standard household tasks,[17] and she could go free by this same law.[18]

Various scholars suggest this legitimate, alternative reading to illustrate this passage's nongender-specific nature: "If you buy a Hebrew servant, *she* is to serve you for six years. But in the seventh year, *she* will go out free. . . . If *her* master *gives her a husband*, and they have sons or daughters, *the husband and the children will belong to her master, and she will go out by herself*." This reading makes perfect sense, and the law's spirit isn't violated at all.

Second, this scenario isn't as harsh as it first appears. Let's stick with a *male* servant scenario. Say the employer arranges for a marriage between this unmarried male servant and a female servant. (In this case of debt servitude, the employer's family would now engage in marriage negotiations.) By taking the male servant into his home to work off a debt, the boss has made an investment. *He would stand to suffer loss if the servant walked out on the contract.* In military service, even if a soldier marries, he can't simply walk away as he still owes the military his time. So it wouldn't make sense to let the man go with his family without paying off the debt.

Third, the released man has three options: (a) He could wait for his wife and children to finish their term of service while he worked elsewhere. No, his wife and children weren't "stuck" in the employer's home the rest of their lives! They could be released when the wife worked off her debt. Yet if the now-free man worked elsewhere, this would mean he would have been separated from his family, and his boss would no longer supply him with food, clothing, and shelter. On the other hand, if he lived *with* his family after release, he'd still have to pay for room and board. So this scenario created its own set of financial challenges.

(b) He could get a decent job elsewhere and save his shekels to pay his boss to release his wife and children from contractual obligations. The problem

---

[17] It is incorrect that this passage implies polygamy or concubinage. The daughter was to be married either to the master (who was divorced or widowed) or to the master's marriageable son—not as a backup wife to provide offspring. We're already told in v. 8 that the man *doesn't choose to take the servant woman as his wife.* In that case, we should understand v. 10 to mean that he marries another *instead of* the servant woman. Also, v. 11 is sometimes misleadingly translated "conjugal rights"; it more likely means "oil" or "shelter/protection." On this, see chap. 11 in Paul Copan, *Is God a Moral Monster?*

[18] Chap. 6 in Chirichigno, *Debt-Slavery in Israel and the Ancient Near East.*

is that it would have been very difficult for the man to support himself *and* to earn enough money for his family's debt-release.

(c) He could commit himself to working permanently for his employer—a lifetime contract (vv. 5–6). He could stay with his family and remain in fairly stable economic circumstances, formalizing his intent in a legal ceremony before the judges ("God") by having his ear pierced with an awl.

In general, destitution in Israel brought about voluntary servitude. In unfortunate circumstances during bleak economic times, Israel's laws provided safety nets for *protection*, not oppression.

Owning Foreign Slaves?

> "[Israelites] are not to be sold in a slave sale. . . . As for your male and female slaves whom you may have—you may acquire male and female slaves from the pagan nations that are around you. Then, too, it is out of the sons of the sojourners who live as aliens among you that you may gain acquisition, and out of their families who are with you, whom they will have produced in your land; they also may become your possession. You may even bequeath them to your sons after you, to receive as a possession; you can use them as permanent slaves. . . ." (Lev 25:42,44–46)

This text troubles many, as it seems that foreigners here could be treated as chattel. But consider the following points. *First, according to Lev 19:33–34, Israel was to love the stranger in the land.* Also, Exodus's laws (Exod 21:20–21,26–27) protect from abuse *all* persons in service to others—not just Israelites.[19] *Second, the verb "acquire* [qanah]*" in Lev 25:39–51 need not involve selling or purchasing foreign servants as property.* This verb appears in Gen 4:1 (Eve's having *"gotten* a manchild" NASB) and 14:19 (God as *"Possessor* of heaven and earth" NASB),[20] and Boaz "acquired" Ruth as a wife (Ruth 4:10)—clearly a full partner and no inferior.

---

[19] Roy Gane, *Leviticus, Numbers*, NIV Application Commentary (Grand Rapids: Zondervan, 2004), 441–42.

[20] John Goldingay, *Israel's Life* (Downers Grove, IL: InterVarsity, 2009), 464 and note.

Third, the very "aliens" in servitude (v. 45) are the same ones capable of sufficient "means" to purchase their own freedom (v. 47)! They weren't inevitably stuck in lifelong servitude. The text continues: "if the means of a stranger or of a sojourner with you becomes sufficient" (v. 47 NASB). The terms *stranger* (*ger*) and *sojourner* (*toshab*) are connected to the terms used in verse 45. That is, these "acquired" foreign servants could potentially better themselves to the point of hiring servants themselves. (Of course, an alien's hiring an Israelite servant was prohibited.) In principle, *all* persons in servitude within Israel could be released, unless they had committed a crime.[21]

Fourth, in some cases, foreign servants could become elevated and apparently fully equal to Israelite citizens. For instance, Caleb's descendant Jarha ended up marrying an Egyptian servant: "Now Sheshan had no sons, only daughters. And Sheshan had an Egyptian servant whose name was Jarha. Sheshan gave his daughter to Jarha his servant in marriage, and she bore him Attai" (1 Chron 2:34–35 NASB). We have marriage between a *foreign* servant and an established *free* person with quite a pedigree, and the key implication is that *inheritance rights* would fall to the servant's offspring, Attai.

Fifth, Israel was required to give foreign runaway slaves protection within Israel's borders and not be returned to their harsh masters (Deut 23:15–16), and kidnapping slaves was also prohibited (Exod 21:16; Deut 24:7). Thus, Leviticus 25 should be understood with these general humanizing protections in mind.

Sixth, since non-Israelites weren't to acquire land in Israel, homeless and landless foreigners wouldn't have much choice but to attach themselves to Israelite households as servants, which might have been the only alternative possible—and not necessarily a bad alternative. John Goldingay writes that "perhaps many people would be reasonably happy to settle for being long-term or lifelong servants. Servants do count as part of the family." He adds: "one can even imagine people who started off as debt servants volunteering to become permanent servants because they love their master and his household" (cf. Deut 15:16–17).[22]

---

[21] Walter C. Kaiser, "A Principlizing Model," in *Four Views of Moving Beyond the Bible to Theology*, ed. Stanley N. Gundry and Gary T. Meadors (Grand Rapids: Zondervan, 2009), 40.
[22] Goldingay, *Israel's Life*, 465–66.

Seventh, various scholars see the "Hebrew" servant of Exod 21:2 as a foreigner without political allegiances who has come to Israel. Note that he wasn't locked in to lifelong servitude (unless he chose this); he had to be released in the seventh year—presumably to go back to his country of origin.

Slavery in the New Testament

In the two sections above, I focused on Old Testament debt-servitude and some of the difficult passages critics commonly raise. In this section, I focus on slavery in the New Testament—a much different world of institutionalized chattel (property) slavery—a topic I address in more detail in *Is God a Moral Monster?* During the first century, a whopping 85–90 percent of Rome's population consisted of slaves with both lowly and prestigious positions. A step backward from the Old Testament, yes, but that was Rome's fault!

Slaves as Persons

The New Testament presupposes a fundamental equality because all humans are created in God's image (Jas 3:9; cf. Gen 1:26–27), yet an even deeper unity in Christ transcends human boundaries and social structures: no Jew or Greek, slave or free, no male and female, as believers are all "one in Christ Jesus" (Gal 3:28 NASB; cf. Col 3:11).

Some critics claim, "Jesus never said anything about the wrongness of slavery." Not so! In his "mission manifesto," He explicitly *opposed* every form of oppression; after all, he came "to proclaim release to the captives . . . to set free those who are oppressed" (Luke 4:18 NASB; cf. Isa 61:1). But just as Jesus didn't press for some economic reform plan in Israel but rather addressed attitudes like greed, materialism, contentment, and generosity, so the New Testament writers addressed underlying attitudes regarding slavery: Christian masters called Christian slaves "brother" or "sister" and were commanded to show compassion, justice, and patience; "master" meant responsibility and service—not oppression and privilege. Thus, the worm was already in the wood for altering the social structures.

The New Testament writers, like Jesus their Master, opposed the dehumanization and oppression of others. In fact, Paul gives "household rules" in Ephesians 6 and Colossians 4 not only for Christian slaves but for Christian *masters* as well. Slaves are ultimately responsible to God, their heavenly Master. But *masters* are to *"treat your slaves in the same way"*—namely, as persons governed by a heavenly Master (Eph 6:9 NIV). Commentator Peter O'Brien points out that "Paul's cryptic exhortation is outrageous" for his day.[23]

Given the spiritual equality of slave and free, slaves could even take on leadership positions in churches or be equal partners in the gospel with, say, Paul. Paul's ministry illustrates how in Christ there is neither slave nor free, greeting people in his epistles by name. Most of these individuals had commonly used slave and freedman names. For example, in Rom 16:7 and 9 he refers to Andronicus and Urbanus (common slave names) as *kinsman, fellow prisoner,* and *fellow worker.* The New Testament's approach to slavery is utterly contrary to that of aristocrats and philosophers like Aristotle, who held that certain humans were slaves by nature (*Politics* I.13).

Paul reminded Christian masters that they, with their slaves, were *fellow slaves* of the same impartial Master; so they weren't to mistreat them but rather deal with them as brothers and sisters in Christ. Paul called on human masters to grant "justice and fairness" to their slaves (Col 4:1 NASB). In unprecedented fashion, Paul treated slaves as morally responsible persons (Col 3:22–25) who, like their Christian masters, are "brothers" and part of Christ's body (1 Tim 6:2).[24] Christian slaves and masters alike belong to Christ (Gal 3:28; Col 3:11). *Spiritual* status is more fundamental and freeing than *social* status.

The "Silence" of the New Testament Writers on Slavery

Though critics claim that the New Testament writers keep quiet about slavery, we see a subtle opposition to it in various ways. We can confidently say that Paul would have considered antebellum slavery with its slave trade to be an abomination—an utter violation of human dignity and an act of human theft. In Paul's "vice list" in 1 Tim 1:9–10, he expounds on the fifth through the ninth commandments (Exodus

---

[23] Peter T. O'Brien, *The Letter to the Ephesians,* Pillar New Testament Commentary (Grand Rapids: Eerdmans, 1999), 454.

[24] Ibid., 455.

20/Deuteronomy 5); there he condemns "slave traders" (NIV) who steal what isn't rightfully theirs.[25]

Critics wonder why Paul or New Testament writers (cf. 1 Pet 2:18–20) didn't condemn slavery outright and tell masters to release their slaves. Yet we should first separate this question out from other considerations. The New Testament writers' position on the negative status of slavery was clear on various points:

- the repudiation of slave trading (1 Tim 1:9–10);
- the affirmation of the full human dignity and equal spiritual status of slaves;
- the encouragement for slaves to acquire their freedom whenever it is possible (1 Cor 7:20–22);
- the revolutionary Christian affirmations (e.g., Gal 3:28) which, if taken seriously, would help to tear apart the fabric of the institution of slavery; indeed, this is precisely what took full effect several centuries later—namely, the eventual eradication of slavery in Europe; and
- the condemnation of treating humans as cargo (Rev 18:11–13, where doomed Babylon—the "city" of God-opposers—stands condemned because she had treated humans as "cargo," having trafficked in "slaves [literally 'bodies'] and human lives," NASB).

Paul along with Peter didn't call for an uprising to overthrow slavery in Rome. On the one hand, they didn't want the Christian faith to be perceived as opposed to social order and harmony. Hence Christian slaves were told to do what is right; even if they were mistreated, their conscience would be clear (1 Pet 2:18–20). Yes, obligations fell to these slaves without their prior agreement. So the path for early Christians to take was tricky—very much unlike the situation of voluntary servitude in Mosaic law.

A slave uprising would do the gospel a disservice—and prove a direct threat to an oppressive Roman establishment (e.g., "Masters, release your slaves!" or "Slaves, throw off your chains!"). Rome would quash flagrant opposition with speedy, lethal force. So Peter's admonition to

---

[25] See Gordon D. Fee, *1 and 2 Timothy, Titus*, NIBC 13 (Peabody, MA: Hendrickson, 1988), 45–46, n49.

unjustly treated slaves implies a suffering endured *without retaliation*. No, suffering in itself is not good—a sadistic, unscriptural attitude; rather, the *right* response in the midst of suffering is commendable.

On the other hand, early Christians undermined slavery indirectly, rejecting many common Greco-Roman assumptions about it (e.g., Aristotle's) and acknowledging the intrinsic, equal worth of slaves. Since the New Testament leveled all distinctions at the foot of the cross, the Christian faith was particularly attractive to slaves and lower classes, being countercultural, revolutionary, and anti-status quo. Thus, like yeast, such Christlike living can have a gradual leavening effect on society so that oppressive institutions like slavery could finally fall away. This is, in fact, what took place throughout Europe: slavery fizzled since "Christianized" Europeans clearly saw that owning another human being was contrary to creation and the new creation in Christ.[26]

This incremental strategy was taken by President Abraham Lincoln, who despised slavery but approached it shrewdly. Being an exceptional student of human nature, he recognized that political realities and predictable reactions to abolition required an incremental approach. The radical abolitionist route of John Brown and William Lloyd Garrison would (and did!) simply create a social backlash against hard-core abolitionists and make emancipation all the more difficult.[27]

Returning Onesimus: A Throw-Back to Hammurabi?

One key portion of the New Testament begs to be discussed—the letter of Philemon. Was Paul's sending Onesimus back to his alleged owner Philemon a moral step backward? Was it more like the oppressive Babylonian Code of Hammurabi, which insisted on returning fugitive slaves to their masters—something prohibited in the Old Testament (Exod 21:16; Deut 23:15–16)? Some charge that Paul was siding with this ancient oppressive code against the Old Testament.

Keep in mind that reading a New Testament epistle like Philemon is like listening to just one party in a phone conversation. We only hear

---

[26] Jonathan Hill, *What Has Christianity Ever Done for Us?* (Downers Grove, IL: InterVarsity, 2005), 176.

[27] See Ronald C. White's *A. Lincoln: A Biography* (New York: Random House, 2009), which explores these themes in detail.

Paul's voice, but plenty of gaps exist that we'd like to have filled in. What was Paul's relation to Philemon ("dear friend and fellow worker" and "partner" [vv. 1,17, NIV])? What debt did Philemon owe Paul? How had Onesimus wronged Philemon (if he even did)?[28] Many interpreters have taken the liberty to "help" us fill in the gaps. The typical result? Too much gets read into the text. The common "fugitive-slave hypothesis" (that Onesimus was a runaway slave of Philemon's) is actually quite late, dating back to the church father John Chrysostom (AD 347–407). However, genuine scholarly disagreement exists about this interpretation. For one thing, the epistle contains no "flight" verbs, as though Onesimus had suddenly gone AWOL. And Paul revealed no hint of fear that Philemon would brutally treat a returning Onesimus, as Roman masters typically did when their runaway slaves were caught.

It's been plausibly suggested that Onesimus and Philemon were *estranged Christian (perhaps biological) brothers.*[29] Paul exhorted Philemon not to receive Onesimus as a slave (whose status in Roman society meant alienation and dishonor); rather, Onesimus was to be welcomed as a beloved brother: "that you might have him back for good— *no longer as a slave, but* better than a slave, *as a dear brother.* He is very dear to me but even dearer to you, both as a man and as a brother in the Lord" (Phlm 1:15–16 NIV, my emphasis).

Notice the similar-sounding language in Gal 4:7: "Therefore you are *no longer a slave, but a son*; and if a son, then an heir through God" (NASB). This may shed further light on how to interpret the epistle of Philemon: Paul wanted to help heal the rift so that Onesimus (*not* an actual slave) would be received back as *a beloved brother in the Lord*— not even simply a biological brother. To do so would be to follow God's own example in receiving us as *sons* and *daughters* rather than *slaves.*

Even if Onesimus *were* an actual slave, this still didn't mean he was a fugitive. If a disagreement or misunderstanding had occurred between Onesimus and Philemon, and Onesimus had sought out Paul to intervene

---

[28] For a fine general discussion, see David B. Capes, Rodney Reeves, and E. Randolph Richards, *Rediscovering Paul* (Downers Grove, IL: IVP Academic, 2007), 237–41. I also borrow insights from Allen Dwight Callahan, "Paul's Epistle to Philemon: Toward an Alternative Argumentum," *Harvard Theological Review* 86 (1993): 357–76; Sarah Winter, "Paul's Letter to Philemon," *New Testament Studies* 33 (1987): 1–15.

[29] See Callahan, "Paul's Epistle to Philemon."

somehow or to arbitrate the dispute, then this wouldn't have rendered Onesimus an official fugitive. And given Paul's knowledge of Philemon's character and track record of Christian dedication, the suggestion that Onesimus's coming back was "Hammurabi Revisited" is way off the mark. Again, if Onesimus *were* a slave in Onesimus's household, Paul's strategy was this: Instead of forbidding slavery, impose fellowship![30]

Concluding Remarks

In the Old Testament, we see a much-improved, humanizing legal system over against other ancient Near Eastern law codes. And when we look at the New Testament, we gain further a deepened perspective. Written during Roman rule with its chattel slavery in place, the Gospels call for freedom from dehumanization and tyranny. Christ's mission is not one of oppression and destruction; rather, he comes to give life, to heal, to redeem, and to release (Luke 4:18). And Paul in Gal 3:28 doesn't abolish slavery; rather, he makes it *ultimately irrelevant*! All the structures that separated Jew and Greek, male and female, slave and free were radically overturned by these Christians sharing a common meal together to celebrate the Lord's death (cf. 1 Cor 11:17–34). Indeed, this was a defiant, countercultural act against Rome's embedded social structures—a far cry from the critics' "passive resignation" argument ("Paul didn't speak out against slavery but accepted it").

Furthermore, the Lord's Supper was also a culturally shameful— yet socially defiant—act: not only did these Christians worship at the table of their once humiliated and crucified Messiah (who rose from the dead!); the lower social status Christians—females, Gentiles, and slaves—were treated as equals with males, Jews, and free persons. In the early church, a social revolution had begun!

In summary, Jesus and the New Testament writers opposed oppression, slave trade, and treating humans as cargo. The earliest Christians were a revolutionary, new community united by Christ—a people transcending racial, social, and sexual barriers—which eventually led to a slavery-free Europe a few centuries later.

---

[30] James Tunstead Burtchaell, *Philemon's Problem: A Theology of Grace* (Grand Rapids: Eerdmans, 1998), 21.

Part 5

CHRISTIAN
UNIQUENESS
AND
OTHER RELIGIONS

Chapter 15

QUESTIONING ISLAMIC TEACHINGS ABOUT THE QUR'AN

Michael H. Edens

I slam claims special status for their holy book, the Qur'an,[1] as divine revelation. For Muslims the book has unquestioned spiritual authority. They make three claims for the book. First, the Qur'an's spiritual authority is drawn from the fact that the Qur'an is solely God-speech completely devoid of human elements. Second, the Qur'an continues and completes the message of the heavenly books before it. Third, the Qur'an is the complete and final revelation.

In light of these claims several Islamic assumptions raise questions. It is beyond the scope of this present project to examine the most serious of these assumptions—the Qur'anic vision of who Allah is and his relationship with and within his creation. Instead, an examination of the internal consistency of Islamic understandings of the Qur'an as special revelation and supreme spiritual authority for humanity is the more modest objective here. This essay will discuss three Islamic claims to supreme authority for the Qur'an and questions arising from these statements.

---

[1] In Arabic, the definite article "the" is part of the name of the book—*al Qur'an.*

Claim #1: "The Qur'an's spiritual authority is drawn from the fact that the Qur'an is solely God-speech completely devoid of human elements."

In this first section, we'll examine the following questions:

1. Can this claim stand in the face of portions of the Qur'an that appear to have a textual history?

2. Is it reasonable to read passages that express interaction with communities and people of Muhammad's day as Allah's eternal speech?

3. Portions of the Qur'an focus on Muhammad's household and his right to marital excess. Does this narrowing of interest argue against the divine nature of the speaker?

4. If the Qur'an is in conflict with respected records of human history, does that negate the claims of eternal authorship?

5. Since at times the text clearly records someone other than Allah speaking, how is that God-speech?

Muslim apologists seek to eliminate any debate concerning the spiritual authority of their scriptures by claiming that it is solely God-speech, devoid of any human content. In their view, stating that the Qur'an is solely God-speech (*ykallimhu Allah*) removes the content from all questioning. For the vast majority of Muslims throughout the complex Islamic world, the Qur'an is the final and complete revelation to humanity from God. Daniel Brown, in *A New Introduction to Islam*, identifies three ways of approaching Islamic scriptures. First, the Qur'an can be studied for the meaning of the message. One also can examine the text as a historical artifact. The final way to approach the Qur'an is as a sacred object, which is an indivisible unit.[2] While all three methods of Qur'anic study can be understood from the Western perspective, most Muslims approach the Qur'an as a unified indivisible sacred object.[3]

The Muslim understanding of the Qur'an as God-speech is drawn from the Qur'an's teaching about itself and the nature of special

---

[2] Daniel Brown, *A New Introduction to Islam* (Oxford: Blackwell, 2009), 53–54.

[3] To better understand this position, see Toby Lester's section "Copyediting God" found in the introduction to his article "What Is the Koran?" *Atlantic Monthly* (January 1999), reprinted in *What the Koran Really Says: Language, Text, and Commentary*, ed. Ibn Warraq (Amherst, NY: Prometheus Books, 2002), 110–15 (107–25).

revelation. The defining text for this concept is the *surah* (chapter) named *Consultation* (surah 42) and *ayah* (verse) 51:[4] "It is not fitting for a man that Allah should speak to him except by inspiration, or from behind a veil, or by the sending of a Messenger to reveal, with Allah's permission, what Allah wills: for He is Most High, Most Wise." All three modes by which Allah addresses a person convey the complete control of Allah on his message without human modification or amendment. Islamic commentators exert great effort to identify Muhammad as Moses' predicted successor in leading humanity on earth.[5] However, this paper only seeks to observe issues arising from Muslim claims for the Qur'an as God-speech devoid of human content. No attempt will be made to compare the modes of special revelation provided to Moses and Muhammad.

1. If portions of the Qur'an have a textual history, does this negate these claims for the Qur'an being solely God-speech?

The Qur'an is the final source for Arabic grammar. It is composed of the purest Arabic language, Islam supposes. Arabic is Allah-language with which he produced a heavenly book. The humanly transcribed Arabic Qur'an is an exact copy of Allah's book. However, many foreign words appear within the text of the Qur'an. This discovery is not new. Alfons Mingana had deduced much of this information in his 1927 work, *Syriac Influence on the Style of the Kur'an*. When Mingana looked at all the foreign words in the book, he discovered five language groups. Ethiopic and Persian words each accounted for 5 percent of the words. Hebrew and Greco-Roman words each comprised 10 percent of the foreign words in the book. However, nearly 70 percent of the words were rooted in Syriac—including Aramaic and Christian Palestinian. The evidence Mingana provided was then divided into six categories: (a) proper names, (b) religious terms, (c) expressions of ordinary language,

---

[4] In this essay references to the text of the Qur'an are cited with the name of the surah followed by the parenthetical reference (surah or chapter number: ayah or verse number), i.e., *Consultation* (42:51). The English text employed in this essay is Abdullah Yusef Ali's translation, *The Meaning of the Holy Qur'an*, 11th ed. (Beltsville, MD: Amana, 2006). This and other renderings of the Qur'an, including the Arabic text, may be accessed at http://al-quran.info.

[5] John Wansbrough, *Quranic Studies: Sources and Methods of Scriptural Interpretation* (Amherst, NY: Prometheus Books, 2004), 33–38.

(d) orthography, (e) sentence constructions, and (f) foreign historical references.[6] The reality displayed by Mingana's tabulations is difficult to explain in a book purposed by Allah to communicate orally with non-literate Arabic speakers. However, modern scholars such as Christoph Luxenberg, John Wansbrough, Jane Dammen McAuliffe, and Andrew Rippin are exploring textual history with recently discovered early copies of the text.[7] These studies point to "hints of a 'concealed' history of the [Qur'anic] text before and during the revelations delivered to Muhammad."[8] For many non-Muslim scholars, the Qur'an is understood to have a textual history and group authorship.[9]

2. If passages express interaction with contemporary humanity, how does this impact the contention that the Qur'an is solely God-speech?

The examples of contemporary conversation in the Qur'an are numerous. For the purposes of this paper, discussion will be limited to three instances. First, the Qur'an contains numerous reports of conflicts with detractors of Muhammad's claim to be the spokesperson for Allah. One example will suffice in *Consultation* (42:24). The text reads, "What! Do they say, 'He has forged a falsehood against Allah'? But if Allah willed, he could seal up thy heart, and Allah blots out vanity, and proves the truth by his words for he knows well the secrets of all hearts."[10] This passage is representative of large blocks of Qur'anic content that defend the prophetic calling of Muhammad in the face of powerful opposition.

---

[6] Alfons Mingana, "Syriac Influence on the Style of the Kur'an," *The Bulletin of the John Rylands Library* 11 (1927): 77–98.

[7] Christoph Luxenberg, *The Syro-Aramaic Reading of the Koran* (Berlin: Verlan Hans Schiler, 2007); John Wansbrough, *Quranic Studies: Sources and Methods of Scriptural Interpretation* (Amherst, NY: Prometheus Books, 2004); Jane Dammen McAuliffe, "Interpretations and Intellectual Traditions," and Andrew Rippin, "Western Scholarship and the Qur'an," in *The Cambridge Companion to the Qur'an,* ed. Jane Dammen McAuliffe (Cambridge: Cambridge University Press, 2007); Andrew Rippin, *Approaches to the History of the Interpretation of the Qur'an* (Oxford: Clarendon, 1988).

[8] Claude Gilliot, "The Creation of a Fixed Text," in *Cambridge Companion to the Qur'an*, 53.

[9] Ibid.

[10] The claim that Muhammad was falsifying his visions was common during his early ministry in Mecca. This surah is thought to have been revealed during that part of his work. On the Islamic understanding of the sequence in which the chapters of the Qur'an was revealed, see: http://www.icbh.org/topics/QuranOrder.htm. The extreme right hand column contains numbers of ayat revealed later than the majority of the surah.

This defense is at variance with the Muslim argument for the book. The essence of their argument is that the Qur'an is solely the dispassionate decree of Allah for humanity in general, written and secured with Allah before time.

In the Islamic argument, the content of the Qur'an is solely and exactly a copy of that book revealed piecemeal to Muhammad. The dialogue with doubters in seventh-century Arabia seems out of touch with that argument, especially when the common understanding of Muslims is that this same revelation is the content of all previous prophets. One assumes that Allah would not have troubled earlier prophets with such revelations, although this is the major subject in many of the 114 surahs of the book. If one compares this content with the opposition Moses, Paul, and Jesus faced, similarities and differences emerge. However, that misses the point. The Bible does not set the context of special revelation solely in the heavens; Muslims make that claim for their holy book. In the Bible, God is speaking into specific human contexts. The coherence and comprehension of these interchanges is enhanced by understanding both those contexts as well as the nature of God. This is not the case with the Qur'an. As a result, this claim for preexisting divine revelation appears to make such "dialogue with doubters" passages at least a minor problem for the Islamic position of the book's spiritual authority.

In at least two instances, the text could demonstrate that cultic practice was changed after failed attempts to gain pagan or Jewish converts to the Islamic community by compromise. It should be noted that, in both cases, Muslims assert that no human causality or dynamic shapes the revelation. The text of the Qur'an is, for them, an exact copy of an eternal book that is with Allah. But is this claim credible?

One of these instances is the factual basis for the novel by Salmon Rushdie, *The Satanic Verses.* The issue is found in two Qur'anic readings. In the surah *The Star* (53:1–25), Muhammad receives the revelation of three female beings with Allah—Lat, Ajja, and Manat. These names were previously associated with three idols worshipped by pre-Islamic Meccans in the Kaaba.[11] In *The Cow* (2:158), the Kaaba is said to contain two symbols of Allah—Safa and Marat—and those who worship these

---

[11] The *Kaaba* is a stone cubical at the center of the pilgrimage to both pre-Islamic and Islamic Mecca. The house is supposed to have been built by Abraham and Ishmael.

images have not sinned. Islamic tradition maintains that the prophet was deceived by a lying spirit in this matter, and a divine messenger corrected Muhammad later; however, the Qur'an does contain these references. The former surah is understood to have been modified by abrogation[12] to the present form, while the latter is left in the text in its original form but understood to have been set aside. Even though *The Star* (53) was revealed much earlier in Mecca than *The Cow* (2), the common fact of these two epochs in the life of Muhammad is that during both he was seeking to win Meccans to his cause and avoid bloody conflicts. If that is not the solution, how can this abrogated content be reconciled with the claim for the Qur'an being solely God-speech?

A possible second instance of human intent behind the text is found in the redirection of daily prayer. In *The Cow* (2:142–50), the word *qibla* refers to the direction to turn in prayer and the geographical location on which prayer is centered. In this passage Muslims turned away from Jerusalem and toward Mecca. This change in worship practice occurred only after the Muslims who migrated to the city of Yathrib (later named Medina) had reached a position of parity with the original ruling tribes of that town, which were Jewish. The revelation is immediately followed by several Muslim sieges of individual Jewish tribes and finally the execution of approximately 700 Jewish men after several Muslim warriors died during the Battle of the Trench.[13] Until that time, Islamic prayers were directed toward Jerusalem, and it appears there was hope of massive Jewish conversion. As conflict replaced hope, worship or ritual prayer turned away from the temple mount in Jerusalem toward the Kaaba in Mecca. The Qur'an explains the original direction of prayer as a test for the Muslim believers who are rewarded with a direction of worship more to their liking. Muslim apologists contend that historical events simply provided the setting for the revelation of the Qur'an but do not affect the content of the ayah (verse or sign) or of the special revelation.[14]

---

[12] Abrogation, the superseding of one revelation to another, as a problem for understanding spiritual authority within Islam will be dealt with in a later section. However, abrogation implies that Qur'anic content evolved during the life of the Muhammad.

[13] Ali Dashti, *23 Years: A Study of the Prophetic Career of Mohammad*, trans. F. R. C. Bagley (Costa Mesa, CA: Mazda, 1994), 87–91.

[14] *Ayah* refers to both a sign from Allah and a division in any surah of the Qur'an.

3. If a portion of the Qur'an focuses on Muhammad's household and his interactions with the Jewish tribes of Medina, does this narrowing of interest argue against the eternal and divine origin of the Qur'an?

In the Qur'an one finds a group of texts referring to conflicts within Muhammad's household and their effect on the Islamic republic. In one of the late Medinan surahs, *Confederates* (33), several passages are devoted to rules for the prophet's marital life. In ayat 37–39, Muhammad is given permission to marry the ex-wife of his adopted son, Zaid, in contrast with previous regulation. This established a practice that persists in the Muslim world today. In ayat 50–54, the prophet is exempted from the normal limits in marriage partners. This passage also established protocols for Muslim men visiting his home. The Qur'an takes pains to establish that the prophet's widows are to remain unmarried after his death. In ayah 59, special rules for modesty are established for those married to Muhammad. Muhammad married thirteen women and left nine widows when he died.[15] These ayat appear to express the desires and contribution of Muhammad rather than Allah. What end would Allah seek to achieve by incorporating such speech in an eternal and universal book?

4. If the Qur'an is in conflict with other historical records, does that negate the claims of eternal authorship?

In *Mary* (19:16–29), one of the Qur'anic accounts of the conception and birth of Jesus the Christ is presented. Allah reports the people addressing Mary in ayah 28 as sister of Aaron, Moses' brother. The Arabic name of both Aaron's sister and the mother of Jesus is Miriam. However, it is a conflation of history to make a single person both sister of Aaron and mother of Jesus Christ. Can this be God-speech?

The second example is found in *Women* (4:157). The text reads, "that they [the Jews] said (in boast), 'We killed Christ Jesus the son of Mary, the apostle of Allah': but they killed him not, nor crucified him, but so it was made to appear to them, and those who differ therein are full of doubts, with no (certain) knowledge, but only conjecture to follow, for

---

[15] Ibn Ishaq, *The Life of Muhammad*, trans. A. Guillaume (Oxford: Oxford University Press, 1987), 792–94.

of a surety they killed him not." The Qur'an is virtually alone in disputing the crucifixion of Jesus Christ. However, conflict with the idea of a sacrificial loving God and humanity in dire need of redemption is inherent in Islam. In the face of Christian and Jewish claims to the crucifixion, the Qur'an denies it as a historical fact.

5. Since at times the Qur'an clearly records someone other than Allah speaking, how is the text God-speech?

The final category is that of passages in the Qur'an that are not God-speech because someone other than Allah is apparently speaking. Richard Bell, following the work of the fourteenth-century Egyptian scholar Al Shyuti, identifies five passages in the Qur'an in which God-speech is precluded.[16] The ending words of *Cattle* (6:104) are Muhammad's for Allah is clearly guarding over the faithful, but the ayah ends with, "I am not (here) to watch over your doings." Muhammad is not the watchman over the faithful, but Allah is. This is not God-speech.

In *Mary* (19:64) the Arabic is translated, "We do not descend without permission of your Lord. Everything between our hands and behind our back and anything between is His. He does not forget." Some English translators, including Ali, add in parentheses at the beginning, "The angels say."[17] This is not in the text. Gabriel is speaking to Mary, and the text is reporting his—not Allah's—speech. A similar pattern is found in *The Scattering Wind* (51:50–51): "Therefore escape to Allah: I was sent from Him to be a clear and plain warning to you. Do not associate anything with Allah in worship. I was sent from Him to be a clear and plain warning to you."

Finally the first surah, *The Opening*, records the pattern prayer of the faithful. It is clearly not God-speech. It is the prayer of believers to Allah.

These questions arising from the claims for the Qur'an based on the idea that it consists solely of God-speech are simply questions. They do not destroy the spiritual authority of the Qur'an to Muslims. However, such discussion may result in other, more meaningful spiritual dialogues.

---

[16] Richard Bell, *A Commentary on the Qur'an*, vol. 1 (Manchester: Victoria University of Manchester, 1995), 201–3.

[17] Likewise, Marmaduke Pickthall and others.

Claim #2: "The Qur'an Possesses Spiritual Authority Because It Continues and Completes the Message of the Bible"

Islam teaches that the Bible of today is to some extent corrupted, yet in some way the Bible is understood to attest to the validity of the Qur'an. Muslims seek to show doctrinal continuity between the Bible and the Qur'an in at least five areas: belief in the unity of God, the nature and foundational purpose of humanity as creature, anticipation of the Qur'an and Muhammad found in the biblical text, belief in angels, and certainty of the Day of Judgment.

1. Are the marks of Islam's concept of Allah coherent with the Old and New Testament teachings about God?
2. Does the Muslim view of human nature and purpose have commonality with the Bible?
3. The Qur'anic claim to spiritual authority partially rests on biblical passages said to anticipate either Muhammad or the Qur'an. Are these claims coherent?
4. Is the Qur'anic presentation of doctrines of angels, office of prophet (*nabi*), and last things consistent with the Bible?

Muslims revere the *Torah* (five books of the Law) of Moses, the *Zabor* (Psalms) of David, and the *Injil* (Gospel) of Jesus since the Qur'an teaches they were each sent down by Allah to his messenger. However, this respect does not carry over to the present books bearing the same name. Yet the claim for spiritual authority for the Qur'an is partially based on the continuity of the message—as Muslims understand it—between the Bible and their holy book. Muslims also believe the Qur'an corrects the Bible. Do these claims prove to be coherent?

Muslims seek to show doctrinal continuity between the two holy books. For Muslims the missing correspondence between the Bible and the Qur'an is proof that the Bible has been altered. However, continuity with previous messages is an Islamic test for the spiritual authority of their holy book. If the core beliefs of Islam are absent from or contradicted by the Bible, the claim for Qur'anic spiritual authority is questionable.

1. Are the marks of Islam's concept of Allah coherent with concepts of God in the Old and New Testaments?

Muslims contend that Allah of the Qur'an is the God of the Bible. Many Qur'anic passages present a dialogue between Muhammad and Jews and Christians. The dialogue in *The Cow* says: "Will ye dispute with us about Allah, seeing that He is our Lord and your Lord: that we are responsible for our doings and ye for yours: and that we are sincere (in our faith) in Him?" (2:139). Many Christian authors have demonstrated aspects of God's self-revelation contained in the Bible that are unknown or denied in Islam. However the issue here is that Islam claims spiritual authority for the Qur'an partly by stating that the original message of the Bible was Islam. Although the Bible, in the teachings of many Muslims, has been corrupted, a vigilant self-revealing God would be expected to retain some relics of the Islamic core in the Bible. However, Allah's willingness to forgive sin in the future based on capriciousness, without justifying the sinner, and his unqualified oneness, *tawhid*, are two marks of Islamic theology that are at the core of the Qur'anic vision of Allah, yet distinct from the Bible.

Contrary to the Islamic expectation, the Bible never vindicates the Islamic teaching that God absolves humans of sin. In fact, the Bible teaches that God refuses to overlook sin. To illustrate, God refuses Moses' request for absolution from sin in the wilderness (Num 14:13–23). Also, the entire Jewish sacrificial system represents the immense importance God places on reconciling, not tacitly overlooking, sinners. Islam strips the redemptive meaning from animal sacrifice, which it borrows from Judaism. Lastly, in the Qur'an, Jesus (*Isa*), son of Mary, although titled the Christ, does not need to die for humanity's sin and is not crucified. Clearly the Qur'anic Allah and the biblical God have no common agreement with regard to the means by which God forgives sin. This central aspect of Allah's nature is contradicted by the biblical record. Allah who simply forgives whom he chooses is not foreshadowed in the Bible.

Because of the biblical emphasis on the oneness of God, one expects to find continuity with the concept of the oneness of Allah in the Qur'an. However, the one God of the Old Testament reveals Himself, rather than just revealing His speech, His will, and His decrees. The oneness of Allah is different: "No vision can grasp Him, but he grasps all visions. He is beyond comprehension, but comprehends all things" (Qur'an, 6:103). The common point between Allah and the God of the Old Testament is that they are other than (or outside their) creation; however, the biblical God is related in such a way to creation that He can reveal Himself to creatures. The *Shema*—"Hear, O Israel! The LORD is our God, the LORD is one!" (Deut 6:4 NASB)—is set in the context of living righteously as a redeemed people. He is not just a distant judge but a loving shepherd to His people. He gives assurance of His covenant-keeping love while maintaining righteousness. He is able to be present within His creation in His love and holiness. The Qur'anic god, Allah, cannot be known by his creature. The 99 noble names of Allah are descriptions of his actions within creation but not his character. He himself is not revealed.

In the gospel, the unity of God (Father, Son, and Spirit) is one of essence but is qualified by the interrelations of the three persons and is not the unqualified singular unit of Allah. God's purpose for humanity is expressed in rebirth, relationship, reconciliation, renewal, and restoration, not merely in human reeducation. In both Old and New Testaments the biblical promise to believers is that they will be present with God after this life—not *near* God, as in Islam, but *with* Him. The contrast between the biblical concept of the oneness of God and the Islamic concept of *tawhid* (oneness) is stark. This central vision of the unknowable Allah found in the Qur'an is not foreshadowed in the Bible. If the text of the Bible bears any resemblance to the original heavenly books Islam says it represents, one would think some remnant of the Islamic doctrine of the oneness of Allah would be preserved by Allah who is great and powerful.

2. Does the Muslim view of human nature and purpose have commonality with the Bible?

In both the Bible and the Qur'an, humanity's first duty is to worship God. In both books God gives Adam and Eve tasks in the garden; however, in the Qur'an, a central task is the establishment of Islamic community. This is a task in and after the garden. Adam and his family must submit to Allah and establish an interrelated worshipping community. This is God's intended purpose and role for humanity, a purpose not derailed by Adam's sin.

The ideal behavior in Islamic community is buttressed and constrained by the principle of honor and shame. Honor/shame differs from innocence/guilt as a basis for a communal value system. Individual behaviors produce honor or shame not primarily for the person but the tribe, clan, or ethnic network—the community. Muslims expect their behavior and that of other Muslims near them to bring honor to their community and to the entire family of Islam. Peer pressure and external reinforcement enhance the Islamic behaviors known as the five pillars of Islam. In the Bible, shame—as well as guilt—for sinful behavior and attitudes is most notably personal, although communal shame and guilt are present.

In the Qur'an there is no substantial difference in the human task, human potential, or the human relationship with God after Adam's disobedience in the garden. The Islamic communities in the created garden and today have the same purpose and potential. However, in the Bible, Adam and Eve began their existence in innocence and on a potential path to perfection through God's provision. They chose to disobey, thereby becoming rebels in need of redemption and a savior. This is one of the stark contrasts between Islamic and Christian understandings of humanity. The two worldviews resulting from this foundational disagreement radically diverge.

Although both the Bible and Qur'an see the original creation as good, the Bible does not agree that humanity is basically good after Adam's sin. Though created good by God, the Bible presents humanity as deeply affected by sin and in need of redemption, while in Islam the need is a guiding book and a worshipping community. Islam's limited view of sin and ignorance of both temporal and eternal consequences of sin for Adam and his descendants prevent Muslims from understanding humanity's precarious position before a holy God who offers redemption through the life and cross of Jesus Christ.

3. The Qur'anic claim to spiritual authority partially rests on biblical passages said to anticipate Muhammad. Are these claims believable?

Islamic writers point to two passages as evidence that Moses and Jesus spoke of Muhammad to their generations. Before dealing with each of these passages, it is important to understand the one thing they hold in common. Both Moses and Jesus spoke to their anxious community as they were departing. For either or both of them to be speaking of Muhammad destroys the comforting impact of the message. The people needing encouragement died hundreds of years before the birth of Muhammad.

God promises Moses and Israel in Deut 18:15–22 a prophet like Moses to lead them. Muslims say this is prophesying Muhammad. They go to great lengths to show that Muhammad is more like Moses than Jesus. However, when comparing the men, Muslim apologists are misunderstanding the text. The text promises a Jewish ("from among your brothers") prophet. The two Jewish prophets that Christians identify with this passage are Joshua—whom Moses identifies as the first to fulfill this role (Deut 31:23)—and Jesus. Muslims ignore this problem when placing Muhammad alongside Moses. Moses was speaking of Jewish prophets, not Arab prophets. Deuteronomy does not speak of Muhammad.

In the middle of ayah 6 of *Al Saff* (surah 61), Jesus proclaims in the Qur'an, "[I am] giving glad tidings of a messenger to come after me, whose name shall be Ahmed." Muslim teachers have pointed to John 14 as evidence that this indeed happened. The teaching uses various Greek spelling errors to make "helper" or "advocate" (*paraklētos*) found in John 14 into "praised one" (*periklutos*), which is the meaning of Ahmed. However, the context of the word stipulates that the one coming will "be with you forever" (John 14:16). By contrast, Muhammad lived long after the death of those who received these comforting words, and he died in the seventh century. He came too late to comfort those who were frightened at the thought of Jesus' departure, and Muhammad has died rather than abiding forever. Contrary to Islamic expectation, Jesus was not prophesying about Muhammad but about the Holy Spirit who has been comforting and abiding with believers from Pentecost (roughly 50 days after this prophesy) until Christ comes again. Muhammad is not mentioned, foreshadowed, or prophesied as prophet or comforter/advocate in the Bible.

4. How much continuity is found between Qur'anic views of angels, office of prophet (*nabi*), and last things when compared with the Bible?

The concept of spirits and angels differs between the Bible and the Qur'an. Spirits play a larger role in the Qur'an than the Bible. In Islam, angels are the primary means for divine interaction with humanity. The Qur'an says of itself that it was delivered to Muhammad by a heavenly messenger. In most passages the messenger is called a spirit: sometimes a holy spirit, at other times an honest spirit. In one or two instances the messenger is identified as the angel Gabriel. Muslim teachers understand all this to be speaking of the same being and he is the angel Gabriel. Only on one occasion in the Qur'anic record does the angel take on a human form—when sent to the Virgin Mary. On none of the many public occasions when Muhammad received part of the Qur'an did any other person see or hear the messenger. However, except for the inability of Muslims to accept that the Qur'anic reference to a holy spirit might be the Spirit of the living God rather than an angel, the views of Islam and the Bible are not strikingly different with regard to angels and the spirit world. The same may be said for the role of prophecy although again there is some difference in emphasis. However, a marked difference remains between the Qur'anic and biblical concepts about the end of time.

Although the nature of god in Islam is beyond the scope of this paper, the concept of Allah is foundational to any Islamic understanding of the final state of human affairs. In contrast with the biblical God, Allah is not concerned by human sin. Sin does not affect him. Most Islamic theologians see Allah's transcendence as virtually precluding his involvement in creation much less being affected in some way by human sin.[18] In the Qur'an, the story of Adam and Eve and their error is told. Sin is reported factually but devoid of terms that could be described as painful to either Adam or Allah. By contrast, emotion courses through the biblical account of Adam and Eve's sin in Eden. The story is dramatic and painful. In the Bible, God is obviously displeased and disappointed

---

[18] Yasin Al Jibouri, *Allah: The Concept of God in Islam* (Qum: Ansariyan Publications, 1997), 5–16. This book provides an example of the inability to conceptualize the person of Allah, not to mention his divine attributes.

by all of humanity except Jesus of Nazareth. Adam is filled with fear and seeks to displace responsibility to someone else for his error.

Death and resurrection are an unstated part of the original creation in Islam. There is no change in this because of Adam or Eve's sin and fall. In the Bible, death was not a stated part of creation but entered creation though human disobedience. Death is a sign of the brokenness of sin in the Bible. The Qur'an, in contrast, presents Adam's descendants as basically good in the sight of Allah. Sin is a concern, but such transgression has not dramatically flawed human nature. Humanity is left in ignorance after the encounter in paradise. However, the Bible presents the human problem as entrenched disobedience and rebellion against God. The Bible, unlike the Qur'an, observes the ravages of sin expressed in marred and broken relationships that play out in human history until God brings all things to His end.

The conflict between biblical and Qur'anic views of the seriousness of human sin, important as it is, points to differences in each book's portrayal of God's nature and His attitude toward the direction the world is going. The Qur'an reveals Allah as willing to blot out sin unimpeded by holiness and justice. He will absolve believers of their sins based on their repentance.

Allah's judgment in the Qur'an in absolving Adam of his sin appears to be based on three tenets. Allah has no problem absolving sin for anyone he chooses.[19] This is his prerogative as sovereign that he exercises without comment. His action is not dependent on either some canon of judgment or human behavior. One of the 99 adjectives for Allah in the Qur'an is *Al-Ghaffar*: "One who has manifested what is beautiful and veiled what is ugly in the life of this world and who does not inflict his penalty on him in the life hereafter. He is the one who forgives sins, veils the shortcomings, wipes out the sins by accepting one's

---

[19] Speaking of Moses, Allah says in surah 7:155–56, "And Moses chose seventy of his people for Our place of meeting: when they were seized with violent quaking, he prayed: 'O my Lord! If it had been Thy Will thou couldst have destroyed, long before, both them and me: wouldst Thou destroy us for the deeds of the foolish ones among us? This is no more than thy trial: by it Thou causest whom Thou wilt stray, and Thou leadest whom Thou wilt into the right path. Thou are our Protector: so forgive us and give us thy mercy; for Thou art the Best of those who forgive.'... He [Allah] said: 'I afflict My Punishment on whom I will; but My Mercy extendeth to all things. That (Mercy) I shall ordain for those who do right, and pay *zakah* [almsgiving], and those who believe in Our Signs.'"

repentance."[20] The second Islamic teaching is that sin is not "against" Allah. Neither Adam's sin nor any human action can "take anything away from Allah." This view is part of the Islamic grand transcendence of Allah that impedes his interaction with creation.

Lastly, the decree of absolution carries with it intertwined teachings of human need for infallible divine instruction[21] and pity for humans who fall prey to Satan's deceptions. In surah 61:5–6 the Qur'an illustrates Satan's deceptions in how both Moses and Jesus were rejected when they presented Allah's message (Islam) to the people of Israel in their day.[22] Thus, the state of humanity after rejecting Islam is rebellion for which the Qur'an has no solution.

Muslims believe that through an elaborate process of judging thoughts, intents, words, and actions each person's piety will be determined. However, Allah simply forgives whom he chooses to forgive; so it is not as if the compilation of good works will earn paradise. Allah is gracious and forgiving. It is impossible to incorporate this view into the biblical account of God's judgment of humanity.

Claim #3: "The Qur'an Is the Complete and Final Revelation from God"

From *al hadith* (the sayings of Muhammad remembered and recorded to guide Muslims) Islam claims that the Arabic Qur'an of today is Muhammad's codex, gathered under the protection of Allah.[23] They teach it was Allah's responsibility to collect it, protect it, and make

---

[20] Al Jibouri, *Allah: The Concept of God in Islam*, 28.

[21] The Qur'an's claim to provide unfailing guidance is observed in 43:2–4, "By the Book that makes things clear—We have made it a Qur'an in Arabic, that ye may be able to understand. And verily, it is in the Mother of the Book, with Us, high (in dignity), full of wisdom."

[22] "And remember, Moses said to his people: 'O my people! Why do ye vex and insult me, though ye know that I am the messenger of Allah (sent) to you?' then when they went wrong, Allah let their hearts go wrong. For Allah guides not those who are rebellious transgressors. And remember Jesus, the son of Mary, said: 'O Children of Israel! I am the messenger of Allah (sent) to you, confirming the Taurat (which came) before me, and giving glad tidings of a messenger to come after me, whose name shall be Ahmad.' But when he came to them with Clear signs they said, 'This is Evident sorcery!'"

[23] "Narrated Abu-Huraira: Gabriel used to repeat the recitation of the Qur'an with the Prophet once a year, but he repeated it twice with him in the year he died. (Book #61, Hadith #520). Accessed from: http://www.searchtruth.com/ book_display.php?book=61&translator=1&start=0&number=520#520.

the meaning clear.[24] The text of the Qur'an is understood to be complete and final. The following questions are skeletal and intended to raise other questions for the Muslim.

1. Since Muslims disagree about what passages are abrogated, how can we know that the Qur'an is complete or even the final revelation?

Muslims understand that an indefinite number of ayat in the written Arabic Qur'an have been superseded.[25] Much Islamic study of abrogating has been done; however, Muslim scholars differ on many aspects of the teaching. There is no consensus. Muslim scholars disagree greatly as to which ayat have been abrogated. Some Muslims believe that abrogation and deletion of unneeded texts was completed in the lifetime of Muhammad. Most point to several passages that they believe were superseded by other ayat, yet the original ayat remain in the text. This is bewildering to studious nontechnical Muslims and all non-Muslims.

According to the Hadith, Uthman was questioned regarding "[t]hose of you who die and leave wives" in *Cow* (2:240). While he

---

[24] The Hadith says, "Narrated Said bin Jubair: Ibn 'Abbas in the explanation of the Statement of Allah. 'Move not your tongue concerning (the Quran) to make haste therewith.'" (75.16). Said [bin Jubair] continues [the narration]: "Allah's Apostle used to bear the revelation with great trouble and used to move his lips (quickly) with the Inspiration." Ibn 'Abbas moved his lips saying, "I am moving my lips in front of you as Allah's Apostle used to move his." Said moved his lips saying: "I am moving my lips, as I saw Ibn 'Abbas moving his." Ibn 'Abbas added, "So Allah revealed 'Move not your tongue concerning (the Qur'an) to make haste therewith. It is for us to collect it and to give you (O Muhammad) the ability to recite it (the Qur'an)'" (75.16–17) which means that Allah will make him (the Prophet) remember the portion of the Qur'an which was revealed at that time by heart and recite it. The Statement of Allah: And 'When we have recited it to you (O Muhammad through Gabriel) then you follow its (Qur'an) recital' (75.18) means 'listen to it and be silent.' Then it is for Us (Allah) to make It clear to you' (75.19) means 'Then it is (for Allah) to make you recite it (and its meaning will be clear by itself through your tongue). Afterwards, Allah's Apostle used to listen to Gabriel whenever he came and after his departure he used to recite it as Gabriel had recited it" (Book 1, Hadith 4; Book 61, Hadith 564). Accessed from: http://www.searchtruth.com/book_display.php?book=1&translator=1&start=0&number=4#4 and http://www.searchtruth.com/book_display.php?book=61&translator=1&start=0&number=564#564 .

[25] Narrated Ibn Abbas: Umar said, "Our best Qur'an reciter is Ubai and our best judge is 'Ali; and in spite of this, we leave some of the statements of Ubai because Ubai says, 'I do not leave anything that I have heard from Allah's Apostle while Allah: "Whatever verse (Revelations) do We abrogate or cause to be forgotten but We bring a better one or similar to it"'" (2.106) (Book 60; Hadith 8). Accessed from: http://www.searchtruth.com/book_display.php?book=60&translator=1&start=0&number=8#8.

was compiling the Qur'an, Ibn Az-Zubair reported his response, "'This Verse was abrogated by another verse.' [he was questioned further] 'So why should you write it? (Or leave it in the Qur'an)?' Uthman said. 'O son of my brother! I will not shift anything of it from its place.'"[26]

Simply put, the Qur'an denies and embraces abrogation. According to surah 6:115, "The words of the Lord are perfect in truth and justice; no person can change His words. He both hears and knows." The message of the Qur'an in 6:34; 10:64; and 18:27 agrees with these words. Abrogation is not possible with the speech of Allah.

However, the same book says of itself: "None of Our revelations do we abrogate or cause to be forgotten but we substitute something better or similar: knowest thou not that Allah hath power over all things?" (2:106). A similar passage says, "And when We exchange a verse in place of another verse—and Allah knows very well what He is sending down—they say, 'Thou art a mere forger!'; Nay, but the most of them have no knowledge" (16:101).

In light of this, the obvious question arises, "Can the text of the Qur'an be known?"

2. Can entire heavenly books be seen as abrogated?

Some Muslims teach that the holy books before the Qur'an are abrogated. Others, realizing that the Qur'an states that these books inform it and that the role of the Qur'an is to affirm the earlier books, avoid this issue. The question needs to be asked, "If you believe that the Bible was abrogated by the Qur'an, why would Allah do that? If he could not keep the Bible uncorrupted, how is the Qur'an kept from corruption?"

3. Was the Qur'an complete at the death of Muhammad?

All except one of the 114 surahs of the Qur'an—namely, surah 9—begins with "in the name of Allah the merciful and beneficent." It is commonly believed among Muslims that when Gabriel confirmed Muhammad's recitation of a surah and it was complete, the angel would amend the surah with this affirmation. Surah 9 was either the last or next to last revelation given Muhammad. Some Muslim teachers deal

---

[26] Ibid., Book 60, Hadith 53.

with this anomaly by saying that the epitaph is missing because surah 9 is actually not a surah but the continuation of the preceding surah although titled and numbered as a surah. Is this a coherent argument?

4. If the Qur'an was compiled under the first three leaders of the community after the death of Muhammad, did Abu Bakr, Umar, or Uthman as the Caliphate (*khalifah*) change the text during compilation?

Muslims cannot frame this question without calling into question the integrity of the book as special speech of Allah. The Muslim is left with a book that claims to be the revealed text of a heavenly book. However, it was not compiled into a corpus until after the death of the person receiving the revelation. At the time of Uthman's work, several other compilations were destroyed. If the correct text was preserved by Allah through this process, why did he allow this to happen?

Conclusion

All spiritual authority in Islam is based on or derived from the Qur'an. Questions such as those posed in this paper undermine that authority in the view of non-Muslims. However, in Islamic worldviews, issues on which these questions are based are unapproachable because of statements purported to be made by Muhammad—their prophet and exemplar of pious life—and because of peer pressure from the Islamic community. As a result of this interlocking authority structure, the questions raised may only provide an opening for a witness to another spiritual authority, the Bible—and the person of Jesus Christ, who is presented in its pages. Apologists should pray to God in Christ that He would guide Muslims to himself. This is what Muslims ask for, unknowingly, daily in ritual prayer. Five times daily they repeat the words of the *Fatiha* (surah 1): "Open the straight path before us, the one of your grace not the one of your wrath. Keep us from going astray." As the Qur'anic path is exposed as questionable, the Holy Spirit will empower the witness to Jesus, the Only Way to the Father.

Chapter 16

ARE WE REALLY ALL HINDUS NOW?

Barbara B. Pemberton

A recent issue of *Newsweek* magazine carried an article by Religion Editor Lisa Miller titled "We Are All Hindus Now." Citing statistics from a 2008 survey, she concluded that while 76 percent of Americans claim to be Christian, "conceptually . . . we are slowly becoming more like Hindus and less like traditional Christians in the ways we think about God, ourselves, each other, and eternity."[1] Miller reported 65 percent of Americans—and a staggering 37 percent of "white *evangelicals*" (italics mine)—agree with Hindus that there are many paths to God.[2] Another disturbing statistic comes from Boston University Professor of Religion Stephen Prothero, who says 20 percent of *evangelicals* believe in reincarnation.[3]

Perhaps we should have seen this coming. I remember when the Beatles first appeared in Indian attire playing what then were considered strange, exotic musical instruments—introducing to the world their newly adopted, self-styled, guru-led spirituality. Of course, the Beatles were not the first Westerners to delve into Indian thought,

---

[1] Lisa Miller, "We Are All Hindus Now," *Newsweek* (Aug. 31, 2009), citing "Radical Western Belief Shift," *Hinduism Today* (Jan.-Mar. 2010), 8; Accessed March 11, 2011, http://www.newsweek.com/2009/08/14/we-are-all-hindus-now.html.

[2] Ibid. *Hinduism Today* expressed delight in finding these statistics in the US media: "Hindus, of course, were gratified to see their philosophy touted at the top of the US mainstream media."

[3] Stephen Prothero, *Religious Literacy: What Americans Need to Know* (Dallas: HarperOne, 2007), 29.

nor were they the first celebrities to introduce Hindu concepts to the West. Eastern thought had been gaining ground through literature and immigration for years but advanced on a larger scale via news and entertainment media after Indian Swami Vivekananda was welcomed at the first Parliament of the World's Religions in Chicago in 1893. The Swami served as an eloquent messenger of many heretofore foreign concepts including karma and reincarnation. Even Christians have waded unawares into the murky waters of Hinduism and have felt right at home thanks to television shows and movies with sometimes subtle, sometimes more obvious, Hindu themes.[4] People browse the current American spiritual buffet, picking and choosing self-oriented concepts and practices they think fit their lifestyles. What they often come out with is a syncretistic concoction with no spiritual nourishment—only artificial ingredients. Such indiscriminant selection leaves many unsuspecting seekers starving—eternally.

From 2005 to 2009 there was even a popular television sit-com (*My Name Is Earl*) based on what has been called "the most distinctive feature of Hinduism": karma.[5] The main character spent each episode trying to undo his own prior bad actions by doing something good for the people he has harmed, hoping his "good deeds" restore his cosmic "karmic" credit rating. Funny stuff—except that there is absolutely nothing funny about karma. In this essay I shall (1) uncover the religious roots of karma, (2) illustrate the complexity of karma theory, including a few of the many problems, and (3) offer reasons why karma is not compatible with a Christian worldview.

Hinduism—Sanatana Dharma

Hinduism, the world's third-largest religious tradition, is actually comprised of several distinct paths or "denominations" so diverse that contemporary scholarship suggests "Hinduism" is a more appropriate term for the entire civilization of India. Although the term "Hindu" was coined from an Arabic word for the people of the Indus Valley,

---

[4] There are many reasons for this trend; contributing factors I have noticed include the lack of adequate teaching of Scripture and doctrine in many of our churches and philosophical postmodernism.

[5] R. C. Zaehner, *Hinduism*, 2nd ed. (London: Oxford University Press, 1966), 59.

devotees continue to use the term as their own self-designation—particularly with outsiders.[6] Adherents traditionally call their faith *sanatana dharma*—"eternal religion" or "eternal duty." At first glance this *dharma* (tradition or duty) looks like "polytheism," for devotees gather in temples filled with images—statues and paintings of many different gods. In practice, the worship is most often henotheism, the belief in one deity without denying the existence of others. For while the believers recognize many gods, each person selects one god, one's *Ishtadeva* (Sanskrit: "chosen god") to serve as the focus of her worship. Some individuals, or entire regions, may focus on *Shiva* or *Vishnu* (or his incarnations or *avatars*—*Krishna* or *Rama*), or even the goddess *Kali*. However, ancient Hindu philosophical texts teach "pantheistic monism":[7] everything that we perceive to exist is of one essence and this oneness is "Ultimate Reality," "Universal Consciousness," or *Brahman*. Yet another strain of the tradition, popular contemporary Hinduism, employs the brand "monotheism," claiming the countless images merely represent the various aspects of the one transcendent *Brahman*. Other professed Hindu monotheists claim their favorite *avatar* as the one, ultimate god who, they argue, must be the same god worshipped by other monotheists—Jews, Christians, and Muslims.

Hinduism has no founder, creed, or what Christians would recognize as divine revelation. It *is* incredibly diverse, though. That said, there are several foundational beliefs all Hindus embrace.[8] Concerning existence, if everything is "one" (of the same essence), and everything is part of "ultimate reality," then it follows that we human beings are also part of ultimate reality. Our problem is epistemological—we just don't know we're "divine"! We are caught in the illusion that this world we live in is real and that we are separate egos; but only *Brahman* is real.

---

[6] For example, "Hindus" participated in the 2009 Parliament of the World's Religions and read a popular magazine: *Hinduism Today*.

[7] Technically, monism and pantheism are distinct, however. For instance, the Hindu philosopher Shankara (d. 820) was a *monist* (there is only one undifferentiated reality); he believed that the Ultimate Reality, Brahman, has no differences or qualities (*nirguna*) and that only Brahman exists; any apparent differentiation is the result of an illusion (*maya*). Thus, India's many deities are not real but ultimately illusory. By contrast, Ramanuja (d. 1137) was a *pantheist* ("all is God"). He claimed that differences do exist (*saguna*), but they are all part of Brahman. Thus, Hindu deities exist in their own right and, therefore, aren't an illusion.

[8] Buddhism and Jainism also developed in India and share basic metaphysical presuppositions with Hinduism; however, they differ considerably in the details of these concepts.

We are ignorant of our true nature (*atman*), which is divine, inseparable from god (*Brahman*)—or as the Hindu texts, the *Upanishads*, declare: *Atman-Brahman*.

Living for ourselves—even clinging to life itself—we commit acts that accrue to our karma that continues to tie us to the cycle of *samsara* or reincarnation, like "moral debts" carrying over from life to life. According to Hindu traditions, the human problem is in our minds. We need to find a way to understand our true identity and rid our lives of karma, thereby escaping the dreadful cycle of death and rebirth so that we may reach our eternal goal, *moksha*—being absorbed into the essence of *Brahman*—like a drop of water into the ocean. The various paths to self-awareness, or enlightenment, account for the numerous strains or denominations within this ancient system.

Karma Theory

What is karma? The earliest Hindu texts, the *Vedas*, assert an inescapable law of justice—*rita* (moral law)—that maintains the natural order, including human activity. Classical Hindu scholars determined karma foundational to the operation of this law in the universe, with reincarnation as a necessary derivative. Originally karma was a technical term for efficacious Vedic rituals; the one who accurately performs the ritual reaps the expected result from the gods—absolute "cause and effect." This concept developed to include acts appropriate to each person's social grouping or class.[9] Eventually karma came to include all actions and now may be defined as intentional *action* that affects your future *and* the attendant *consequences*, either in this life or later incarnations.[10] Ancient texts record detailed consequences: for good actions one may expect to be reborn into a higher class, but "those whose conduct is 'evil-smelling' will enter the womb of a dog, a pig, or, what is quite unclean and vile, an outcaste."[11]

---

[9] The traditional Hindu hierarchical social structure consists of four segregated classes or *varnas* divided according to occupation: Brahmin—priests, teachers, doctors, etc.; Kshatriyas—warriors and leaders; Vaishyas—producers, farmers, traders; and Sudras—laborers. Each of these classes is comprised of many "castes" or *jatis*.

[10] Zaehner, *Hinduism*, 59–60.

[11] Ibid., 59. A "outcaste" is a person whose social standing is below the four recognized occupational classes, therefore relegated to performing duties seen as irrevocably polluting—like

In relating karma to responsibility, the compiler of the *Yoga Sutras*, Patanjali (ca. 150 BC) taught that nothing within the universe is inherently good or evil; "good" and "evil" are relative value judgments made by individuals according to their life situations as determined by the law of karma. "Good" (as in doing one's class duty) is whatever takes an individual closer to awareness of the real Self (*Atman-Brahman*); "evil" is whatever removes the individual from such awareness. Karma acts as a law of automatic justice. The person acts, and then enjoys or suffers the consequences, according to karma—including the possibility of reincarnation in the animal or plant realm.[12] According to Patanjali, only humans accrue karma in pursuit of *moksha*; so birth as a human is a great privilege not to be wasted.

Other early texts, such as the *Puranas*, also describe this law of cause and effect as impersonal, inescapable, and exacting, with reincarnation needed to provide the time necessary for the moral order to be worked out for each individual. Popular belief has always had a considerably less fatalistic view, hoping to mitigate the dread consequences of wrongdoing by embracing practices such as worship. Several questions come to mind: "If we are the sum of our yesterdays, how can we affect our tomorrows?"[13] To what extent are humans free? Do we really get what we deserve?

From at least the beginning of the twentieth century, Indian philosophers have felt compelled to respond to charges of determinism with all the socioeconomic implications inherent in their system. One of the best-known responses came from philosopher and past president of India, Sarvepalli Radhakrishnan (1888–1975). In 1908 the statesman published an influential article titled "Karma and Free Will" in which he offered his now well-used analogy of a game of bridge to explain how karma constructs the circumstances of life without setting limits. He explained that the universe is orderly and predictable as a deck of cards. Humans do not choose their cards but are dealt a "hand of cards"

---

cleaning toilets—rendering these people "untouchable."

[12] Ever optimistic New Agers teach that humans face reincarnation only as humans—never rebirths down the ladder of existence. Most Hindus believe return as a lower life-form is always a possibility—if deserved.

[13] Austin B. Creel, "Contemporary Philosophical Treatments of Karma and Rebirth," in *Karma and Rebirth: Post Classical Developments*, SUNY Series in Religious Studies, ed. Ronald W. Neufeldt (Albany: State University of New York Press, 1986), 3.

according to past karma. You may make any play you desire—choose any option—within the rules established by the game. People with greater skills will recognize more potential plays and will be able to make the most of the cards available.[14]

Radhakrishnan also rejected what he saw as a common misconception of karma as merely a fatalistic law of retribution—preferring the more positive term: "continuity." He argued that ties to the past need not eliminate the possibility of freedom, asserting karma as a powerful case for personal responsibility. A subsidiary doctrine, *niskama-karma*, or "non-attached" living (unselfish action), states that not only may people "undo" their karmic consequences, but they may also work toward spiritual progress.[15] Employing this evolutionary perspective, Radhakrishnan taught that reincarnation is educational and progressive—an "evolution of the self." In answer to those who asked how rebirth can be of any pedagogic value if the individual retains no memory of past existences, he countered that it is more significant to focus on what does continue—the "dispositions and tendencies" of the person. He speculated that specific memories from past lives would be a "nuisance" and complicate one's personal life.[16]

Radhakrishnan also responded to the related charge that the doctrines of karma and rebirth are "life-denying," that the Hindu worldview focuses on escape from a meaningless existence in a realm that is really illusory. He appealed again to the evolutionary view of self-development through which individuals work their way up to the human realm—and beyond—out of their beginnings as lower life-forms. His progressive model of "successive spiritual opportunities" rejects the possibility of human reincarnation into the animal realm, claiming such ideas found in religious texts are merely metaphorical. This means that karma bestows on all individuals an opportunity—a "life context" in which to operate (a hand of cards). Human free will is therefore limited to life within that context, including the limitations of character that he

---

[14] Ibid., 3–4.

[15] Ibid., 10. However, Gajanan Wasudeo Kaveeshwar noted that it seems ludicrous to hold someone responsible for "doing his duty" while insisting that he is not to give any thought to the consequences of his actions. Giving no thought to your actions is "unnatural" (*The Law of Karma* [Poona: University of Poona, 1975], 1).

[16] Robert N. Minor, "In Defense of Karma and Rebirth: Evolutionary Karma," in Neufeldt, *Karma and Rebirth*, 31–32.

saw as the "condensation" of one's previous lives. Character is shaped in past lives but is continually developed in the current life toward ultimate *self-fulfillment*. Each life should be seen as progressing to the infinite, with the ultimate goal of leaving the process altogether—*moksha*.[17]

Other Hindu thinkers have also tackled the issue of free will, and with it moral responsibility, arguing that although one's life is the product of past thoughts and actions, the concept of karma does not say individuals are *solely* responsible—leaving room for other factors. Karma may be responsible only for one's basic existence and life-situation, leaving all people the opportunity within their "karmic circumstances" to make changes and improve themselves.[18]

While scholars wrestle with the concept of karma, religious communities throughout India *apply* the doctrine of karma in a variety of ways. For example, among the Tamil people of Kalappur, South India, some villagers believe strongly in fate. Traditional understanding describes the god *Shiva* as creating and molding the personality and nature of each person and also writing on each person's head all the details of that life. These people believe that with each successive life individuals add to their own "headwriting." This deterministic view has led some villagers to pity criminals and discount accomplishments. Other villagers have concluded that while destiny is *influenced* by karma, an individual may redirect it through personal choices. These villagers say people are responsible for their actions, not karma or "headwriting." Interestingly, researchers found that many of the Tamil people employ what I call "selective determinism"—taking one view or the other according to the circumstances. For example, when disaster strikes, a villager may find determinism more comforting, but the same villager may embrace "free will" when achieving personal success.[19]

There are numerous complications; for example, is there such a thing as "group karma"? When a whole community is lost in a natural disaster,

---

[17] Ibid., 34–36.

[18] Ramakrishna Puliganda, "Karma, Operational Definitions and Freedom," in *The Dimensions of Karma*, ed. S. S. Rama Rao Pappu (Delhi: Chanakya Publications, 1987), 133–36. The author adds that karma is not "potentially falsifiable" and therefore is unscientific, yet many scientists adhere to it on faith.

[19] Sheryl B. Daniel, "The Tool Box Approach of the Tamil to the Issues of Moral Responsibility and Human Destiny," in *Karma: An Anthropological Inquiry*, ed. Charles F. Keyes and E. Valentine Daniel (Berkeley: University of California Press, 1983), 27–28, 1.

such as a *tsunami*, was this each individual's karma? Had the community done something as a group to bring about such a consequence? Gandhi declared the Bihar earthquake "group karma" or group consequences from the mistreatment of the lower classes. Expanding this concept of group karma, Vivekananda espoused "national karma." Does this mean then, since no one lives in a bubble, we all affect other people's karma? Are we our brother's karma-keeper? Not all thinkers agree with the notion of collective karma, arguing one should not suffer the consequences of others' actions.[20]

Does *karma* theory support a form of "merit transfer"? Can "good karma" be bought or acquired from someone with a surplus from pilgrimages or worship? For example, if your child is sick, can you obtain "good karma" from a holy man to heal the child, or at least ensure a better rebirth for the child should he die? Classical Hinduism has no concept of passing karma from one person to another; however, popular Hinduism offers just such an opportunity—merit may be transferred but not guilt. Holy men are often approached to transfer their merit ritually to the sick or otherwise needy. Many Hindus believe your surplus of merit or demerit can "pile up" from numerous lives, which means you may be experiencing consequences now from actions several lives ago or you may have good karma to share.

Is there an element of "hope" in this system? One popular religious expression of Hinduism, devotionalism, while not systematic, has certain widely held understandings that are not necessarily in line with the more traditional deterministic philosophical assertions. Karma and rebirth are not considered by most of the devotionalists as an "ultimate metaphysical horror" or an "impersonal, inescapable absolute law of the universe." These devotees reject classic expressions of retribution and focus instead on concepts of "sin" and "grace." Most believe the Ultimate (*Brahman*) is a "Supreme Person" with whom one may have a personal Lord-servant relationship forever, rather than an impersonal, unknowable force into which one seeks absorption. The beloved Hindu text, the *Bhagavad Gita,* teaches *bhakti* (devotion) love is available for all men and women of any social group. In this epic, Lord Krishna (one *avatar* of the god Vishnu) reveals that he can suspend the rules and reward

---

[20] Creel, "Contemporary Philosophical Treatments," in Neufeldt, *Karma and Rebirth*, 5.

good and punish evil as he will—making personal faith and practices efficacious for "saving grace."[21] However, *bhakti* devotion to Krishna (or any other Hindu god) does not displace *karma* as the driving force behind reincarnation. In fact, everyone faces double retribution: "grace" from Krishna may provide a temporary reprieve in some heavenly state (or without it you may suffer in a hellish state), but you will still return time and time again until release—*moksha*—is achieved.[22]

Karma Difficulties

Most Hindu thinkers describe karma as "self-determination" as opposed to determination by "external agency" or "luck"—each person causes what she experiences. This stark understanding of a dispassionate, impersonal karma working in each individual life can be used to rationalize a lack of social concern. Taken to the extreme, karma may even lead one to believe it inappropriate to step in and mitigate another person's karmic circumstance; perhaps intervention is hopeless in the face of such a law. This has important sociopolitical ramifications. For example, are the Indian government's various quota systems and efforts toward improvement of living conditions within the country legitimate in light of karma? At least two components of karma contradict notions of modern social justice: (1) ability according to birth, and (2) societal role according to birth. While many Hindus no longer accept these limitations, the doctrines of karma and rebirth seem to have provided little incentive for social reform but rather have historically provided India a profound justification for maintaining the socioeconomic status quo: do your duty—"bloom where you are planted."[23]

---

[21] Klaus K. Klostermaier, "Contemporary Conceptions of Karma and Rebirth Among North Indian Vaisnavas," in Neufeldt, *Karma and Rebirth*, 84.

[22] Many contemporary devotees no longer believe in *moksha*, believing rather in an eternal heavenly existence. *Bhakti* devotion to Krishna is the focus of the International Society for Krishna Consciousness (ISKCON, popularly known as "Hare Krishnas") founded in 1966. This group teaches that fervent adoration of Krishna saves from future undesirable consequences.

[23] Creel, "Contemporary Philosophical Treatments," in Neufeldt, *Karma and Rebirth*, 5–9. Your caste, immediately evident by your last name, pigeonholes you for life. Caste discrimination is illegal in India, but continues to cause problems, particularly in family life, and the stigma of outcaste status endures. "Radical Western Belief Shift," *Hinduism Today*, 8.

Furthermore, since the human problem is *ignorance,* your social class situation is an indication of just how ignorant you were in past lives. The very idea that your life situation directly reflects your knowledge and actions in previous lives leads others to see your predicament and leave well enough alone. Bottom line: people are not born equal. Perhaps it's better for suffering communities to work through their situation for better karma next time; the beggar, cripple, and outcaste, according to karma, brought their situation upon themselves. This means the social system supports a deterministic interpretation of the doctrines with all the pain and associated inequities and social stigmas, whether they are verbalized as such or not. Rationalization is found within the doctrine of karma:

> The law of evolution called Karma explains the apparent injustice in the world with sublime simplicity. There is a law of cause and effect in the moral world. We are the builders of our own destiny, and the results are not limited to one life, since our Spirit that was never born and will never die must come again and take to itself a body, that the lower self may have the reward of its works. Good shall lead to good, and evil to evil. From good, joy shall come and from evil shall come suffering. And thus the great evolution flows on to perfection.[24]

But note the contradiction: if each soul (*atman*) *is* Brahman (ultimate reality), that is, all humans are divine, then why are the outcastes—people on the lowest rung of society's ladder—treated as they are? Contemporary scholarship stresses the *equality* and *justice* found in karma! From the nondualist *advaitans* clinging to *Atman-Brahman,* to the dualists arguing individuals are not identical to god but *equally dependent* on god—in one sense all schools of thought agree: people *are* treated equally by karma, for it is impersonal and you do get just what you deserve. However, once reincarnated, human beings are not treated equally by society—try as hard as contemporary Indians are doing to make it happen.

Although the ancient Brahminical priesthood, the highest class, considered this system the best hope for social stability, what it really

---

[24] Juan Mascaró, *The Upanishads: Translations from the Sanskrit with an Introduction* (London: Penguin Books, 1965), 13.

achieved was a stagnant society stripped of ambition, institutionalizing the notion that people are not born equal. And what may be drawn from the "evolutionary" concept of karma? In spite of arguments to the contrary, "karmic amnesia" leaves reincarnation with no pedagogical value. Radhakrishnan maintained human "tendencies" are improving through the process; however, does history bear this out? How can "evolutionary karma theory" be supported in light of the apparent human proclivity toward war and violence? Can humanity ever overcome these karmic tendencies? Perhaps human nature is not divine as Hinduism presupposes.

Social class is not the only institutionalized inequity fostered by karma theory. Gender discrimination, rooted in revered ancient texts, has led to horrors such as female infanticide, and legitimized withholding educational opportunities from girls. The ancient *Manu Dharma Shastra* (*Laws of Manu*) describes the three states of obedience for women: first as a daughter; then as a wife; then if widowed, life under the authority of the eldest son. "In the married state the wife is wholly subject to her husband whom she should revere as a god."[25] According to the text, to be born female means to be forever under male authorities to prevent the women from causing evil and destruction. Ironically, goddess worship has not appreciably helped the plight of women throughout India, nor has the rise of female political leaders.

"Untouchables" and females are not the only people who suffer in life. Does karma offer an adequate contemporary explanation for innocent suffering—a satisfactory theodicy? Who can tell abused children that according to karma they received just what they deserved, that their situation was prescribed by karma? What do you tell the victims of natural disasters? Does the notion that "the world we perceive and inappropriately cling to as 'reality' is actually illusion" really provide comfort? And should those in abusive relationships be told they deserve their treatment? Are suffering people in the Hindu system left to believe they deserve their plight?

Contemporary guru Yogananda teaches:

---

[25] Zaehner, *Hinduism*, 111. Contemporary Hindu scholars wrestle with these ancient texts that contain passages on women. It should be noted: the laws present an idealized view not always followed in practice.

Today if anyone behaves badly toward us, it is him we blame
for our hurt. That we might in some way have *attracted* that
hurt never enters our minds. If our "luck" turns against us, *we*
blame anything and anyone but ourselves. Yet it is we by the
magnetism projected by our own karma, who drew that hurt-
ful behavior, or that "rotten luck," to ourselves.[26]

Hindus will argue that the Christian God is cruel to allow innocents
to suffer. Karma theory asserts no one is innocent: we all must accept
responsibility for our lives. We cannot blame others, even parents, for
our misfortunes, because a wrongdoer in a previous life will attract
wicked parents for this present life. "[T]hose who created poverty, disease, and ignorance through negligence in past lives will meet those conditions from the very beginning of their present lives."[27]

Karma theory has problems on the societal level in terms of class and
gender discrimination and with theodicy in general. On a more personal
level, what does karma do for the individual who has "bad karma" (and
that would be all of us) other than offer paths to accrue good karma to
offset it in another life? Classical Hinduism has no concept of personal
sin; instead we do things that have unfortunate consequences—"bad
karma." *Brahman* is beyond good and evil—which means, since we are
inseparable from the divine, our "real Selves" are also beyond good and
evil (and untouched by karma). We *should* feel no guilt for what we do
if there is no personal god to whom we are accountable. However, at
least as far back as the sixth century, Hindu devotionalists have wrestled
with "sin" and sought "grace"—revealing people innately know they sin
and need forgiveness (not impersonal karma). Some devotionalists seek
grace for relief from reincarnation, but many worship in search of an
eternal relationship with God. Radhakrishnan taught Hindus the universal judge is within each person.[28] How does seeking grace from the
divine, which is technically yourself (*Atman-Brahman*), make sense?

---

[26] Paramhansa Yogananda, *Karma & Reincarnation* (Nevada City, CA: Crystal Clarity
Publishers, 2007), 34–35.

[27] Ibid., 100–101. It should be noted that some Hindus see embracing karma as psychologically beneficial: the concept should remove bitterness—you are responsible for your life and,
after all, everyone has another chance at life. Karma theory has also been said to eliminate the
"stress" of personal ambition.

[28] Minor, "In Defense of Karma," in Neufeldt, *Karma and Rebirth*, 34.

This pantheistic monism of early Hindu texts did not provide a divine being to worship and to whom the people could relate. The concept of a god who encounters humankind came later in the form of *avatars*: a deity-indwelt image, or more apt for our comparison, the deity revealed in human form. Many devotees came to cling to Krishna, but is he worthy of such trust and devotion? Both Hindu and Christian scholars have compared Krishna and Jesus Christ.[29] Many Hindus think of Jesus as an avatar, but the differences are too numerous to include here. Essentially, Krishna does not actually participate in Hinduism's most dreaded plight of humankind—as an incarnation of Vishnu, he did not become a historical human being through the karmic process. In that regard he is not participating in the illusion all life faces. Having four arms, he definitely is unlike humans in appearance.[30] But Jesus, eternal God, became perfect man in order to mediate between God and humans (1 Tim 2:4–5). He shared in our humanity in order to represent us (Heb 2:14).

The greatest difference lies in the purpose of their manifestations. Why do Hindus believe Krishna appeared and what did he accomplish? Krishna entered the world to confront evil from both demons and the natural world. Wrongdoers are changed into loving followers after contact with the all-forgiving Krishna.[31] Christ also came to confront evil, but

> Christ came to save evildoers, via atonement for sin, before the eschatological judgment in a once-for-all establishing of righteousness. Krishna came to destroy them (ensuring rebirth), thus establishing righteousness for a particular age among countless others, not by atonement for sin but by a didactic of various spiritual disciplines, culminating with the discipline of single-minded devotion to Krishna.[32]

[29] For example, *Song Divine: Christian Commentaries on the Bhagavad Gītā*, ed. Catherine Cornille (Leuven: Peeters, 2006).

[30] Steven Tsoukalas, "Krishna and Christ: The Body-Divine Relation in the Human Form," in ibid., 151. While many Hindus believe Krishna came into the world historically, there is little proof. Furthermore, with or without any shred of historical evidence for a Krishna-figure, this makes no material difference in the worship of Krishna. Historicity is ultimately irrelevant.

[31] John Renard, *Responses to 101 Questions on Hinduism* (New York: Paulist Press, 1999), 25–26.

[32] Tsoukalas, "Krishna and Christ," in Cornille, *Song Divine*, 155.

All people sin; no one could ever do enough to mitigate every wrong action of life. Hindus turn to the god offered through their sacred literature—a god who has never actually entered into time and space, a god who provides no definitive revelation. What is claimed concerning the Hindu god has been "intuited" by ancient seers and interpreted through experience by contemporary gurus. Christians have a very different source: God who reveals Himself through word and deed historically and ultimately entering into our world in human form: "God's love was revealed among us in this way: God sent his One and Only Son into the world so that we might live through Him. Love consists in this: not that we loved God, but that He loved us and sent His Son to be the propitiation for our sins" (1 John 4:9–10 HCSB).

Do We Get What We Deserve?

Yes and no. We know there are consequences to our actions in this life, but these are consequences overseen by our holy and just yet personal God who loves us enough to die for us (John 3:16). He can be trusted always to have our best interest in mind—no matter how unpleasant the experience. We may be chastened *for* our bad deeds—but we are not left on our own to be punished *by* our deeds. Those who are *not* in Christ get exactly what we *all* deserve—eternal separation from God (Col 2:14; 2 Thess 1:7–9).

Many people, even some church members, believe that after death we all face a situation reminiscent of karma—getting just what we deserve. Some folks imagine in the balance their own good deeds versus their bad deeds. I have talked to many dear people who have told me they "hope" they will be in heaven with God one day because they're "pretty good," haven't done anything *really* bad, and have attended church ever since they were children. Other people think their lives will be compared to other people. I've heard neighbors say, "I'm doing OK. I'm better than most people."

But neither picture is biblical. We will not be compared to other people, nor will our deeds be weighed in the cosmic balance to determine our eternal standing. We will be judged according to God's righteousness—and every one of us falls short (Rom 3:10). The good news is those who have put their faith in Christ do not stand on their own—but in Christ's righteousness (Phil 3:9). The outcome of judgment depends on your relationship to Jesus (John 3:16; 11:25; cf. Rom 8:1). No one *earns* salvation; it is a gift for which we will be eternally grateful (Eph 2:8–9).

Hinduism is not the only tradition to offer individuals what they deserve. That is all most religions have to offer, either in the form of karma or works to merit some eternal reward. Hindu devotionalists live lives of simple trust in a savior figure who offers what they call "grace." But this is grace without a cost—an empty appeal to follow a powerless imposter. Where is the justice in that? I have always loved the definition of *grace* I heard as a child: God's Riches at Christ's Expense. Christ paid the ultimate price on the cross to offer us true escape from a reality of sin and sorrow—drawing us to Himself (Mark 10:45; 1 Pet 3:18).

What about reincarnation? Do we get a second chance? In the absence of more definitive justification, it's one huge metaphysical gamble to assume that we have multiple chances to "get it right." Moreover, the Scripture utterly contradicts reincarnation (Heb 9:27). But we are not on our own trying to improve ourselves in order to merit some heavenly abode or state of being. Christians do talk about being "born again," but this means becoming a permanent member of God's family by grace through faith (John 3:7; 1 Pet 1:3–5). The emphasis of the Bible is resurrection, not reincarnation (John 11:25). The historical evidence for Jesus' resurrection is superior to that offered for reincarnation.

Many Hindus believe that eventually all souls, actually divine already, will reach the ultimate goal of *moksha*—regardless of the religious path they take. This fits in with the evolution argument—and again, I don't believe history indicates any such moral development by humankind. Unlike Buddhists who do not believe in transmigration of the soul, most Hindus trust each individual will in some way enjoy this eternal state of absorption. But note: not all Hindu scholars believe there will be continued self-awareness when merged with the "Ultimate Consciousness"—therefore, no self, no awareness, no joy. By contrast, Christians contend that humans are not divine. We are sinners in need of forgiveness, and with that forgiveness also comes an eternity, not of absorption, but in the presence of a loving God (1 Cor 15:53–54). The Bible is also clear that all paths do not lead to this eternity with God—faith in Christ alone saves (Matt 7:13–14; John 14:6; Acts 4:12).

Hinduism as classically expressed is life-denying—the futile attempt to escape never-ending death. For many adherents, the opportunity eventually to escape rebirth into this world gives relief from the possibility of returning to hopeless lives. While Christians look forward to eternity with Christ, they are not eager to "escape" this world. Followers of Christ seek to serve and enjoy fellowship with God here in the world He created. Life has meaning both *now* and *eternally* for the Christian (John 10:10).

Bottom line: karma is incompatible with a Christian worldview which alone offers "a transcendent and personal deity, irrevocable forgiveness of sin, triumph over death, egalitarian spiritual community and the simple joy of accepting our unchangeable status as infinitely valuable but fallen creatures of a living and holy God."[33]

On the cross Jesus paid our debt in full. There is no karma to face—Christ's work is sufficient. Christians have this message of joy and hope for our Hindu friends, who would agree: there's absolutely nothing funny about karma.

---

[33] James A. Herrick, *The Making of the New Spirituality* (Downers Grove, IL: InterVarsity Press, 2003), 279–80.

CONTRIBUTORS

Toni Allen (D.Min. philosophy and culture [ABD], Talbot School of Theology) is adjunct professor of philosophy at Northern Virginia Community College and the United States Pentagon in Arlington, Virginia. She earned her M.A. in philosophy of religion and ethics from Talbot School of Theology. She is the director of Thought Life Ministries, LLC—a ministry devoted to teaching women to love God noetically by helping them to develop a well-formed thought life. She enjoys speaking, writing, and producing social media. She resides in Alexandria, Virginia, with her husband Jay and twin children, John and Zoe.

Paul Copan (Ph.D. philosophy, Marquette University) is professor and Pledger Family Chair of Philosophy and Ethics at Palm Beach Atlantic University (West Palm Beach, Florida). In addition to writing popular-level apologetic books such as *Is God a Moral Monster? Understanding the Old Testament God* (Baker), he is coauthor (with William Lane Craig) of *Creation Out of Nothing: A Biblical, Philosophical, and Scientific Exploration* (Baker Academic). He is coeditor (with Paul K. Moser) of *The Rationality of Theism* (Routledge), as well as the coeditor (both with Chad V. Meister) of *The Routledge Companion to Philosophy of Religion* (Routledge) and *Philosophy of Religion: Classic and*

Contemporary Issues (Blackwell). He has coedited *Passionate Conviction* and *Contending with Christianity's Critics* (B&H Academic) with William Lane Craig and coedited the *Apologetics Study Bible* (B&H Academic). He has authored and edited several other books and contributed essays and written reviews for journals such as *The Review of Metaphysics*, *Faith and Philosophy*, *Philosophia Christi*, and *Trinity Journal*. He lives with his wife Jacqueline and their six children in West Palm Beach, Florida.

William Lane Craig (Ph.D. philosophy, University of Birmingham; D.Theol., Ludwig-Maximilians-Universität München) is research professor of philosophy at Talbot School of Theology (La Mirada, California). Prior to his appointment at Talbot he spent seven years at the Higher Institute of Philosophy of the Katholike Universiteit Leuven, Belgium. He has authored or edited more than 30 books, including *Reasonable Faith: Christian Truth and Apologetics* (Crossway); *The* Kalam *Cosmological Argument* (Macmillan); *Divine Foreknowledge and Human Freedom* (Brill); *Theism, Atheism, and Big Bang Cosmology* (Clarendon); *God, Time, and Eternity* (Kluwer); and *Einstein, Relativity, and Absolute Simultaneity* (Routledge, forthcoming). Craig is also the author of more than 100 articles in professional journals of philosophy and theology, including *The Journal of Philosophy*, *Philosophy*, *American Philosophical Quarterly*, *Philosophical Studies*, *British Journal for Philosophy of Science*, and *International Studies in the Philosophy of Science*.

Michael H. Edens (Ph.D. theology, New Orleans Baptist Theological Seminary) recently returned to the USA after living and teaching in the Middle East for 27 years. He is professor of theology and Islamic Studies at New Orleans Baptist Theological Seminary.

Matthew Flannagan (Ph.D. theology, University of Otago) is an independent scholar based in Auckland, New Zealand. His areas of expertise include divine command meta-ethics, applied ethics, bio-ethics, Old Testament ethics, philosophy of religion, critical thinking, and apologetics. He has contributed essays to various books, includ-ing *Old Testament "Holy War" and Christian Morality: Perspectives and Prospects*, edited by Paul Copan, Jeremy Evans, and Heath Thomas (InterVarsity Press), and *In Defense of the Bible: A Comprehensive*

Apologetic for the Authority of Scripture, edited by Steven B. Cowan and Terry L. Wilder (B&H Academic). He has written journal articles, engaged in debates, and presented papers at annual meetings of the Evangelical Philosophical Society and the Society of Biblical Literature.

Mark W. Foreman (Ph.D. philosophy, University of Virginia) is professor of philosophy and religion at Liberty University, where he has taught philosophy, apologetics, and bioethics for more than 20 years. He is the author of *Christianity and Bioethics* (College Press [reprint Wipf and Stock]), *Prelude to Philosophy: Critical Thinking about Basic Beliefs* (InterVarsity Press, forthcoming), and *How Do We Know: A Short Introduction to the Issues of Knowledge* (with James K. Dew Jr., InterVarsity Press, forthcoming). He has also contributed articles to the *Popular Encyclopedia of Apologetics* (Harvest House) as well as chapters for *Steven Spielberg and Philosophy* (with David Baggett, University of Kentucky Press) and *Tennis and Philosophy* (University of Kentucky Press).

Gregory Ganssle (Ph.D. philosophy, Syracuse University) is a senior fellow at the Rivendell Institute. He has been a part-time lecturer in philosophy at Yale University. Greg has authored and edited several books, including *God and Time: Essays on the Nature of God* (Oxford), *God and Time: Four Views* (InterVarsity Press), *Thinking About God: First Steps in Philosophy* (InterVarsity Press), and *A Reasonable God: Engaging the New Face of Atheism* (Baylor University Press). His main areas of interest have been contemporary analytic philosophy of religion, particularly God's relation to time, the problem of evil, metaphysics, and the history of early modern philosophy.

Gary R. Habermas (Ph.D., Michigan State University) has authored, coauthored, or edited some 35 books, of which 18 center on various aspects of the resurrection of Jesus. These include *Did Jesus Rise from the Dead?* (Harper & Row) and *The Risen Jesus and Future Hope* (Rowman & Littlefield). Other topics concern religious doubt, personal suffering, and near-death experiences. He has also contributed more than 60 chapters and essays to additional books, plus more than 100 articles and reviews in journals and other publications. In recent years, he has been a visiting or adjunct professor at about 15 different graduate schools and seminaries in the United States and other countries. He is currently distinguished research professor of apologetics and philosophy, as well as chair of the Department of Philosophy, at Liberty University, where he has taught since 1981. His primary teaching responsibility is in Liberty's Ph.D. program in theology and apologetics.

Richard S. Hess (Ph.D. Old Testament, Hebrew Union College) is professor of Old Testament and semitic languages at Denver Seminary. He has authored eight books, including volumes on religion (*Israelite Religions: A Biblical and Archaeological Survey*), ancient Near Eastern subjects (*Amarna Personal Names* and *Names in the Study of Biblical History*), Genesis (*Studies in the Personal Names of Genesis 1–11*), and commentaries on Leviticus, Joshua, and the Song of Songs. He has edited 13 books, most recently collections of studies on *War in the Bible and Terrorism in the 21st Century, Issues in Bible Translation*, and *The Family in the Bible*; and commentaries on the Septuagint texts of Genesis and Joshua. In addition to several hundred book reviews and dictionary articles, Dr. Hess has published more than 100 scholarly articles in collected essays and journals such as *Biblica, Biblical Archaeologist, Bulletin for Biblical Research, Catholic Biblical Quarterly, Themelios, Tyndale Bulletin, Vetus Testamentum*, and *Zeitschrift für die alttestamentliche Wissenschaft*. Current research projects include commentaries on the books of Genesis and Kings, an introduction to the Old Testament, Hebrew grammar, and the study of ancient Near Eastern texts related to the Old Testament.

Craig S. Keener (Ph.D. New Testament, Duke University) is professor of New Testament at Asbury Theological Seminary in Wilmore, Kentucky. Prior to this, he was professor of New Testament at Palmer Theological Seminary. He is author of more than 100 articles and 15 books, including three award-winning commentaries. Together, his books have sold more than half a million copies. The most relevant of his books to this project is *The Historical Jesus of the Gospels* (Eerdmans). He is married to Dr. Medine Moussounga Keener, from Congo, Central Africa.

Michael Licona (Ph.D. New Testament Studies, University of Pretoria) serves as external research collaborator at North-West University (Potchefstroom). Mike was interviewed by Lee Strobel in his book *The Case for the Real Jesus* and appeared in Strobel's video *The Case for Christ*. He is the author of numerous books including *The Resurrection of Jesus: A New Historiographical Approach* (IVP Academic, 2010), and *Paul Meets Muhammad* (Baker, 2006), coauthor with Gary Habermas of the award-winning book *The Case for the Resurrection of Jesus* (Kregel, 2004), and coeditor with William Dembski of *Evidence for God: 50 Arguments for Faith from the Bible, History, Philosophy, and Science* (Baker, 2010). Mike is a member of the Evangelical Philosophical Society, the Institute for Biblical Research, and the Society of Biblical Literature. He has spoken on more than 50 university campuses, and has appeared on dozens of radio and television programs.

J. P. Moreland (Ph.D. philosophy, University of California-Riverside) is distinguished professor of philosophy at Talbot School of Theology, Biola University in La Mirada, California. He has authored, edited, or contributed papers to 35 books, including *Does God Exist?* (Prometheus), *Universals* (McGill-Queen's), *Consciousness and the Existence of God* (Routledge), and *Blackwell Companion to Natural Theology* (Blackwell). He has also published more than 80 articles in journals such as *Philosophy and Phenomenological Research, American Philosophical Quarterly, Australasian Journal of Philosophy, Metaphilosophy, Philosophia Christi, Religious Studies*, and *Faith and Philosophy*.

Barbara B. Pemberton (Ph.D. world religions, Baylor University) is associate professor at Ouachita Baptist University, where she is the director of the Carl Goodson Honors Program. She has contributed to the *Apologetics Study Bible* and is a frequent conference speaker.

E. Randolph Richards (Ph.D. New Testament, Southwestern Baptist Theological Seminary) is the professor of biblical studies and dean of the School of Ministry at Palm Beach Atlantic University. He has written two major monographs (*The Secretary in the Letters of Paul*, Wissenschaftliche Untersuchungen zum Neuen Testament 2/42; and *Paul and First Century Letter Writing*, InterVarsity Press) and coauthored two others (*The Story of Israel: a Biblical Theology* and *Rediscovering Paul: An Introduction to His Life and Work* [both with InterVarsity Press]). He has published dozens of articles. His most recent projects include *(Mis)Reading Scripture with Western Eyes*, with Brandon O'Brien (InterVarsity Press, forthcoming); "Reading, Writing, and the Production and Transmission of Manuscripts," in *The Background of the New Testament: An Examination of the Context of Early Christianity*, ed. Joel B. Green and Lee Martin McDonald (Baker, forthcoming); "Pauline Prescripts and Greco-Roman Epistolary Convention" in *Christian Origins and Classical Culture: Social and Literary Contexts for the New Testament*, ed. Stanley Porter and Andrew Pitts, Texts and Editions for New Testament Study 1 (Brill); "(Mis)Reading Paul's Letters through Western Eyes," in *Paul as Missionary: His Identity, Activity, Theology and Practice*, ed. Trevor Burke, LNTS (formerly JSNTS) 420 (T & T Clark); "Flattery, Favors and Obligations: Patrons and Clients in Greco-Roman Culture," *The Biblical Illustrator*; and various articles in *The Baker Handbook for the Bible*, ed. J. Daniel Hays and J. Scott Duvall (Baker Academic), and in *The Baker Illustrated Bible Dictionary*, ed. Tremper Longman (Baker Academic). He also serves as the teaching pastor at Grace Fellowship Church in West Palm Beach, Florida.

Mary Jo Sharp (M.A. Christian apologetics, Biola University) is the founder of Confident Christianity Apologetics Ministry. She is a visiting professor at Oklahoma Baptist University and is a debater (on Islam and Christianity) and experienced speaker in apologetics. Mary Jo's book on implementing the study of apologetics in women's ministries is forthcoming with Kregel Publishers. She is a member of the Evangelical Philosophical Society and the Evangelical Theological Society. She is a certified apologetics instructor with the North American Mission Board of the Southern Baptist Convention.

Robert B. Stewart (Ph.D. Southwestern Baptist Theological Seminary) is professor of philosophy and theology at New Orleans Baptist Theological Seminary where he is Greer-Heard Professor of Faith and Culture. He is editor of *The Resurrection of Jesus: John Dominic Crossan and N. T. Wright in Dialogue* (Fortress and SPCK), *Intelligent*

Design: William A. Dembski and Michael Ruse in Dialogue (Fortress), *The Future of Atheism: Alister McGrath and Daniel Dennett in Dialogue* (Fortress and SPCK), and *Memories of Jesus: A Critical Appraisal of James D. G. Dunn's Jesus Remembered* (B&H Academic). He is the author of *The Quest of the Hermeneutical Jesus: The Impact of Hermeneutics on the Jesus Research of John Dominic Crossan and N. T. Wright* (University Press of America). A contributor to the *Cambridge Dictionary of Christianity* and the *Revised Holman Bible Dictionary,* he has published articles or book reviews in numerous journals.

NAME INDEX ·

SCRIPTURE INDEX

Joshua

Judges